HEYDAYS

i

This edition of *Heydays: Great Stories in Chicago Sports* is an updated and expanded version of the edition published in 2009.

———————————

OTHER BOOKS BY CHRISTOPHER TABBERT

Ghosts of Birch Lake
978-0-692-70759-3

The Lives of Lincoln
978-0-692-77678-0

HEYDAYS

GREAT STORIES IN CHICAGO SPORTS

by

CHRISTOPHER TABBERT

Bristol & Lynden

Bristol & Lynden Press
233 Wood Creek Road, Unit 503
Wheeling, IL 60090

www.bristolandlyndenpress.com

ISBN: 978-0-692-81833-6

This book is dedicated to

the great sports fans of Chicago—

past, present, and future.

Contents

CHAPTER 1

Crosstown Classic

"The intermingling of south and west side fans was productive of much repartee, but the joshing was generally good natured."
                              -- The Chicago Tribune, *describing the 1906 World Series*

By the dawn of the 21st century, few fans were old enough to remember either Chicago team playing in a World Series, so it was hard to imagine the Cubs and White Sox facing *one another* in the fall classic. But that is exactly what happened in 1906.

The two clubs took divergent paths to the first single-city World Series. The Cubs blasted out of the gate and never looked back, racking up a phenomenal record of 116-36—still the best of all time—and outdistancing the defending world-champion New York Giants by 20 games. The White Sox started slowly, crept over .500 in mid-June, won 19 straight in August to assume first place, fell back into second several times in September, and finally surged to the finish line three games ahead of the New York Yankees (then known as the Highlanders).

The Cubs led the National League in hitting, fielding, and pitching. They scored 80 more runs than the second-best offensive team and yielded 89 fewer than the second-best defensive team. They got better as the season went on, winning 50 of their last 57 games. They were 56-21 at home and 60-15 on the road. When asked whether he was amazed that the Cubs had won 116 games, pitcher Ed Reulbach said, "I wonder how we came to *lose* 36." First baseman and manager Frank Chance led the league in stolen bases with 57 and runs scored with 102; third baseman Harry Steinfeldt tied for the lead in runs batted in with 83. Between them on the infield were Joe Tinker and Johnny Evers, the shortstop and second baseman later immortalized with Chance in the

1

most famous baseball poem after "Casey at the Bat." Johnny Kling was one of the finest catchers of his day, the first in the majors to throw from a crouch. Pitchers Mordecai "Three-Finger" Brown, Jack Pfiester, and Reulbach finished one-two-three in the league in earned-run average; Brown's figure of 1.04 remains the best ever by a National Leaguer.

Against this juggernaut stood a White Sox club disparagingly nicknamed "the Hitless Wonders." Their anemic .230 team batting average and puny total of seven home runs both ranked last in the American League. "It must be admitted," Fred Lieb wrote, "that [manager] Fielder Jones won his pennant with mirrors." Lieb should have said mirrors and pitching, for the Sox posted 32 shutouts. Frank Owen, Nick Altrock, and Doc White won 22, 20, and 18 games, respectively, and White's ERA of 1.52 led the league. Ed Walsh added 17 victories, 10 of them shutouts. The cocky 25-year-old Walsh, described as "the only man who could strut while standing still," had just mastered the spitball (which was then legal) after two years of trial and error. He was destined for the Hall of Fame.

To an extent that has probably not been equaled since, Chicagoans in the first decade of the 20th century were absolutely mad about baseball. "All the honors worth winning," an anonymous *Tribune* writer gushed, "in the most sensational, record-breaking, and most financially successful season in baseball's history belong to Chicago, admittedly the greatest, most loyal, and enthusiastic baseball city in the world."

The *Tribune* offered mechanical "recreations" of each Series game in an armory building and at the Auditorium and McVickers theaters. "The plan," the newspaper explained, "is to reproduce the games, play by play, with that remarkable accuracy which ingenuity has made possible." The result of each play was flashed by telegraph from the ballpark to the sites, where it was represented on simulated baseball diamonds. Thousands of fans took advantage of this service, and thousands more kept up with the games by hanging around outside the ballparks or telegraph offices.

Chicago's huge population of recent immigrants from Germany and Ireland was neatly divided in its loyalties. The Germans favored the Cubs, whose roster included Solly Hofman, Kling, Pfiester, Reulbach, Steinfeldt, Jimmy Sheckard, and Frank "Wildfire" Schulte. The Irish

2

supported the White Sox, who featured Jiggs Donahue, Patsy Dougherty, Ed McFarland, Bill O'Neill, Billy Sullivan, Walsh, and White.

Although the Sox' record of 93-58 was excellent, it nonetheless would have placed them 17½ games off the pace set by the Cubs. It was no surprise, then, that the South Siders were overwhelming underdogs to their West Side rivals (the Cubs didn't move to the North Side until 1916). But Giants manager John McGraw, for one, wasn't so sure. "They say the White Sox won the flag without hitting," he said, "but I know better. Their grounds prevent anyone from hitting heavily, and as they played 77 games there, it made their averages look very small. On the road, they hit as hard as anybody." It was true that the Sox' very spacious home field, South Side Park at 39th and Princeton, contributed substantially to the apparent futility of their hitters and mastery of their pitchers. When owner Charles Comiskey built his new park in 1910, he gave it, at Walsh's urging, similarly gargantuan dimensions.

The Cubs were being called the mightiest ballclub ever to take the field. They had good reason to be confident as they opened the Series with their ace, Mordecai Brown, on the mound. He'd had 26 victories in this first of his six consecutive years with 20 or more. Walsh was slated to oppose Brown in what would have been a dream matchup, but according to legend Sox manager Jones changed his mind at the last minute because he believed that Walsh's spitballs would freeze in the unseasonably cold air. So the two greatest pitchers in Chicago history did not face each other. Altrock went to the hill for the Sox.

Game 1 was played in the Cubs' park, the West Side Grounds at Polk and Lincoln (now Wolcott), on October 9. "Never was such a contest, for such high stakes, played under worse conditions," the *Tribune* reported. "A cold, raw day was made more disagreeable by a chilling wind, and cold gray clouds denied the sun more than a single, fleeting chance to light up the picture." Snowflakes floated over the crowd of 12,693.

Brown and Altrock were sharp, and the game was scoreless for four innings. In the fifth, Sox third baseman George Rohe drove one past Cubs left fielder Sheckard for a triple. Rohe, a seldom-used reserve who was playing only because George Davis was injured, would figure prominently throughout the Series. He scored the Sox' first run when

Dougherty tapped a weak bouncer back to Brown, whose throw home somehow eluded the usually sure-handed Kling.

Brown committed the cardinal sin of walking Altrock, a .152 hitter, to lead off the sixth. Altrock moved to second on a sacrifice by Eddie Hahn, then tried to score on Jones's single to center. But Hofman's throw to Kling was perfect, retiring Altrock while Jones took second. Jones advanced to third on a passed ball by Kling and scored on Frank Isbell's single to left.

Leading off the bottom of the sixth, Kling walked. Brown twice failed to bunt him to second, then swung away and singled over the middle. After Hofman sacrificed, Altrock threw a wild pitch that scored Kling and pushed Brown to third. But Brown, representing the tying run, went no further. First, shortstop Lee Tannehill raced back into shallow left to make an over-the-shoulder grab of a blooper by Sheckard. Then first baseman Donahue stretched to scoop Rohe's low throw out of the dirt, retiring Schulte and the side.

Altrock clung to the narrow lead for three more innings, and when it was over he and the Sox had escaped with a 2-1 win. "One swallow does not make a summer," Cubs owner Charles W. Murphy remarked. "I might add one snowstorm does not make a winter, but it keeps fans away from ball games."

Game 2 was played before 12,595 at South Side Park, also amid snow flurries. The Cubs scored early and often, knocking White out after three innings and roughing up his successor, Owen, as well. They pounded out 10 hits and seven runs. Reulbach, meanwhile, allowed but one hit and one unearned run. In three different innings he walked the first batter and in another he hit the first man up, but only in one of these instances did the man reach second base. Brilliant fielding by the Cubs repeatedly rescued Reulbach from his self-imposed peril, and the Series was tied up. "That's one and one," said Comiskey. "And we'll be there with the right kind of goods tomorrow."

Walsh, the right kind of goods, started Game 3 against the Cubs' Pfiester. The weather had improved markedly, and 13,667 showed up at the West Side Grounds. They saw a superb pitching duel in which neither team scored for five innings. In the top of the sixth, the Sox loaded the bases with none out. Pfiester didn't give in. He got Jones on a foul pop-up to Kling, who leaned well into the crowd behind the plate to make a fine catch. Then Pfiester fanned Isbell. He was on the verge of squeezing out of the jam when the unknown Rohe came up. Rohe hit the first pitch down the left-field line, where it bounced into the crowd for a ground-rule triple. The three runs were all that Walsh needed as he scattered two harmless hits and struck out 12. The Sox won 3-0.

Game 4, played before 18,384 at South Side Park on October 12, featured a rematch between Brown and Altrock, who had battled memorably in Game 1. George Davis was back in action for the Sox, replacing Tannehill at shortstop while Rohe remained at third base. Right fielder and leadoff man Hahn was also in the lineup, unfazed by the broken nose sustained when he was hit by a pitch in the previous game. "They can hand me the beanball or push my nose aside every day in the week," he said, "if the Sox can only win." Hahn singled with two outs in the sixth for the Sox' first hit off Brown, but he was stranded. In the seventh, he lost Chance's drive in the sun and allowed it to fall for a single. Two successive bunts moved Chance to third, and Evers's solid single to left scored him with the only run of the game.

Brown blanked the Sox on two hits. In the ninth inning, with two out and the potential tying and winning runs on base, he was literally knocked down by a vicious shot off the bat of Isbell. He recovered both his bearings and the ball in time to throw to Chance for the game's final out.

Altrock was philosophical about finding himself on the short end of the 1-0 score. "There is no great loss," he said, "without its compensating gain. Had I won this game and another, the irksome ethics of this profession would compel me to wear a collar and necktie all winter."

For four games, the Hitless Wonders had been true to form, with just 11 hits in 113 at-bats for an average of .097—yet the upstarts had given the vaunted Cubs all they could handle. In the latter respect only, the remaining games of the Series would be no different.

A throng of 23,257 filled every nook and cranny of the West Side Grounds for Game 5. Thousands more were outside, the *Tribune* noted, "packed on adjoining roofs, clinging to telegraph poles and wires like monkeys, or fretting behind locked gates and trying to gain from the incessant yelling some idea of how the tide of battle was going within."

Walsh was back on the mound for the Sox, just two days after his complete-game shutout in Game 3, and Reulbach went for the Cubs. Both pitchers had trouble in the first inning. Reulbach was touched for a run on three hits before he wriggled out of a bases-loaded jam. Walsh allowed his first runs of the Series, through no fault of his own, when errors by Isbell and Donahue led to three tallies by the Cubs.

Cubs fans were ecstatic, figuring that the three runs would be sufficient to subdue the Sox, who'd scored only six times in the first four games. But suddenly the South Siders' popgun attack erupted. When Isbell and Davis rapped back-to-back doubles to lead off the third, Reulbach was through. The Sox weren't. Pfiester came on for the Cubs and retired the side, but not before Isbell and Davis scored. In the fourth, Pfiester got only one man out before he too was sent to the showers. By the time Orval Overall finally got the third out, the score was 7-3, and it was the Sox fans who had something to shout about.

The Cubs scored once in the fourth and twice in the sixth, again on miscues by the Sox infielders (who committed an astounding six errors among them). White relieved a tiring Walsh in the seventh and yielded just one scratch single over the final three innings to preserve Big Ed's second win of the Series. The final score was 8-6; it could have been 8-0 if not for what the *Tribune* called "the rankest exhibition of fielding a team of champions ever gave in public."

With the heavily favored Cubs now at the brink of elimination, Brown returned for Game 6 on two days' rest. And despite his own rather lengthy stint just the day before, White started for the Sox. Like most managers in those days, neither Chance nor Jones was shy about using his best pitchers to, and often past, the point of exhaustion.

A crowd of 19,249 packed South Side Park to see whether the Sox could pull off their miracle. The answer was not long in coming. Trailing 1-0 in the bottom of the first, the Sox had two on and one out when Davis banged a long fly to right. Schulte drifted back, circled, and then stumbled as the ball fell safely behind him for a double. The Cubs claimed that a policeman placed on the field for crowd control had purposefully kicked Schulte in the pants as he reached for the ball, but their pleas fell on deaf ears, and the game was tied. Shortly thereafter, Donahue doubled to left, scoring two more runs. He wouldn't have batted if Davis's ball had been caught. "Three runs scored where there should have been none," Charles Dryden wrote in the *Tribune*, "and more disaster followed."

When Brown easily retired the first two Sox hitters in the second, it seemed that he had settled down, as Dryden wrote, and "might yet finish the game in his usual form." But then he unraveled completely. Hahn singled, Jones walked, and Isbell singled to load the bases. Tinker leaped and almost made a sensational catch of a line drive by Davis, but the ball ticked off his glove as two runs scored. Rohe then singled, loading the bases again. With this, Overall replaced Brown. He promptly yielded a single to Donahue and a walk to Dougherty for two more runs before retiring Sullivan (who had the dubious distinction of making two outs in the inning).

The White Sox' stunning two-out rally produced seven successive base runners and four runs. It also put the game out of reach. "Realizing only the most unexpected events could rob their heroes of the hard fought for honors," the *Tribune* reported, "the thousands whose sympathies were with the Sox turned the affair into a jubilee of noise. The waving banners, the tin horns, the dinner bells, the megaphones, the counting of the score in unison—all were suggestive of a gridiron contest. Nothing like it ever before was seen on a baseball diamond."

For the first time in the Series, the home team won. The final score was 8-3. Against the pitching staff whose collective earned-run average of 1.76 remains the best of all time, the Hitless Wonders had exploded for 16 runs on 26 hits in the two games that decided the world championship. Their triumph still ranks among the greatest upsets in World Series history.

Sox owner Comiskey handed Jones a check for $15,000 and told him to split it evenly among the White Sox; this was in addition to the $25,052 they were to share from the gate receipts. Jones and the players, naturally, regarded the extra $15,000 as a gift from their grateful boss. They didn't learn until later, and much to their chagrin, that it was really intended as an advance against their 1907 salaries.

Amazingly, sportswriter Hugh Fullerton had predicted a White Sox victory and even the number of games it would require, but editors at the *Tribune* refused to print his analysis for fear that it would make the paper a laughingstock. Fullerton's scouting report on the two clubs wasn't printed until the day after Game 6, by which time events had vindicated him (and by which time, of course, his prediction was of no use except as a curiosity).

"The Sox played grand, game baseball," said Chance, "and outclassed us in the Series just ended. But there is one thing I never will believe, and that is that the White Sox are a better ballclub than the Cubs. They fought so hard that they made us like it and like it well. We played our hardest to win, but in this Series we did not show we were the best club."

Torchlight celebrations continued on the South Side into the wee hours, as Sox players were paraded through the streets on horse-drawn carts and on the shoulders of their fans. A crowd gathered outside Jones's house on Cottage Grove Avenue, demanding a speech. "I thank you," Jones said, "and all the other friends whose hearty support as been as vital as good ball playing."

Comiskey hosted a victory party at a nearby hotel and vowed that he would not sleep that night. "All I can say, boys," he said after several rounds, "is that I'd rather [have] beaten any team on Earth than Chance's. He's got a lot of fine fellows, and I wish I could find him to-night, for he's game enough to help me celebrate."

His polite public utterances notwithstanding, Chance was in no mood to celebrate. Nor did he soon forgive the Cubs for losing. When they gathered for the first day of spring training in 1907, he welcomed them with this comment: "You're a fine bunch of shits."

CHAPTER 2

Giant Killers

"If you didn't honestly and furiously hate the Giants, you weren't a real Cub."

-- Joe Tinker, Cubs shortstop, 1902-1912

From 1901 through 1913, the New York Giants, the Pittsburgh Pirates, and the Cubs were the only teams to capture the National League pennant, and they engaged in fierce battles for supremacy almost every year. While no one could work up much of a dislike for the Pirates, whose star was the beloved Honus Wagner, there was genuine bad blood between the Giants and Cubs. Their enmity was driven in part by the natural competition between the nation's first and second cities, but more by the combative personalities of the two managers, John McGraw of the Giants and Frank Chance of the Cubs.

Both clubs were replete with names that have become immortal in baseball annals. For New York, McGraw was in the seventh of his 31 seasons at the helm—during which time he would win 10 pennants. "With my team," he said, "I am an absolute czar. My men know it. I order plays and they obey." His players called him Mr. McGraw, not John or Mac. Though he was ruthless in trading or releasing players who could no longer measure up to his exacting standards, he often hired these same castoffs back as groundskeepers or ticket takers after their playing days. "He was a man in every old-fashioned sense of the word," umpire Bill Klem wrote. "He helped his friends; he fought for his rightful due with words, fists or whatever came readily to hand; his charity knew neither restraint nor publicity."

McGraw's ace pitcher was Christy Mathewson. "He had knowledge, judgment, perfect control, and form," said Connie Mack. "It was won-

9

derful to watch him pitch—when he wasn't pitching against you." Even though the handsome, articulate, and college-educated "Matty" could hardly have been more different from the squat, pugnacious McGraw, the older man loved him like a son. Mathewson's teammates also adored him. "How we loved to play for him!" said catcher Chief Meyers. "We'd break our necks for that guy. If you made an error behind him or anything of that sort, he'd never get mad or sulk. He'd come over and pat you on the back."

Chicago, of course, had the fabled double-play combination of Joe Tinker, Johnny Evers, and Chance, immortalized by New York writer Franklin P. Adams:

> *These are the saddest of possible words:*
> *"Tinker to Evers to Chance."*
> *Trio of bear cubs fleeter than birds,*
> *"Tinker and Evers and Chance."*
> *Ruthlessly pricking our gonfalon bubble,*
> *Making a Giant hit into a double—*
> *Words that are weighty with nothing but trouble:*
> *"Tinker to Evers to Chance."*

Although they were forever linked in the public imagination by the poem, Tinker and Evers did not get along. Off the field, they once went two years without speaking, reportedly because of a dispute over cab-fare. For his part, Chance—known as "The Peerless Leader" or simply "P.L." in Chicago newspapers—was not a warm and fuzzy presence in the Cubs' dugout; he fined his players for merely saying hello to opponents. Few gave him any lip, since he was, according to former heavyweight champion John L. Sullivan, "the greatest amateur brawler in the world."

The Cubs also possessed a sterling pitching staff anchored by Mordecai Brown, whose lifetime earned-run average of 2.06 is the third best in history. An accident with a grain-cutting machine when he was seven had severed the index finger and mangled the little finger of Brown's right hand—hence his nickname, "Three-Finger." Ironically, the injury made Brown a great pitcher, enabling him to impart a ferocious break to his curveball, which Ty Cobb called "the most devastating pitch I ever faced." Brown was once asked whether it was difficult to pitch with three fingers. "I don't know," he replied. "I've never done it any other way."

The Cubs-Giants rivalry reached its peak during the unforgettable pennant race of 1908. With only two weeks remaining in the campaign, the Cubs' drive for a third straight flag appeared to be running out of steam; they trailed New York by three and a half games. On September 21, though, the Cubs took two at Philadelphia while the Giants lost to Pittsburgh. The very next day, the Cubs visited the Polo Grounds for a crucial doubleheader with the Giants. Brown worked the last three innings of the first game to save a 4-3 decision, then went the distance in the nightcap to prevail 3-1. The sweep moved the Cubs into a virtual tie for first place and paved the way for the contest of September 23, which remains among the most famous games in major-league history.

The game was scoreless until the fifth, when Tinker's line drive into the gap eluded right fielder Mike Donlin and went for an inside-the-park home run. Donlin made amends the next inning by singling in the tying run. The Cubs' Jack Pfiester held his own against Mathewson, and the game remained deadlocked 1-1 into the bottom of the ninth. With two out and Moose McCormick on first, Fred Merkle came to bat for the Giants. Merkle, a 19-year-old rookie, was in the lineup only because regular first baseman Fred Tenney was hurt.

Merkle came through with a single to right, sending McCormick around to third. That brought Al Bridwell to the plate. "Well, the first pitch came into me," Bridwell recalled, "a fastball, waist high, right over the center of the plate, and I promptly drilled a line drive past Johnny Evers and out into right center field. Bob Emslie was umpiring on the bases and he fell on his can to avoid being hit by the ball. I really socked that one on the nose. A clean single."

McCormick crossed home plate, and New York had seemingly won the ballgame. Merkle jogged only about halfway to second base before he became unnerved by the thousands of jubilant fans who were swarming onto the field. He peeled off and sprinted for the Giants' clubhouse. Evers immediately recognized the youngster's mistake; if he could get hold of the ball and step on second base, Merkle would be forced out to retire the side, and the game would still be tied. He began yelling for center fielder Solly Hofman to throw him the ball.

11

Three weeks earlier in Pittsburgh, another rookie, Warren Gill, had failed to touch second base on an apparent game-winning hit against the Cubs. On that occasion, Evers screamed bloody murder but umpire Hank O'Day was unmoved, and the Pirates' victory was allowed to stand.

O'Day now found himself confronted with the exact same situation. Rather than leave the field, he watched intently as Hofman grappled with fans for the ball and threw it toward the infield. Realizing what the Cubs were up to, third-base coach Joe McGinnity grabbed the ball and chucked it into the crowd, where it was caught, according to Evers, by "a tall, stringy middle-aged gent with a brown bowler hat on." The Cubs' Harry Steinfeldt and Rube Kroh chased this fellow, Kroh finally knocking him to the ground and retrieving the ball. (Kroh, a seldom-used pitcher, had been in charge of the bag in which the Cubs stored their valuables for safekeeping. He forgot all about it when he left the bench to pursue the man in the bowler hat. The bag and its contents, about $5,000 in cash and jewelry, were never seen again.)

Kroh flipped the ball to Tinker. "I was yelling and waving my hands by second base," said Evers, "and Tinker relayed it over to me and I stepped on the bag and made sure O'Day saw me." O'Day ruled that Merkle was out and the run did not count. Accordingly, the game should have continued into extra innings, but clearing the field was out of the question. While the Cubs and the umpires ran a gauntlet of irate Giants fans to the clubhouse, Chance took the opportunity to berate O'Day, claiming that because the chaos on the field prevented extra innings, the Cubs should be declared the winners by forfeit.

Neither team was satisfied by the outcome, although the Cubs were well aware that they had gotten the better of it. Evers, for one, understood that O'Day could have taken the easy way out by assuming that Bridwell's hit had ended the game. He said that O'Day's call was "one of the greatest examples of individual heroism the game has known."

O'Day advised both teams to take up their arguments with league president Harry C. Pulliam. They did, and while Pulliam deliberated, the season continued.

The Cubs and Giants returned to the Polo Grounds the next day for their last scheduled meeting of the season. Howls of derision greeted the Cubs' every move, and Evers jawed with McGraw from the first pitch to the last. When it was over, Mathewson had bested Brown 5-4, and the Giants were back in first place. The Pirates, meanwhile, had surged back into contention and were now tied with the Cubs for second.

On Saturday, September 26, Ed Reulbach took the mound for the Cubs in the first game of a doubleheader at Brooklyn. Reulbach had led the league in winning percentage in 1906 and 1907 and was on his way to doing so again in 1908; he ended up going 50-15 over the three years. Unfortunately, he toiled in the long shadow cast by Brown and is rarely remembered today. Yet he was indispensable to the greatest teams in Cubs history, and never more so than on this occasion.

Reulbach tossed a shutout as the Cubs won 5-0. He yielded just five hits, all singles, while striking out seven and walking one. The job was done in an hour and 45 minutes. "The grace, style, endurance, and speed of Mr. Reulbach fits into this remarkable baseball race," Charles Dryden wrote in the *Tribune*. "He put the locals away so easily in the curtain raiser that Chance granted his request to go in and bring them in again."

Having asked for the ball again, Reulbach dispatched the Dodgers even more effectively in the nightcap, surrendering only three singles as he earned another shutout. He was, Dryden wrote, "even better in the second go and his speed fairly blinded the dizzy young men of Brooklyn." The Cubs won 3-0 in an hour and 15 minutes. This time Reulbach fanned four and walked one.

Meanwhile, the Giants swept a doubleheader and the Pirates also won. Reulbach's feat, then, was as necessary as it was exhilarating, allowing the Cubs to keep pace with the other contenders. It marked the first and last time in major-league history that anyone pitched two complete-game shutouts in the same day.

In this time before radio, fans would gather by the hundreds outside telegraph and newspaper offices for play-by-play updates. Those who did so in the waning days of the 1908 season "witnessed" a thrilling three-way struggle for the pennant.

September 28: Giants beat Philadelphia; Cubs and Pirates idle. New York 91-52, Chicago 93-54, Pittsburgh 92-55.

September 29: Cubs beat Cincinnati; Giants split doubleheader with Philadelphia; Pirates sweep doubleheader from St. Louis. Chicago 94-54, New York 92-53, Pittsburgh 94-55.

September 30: Cubs lose to Cincinnati; Giants beat Philadelphia; Pirates beat St. Louis. New York 93-53, Pittsburgh 95-55, Chicago 94-55.

October 1: Cubs beat Cincinnati (Reulbach tosses another shutout); Giants split doubleheader with Philadelphia; Pirates idle. New York 94-54, Pittsburgh 95-55, Chicago 95-55.

October 2: Cubs beat Cincinnati; Giants beat Philadelphia; Pirates sweep doubleheader from St. Louis. Pittsburgh 97-55, New York 95-54, Chicago 96-55.

October 3: Cubs beat Cincinnati; Giants lose to Philadelphia; Pirates beat St. Louis. Pittsburgh 98-55, Chicago 97-55, New York 95-55.

On Sunday, October 4, the Pirates came to Chicago to make up a game that had been rained out earlier. While the Cubs and Giants were worrying about each other, the Pirates had won 12 of their last 13 games to pass both clubs. They needed one more victory to make the Cubs-Giants race moot.

The West Side Grounds were packed beyond capacity, with the overflow fans placed along both foul lines and in the far reaches of the outfield. The crowd of 30,247 was the largest ever to see a baseball game anywhere up to that time—a record that would stand for four days.

The game was tied 2-2 in the bottom of the sixth when Three-Finger Brown singled to score Tinker with the lead run. Brown also singled and scored an insurance tally in the eighth, giving the Cubs their final margin of 5-2. As if that weren't enough, he pitched a complete game for the second time in three days (he had blanked Cincinnati on Friday). "We simply had to win," said Chance, "and we did. That's all there was to it." After the game, Cubs players were carried around the field atop the shoulders of exultant fans, and Chance was mobbed as he tried to get into his car.

Pittsburgh's season was over. At 98-56, the Pirates could not win the pennant. New York still had three games left to play. If the Giants lost even one of them, they would be eliminated. If they won them all, they would draw even with the Cubs and force a replay of the disputed "Merkle game" of September 23—which league president Pulliam had finally declared officially a tie. (The stress Pulliam endured before making his decision, and the abuse he was subject to after, almost certainly contributed to his suicide the following year.)

The Giants beat Boston on Monday and on Tuesday. On Wednesday morning, the Cubs boarded the 20th Century Limited bound for New York. Late in the afternoon they learned that their journey would not be in vain; the Giants had taken care of business, defeating the Braves yet again to move into a first-place tie with Chicago. The Cubs and Giants would meet the next day to decide the pennant. On the train, Chance was as cocky as ever. "Whoever heard of the Cubs losing a game they had to have?" he asked. "Chicago is going to win this flag. To do it we must beat New York, and we are going to do it."

"It is clear," the *Tribune* asserted, "that the stage is being fittingly set for what is undoubtedly to be the most dramatic baseball event in the game's history."

It was a warm, crystal-clear afternoon in New York. The park was completely full more than two hours before game time, and the police ordered the gates closed. "Thousands who held tickets couldn't force their way through the street mobs to the entrances," Brown remembered. "By game time there were thousands on the field in front of the bleachers, the stands were jammed with people standing and sitting in the aisles. The elevated lines couldn't run for people who had climbed up and were sitting on the tracks." Tens of thousands lined the rocky cliff known as Coogan's Bluff, from which only parts of the field could be seen. Thousands more tried to break down the gates and enter the park itself, but they were held off by mounted police.

The Cubs arrived at the Polo Grounds a bit groggy after an 18-hour train trip and a restless stay in their hotel, where a gang of Giants fans had stood outside with horns and noisemakers all night. Then, just when the Cubs had started batting practice, the Giants abruptly changed the game time from 3:00 to 2:45. As Chance led the Cubs back to their dugout, New York's Joe McGinnity tried to pick a fight with him so that both would be ejected. He not only brandished a bat at Chance and called him names, according to the Giants' Fred Snodgrass, but also "stepped on his shoes, pushed him, actually spit on him. But Frank wouldn't fight. He was too smart."

The Giants, naturally, had tapped Mathewson as their starting pitcher, while Chance had chosen Jack Pfiester, who'd shown well against Matty in the Merkle game. Mathewson, 37-10 on the season, dispatched the Cubs easily in the first. In the bottom half of the inning, Pfiester looked rattled. He hit Fred Tenney with his first pitch, then walked Buck Herzog on four pitches. He settled down sufficiently to fan Roger Bresnahan; on the third strike, catcher Johnny Kling caught Herzog straying from first base and picked him off. But then came more trouble. Mike Donlin doubled to score Tenney, and Cy Seymour walked. Chance had seen enough. He called for Three-Finger Brown.

Brown had received a number of letters suggesting he would be killed if he dared to pitch against the Giants. Nonetheless, here he came wending his way from the bullpen through the hostile crowd. There were two on and two out. "Arthur Devlin was up," said Brown, "a low-average hitter but tough in the pinches. I fanned him, and then you should have heard the names that flew around me as I walked to the bench. I never heard anybody or any set of men called as many foul names as the Giants fans called us that day, from the time we showed up till it was over."

Chance, the primary target of the fans' ire, led off the second with a sharp single to center. But when the ball came back to the infield, he was caught off first base and tagged out on a close play. Cubs center fielder Solly Hofman argued the call too strenuously and was thrown out of the game. Mathewson then struck out Harry Steinfeldt and Del Howard, who was pinch-hitting for Hofman.

The turning point came in the third, when Tinker lined the first pitch over Seymour's head in center field for a triple. Kling's single to left center scored Tinker to tie the game 1-1. After Brown sacrificed Kling to second, Evers was intentionally walked. Wildfire Schulte's liner over third ended up in the crowd down the left-field line for a ground-rule double, scoring Kling and sending Evers to third. Up came Chance. Amidst a cacophony of jeers, he banged a double to right, scoring Evers and Schulte.

While the Giants and their fans grew progressively more desperate, Brown and the Cubs maintained the 4-1 advantage through the sixth inning. In the bottom of the seventh, New York mounted a threat. Devlin and McCormick singled and Bridwell walked to load the bases with nobody out. McGraw sent Larry Doyle in to pinch-hit for Mathewson.

This was the kind of situation that brought out the best in Three-Finger Brown. With 50,000 voices screaming for him to fail, he triumphed. First, Doyle lofted a foul pop-up behind the plate. Kling had to dodge a number of projectiles while circling under the ball, but he made the catch. Then Tenney flied to Schulte in right, scoring Devlin. Finally, Herzog smashed a hot grounder toward left, but Tinker gloved it and threw him out. The would-be rally had produced only one run, the mighty Mathewson was out of the game, and Brown was in control.

A Cubs victory began to seem inevitable. "I was about as good that day," said Brown, "as I ever was in my life." He retired the Giants in order in the eighth. By the bottom of the ninth, the fans had given up booing and hissing the Cubs and had taken to fighting amongst themselves. "It was as near a lunatic asylum as I ever saw," Brown recalled. After a semblance of order had been restored, Brown needed but four pitches to subdue the Giants. The final out was recorded when Bridwell, whose hit had precipitated the Merkle incident, grounded to Tinker.

"As the ninth ended with the Giants going one-two-three," said Brown, "we all ran for our lives with the pack at our heels. Some of our boys got caught by the mob and beaten up some." Chance was punched in the throat, Hofman was hit in the face with a bottle, and Pfiester was slashed on the shoulder with a knife. The Cubs rode back to their hotel in paddy wagons with armed policemen lining the running boards.

"My team," said John McGraw, "merely lost something it had honestly won three weeks ago." Thus he blamed the Merkle incident of September 23, but not Merkle himself, for the loss of the pennant. Merkle's teammates also understood that any one of them could have made the same mistake. Even Al Bridwell, the man who was deprived of the biggest hit of his career and credited with a fielder's choice instead, had only empathy for the rookie. "I think anyone would have done the same thing that Fred Merkle did," he said.

New York fans, though, blamed Merkle's "bonehead" play and the "villainy" of the Cubs for giving Chicago the title. Although he played usefully in the majors for a dozen more years (including four with the

17

Cubs), Merkle never lived it down. "I wish I'd never gotten that hit," Bridwell said many years later. "I wish I'd struck out instead. If I'd have done that, then it would have spared Fred a lot of unfair humiliation."

Those who hung it all on Fred Merkle didn't notice that the Giants lost six times *after* the disputed game and went only 11-9 down the stretch (while the Cubs went 13-2 and the Pirates 12-2). They didn't remember that Harry Coveleski of the also-ran Phillies beat the Giants *three times* between Tuesday, September 29, and Saturday, October 3. And they didn't understand that Three-Finger Brown wouldn't be defeated when it mattered most, even by Christy Mathewson. "He was one of the wonders of baseball," Bridwell said of Brown. "What a tremendous pitcher he was!"

After the most bitterly contested pennant race ever seen, the World Series was bound to be something of an anticlimax. It offered a rematch of the previous year's fall classic, in which the Cubs had swept Ty Cobb and the Detroit Tigers four games to none. (The Cubs' hopes for another crack at the White Sox were foiled when the Sox finished a game and a half out.) "We will beat Detroit easily," declared Mrs. Frank Chance, and she was right. This time, Detroit managed to win one game. Brown and Orval Overall each won twice to lead the Cubs to their second World Series championship.

Who could have known that even the youngest of Cubs fans would never see a third?

CHAPTER 3

A League of His Own

We are the ship, all else the sea.

-- Slogan of the Negro National League, 1920

As an African-American, Andrew Foster found few doors open to him in the early days of the 20th century, but he was not fazed. He carved out a long and influential career in baseball that would stand up to comparison with anyone's.

Foster was the son of a preacher from the rural hamlet of Calvert, Texas, about halfway between Dallas and Houston, who decided early in life not to follow in his father's footsteps. He dropped out of school after the eighth grade (when he was already six feet tall and fast approaching 200 pounds), and soon after he was making a modest living pitching for a black semipro club in Waco. Even in his teens, Foster had a full repertoire of pitches—a blistering fastball, tantalizing curve, and what he called the "fadeaway" (now known as the screwball). His reputation spread rapidly, and he was brought to Chicago by South-Side impresario Frank Leland in 1901. In the midst of his first barnstorming tour with Leland's Union Giants, Foster quit and signed up with an integrated semipro league in the wilds of Michigan.

Foster joined the all-black Philadelphia Cuban X-Giants in 1902. He was bombed 13-0 by a team from Hoboken in his first start, but he was all but unbeatable thereafter, reportedly winning 44 games in a row at one point. In the series for the "Colored World's Championship" in 1903, Foster won four games as the X-Giants beat the Philadelphia Giants five games to two. A year of trash talking between the two clubs followed; they did not meet again until a ballyhooed three-game series after the 1904 season. Foster struck out 18 batters in Game 1 and tossed a two-hitter in Game 3 as the X-Giants swept the three games. In 1905, he jumped over to the Philadelphia Giants and went 51-5.

Foster was easily the finest black pitcher before Satchel Paige, and perhaps the best, black or white, of his day. Alas, he was born a couple generations too early to play in the white major leagues. Foster was a master of the psychological aspects of pitching. "The real test comes when you are pitching with men on bases," he explained. "Do not worry. Try to appear jolly and unconcerned. I have smiled often with the bases full with two strikes and three balls on the batter. This seems to unnerve them. In other instances, where the batter appears anxious to hit waste a little time on him, and when you think he realizes his position and everybody is yelling at him to hit it out, waste a few balls and try his nerve. The majority of times you will win out by drawing him into hitting at a wide one."

In 1901, manager John McGraw of the Baltimore Orioles wanted a second baseman named Charlie Grant in the worst way. But there was a problem: Grant was black. McGraw hatched a scheme that would have been comical if it weren't so tragic. He tried to pass the light-skinned Grant off as a Native American. Charles Comiskey, owner of the White Sox, would have none of it. "If McGraw really keeps this 'Indian,'" Comiskey said, "I will get a Chinaman of my acquaintance and put him on third. Somebody told me that this Cherokee of McGraw's is really Grant, the crack Negro second baseman from Cincinnati, fixed up with war paint and a bunch of feathers." McGraw backed down. Grant was let go after playing in a couple of intrasquad games.

After McGraw took over the New York Giants, he set his sights on acquiring Foster. But as the Grant incident should have taught him, there was absolutely no chance of that. While black players were never *officially* barred from the major leagues, a tacit agreement among the club owners ensured that segregation remained in effect until after World War II. In 1933, for example, National League president John Heydler said, "I do not recall one instance where baseball has allowed race, creed, or color to enter into its selection of players." At the same time, though, he and other executives were working behind the scenes to preserve the status quo.

Foster never pitched in the majors, but he often faced white stars in exhibition games and more than held his own. After he bested the great Rube Waddell of the Philadelphia Athletics one day, no one ever called him Andrew again. From then on, he was Rube.

One of the tenets of Foster's philosophy was that the pitcher shouldn't resort to the fastball in a tough jam. "Some pitchers when they have three balls and two strikes on a batter," he wrote, "bring the ball straight over the plate and as the batter is always looking for it that way he will possibly 'break up the game' for you. I use a curve ball mostly when in the hole. In the first place, the batter is not looking for it, and secondly, they will hit at a curve quicker as it may come over the plate, and if not, they are liable to be fooled." Foster's principles of pitching resonated throughout baseball; he often claimed to be a sort of freelance coach for McGraw's Giants and Connie Mack's Athletics.

Foster returned to Chicago in 1907 to join Frank Leland's new team, the Leland Giants. Before signing on, he demanded to be appointed manager and booking agent for the club. These demands were accepted, and Foster was on his way to becoming black baseball's most powerful mogul as well as its most famous player.

Under Foster, the Leland Giants introduced a style of baseball that hadn't been seen before. They used the hit-and-run, bunt-and-run, and other plays not in special situations, but all the time. When they got a man on first base, they would steal second, or pull off a hit-and-run or bunt-and-run. The Leland Giants often advanced two bases on a well-executed bunt. The more rattled his opponents got, the more tricks Foster would use to torment them.

"You don't have to get three hits a day for me, or even two," Foster told his players. "I only want one at the right time." The Leland Giants were said to have won 90 percent of their games from 1907 through 1909. At the same time, Foster negotiated ever-larger shares of the gate receipts, so that the club collected about $500 per game—not bad money in those days.

White major leaguers often played, under assumed names, against the Leland Giants in the Chicago City League, whose clubs represented various neighborhoods (Logan Square and Rogers Park, for example) and were sponsored by local businessmen. These Saturday- and Sunday-morning games were over early enough that the big leaguers could get to their real jobs in plenty of time, with some extra cash in their pockets. Joe Tinker and Johnny Evers of the Cubs, among others, were regulars in the Chicago City League. But when Cubs owner Charles W. Murphy scheduled a three-game exhibition series with the Leland Giants in 1909, Evers refused to play. So did player-manager Frank Chance, who earlier, in an unguarded moment, had called Foster "the most finished product I have ever seen in the pitcher's box."

By this time Foster was feuding with Frank Leland, and he pronounced himself unfit to play in the series because of a broken leg. In the first game, Cubs ace Three-Finger Brown outdueled Walter Ball 4-2, "with the help of the umpires" (according to black newspapers), "who were more than favorable to the Cubs." The Cubs won the second game 1-0 behind Ed Reulbach. Suddenly, Foster declared that he was ready to go, his "broken leg" having miraculously healed. Perhaps this dramatic comeback had been planned all along. In any event, Foster received a tremendous ovation from the integrated crowd when he appeared on the mound for the third game.

The Leland Giants staked Foster to a 5-0 lead against Orval Overall. It seemed for a while that he would make short work of the Cubs, but by the ninth inning he was in trouble and tiring badly. Leading 5-2 now, with the bases loaded and one out, Foster walked in a run. He got the second out on a force play at the plate. Then light-hitting outfielder Del Howard stroked a double that tied the score and sent the winning run to third.

"What happened next has become a matter of conjecture," Mark Ribowsky wrote in his history of the Negro Leagues. "What is known is that Foster walked off the mound and to his dugout, in order, he said later, to bring in a reliever, and only after calling time-out. But since no one on the field heard Rube call time, and with no sign from any umpire, Frank 'Wildfire' Schulte bolted from third and crossed the plate with the winning run." Foster blamed the bizarre ending on the white umpiring crew, but he never explained why he had left the mound with the game on the line—a very uncharacteristic act for a man who normally relished these situations.

Although he was only 30, Foster had become grossly overweight by 1909, and his playing days were all but over. His infrequent appearances on the mound were promoted in black newspapers for days in advance, ensuring good crowds, but he was increasingly ineffective. He didn't really mind, having already concluded that his future in baseball depended more on his managerial, administrative, and selling skills than on his waning physical ability.

The debacle against the Cubs marked the end of Foster's association with Leland. Foster started up his own club, the Chicago American Giants, in 1910. He leased South Side Park, an 8,000-seat facility at 39th and Wentworth, from John Schorling, a saloonkeeper and the son-in-law of Charles Comiskey (whose White Sox were just moving into their palatial new home at 35th and Shields). For years, Comiskey would happily reap tidy profits from black baseball while stressing the need to keep the major leagues all-white.

Since Foster was legally enjoined from taking any of Leland's players with him, he raided the best black clubs in the East and put together a juggernaut. "He put on all the plays and he had the type of men that could do just what he wanted them to do," Negro Leagues veteran Buck O'Neil said. "Can you imagine a ballclub with eight or nine Rickey Hendersons? This was the Chicago American Giants in 1911, 1912. Everybody could go to first base in under four seconds, and Rube would score runs without a base hit."

The American Giants played few games in Chicago. Instead, they traveled throughout the Midwest, West, and even the South, going to places where few black teams had dared to play. They dressed in the most stylish suits, rode the rails in a private Pullman car, and became black America's team. In every dusty town they went through, the African-American community greeted Foster as a conquering hero. "I shall never forget the first time I saw Rube Foster," said Dave Malarcher of Louisiana. "I never saw such a well-equipped ballclub in my whole life. I was astounded. Every day they came out in a different set of beautiful uniforms, all kinds of bats and balls, all the best of equipment." If one of the local players showed especially well against his club, Foster was liable to sign him up on the spot; this was the equivalent of winning the lottery for a young black man living in the Deep South at the time. Malarcher was among the players who experienced this miracle.

The American Giants went 123-6 in 1910. They were the dominant force in black baseball throughout the teens, although they were challenged for supremacy by clubs such as the Indianapolis ABCs, Detroit Stars, and St. Louis Giants. These stronger clubs tended to play each other only rarely, because games against white semipro and industrial teams generally drew better crowds than all-black contests. Taking note of this, the *Chicago Defender* complained that it would not be surprising if the American Giants soon "depended on the other race altogether." But the Great Migration of African Americans from the rural South into northern cities during and immediately after World War I changed all that. Suddenly there were hundreds of thousands of new fans available for black baseball.

Throughout 1919, Foster loudly campaigned for a league that would serve this burgeoning pool of potential fans, stop the merry-go-round of players jumping from club to club for a few extra dollars, and eliminate the presence of white investors in the black game. (On these last two points, Foster would have had to be taken with a large pinch of salt. He had built his club by blithely raiding the rosters of others, and he remained heavily dependent on the financial backing of his silent partners, Schorling and Comiskey.)

The Negro National League was founded in February 1920 in Kansas City. In addition to the American Giants, the league included the Chicago Giants, Cincinnati Cuban Giants, Dayton Marcos, Detroit Stars, Indianapolis ABCs, Kansas City Monarchs, and St. Louis Giants. Its letterhead proclaimed "A.R. Foster" as Chairman of the Board of Directors and as Chairman of the league's governing body, the National Association of Colored Professional Base Ball Clubs. It also carried, in a swirling script, the motto "We Are the Ship, All Else the Sea." Foster immediately dictated a series of personnel moves to balance the league. He sent his own star outfielders, Oscar Charleston and Jimmie Lyons, to Indianapolis and Detroit, respectively. He sent pitchers Jose Mendez and Sam Crawford from Indianapolis to Kansas City. He sent pitcher John Donaldson from Kansas City to Detroit, and so on.

The NNL's first game was played on May 2, 1920, with the Indianapolis ABCs beating the American Giants 4-2. Each of the eight teams was supposed to have a permanent home ballpark and was scheduled to play 100 games, but these plans soon went awry. The Cincinnati Cuban Giants never did line up a suitable ballpark, so they played all their games on the road. Some teams skipped league games on Saturdays and Sundays in favor of more lucrative dates with local white clubs. "Foster spent long hours in his office," Ribowsky wrote, "seeking to solve every problem in the operation. When teams ran out of money and were stranded on the road, Rube would wire them enough to get home. When teams were on the verge of going bankrupt, Rube would send a payroll advance to keep them afloat. Still trying to pump up weak clubs, he continued to rearrange player rosters."

It was rocky going at first, but the Negro National League survived and even flourished. The eight teams drew a total of 616,000 fans the first year, and each made a profit. Foster did not take a salary to run the league, but an entity called the Western Booking Agency, of which he was sole owner, collected 10 percent of all gate receipts; this meant an $11,000 windfall for Rube in 1920, and considerably more in later years. Foster stayed on as manager of the American Giants for the first two years of the NNL's existence. In the absence of a balanced schedule or official record keeping, and with newspaper coverage of the league spotty at best, no one could say for sure which team had won the first NNL pennant. When the league office declared that the American Giants had, no one complained.

Foster's league prospered throughout the early twenties. Total player salaries soared from $30,000 in 1920 to $275,000 in 1925. The first Negro World Series was played in 1924. It matched the Kansas City Monarchs against the Philadelphia Hilldales of the new Eastern Colored League. The 10-game series was a traveling show, with two games played in Philadelphia, two in Baltimore, three in Kansas City, and three in Chicago. In the final game, with Foster calling the pitches for him from the Monarchs' dugout, Jose Mendez tossed a three-hit shutout as Kansas City claimed the series five games to four with one tie.

The series was a huge success, both artistically and financially, but it marked the last hurrah for Rube Foster. The Eastern Colored League, which had been formed by white entrepreneurs impressed by the profits Foster's league had rung up, soon began luring NNL players with its higher salaries. Foster worked harder and harder trying to stanch the flow of stars to the rival league. By 1926 he was physically and mentally exhausted; he had to be institutionalized. He had periods of lucidity thereafter, but eventually dementia took hold of him. He remained in the state hospital at Kankakee for the rest of his life, convinced that he would soon be summoned to pitch in the white World Series. On December 9, 1930, Foster suffered a heart attack and died at the age of 51.

Foster's body lay in state at a Chicago funeral parlor for three days, while lines of mourners stretched for blocks in the icy winds. Each day the casket was closed, according to a contemporary reporter, "at the usual hour a ballgame ends." Three thousand people attended the funeral.

Foster had aimed for nothing less than creating a stable, self-sustaining league for black ballplayers that was on a par with the white major leagues. He didn't quite pull it off, but he came as close as anyone ever would. In the thirties and forties, the Negro Leagues featured players such as Cool Papa Bell, Josh Gibson, Buck Leonard, Satchel Paige, and a few dozen others who were at least the equal of their white counterparts. The undeniable quality of the play on the field, however, was usually accompanied by the same casual approach to contractual commitments, financial management, and other formalities that Foster had fought so hard to overcome.

After Jackie Robinson's debut with the Brooklyn Dodgers in 1947, the black leagues survived, barely, for another decade while the likes of Larry Doby, Roy Campanella, Joe Black, Don Newcombe, Luke Easter, Sam Jethroe, Monte Irvin, Willie Mays, Ernie Banks, Hank Aaron, and even the forty-something Paige became part of a mass exodus to the major leagues.

CHAPTER 4

Moments, 1917-1922

May 2, 1917
Double No-Hitter

The cold, blustery afternoon of Wednesday, May 2, 1917, was not a promising one for baseball, and only about 2,500 fans came to Wrigley Field (then known as Weeghman Park) for the privilege of seeing something unique in baseball history.

The Cubs and Reds each sent their ace to the mound—Hippo Vaughn for Chicago and Fred Toney for Cincinnati. Vaughn walked Heinie Groh twice, but each time the Cubs turned a double play to end the threat. Toney, a former Cub, walked Cy Williams twice, but allowed no other baserunners. An error by the Cubs put Greasy Neale on base, but he was promptly caught stealing.

On and on it went, inning after inning, with neither team managing a hit. It was the ultimate pitcher's duel. When the Reds were retired in the ninth (with Toney fanning for the final out), the sparse crowd cheered lustily, both for Vaughn's magnificent pitching and for the prospect of a Cub rally in the bottom half of the inning. But the Cubs went down easily. Both Vaughn and Toney had gone a full nine innings without yielding a hit. But only Toney would go into the record books as having pitched an official no-hitter.

Vaughn got the first batter in the 10th to pop out. Then Larry Kopf drilled the first hit of the game, a single to left center. After Neale flied out to Williams in center, Hal Chase hit another fly to Williams for the apparent third out. But Williams muffed it. Kopf took third on the error, and Chase stole second on the next pitch. Jim Thorpe was at bat (yes, the same Jim Thorpe to whom King Gustav V of Sweden said, at

27

the 1912 Olympic Games in Stockholm, "You, sir, are the greatest athlete in the world").

Thorpe swung and topped a little dribbler down the third-base line. "I knew the minute it was hit," Vaughn said, "that I couldn't get Thorpe at first. He was fast as a racehorse. So I went over to the line, fielded the ball, and scooped it toward the plate. Kopf, running in, was right behind me and he stopped when he saw me make the throw to the plate. I didn't see him or I could have just turned around and tagged him out." Catcher Art Wilson wasn't able to handle Vaughn's throw; it hit his chest protector and bounded away, allowing Neale to score. When Chase rounded third and tried to score too, Wilson finally recovered the ball and tagged him out. But the damage had been done.

Toney set the Cubs down one-two-three in the bottom half of the inning to preserve a 1-0 victory and a 10-inning no-hitter. Vaughn went on to win 23 games that year, but there again he came up just shy of Toney, who won 24.

October 13, 1917
Workhorse

The 1917 White Sox won 100 games (still a franchise record) and cruised to the American League pennant by nine games. In the World Series against the New York Giants, they won the first two games at Comiskey Park, 2-1 and 7-2, with Eddie Cicotte going the distance in Game 1 and Red Faber doing likewise in Game 2. The Sox pounded out 14 hits in Game 2, and even Faber—an .058 hitter for the regular season—joined in the fun, rapping a single to right in the fifth inning. When Giant right fielder Davy Robertson threw home to hold Buck Weaver at third on the play, Faber alertly took second. Then, seeing that pitcher Pol Perritt was ignoring him, Faber took off for third on the next pitch. He slid in, apparently safe, only to come face-to-face with Weaver, who was still occupying the base. "Where the hell are *you* going?" Weaver asked. The sheepish Faber replied, "Why, back to pitch, of course."

Faber could afford to laugh at his baserunning blunder after the Sox scored an easy victory in the game, but the Sox weren't laughing when they were shut out in Games 3 and 4 at New York. In the pivotal Game 5 on October 13, back at Comiskey Park, they were down 5-2 heading into the bottom of the seventh, and their hopes for a world championship seemed to be fading fast. But the Sox rallied for three to tie the score.

When the Sox took the field for the eighth, manager Pants Rowland called on Faber, even though he had pitched seven tough innings just two days before. Faber set the Giants down in order. The Sox scored three times in their half of the eighth to take the lead. Faber was again perfect in the top of the ninth, and the Sox won 8-5. It was the turning point of the Series: the momentum had shifted back in Chicago's favor.

For Game 6 in New York, Rowland *again* elected to go with Faber. In the top of the fourth, the Giants fell apart defensively. Eddie Collins reached on a bad throw by third baseman Heinie Zimmerman, who, it was said, "fielded by ear." Joe Jackson lofted an easy fly ball that Robertson dropped. Then Happy Felsch hit a bouncer to Zimmerman, and it appeared that Collins was hung up between third and home. Inexplicably, however, catcher Bill Rariden and pitcher Rube Benton both left the plate unattended. With the unfortunate Zimmerman chasing him, Collins streaked home with the first run of the game. Jackson and Felsch scored on a single by Chick Gandil, and the White Sox were on their way. Faber went all the way, scattering six hits, as the Sox won 4-2 to claim the Series.

Faber pitched 27 innings in the Series, winning three games and losing one. He and Cicotte pitched 50 of the 52 innings between them. Faber went on to star for the South Siders until 1933, but he missed the infamous 1919 World Series with an injury. "If Red had been available," catcher Ray Schalk said, "there would never have been a Black Sox scandal."

April 30, 1922
Perfect

On April 30, 1922, White Sox pitcher Charlie Robertson took the hill in Detroit to face a formidable assemblage led by 12-time batting champion Ty Cobb. Cobb, the Tigers' center fielder and manager, was showing no signs of slowing down at age thirty-five. Flanking him in the outfield were Bobby Veach in left and Harry Heilmann in right. This trio comprised the three-four-five combination in the batting order and was responsible for most of Detroit's offensive production. Cobb would hit .401 that year, Veach .327, and Heilmann .356, and the three would combine for 317 runs batted in.

A crowd in excess of 25,000 was on hand, and officials at Navin Field (as Tiger Stadium was known in those days) found themselves with more fans than seats. As was common practice at the time, they simply roped off sections of the outfield and put the extra fans there. Any ball that rolled or bounced beyond the ropes would be called a ground-rule double.

Robertson was still a rookie, having spent the past three years in the minors after pitching (and losing) one game for the Sox in 1919. But he pitched like a wily old veteran against the Tigers, mixing a lively fastball with an assortment of slower stuff and demonstrating pinpoint control. He retired Cobb on a grounder to third, a fly to short left, and a strikeout. He retired Veach on a deep drive to left (Johnny Mostil making the catch just inside the ropes), a high pop fly to right, and a strikeout. He retired Heilmann on a fly to right, a tap back to the mound, and a foul pop to first.

You get the picture. Robertson faced 27 batters and retired them all for a perfect game. Six Tigers fanned, seven grounded out, six flied out, and—this was the real measure of Robertson's effectiveness—*eight* hit pop-ups on the infield. The more frustrated the Tigers got, the harder they swung; and the harder they swung, the more weak pop flies they hit.

Hoping in vain to upset the rookie, the Tigers complained ceaselessly from the fifth inning on that he was illegally doctoring the ball. First Heilmann, then Cobb, demanded that the home-plate umpire search Robertson's cap and uniform for a foreign substance. When nothing was found, Cobb had the umpire inspect the Sox first baseman, Earl Sheely, also to no avail. (It was Sheely whose second-inning single had knocked in Harry Hooper and Mostil with what proved to be the only runs of the game).

Late in the game, the Detroit fans took to cheering for Robertson. When pinch-hitter Johnny Bassler flied to Mostil for the final out, a group of fans carried Robertson off the field on their shoulders. He had pitched the third perfect game of the modern era, joining Cy Young and Addie Joss in a very exclusive club (there would be no new members until 1956, when Don Larsen pitched his famous perfect game in the World Series).

From absolute perfection, of course, there is only one direction to go, and Charlie Robertson's subsequent career proved the point nicely. He lost more games than he won every year, allowing better than a hit per inning and walking more batters than he struck out. He finished up with a record of 49-80 over eight seasons. Later he regretted having played major-league baseball at all. "It is ridiculous," he said, "for any young man with qualifications to make good in another profession to waste time in professional athletics." But where else could one be perfect, even if only for one day?

CHAPTER 5

Fix

"We've sold ourselves and our jobs—the only jobs we know anything about.
We've gotten in return only a few dollars, while a lot of gamblers have gotten
rich. Looks like the joke's on us, don't it?"

-- Happy Felsch, White Sox center fielder, 1915-1920

"There never was a better ballclub," White Sox second baseman Eddie Collins said before the 1919 World Series against the Cincinnati Reds. Most experts agreed: the Sox were loaded.

The Sox' top three starting pitchers won 65 games and lost 25. Eddie Cicotte was 29-7 with a 1.82 earned-run average. He led the league in wins, winning percentage, innings pitched, complete games, and fewest walks per nine innings. If Cicotte wasn't the best pitcher in the league, he was a *very* close second to the immortal Walter Johnson. Lefty Williams was only slightly less dominant, at 23-11 and 2.64. Rookie Dickie Kerr was 13-7 and 2.88.

On the offensive side, the Sox led the league in hits, runs scored, batting average, and stolen bases. Collins hit .319, scored 87 runs, knocked in 80, and swiped a league-leading 33 bases. Third baseman Buck Weaver batted .296 and led the club in runs scored with 89. Catcher Ray Schalk (like Collins a future Hall of Famer) contributed excellent defense while hitting .282. Left fielder Shoeless Joe Jackson, the best of them all, hit .351 with a team-leading 96 runs batted in. He struck out only 10 times in 599 plate appearances.

"We've got everything," said Collins. "We ought to win."

But the Reds won the Series five games to three (in 1903 and from 1919 to 1921, the World Series was best of nine). That the Sox lost was shocking. *How* they lost was appalling, with some star players performing in a manner that was almost comically inept. *Why* they lost became known a year later, touching off the greatest scandal in the history of American sports.

In Game 1 at Cincinnati, Cicotte, the American League's leader in wins and complete games during the regular season, was bombed 9-1. The next day, Williams, who hadn't walked more than two batters in a game all season, walked three in one *inning*, providing the impetus for the Reds' 4-2 win.

The Series then shifted to Chicago, and the Sox looked more like themselves as Kerr blanked the Reds 3-0 in Game 3. With two more home games coming up, Sox fans had reason to be optimistic. But inexplicably bad play returned in Game 4. Cicotte pitched creditably enough but committed two errors to give the Reds their only runs in a 2-0 decision.

In Game 5, the Sox were again listless as Cincinnati pounded Williams 5-0.

The Reds had taken four of the first five games with astonishing ease. Sox manager Kid Gleason was beside himself. "I don't know what's the matter, but I do know that something is wrong with my gang," he told reporters. "The bunch I had in August fighting for the pennant would have trimmed this Cincinnati bunch without a struggle. The bunch I have now couldn't beat a high school team."

"There is more ugly talk and more suspicion among the fans than there ever has been in any World's Series," sportswriter Hugh Fullerton wrote. "The rumors of crookedness, of fixed games and plots, are thick."

Fullerton and Ring Lardner took to circling suspicious plays on their scorecards and then comparing notes with Christy Mathewson, the former Giants ace who was covering the series for a New York newspaper. All three agreed that something fishy was going on. They even made a list of White Sox players who appeared to be giving less than their best effort.

Meanwhile, the Sox clubhouse, several players were openly accused of having thrown the games. On one occasion, Gleason tried to strangle first baseman Chick Gandil; on another, Schalk jumped Williams and pummeled him before being restrained.

The teams returned to Cincinnati, where a huge crowd gave the Reds a heroes' welcome at the train station. It seemed that the Reds would have the pleasure of closing out the Series before the home folks, who were ecstatic at their club's surprising good fortune. But in Game 6, behind another determined effort by Kerr, the Sox prevailed 5-4 in 10 innings to stave off elimination. Then Cicotte displayed his regular-season form as he cruised to a 4-1 victory in Game 7.

"For the second day in a row," Gleason told reporters on the train back to Chicago, "my gang played the kind of baseball it has been playing all season. Even though we are still one game behind, we will win for sure."

It was not to be. On October 9 at Comiskey Park, with Lefty Williams back on the hill for the Sox, any doubts about the outcome of the Series were put to rest. Williams retired only one batter, and yielded four runs, before heading off to the showers in the first inning. The Sox were not in the game thereafter, and the Reds won 10-5 to become world champions.

"The Reds beat the greatest ball team that ever went into a World's Series," Gleason said after the final game. "But it wasn't the real White Sox. They played baseball for me only a couple or three of the eight days."

In the weeks following the Series, allegations that the games had been fixed became widespread. This was not the first whiff of a gambling scandal affecting the national pastime. Far from it. In those days betting on major-league games was roughly as popular as betting on NFL games became decades later. There was a lot of money involved, which inevitably led to the corruption of certain players. But previous episodes had been on a much smaller scale and were brushed under the rug rather easily.

For a time, Fullerton's articles detailing his concerns about the Series were dismissed as mere sensationalism. "These yarns are manufactured out of whole cloth," Comiskey said.

Despite his public pronoucements, however, Comiskey had actually been suspicious from the beginning. He had even delayed sending out the players' World Series checks until the initial controversy died down somewhat. From then on, he kept his fingers crossed. "I believe my boys fought the battles of the recent World's Series on the level," he said. "And I would be the first to want information to the contrary."

Comiskey grandly announced that he would pay $10,000 to anyone who produced proof of a fix. When a number of people came forward to take him up on it, though, he rejected all the information offered as "hearsay."

But the matter ultimately couldn't be wished away. By late summer of 1920, separate investigations had been launched by American League president Ban Johnson and, more ominously, a Cook County grand jury. Although the grand jury's inquiry was into the influence of gamblers and gambling throughout baseball, it eventually focused on eight White Sox players and their role in the events of 1919.

With his players being hauled before the grand jury and the whole squalid story about to be revealed, Comiskey had little choice but to suspend the seven men who'd been implicated: Cicotte, Williams, Weaver, Jackson, center fielder Happy Felsch, shortstop Swede Risberg, and infielder Fred McMullin. (Gandil had retired after the Series.)

The Sox trailed Cleveland by only one game with three left to play when the suspensions were announced on September 28, 1920. The Indians won the pennant and went on to take the World Series.

Losing the pennant was now the least of the White Sox' problems. In the grand jury room, the players told their tale of greed and betrayal. It began in a New York hotel during the waning days of the 1919 regular season. Gandil announced to several teammates that they could collect $20,000 for each losing game in the impending World Series, for a total of $100,000. It was a tempting offer—for although they were the best team in baseball, the Sox were among the lowest paid. Their nickname, "Black Sox," was later used to refer to the scandal, but it actually originated in 1918 to describe the filthy uniforms the players wore to protest Comiskey's refusal to pay for laundering.

Cicotte had been promised a $10,000 bonus if he won 30 games in 1919—but after he won his 29th, Comiskey ordered him benched for the remainder of the regular season. Cicotte had counted on the bonus money to pay off the mortgage on his new farm. Before the grand jury, he confessed that he had taken part in the fix for $10,000 in cash, up front. Cicotte had found the cash under his pillow the night before

Game 1. The next afternoon, he'd signaled to the other conspirators that the fix was on by hitting Cincinnati's leadoff batter, Morrie Rath, with his second pitch in the first inning.

"It is hard to tell when a game is on the square and when it is not," Cicotte advised the grand jury. "A player can make a crooked error that will look on the square as easy as he can make a square one." As for his own pitching in the two games he had lost, Cicotte said, "You could have read the trademark on [the ball], the way I lobbed it over the plate. Why, a baby could have hit 'em. Schalk was wise the moment I started pitching."

Lefty Williams claimed that he had gone along only because of threats on his life. After Game 5, by which time it was apparent that not all of the agreed-upon payments were being delivered, the players had decided to double cross the gamblers and play Games 6 and 7 to win. They *had* won both games, and Williams testified that a stranger had visited him the night before Game 8 to tell him that he would be killed if the Sox won again. The next day, Lefty had failed to make it through the first inning, becoming the first pitcher to lose three games in a single World Series (this record went unequaled for 62 years).

Happy Felsch admitted that he had been paid $5,000. "I could have got just about that much," he said ruefully, "by being on the level if the Sox had won the Series." A .275 hitter during the regular season, Felsch had hit .192 in the Series.

Fred McMullin, a benchwarmer who could not have affected the outcome, had been let in on the plot after overhearing Gandil and Risberg talking about it in the Sox clubhouse. Promised a full share in exchange for keeping quiet, he'd received nothing.

Buck Weaver also hadn't gotten a penny, but he admitted that he had attended meetings with the others and had failed to blow the whistle on them. He had played superbly throughout the Series; his 11 hits were second only to Jackson's 12 among players on both clubs.

Joe Jackson testified that he had been promised $20,000 but had collected only $5,000. A virtually illiterate country boy from South Carolina, Jackson was Ty Cobb's only rival as the finest hitter of the era; his .356 career mark remains the third-highest of all time. He had batted .385 in the Series. Shoeless Joe stood at the pinnacle of his career when he and the others were suspended—in 1920, he hit for a .382 average, with 105 runs scored, 12 homers, and 121 RBIs.

Cicotte, Williams, Felsch, and Jackson all agreed that they had received but a fraction of the money promised them. They believed that the rest had been siphoned by Gandil and his roommate Risberg. "I told Williams after the first day it was a crooked deal all the way through," Jackson said. "Gandil was not on the square with us."

Gandil, whom Cicotte called the "master of ceremonies" for the scheme, denied everything. He had batted .233 in the Series, with most of his hits coming late in games that had already been decided. He had turned down Comiskey's offer of a contract for 1920 and had retired from baseball—according to Jackson, because he could no longer face the others and because he had plenty to retire on.

Risberg had managed only two hits in the Series for an average of .080, while experiencing a variety of lapses at shortstop.

It is difficult to imagine today how traumatic the Black Sox revelations were at the time. Americans still had unqualified faith in their institutions, perhaps the most sacred of which was the national pastime. The nation's sense of betrayed trust was captured in the single sentence that a young boy is supposed to have uttered to Jackson on the courthouse steps: "Say it ain't so, Joe."

A gambler named Arnold Rothstein was widely suspected of having pulled all the strings. He was said to have made hundreds of thousands betting on the Reds, but he would have made two or three times as much if the fix had not been so blatant as to drive the odds down to even money. Called to testify when the scandal broke, Rothstein came away from his encounter with the grand jury unscathed, and went on to a long career in organized crime in New York before being shot to death in a dispute over a poker game.

On October 22, 1920, the grand jury returned indictments against the eight players, former featherweight boxing champion Abe Attell (purportedly Rothstein's liaison to the players), former pitcher Sleepy Bill Burns, and a handful of others. Fixing a baseball game was not illegal in Illinois; the men were indicted for conspiracy to defraud the public and do injury to Charles Comiskey's business.

The trial, which began in June 1921, quickly proved a farce as the grand jury's records disappeared, witnesses recanted their earlier testimony, and the confessions of Cicotte, Jackson, Williams, and Weaver also turned up missing. Not surprisingly under the circumstances, the defendants were acquitted. When the charges against them were dismissed on August 2, the players were carried off to a nearby restaurant on the shoulders of courtroom spectators and even jurors for a post-trial party.

Though raucous, the celebration was short-lived. The very day after the trial concluded, commissioner Kenesaw Mountain Landis declared that the eight Black Sox would be banned from baseball for life. "Regardless of the verdict of juries," Landis intoned, "no player who throws a ballgame, no player that undertakes or promises to throw a ballgame, no player that sits in conference with a bunch of crooked ballplayers and gamblers where the ways and means of throwing a ballgame are discussed and does not promptly tell his club about it, will ever play professional baseball."

Desperate to restore the public's faith in the integrity of the game and its players, baseball had ordained Landis, a federal judge, as its first commissioner in November 1920. This slightly built, stern-faced fellow with a mane of snow-white hair had been granted absolute authority over owners, umpires, and players, along with the assurance that his decisions would not be subject to appeal. He retained these powers until his death in 1944.

Judge Landis and his successors saw to it that none of the eight Black Sox ever held a job in organized baseball again. As late as 1953, Buck Weaver was still writing to commissioner Ford Frick, pleading for reinstatement. None of his letters was ever answered.

CHAPTER 6

Birth of the Bears

"Nothing is work unless you'd rather be doing something else."
-- *George Halas, Bears founder and owner, 1920-1983*

On May 6, 1919, 24-year-old George Halas made his debut as a right fielder with the New York Yankees. In his first 12 games, he managed just two hits in 22 at-bats, for a batting average of .091. He had no doubles, no triples, no home runs, no runs batted in, and had struck out eight times. Manager Miller Huggins took him aside and told him that he was being sent down to the minor leagues for more seasoning.

Halas never appeared in another major-league game. By 1920, his baseball career was over. Babe Ruth had taken over right field for the Yankees, and Halas had embarked on a new career, to which he would devote his considerable energies for the next six decades.

In those days, games in industrial and semi-pro baseball leagues sometimes drew thousands of spectators. A.E. Staley, a manufacturer of corn starch and related products in Decatur, Illinois, had the idea that football games could be just as popular. He decided to sponsor a football team to represent his company, and he hired Halas to organize, coach, and play for it. Halas had made a name for himself on the gridiron at the University of Illinois, where he'd also lettered in baseball and basketball. He had been Most Valuable Player of the 1919 Rose Bowl game—but not in the orange and blue of Illinois. Halas had enlisted in the Navy when the United States entered World War I, and he was a member of the Great Lakes Naval Station team that defeated another group of servicemen, the Mare Island Marines, in the Rose Bowl.

Halas arrived in Decatur in March 1920. He had never forgotten something Illini coach Bob Zuppke had once said: "Just when I teach you fellows how to play football, you graduate and I lose you." Halas believed that "post-graduate football," as it was then called, had a future. But he was far from certain. College games routinely drew crowds of fifty, sixty, even seventy thousand spectators. The pro game was merely a curiosity to most fans, and pro players were generally regarded as nothing more than a bunch of hooligans. College coaches like the fabled Amos Alonzo Stagg condemned pro games as a scourge that corrupted the athletes and demeaned football itself. Halas's mind was made up, however, and even his mentor and idol Zuppke could not dissuade him from going forward—though he tried.

Halas got to work building his team by recruiting men he had played with or against in college. Among the notables he landed were center George Trafton of Notre Dame, halfback Jimmy Conzelman of Washington University (St. Louis), halfback Dutch Sternaman of Illinois, fullback Bob Koehler of Northwestern, tackle Hugh Blacklock of Michigan State, and All-American end Guy Chamberlin of Nebraska. Charlie Dressen, a Decatur native who hadn't played college football, would share the quarterback chores with Pard Pearce of Penn. (Dressen was soon to make the same career move Halas had, in reverse. After a brief stint in pro football, he switched to baseball and had an eight-year career as a third baseman with the Cincinnati Reds and New York Giants. He also managed for 16 years, winning pennants with the Brooklyn Dodgers in 1952 and 1953.)

Halas and the other players he'd signed up were placed on the Staley Company payroll, but they had few duties other than playing football. Their main job was to win games and bring favorable publicity to the company.

When Halas began trying to line up opponents for his new team, he ran into difficulty. He wrote to several of the better-known teams, but received noncommittal responses. "Paid football was pretty much of a catch-as-catch-can affair," Halas recalled many years later. "Teams appeared one week and disappeared the next. Players came and went, drawn by the pleasure of playing. If others came to watch, that was fine. If they bought tickets or tossed coins into a helmet passed by the most popular player, that was helpful."

Halas was thrilled when he learned that plans were afoot to organize a genuine league. Creating at least a semblance of order would be pro football's first step in building credibility with the public. On September 17, 1920, the American Professional Football Association was founded in Ralph Hay's Canton, Ohio, automobile showroom. Halas was there, representing the Decatur Staleys. Ten other teams became charter members of the fledgling league that day: Akron Pros, Canton Bulldogs, Chicago Cardinals, Cleveland Indians, Dayton Triangles, Hammond Pros, Massillon (Ohio) Tigers, Muncie Flyers, Rochester Jeffersons, and Rock Island Independents. Each agreed to pay $100 for a franchise. "To give the new organization an appearance of financial stability," Halas recalled, "we announced that the membership fee for individual clubs had been set at $100. However, I can testify that no money changed hands. Why, I doubt if there was a hundred bucks in the whole room."

The Buffalo All-Americans, Chicago Tigers, Columbus Panhandles, and Detroit Heralds also joined the APFA before its inaugural season. The Massillon club folded before playing a game; Muncie dropped out after a few games. The APFA was not a league in any real sense in 1920—it had no official schedule and kept no standings. League president Jim Thorpe, the legendary "world's greatest athlete," was purely a figurehead, chosen for his name. He was still an active player with Canton and hadn't the time, inclination, or authority to handle any larger issues. Teams still scheduled games as they pleased, traveling only within 150 miles or so of home. The Staleys, for example, played only four league teams all season—the Cardinals, Tigers, and Rock Island twice each, and Hammond once.

The Staleys opened their season on October 3 by easily subduing a non-league team, the Moline Tractors, 20-0 before about 1,000 fans at Staley Field in Decatur. They won their first seven games and weren't scored upon until the seventh, a 28-7 win over Hammond. They were scored upon only once more all season, in a 7-6 loss to the Cardinals in Chicago. That game drew a capacity crowd of 5,400 to the Cardinals' field at 61st and Racine, with more spectators watching from rooftops and even from trees. When the two teams played again in Wrigley Field (then known as Cubs Park), about 8,500 fans showed up to see the Staleys prevail 10-0.

Decatur finished 5-1-1 in league games, and Akron was 6-0-1. The teams had not met during the season, so they rented out Wrigley Field for the first "world's professional football championship game." The weather was atrocious, and the 11,000 fans who turned out were treated to a duel between the two punters, as the offenses of both teams bogged down in the mud. Akron's star player/coach Fritz Pollard—the first black All-American and the first black head coach in pro football by 60 years—was neutralized by the sloppy footing. So was Dutch Sternaman, the Staleys' main offensive threat. So, too, was Paddy Driscoll, the great star of the Cardinals, who had suited up for the Staleys. "Driscoll had already proved himself one of the best backs and kickers in the game," wrote Richard Whittingham, "and his team had ended [its] season the week before. The Decatur coaches put him in a Staley uniform, choosing to ignore the unwritten agreement about not tampering with another team's players, but in the end it did them no good." The game ended in a scoreless tie. Halas proposed a rematch, but Akron refused. Both teams claimed to be world champions.

The Staleys were off to an auspicious start. Including non-league games, they had compiled a record of 10-1-2, scoring 166 points while yielding only 14. Each player had earned about $1,900 for his efforts. Halas began planning for an even better year in 1921. But one day A.E. Staley suddenly informed him that he could no longer afford to subsidize the football team.

Halas was stunned. Staley, though, was about to do him the greatest favor of his life. "Mr. Staley was a good businessman," Halas wrote in his autobiography. "I assume he went over the books carefully. One glance must have shown him the way to the future did not lie in Decatur. The three games played there brought in $1,982.49, while the five Chicago games produced $20,162.06." Staley suggested that Halas and Sternaman take over ownership of the team and move it to Chicago. He even offered them $5,000 to get started, in return for a promise to retain the name "Staleys" for one more year. Halas and Sternaman eagerly took him up on it.

Shortly before the 1921 season, Halas called on Bill Veeck, Sr., president of the Cubs. He wanted to make Wrigley Field his team's permanent home. According to Halas, the negotiations lasted less than two minutes. Veeck asked for no cash up front—probably recognizing that the young entrepreneur had none anyway. Instead, he asked for a straight 15 percent of the gate receipts and all concessions. Halas, inwardly delighted but not wanting to accede too easily, said the Cubs could have all the concessions except the game programs. Veeck agreed. Veeck suggested that the Cubs' take should be raised to 20 percent whenever the gate exceeded $10,000. Halas agreed. The deal was sealed with a handshake, and, according to Halas, never committed to paper. It remained in effect until the Bears moved to Soldier Field half a century later.

The APFA was reorganized in 1921, becoming a league in the true sense of the word. Under its new president, Joe Carr, the APFA established an official schedule and began to keep standings and other statistics. It also enacted sanctions against tampering with players on other teams. The Staleys' recent misappropriation of Paddy Driscoll might have been the straw that broke the camel's back, but virtually every team had been guilty of using ringers on occasion. Players had casually jumped from club to club for the slightest inducements. Carr saw to it that this practice was discontinued.

The Staleys opened the 1921 season with an apparently meaningless exhibition game against the Waukegan American Legion team, winning 35-0. Then they played their first, and last, official league game in Decatur. A capacity crowd of 4,000 came out for the team's farewell appearance at Staley Field. The Staleys beat Rock Island 14-10, then boarded the train to Chicago. Halas rented out rooms for his players in a boarding house at 4414 N. Clarendon, for two dollars per man per week. The players walked to Wrigley Field for practices and games.

Through their first six league games, the Staleys were undefeated and untied. In the sixth, they dispatched Jim Thorpe's new team, the Cleveland Indians, 22-7 before a crowd estimated at 10,000. On Thanksgiving Day, the unbeaten Buffalo All-Americans invaded Wrigley Field and handed the Staleys a tough 7-6 defeat. On November 27, quarterback and coach Curly Lambeau led his Green Bay Packers into Chicago for the first game in what would become the greatest rivalry in pro football. The Staleys won 20-0. Then, in the biggest game of the season, a rematch with Buffalo, Guy Chamberlin scored a touchdown and kicked a field goal to carry the Staleys to a 10-7 victory.

Now Chicago and Buffalo each had suffered one loss. The Staleys beat Canton 10-0 on December 11, then closed out the season the next Sunday against the Cardinals. On a frozen field, the teams slipped and skidded to a scoreless tie. The Staleys finished 9-1-1 in league games, while Buffalo was 9-1-2. Joe Carr ruled that the Staleys' game with the semi-pro Waukegan team would count in the APFA standings. Thus the Staleys were 10-1-1 and the first official champions of pro football.

Although they triumphed on the field and were reasonably success-ful at the box office, the 1921 Staleys did little to justify Halas's faith in the ultimate profitability of pro football. They lost $71.63 for the sea-son.

In 1922, the Chicago Staleys became the Bears. "I considered nam-ing the team the Chicago Cubs," Halas remembered, "out of respect for Mr. William Veeck, Sr., and Mr. William Wrigley, who had been such a great help. But I noted football players are bigger than baseball players; so if baseball players are cubs, then certainly football players are bears!" The Staley franchise was officially transferred to the Chicago Bears Football Club, Inc. A year later, the American Professional Football As-sociation also adopted a new name—the National Football League.

On November 22, 1925, the Bears blanked the Packers 21-0 at Wrigley Field. Observing from the Bears' bench was Harold "Red" Grange, the Wheaton native whose sensational career at the University of Illinois had concluded less than 24 hours earlier. Immediately after the Illini's season-ending 14-9 victory at Ohio State, the three-time All-American had secretly boarded a train for Chicago to join the Bears. Thus he was at their game the very next day—but not in uniform, be-cause the final details of his contract had not been settled.

When Grange officially signed with the Bears on Monday morning, it was a monumental coup for Halas. He announced that "the Galloping Ghost" would make his debut on November 26, Thanksgiving Day, against the Cardinals. Tickets went on sale Monday afternoon, and the 20,000 that had been printed were sold within three hours. Mounted police were called to quell a potential riot among fans who were still in line when the supply ran out. More tickets were printed the following day, and another 16,000 were sold.

Thursday afternoon was damp and chilly, but Wrigley Field was filled to the rafters. 17 people were arrested outside the park for selling counterfeit tickets. Grange took the field wearing a Bears' jersey onto which his familiar No. 77 had been hastily stitched.

In the first quarter, Grange brought the fans to their feet when he fielded a punt and zigzagged 30 yards before being wrestled down. The rest of his afternoon was less eventful. He ended up with 66 yards on three punt returns and 36 yards on 13 carries from scrimmage. He also attempted six passes, all of which fell incomplete, and caught one pass. His interception thwarted one of the Cardinals' two scoring threats (the other was a field-goal attempt by Paddy Driscoll that ricocheted off one of the uprights).

Although the Bears failed to mount a serious assault on the Cardinal goal line and the game ended in a scoreless tie, no one seemed too disappointed. When the gun sounded, Cardinal players lined up to shake Grange's hand, knowing that his presence in the league was likely to make them all more prosperous. Hundreds of fans swarmed onto the field, and only quick work by a cordon of policemen saved Grange from being stampeded by the well wishers.

"The Bears and the Cardinals are great pro teams," the *Tribune*'s Don Maxwell wrote the next morning. "They have thousands of enthusiastic followers. But the more than 36,000 folk who made the turkey wait until the game was over weren't there to see their teams play. They were there to see the redhead of Wheaton. They cheered when Grange gained ground; they cheered when he lost ground. They went into vocal hysterics when he trotted on the field, and they almost mobbed him when he left it."

To exploit Grange's tremendous popularity, the Bears played exhibition games in St. Louis, Washington, and Pittsburgh in addition to their five regularly scheduled league games between December 2 and December 13—for a total of eight games in 12 days. Late in December, they set off on a coast-to-coast barnstorming tour that saw them play nine more games before the end of January. As a result of these games, Halas said, "Pro football for the first time took on true national stature."

Pro football was here to stay. By the time of his death in 1983, Halas had seen the value of a franchise increase from $100 to roughly $100 million. He had also done more than anyone to make it happen.

CHAPTER 7

The Long Count

"I don't think the public is any too well satisfied with a champion who gets knocked down for a count of from 13 to 16 seconds and then dances around the ring trying to keep out of the challenger's way."
-- Jack Dempsey, world heavyweight champion, 1919-1926

"All that argument about the long count is useless, as I could have arisen several seconds sooner than I did."
-- Gene Tunney, world heavyweight champion, 1926-1928

Although it took place more than 80 years ago, the bout between Gene Tunney and Jack Dempsey at Soldier Field on September 22, 1927, still resonates. It remains among the most famous heavyweight title fights of all time, arguably exceeded only by the epic first meeting of Joe Frazier and Muhammad Ali in 1971. There are several reasons why this is so.

First, 1927 was the year that the American cult of celebrity was born. Not coincidentally, it was the year of Charles Lindbergh's solo flight across the Atlantic and Babe Ruth's 60 home runs, as well as the Tunney-Dempsey contest. Because exhaustive coverage by newspapers, newsreels, and radio enabled millions of people to follow these events much more closely than would have been possible just a few years before, Lindbergh and the rest became the first modern superstars.

Second, the Tunney-Dempsey fight took on aspects of a morality play. Tunney had served with the Marine Corps in France during World War I; Dempsey had remained out of uniform and in the States (that he was the sole support of his mother and siblings did not sway those who called him a "slacker"). Tunney was a devotee of Shakespeare who spent his spare time in quiet contemplation; Dempsey was a high-living lover of wine, women, and song. Tunney was nicknamed "Gentleman Gene," Dempsey "the Manassa Mauler." The fight was described in the press as brains vs. brawn, cunning vs. brute strength, craftsman vs. killer.

Third, and most importantly, the bout featured the notorious "long count"—perhaps the single most controversial incident in the ancient and invariably controversial history of boxing.

Dempsey was a copper miner, lumberjack, and dance-hall bouncer near his family home in Manassa, Colorado, before he entered the fight game. He rose like a rocket through the heavyweight ranks, earning a shot against champion Jess Willard on July 4, 1919.

The six-foot-six, 245-pound Willard had fought only once since wresting the title from the legendary Jack Johnson in 1915, and he was no match for Dempsey. The 187-pound challenger floored Willard seven times *in the first round*, then left the ring in triumph as the champion was counted out. It was determined, though, that the count of 10 had come after the bell, so the fight continued. Willard's reprieve was brief and painful; Dempsey battered him mercilessly for two more rounds before Jess murmured "I guess I'm beaten" prior to the fourth.

Dempsey had a grand time as champion. He married a gorgeous actress, Estelle Taylor, and the two toured the country, appearing on stage for $7,000 a week. He also played himself in a series of low-budget movies. He managed to find the time to defend his title just five times in seven years, studiously avoiding the most formidable contender, Harry Wills, who happened to be black. Dempsey later asserted that he'd been ordered by the government not to take on Wills in light of the racial climate in the country at that time; Johnson's incendiary reign as champion had aroused white racists from coast to coast.

Dempsey had been idle for more than three years when he stepped into the ring against Tunney on September 23, 1926, in Philadelphia. He was only 31, but his lax approach to training had taken its toll. Tunney, a 29-year-old New Yorker, peppered Dempsey with jabs, crosses, and an occasional hook while adroitly steering clear of danger himself. Dempsey spent much of the time flailing at empty spaces left by the quick, evasive Tunney. At the end of the 10 rounds, Dempsey's left eye was closed and his face a bloody mask. He was thoroughly beaten, and no one questioned the judges when they awarded Tunney a unanimous decision.

Tunney had hardly climbed out of the ring with the title when the public began hollering for a rematch. His excellent performance was not considered a fluke, but Dempsey's dismal showing was.

The clamor for a rematch and, especially, the huge sums of money offered proved irresistible. The second Tunney-Dempsey fight was scheduled for Chicago, 364 days after their initial encounter. It would be Tunney's first title defense and Dempsey's chance to become the first man to win the title for a second time.

The rematch was the most ballyhooed sporting event ever seen up to that time. For weeks prior to the bout, newspapers reported every detail from Tunney's training camp at Cedar Crest Country Club in Lake Villa and Dempsey's at the Lincoln Fields racetrack (later known as Balmoral Park) in Crete. The *Tribune*, for example, recited Tunney's complete activities, such as they were, of September 16: "Arose at 10 o'clock and took a bath. Had breakfast at 10:30 o'clock and came out of the dining room at 11:15. Read books and paper until 12:30, when he took a nap until 3:00. Reported at training quarters at 3:30 after holding a conversation with [heavyweight contender] Jack Sharkey on the steps of the house. Came out of training quarters at 4 o'clock and posed for pictures. Engaged in his workout from 4:10 until 4:45. Given treatment by Trainer Lou Fink until 5 o'clock. Conferred with Promoter George Getz and John Righeimer, chairman of the boxing commission, until 5:30. Returned to the club house to read and had dinner at 7:30. Came out of the dining room at 8:45 o'clock. Talked with friends, and retired at 10."

Both fighters closed camp the morning of the bout and drove to Chicago for the weigh-in. Tunney tipped the scales at 189½ pounds, Dempsey was three pounds heavier. Each man, of course, expressed total confidence in the outcome.

Dempsey: "I am ready for Gene Tunney this time. I will win decisively. I think I am good enough now to finish Tunney inside of seven rounds. If he happens to last the limit, I am sure I will be far enough out in front to win the decision. If Tunney will stand up and fight, it will not take long. If I have to chase him I will catch up with him. I want the referee, whoever he is, to make us fight and give me all that is coming to me, nothing more."

Tunney: "I have reached the very peak of condition and am without a bruise or any hurt on the eve of the battle. I am even more certain I will win than I was when I first engaged Dempsey at Philadelphia last year. I feel as a result of another year of study and application, I have improved considerably and will win without any great difficulty. I hope and expect our contest will be a fairly and cleanly waged battle which will merit the attention given it by the greatest crowd ever gathered to see a sporting event."

At Soldier Field, folding chairs and wooden plank benches were arrayed in the grass around the ring, augmenting the permanent stands and swelling capacity to 163,000 (assuming, as the promoters did, that the average spectator on the plank benches was only 17 inches wide). The $40 "ringside" seats extended for 117 rows from the ring. The top row of seats in the north end zone was 313 rows, or about 600 feet, from the action; these seats went for $5.

People who were there said what they remembered most was the brilliant light in which the fighters were bathed. Dozens of cone-shaped fixtures were suspended directly above the ring, sending columns of white light onto the canvas. "All is darkness in the muttering mass of crowd beyond the spotlight," Graham McNamee intoned to the radio audience. "The crowd is thickening in the seats. It's like the Roman Colosseum."

Estimates of the crowd varied widely, from a low of 105,000 to a high of 150,000. This mass of humanity produced gate receipts of $2,658,600—establishing a record that stood for over 40 years. Dempsey received $450,000, Tunney slightly less than $1 million. (Dempsey had earned about $900,000 to Tunney's $200,000 in their first fight, the most lucrative in history prior to their second.)

The weather was cool, around 55 degrees, with a gentle breeze from the lake. The crowd paid almost no attention to the four preliminary bouts, but came to life when Dempsey appeared at 9:55 p.m. He bounced around the ring and chatted nonchalantly with Mayor Big Bill Thompson while waiting for Tunney, who made his entrance some five minutes later. Dempsey and Tunney shook hands and said a few words to one another.

"They're getting the gloves out of a box tied with pretty blue ribbon," McNamee informed his listeners. Then it was time to get down to business. "Robes are off," he cried. "The bell!" As in the earlier fight, Dempsey was the aggressor. The methodical Tunney was content to backpedal and feint, patiently looking for openings. When he saw one, he struck quickly and danced away before Dempsey could effectively retaliate. Throughout the early rounds, Tunney stayed out of trouble and piled up points. Time and again, he lured Dempsey in too close, then nailed him with a straight left to the forehead followed by a right cross to the jaw. By general consensus, the champion won each of the first five rounds.

Dempsey emphasized body blows early in the fight, but these had little impact. He went for the head from the sixth round on, realizing that he would probably need a knockout in order to win. He scored twice in the sixth with wicked lefts to the jaw, and most observers gave him a narrow edge in that round.

Dempsey continued to attack in the seventh. He came out of his corner with renewed enthusiasm and caught Tunney against the west ropes almost at once. Tunney missed with a right cross. Then Dempsey delivered a left hook to the jaw, followed by a right cross that landed as Tunney was already falling to the canvas. "What a surprise!" Tunney wrote in his autobiography. Dazed, Tunney sat on his haunches with his left arm looped around the middle rope. Dempsey stood over him menacingly, eager to finish him off if and when he got back to his feet.

Referee Dave Barry did not begin to count over Tunney until Dempsey retreated to a neutral corner, per the rule that is meant to prevent a man from being struck while he's down. Between four and five seconds elapsed before Barry began counting. "Meantime," Harvey Woodruff wrote in the *Tribune*, "champion Gene, whose title seemed [to be] slipping from his grasp, rose on one knee and, with his senses rapidly recuperating, coolly awaited the count of nine before arising to his feet."

The notorious "long count" was that simple. There was no question that Tunney was on the floor for 13 to 14 seconds—when 10, of course, is enough to register a knockout. But there was also no question that Dempsey was tardy in moving away from his fallen opponent. He had stood over Tunney for several seconds with his right arm cocked. Barry correctly interpreted the rule which stated, "Should the boxer on his feet fail to stay in the [neutral] corner, the referee and the timekeeper shall cease counting until he has so retired."

Tunney always maintained that he could have gotten up whenever he pleased. "I was not hurt," he claimed, "but considered it just as well to take my time about arising." When the fight resumed, Dempsey attacked relentlessly, but Tunney held him off with body blows. Dempsey chased Tunney around the ring, derisively motioning for him to stand and fight. Tunney kept on moving. Soon his head was clear of cobwebs, and he managed to deliver a right to Dempsey's jaw and a left to the midsection just before the bell.

By surviving the seventh round, Tunney had recovered the momentum. He scored a knockdown of his own in the eighth with an overhand right cross to Dempsey's head. Jack popped back up after a count of one, but he was wobbly as the bout continued. Tunney shot a series of lefts to the jaw, then rocked Dempsey with lefts and rights to the head. The bell sounded with the two fighters toe-to-toe in the center of the ring and the fans on their feet, roaring.

Tunney was in command the rest of the way. Dempsey, desperate by now, repeatedly resorted to illegal "rabbit punches" to the back of the champion's head throughout the later rounds. Like his legitimate blows, however, they did little damage. Most uncharacteristically, Tunney threw caution to the wind. Sensing that Dempsey was tired and wounded, he abandoned his dancing and forced the issue. He advanced on the challenger and banged away virtually at will in the ninth round, opening a nasty cut above Dempsey's left eye. In the 10th, the frustrated Dempsey wrestled Tunney to the floor. When he got back up, Tunney landed five left jabs to the face without being hit in return.

Dempsey knew he needed a knockout, but as the clock ticked down he simply did not have the strength to throw anything but a few token punches. Tunney showered him with a barrage of left and right hooks in the closing seconds. If the bell had come any later, Dempsey almost certainly would have ended up on the canvas.

Tunney won a unanimous decision. "It simply was a case," Walter Eckersall wrote in the *Tribune*, "of a boxer, who was much faster, winning a 10-round decision over a fighter who always commands respect because of his punching power."

Dempsey and his supporters, naturally, complained bitterly about the long count. "It appeared they gave Tunney a generous count in the seventh," Dempsey said, "just enough extra time to let him get his bearings and climb back on his bicycle." Dempsey's manager, Leo P. Flynn, declared that Tunney had retained the title "by grace of what was either a queer decision or a colossal case of inefficiency in the simple matter of counting seconds." Flynn was just warming up. "Even if Tunney could have got to his feet at the end of an up-and-up count," he said, "Jack would have floored him again. He needed those extra five seconds mighty bad."

Flynn filed a formal protest, which was denied. At the time, his and Dempsey's grievances were written off as sour grapes. Over the years, though, the controversy surrounding the long count grew until it nearly overshadowed the estimable careers of the two principals, both of whom deserved to be ranked among the great heavyweights.

"Some folks are saying that I should fight Dempsey again," Tunney said the day after the fight in Soldier Field. "I don't agree with them. I have beaten him twice and I see no reason why the public should want to see us matched again." With that, Dempsey retired; his record was 62-6-10, with 49 knockouts. He became a sort of professional celebrity and opened a successful nightclub in New York. Tunney fought only once more, earning a technical knockout of Tom Heeney on July 26, 1928. He then hung up his gloves, married a Connecticut society woman, and embarked on a tour of Europe's art museums and literary haunts. His record was 65-1-1, with 47 knockouts.

Tunney and Dempsey had a reunion of sorts during World War II. Both served in the Pacific (Tunney as a commander in the Navy and Dempsey as a commander in the Coast Guard), conducting physical training courses. Dempsey even saw combat duty on the island of Tarawa, putting to rest once and for all the questions about his patriotism that had dogged him for over 25 years.

CHAPTER 8

Powerhouse

"Bronko Nagurski was probably the greatest player I ever went up against. I thought to myself, 'You either better start moving and go after him or just get the hell out of the way, because otherwise you are going to get killed.'"
-- *Clarke Hinkle, Green Bay Packers fullback and linebacker, 1932-1941*

Bronko Nagurski grew up in International Falls, Minnesota, a remote outpost along the Canadian border, and from the time he was very young he was regarded as a sort of real-life Paul Bunyan. Clarence "Doc" Spears, his coach at the University of Minnesota, had a colorful account of how he recruited Nagurski. "I saw this young kid pushing a plow," Spears said. "There was no horse or anything else, just this kid pushing a plow. I asked directions of him and he picked up the plow and pointed with it. I decided then and there he should go to Minnesota."

Bronko went on to perform spectacularly at Minnesota, and he joined the Bears in 1930. He weighed about 235 pounds at a time when very few players exceeded 210. A fullback on offense and a tackle on defense, he was easily the best player in the NFL at both positions. He was the heart and soul of the Bears' powerhouse teams of the early thirties.

In the final game of the 1932 regular season, Nagurski's 56-yard touchdown gallop led the Bears to a 9-0 victory over the Green Bay Packers amid swirling snows at Wrigley Field. The win moved the Bears into a tie with the Portsmouth (Ohio) Spartans for first place in the NFL, and league president Joe Carr decided to have a playoff game to settle the issue. Because Portsmouth's stadium seated only 8,000, the first postseason game in pro football history was scheduled for Chicago.

That the NFL was still in its infancy was demonstrated by the fact that Portsmouth's star tailback Dutch Clark, the league's leading scorer, was not available for the game. His contract as basketball coach at Colorado College called for him to report immediately after the Spartans' season was concluded, and it had no provision for an extra week.

The weather worsened in the days leading up to the game, with snow continuing intermittently and the temperature plummeting to below zero. George Halas recognized that few hardy souls were likely to pay hard-earned Depression dollars to sit out in a blizzard at Wrigley Field, so he got approval from the league to play the game indoors at Chicago Stadium. Inside the Stadium, a field was set up that was 20 yards shorter and 15 feet narrower than the standard.

A circus had come through the week before, and a six-inch layer of dirt remained on the Stadium's cement floor. With rolls of sod laid on top of the dirt, the playing surface was passable and certainly safer than the frozen ground at Wrigley Field. One observer reported, however, that the arena "was a little too aromatic, what with the horses and elephants that had traipsed around there a few days before the game."

More than 11,000 people showed up, vindicating the decision to play the game indoors. "They were exposed to the violence of professional football," Richard Whittingham wrote, "in a way that spectators in outdoor stadiums never were. In the enclosed stadium, the sounds of impact when players blocked or tackled each other resounded through the acoustically controlled hall."

Both defenses held sway for the first three quarters. There was only one punt returned all day, as most of them flew well into the seats. The Bears' Red Grange was knocked out cold when he was thrown out of bounds and into the hockey boards after an end run of 15 yards. He was carted off, but soon returned. In the fourth quarter, Dick Nesbitt of the Bears intercepted a pass at the Spartans' seven-yard line. Nagurski bulled his way down to the two on first down, but then he was stopped for virtually no gain on his next two attempts.

On fourth down and goal, the Portsmouth defenders massed in the middle of the line, convinced that Nagurski would carry the ball again. Bronko did take the handoff from quarterback Carl Brumbaugh, but instead of charging ahead, he backpedaled and lofted a pass over the scrum at the goal line. Grange was alone in the end zone to gather it in for a touchdown. Portsmouth coach Potsy Clark was apoplectic, arguing that Bronko had been too close to the line of scrimmage when he delivered the ball (at the time, one had to be at least five yards behind the line in order to throw a legal forward pass). Potsy may have been right, but the call stood.

When Clark finally calmed down and left the field, Tiny Engebretsen kicked the extra point for the Bears. Several minutes later, a Spartan fumble rolled out of the end zone for a safety. The score of 9-0 held up, and the Bears were world champions.

George Preston Marshall, owner of the Boston Redskins (who would soon move to Washington), had an idea. Since the postseason playoff had stirred up so much interest, he suggested, why not make it an annual event? Marshall's proposal was immediately adopted. The NFL was split into two five-team divisions whose winners would meet after the season for the championship.

Despite winning the improvised championship game in 1932, the Bears lost $18,000 for the year. The partnership of owners Halas and Dutch Sternaman did not survive the financial reversal; the two decided to part ways. Halas borrowed from every friend and acquaintance who had a few dollars to spare, and he bought Sternaman out. He also appointed himself head coach, a position he had relinquished upon his retirement as a player after the 1929 season. "I will coach for this year only," Halas told the press. He later joked that it turned out to be an awfully long year.

Halas, chairman of the NFL rules committee, pushed through several new wrinkles to provide for a more wide-open and entertaining game. First, a ball carried out of bounds would no longer be placed right on the sideline for the next play, but would be spotted on hash marks 10 yards inside the line. Second, the goal posts were moved up to the goal line to enable more field goals. Third, a forward pass could now be thrown from anywhere behind the line of scrimmage.

The controversial play that had won the title for the Bears in Chicago Stadium now became a staple of Halas's offense. Nagurski would take a handoff from Brumbaugh and either blast through the line himself or zip a quick jump pass to Bill Hewitt, Bill Karr, or Luke Johnsos. The play and many variations thereof worked like a charm time and again in 1933.

The Bears won their first three games of the season, at Green Bay, at home against Boston, and at Brooklyn. In the fourth game, at Wrigley Field, they found themselves trailing the lowly Chicago Cardinals 9-0 in the final minutes. Brumbaugh gave to Hewitt on an end-around. Hewitt continued toward the sideline and purposely slowed up to allow the Cardinals' pursuit to close in on him. At the last instant, he lofted a long pass to Johnsos for a touchdown. Rookie "Automatic Jack" Manders kicked the point after. The Cardinals' next possession resulted in a safety that tied the score. Finally, with just over a minute left, Manders booted a field goal to give the Bears a 12-9 win.

The Bears won their next two games, also at home, 10-7 over the Packers and 14-10 over the New York Giants, running their record to 6-0. But just when they began to seem invincible, the Bears endured a dismal stretch of three games on the road. Their offense inexplicably deserted them as they lost 3-0 at Boston, tied 3-3 at Philadelphia, and lost 3-0 at New York.

Happily, the Bears soon returned to form, winning their last four games to finish the regular season at 10-2-1. The Giants were champions of the East at 11-3. The two clubs were clearly the class of the league (of the other seven teams, only Portsmouth won as many as six games) and were worthy participants in the first official NFL championship game. Each roster included five future Hall-of-Famers: tackle and coach Steve Owen, halfback Ken Strong, center Mel Hein, and ends Ray Flaherty and Red Badgro for the Giants, and Nagurski, Grange, Hewitt, and tackles George Musso and Link Lyman for the Bears. One New York writer termed the contest "the Title Tilt of the Titans."

The game was played on December 17 at Wrigley Field, and the 21,000 fans who braved the cold and drizzle got their money's worth. "Marshal your adjectives," Wilfrid Smith wrote in the *Tribune*. "Bring out all the superlatives and shift them as you would juggle a jigsaw puzzle. All will fit in a description of the championship battle."

The Giants opened their very first possession with a bit of trickery. Quarterback Harry Newman took the snap from Hein, then immediately handed it back to him. Newman dropped back as if to pass and was buried under a swarm of Bear tacklers. Meanwhile, Hein had stuffed the ball under his jersey and started nonchalantly walking downfield. "After a few yards," Hein recalled, "I got excited and started to run, and the Bear safety Keith Molesworth saw me and knocked me down. I got about 30 yards but we didn't score."

The Bears scored first on a field goal by Manders after Nagurski faked a jump pass and barreled 14 yards deep into New York territory. Manders kicked another field goal in the second quarter, but Newman connected with Badgro on a 29-yard touchdown strike, and Strong's extra point put the Giants ahead 7-6 at halftime.

A third Manders field goal capped a drive on which Nagurski rushed for 22 yards. Newman, the league's best passer, came right back with five straight completions to set up a one-yard touchdown plunge by Max Krause. Strong kicked the extra point to give the Giants a 14-9 lead.

Still in the third quarter, Bear halfback George Corbett passed to Brumbaugh, from whom he'd taken a handoff, for a 67-yard gain to New York's eight-yard line. On the next play, Nagurski took a handoff and charged toward the line, then—just as he had done in the Stadium a year before—stopped and flipped a pass over the line and into the end zone, where Karr caught it for a touchdown. Manders's extra point gave the Bears a 16-14 edge.

Newman wasn't through. On New York's next possession, he completed four straight aerials, and the Giants were on the Bears' eight-yard line when the third quarter ended. The first play of the fourth quarter featured more razzle-dazzle by the Giants. "Newman handed off to me on a reverse to the left," Strong recalled, "but the line was jammed up. I turned around and saw Newman standing there, so I threw him the ball. He was bottled up. By now, I had crossed into the end zone and the Bears had forgotten me. Newman saw me wildly waving my hands and threw me the ball." Strong's touchdown reception and his own extra-point kick put the Giants ahead 21-16.

Time was running out when the Bears turned to what they came to call the "victory play." Nagurski took a handoff from Brumbaugh at the New York 33 and fired one of his patented jump passes to Hewitt. Hewitt, the last NFL player who never wore a helmet, then flipped a lateral to Karr. Gene Ronzani's block leveled Strong and another would-be tackler as Karr flashed down the sideline for a touchdown. Brumbaugh kicked the extra point, and the Bears led 23-21.

The Giants had one more chance in the final seconds. Badgro received a pass from Newman, then looked to lateral to Hein, who would have had clear sailing to the Bears' end zone. Red Grange had other ideas. "Instead of going low for a conventional tackle," Badgro said, "he grabbed me around the arms and the upper body, pinning the ball to me so I couldn't lateral."

It was, said Halas, "the greatest defensive play I ever saw."

"Had I been able to get the ball to Hein," Badgro lamented, "we would have won the championship." Grange's heroics not only deprived the Giants of the title, but also cost them 70 dollars and 12 cents apiece. Each member of the victorious Bears received $210.34 for his trouble, while each Giant got $140.22.

Nineteen-thirty-four saw the advent of the College All-Star Game, which would be a Chicago summertime fixture for the next 42 years. In the series' first installment, the Bears and the All-Stars struggled to a scoreless tie before 79,432 at Soldier Field. It was a mundane prelude to one of the greatest seasons in Bears' annals.

The first five games, all on the road, were won by scores of 24-10, 21-3, 21-7, 28-0, and 20-0. The home opener was a 41-7 triumph. After nine games, the *closest* had been decided by 13 points. The Bears subdued the Giants 10-9 in New York to make it 10 straight. Their next win, a 17-6 decision over the Cardinals at Wrigley Field, was costly. Beattie Feathers, the sensational rookie halfback from Tennessee, suffered a separated shoulder that put him out for the year. Running behind the ferocious lead blocking of Nagurski, Feathers had rushed for 1,004 yards and eight touchdowns. He was pro football's first 1,000-yard rusher, and his per-carry average of 8.4 set a record that still stands.

The last two games of the season were a home-and-home set against the Detroit Lions, the former Spartans who had just moved from Portsmouth. The Bears were 11-0; the Lions were 10-1 and had posted seven consecutive shutouts. The Lions were tough—but even without Beattie Feathers, the Bears were tougher. They had Bronko Nagurski. His late touchdown pass to Hewitt beat the Lions 19-16 in Detroit, and his seven straight carries from the Lions' 26-yard line into their end zone beat them 10-7 at Wrigley Field. Thus the Bears completed a perfect regular season, the first in league history.

Not counting the exhibition against the College All-Stars, the Bears had now won 18 games in a row since their disastrous East Coast road trip more than a year earlier. They were prohibitive favorites in their title rematch against the Giants, whose dull 8-5 mark had been good enough to win the East. New York would be missing Newman, Badgro, and halfback Stuart Clancy, all of whom had been injured in the closing weeks of the regular season.

The championship game was played at the Polo Grounds on December 9, before a smaller-than-expected crowd of 35,059. The ground was frozen solid, and a stiff breeze from the northwest pushed the wind-chill factor well below zero. As the Giants slipped and slid around the field during the pre-game warmups, Ray Flaherty suggested that they don basketball shoes for better footing. Trainer Gus Mauch was also trainer of Manhattan College's basketball team, and he sent Abe Cohen, an elderly tailor and rabid Giant fan, to the Manhattan campus to fetch some sneakers.

Meanwhile, the game began. Ken Strong's 38-yard field goal gave the Giants an early 3-0 lead. A one-yard dive by Nagurski and a 17-yard field goal by Manders put the Bears on top 10-3, but they missed several opportunities to pad their advantage before halftime. An eight-yard touchdown run by Nagurski was called back, and Manders missed field-goal attempts of 24 and 38 yards.

Abe Cohen returned from Manhattan College during the intermission with nine pairs of sneakers. He later claimed to have broken into lockers with a hammer to appropriate the shoes, while Mauch maintained that he'd given Cohen a master key. In any event, the Giants' key players came onto the field for the second half sporting the rubber-soled footwear. The change had no immediate effect, as the Bears were able to control the ball for most of the third quarter.

In the fourth quarter, though, the Giants exploded. Trailing 13-3 with less than 10 minutes remaining, they pulled off one of the most stunning turnabouts ever seen. The fierce wind was at their backs now, and their sneakers enabled them to run circles around the Bears. Ed Danowski passed 28 yards to Ike Frankian for New York's first touchdown. Strong booted the extra point. After the Bears went three-and-out on their next possession, the Giants took over on Chicago's 46. Strong plowed ahead for four yards on the first play. On the next, he swung around right end and sprinted 42 yards for the touchdown that put the Giants ahead. Hundreds of fans stormed the field to congratulate him. After order was restored, he kicked the extra point to make it 17-13. A cordon of police ringed the field for the rest of the game. Even so, each good play by the Giants triggered a demonstration that delayed the proceedings.

The Bears' next drive stalled when Nagurski was stopped on fourth-and-two at midfield. Four rushes by Strong and two by Danowski pushed the Giants to the Bears' nine-yard line. By now it seemed that the Giants could move the ball at will. Danowski took the snap, faked a run up the middle, and gave to Strong on a reverse. Strong cruised into the end zone unmolested. The point after was no good, but the Giants had a commanding 23-13 lead.

As if to add insult to injury, the Giants' Bo Molenda intercepted on the very first play of the Bears' next possession. Four plays later, Danowski was in the end zone. Molenda's kick made it 30-13. After the kickoff, New York intercepted again and returned the ball to Chicago's 15-yard line. Only the clock prevented further humiliation for the Bears; time expired before the Giants could score yet again.

New York's phenomenal upset went down in football lore as "the Sneakers Game," and Abe Cohen was hailed as a hero by his fellow Giant fans. For the Bears, there was a kind of symmetry in the fact that their reign as NFL champions had begun in a hockey rink and ended on a sheet of ice.

CHAPTER 9

Gardiner's Finest Hour

"He's the greatest goalie that ever donned the pads."
-- *Tommy Gorman, Blackhawks coach, 1933-34*

The Blackhawks came into being on May 15, 1926, when Major Frederic McLaughlin was awarded a National Hockey League franchise in Chicago. McLaughlin named his new team after the division in which he had served during World War I—the 85th Division of the U.S. Army was nicknamed the "Blackhawk" division in honor of the Sac and Fox chief of the early 19th century.

As the season opener approached, McLaughlin's team had a place to play (the ancient Chicago Coliseum at 14th and Wabash) and a striking logo for the uniforms (the profile of Chief Blackhawk that remains essentially unchanged to this day), but what it didn't have was players. Unfazed, McLaughlin went first for quantity, buying the entire Portland Rosebuds team of the financially strapped Western Hockey League and importing its players to Chicago. Then he added quality through a series of separate transactions.

McLaughlin's frenetic dealing paid off. The original Blackhawks who took the ice on November 17, 1926, and defeated Toronto 4-1, included five future Hall of Famers: forwards Babe Dye, George Hay, Dick Irvin, and Mickey MacKay, and goalie Hughie Lehman. The 41-year-old Lehman played between the pipes for every minute of the 1926-27 season. He and the Hawks won 19 games, lost 22, and tied 3 that first year, with Lehman logging five shutouts in the process.

Today, people refer to the "original six" teams of the NHL, by which they mean the Blackhawks, Boston Bruins, Detroit Red Wings, Montreal Canadiens, New York Rangers, and Toronto Maple Leafs—because these clubs pre-date the era of expansion that began in 1967. But in the Hawks' first season, the league also included the Montreal Maroons, New York Americans, Ottawa Senators, and Pittsburgh Pirates.

It was a 10-team league of two divisions in 1926-27, and the Hawks finished third in the American division with 41 points. A respectable showing, but McLaughlin was incredulous that the talent he had assembled hadn't finished higher. When he fired coach Pete Muldoon and replaced him with Barney Stanley, McLaughlin established a precedent that he faithfully followed from then on. In their first 10 years, the Hawks would go through 12 coaches—13 if you count the two separate stints by Bill Tobin.

Barney Stanley's regime lasted only half a season, but it was noteworthy in one respect. Rookie Chuck Gardiner supplanted Lehman as the Hawks' regular goalie, with Lehman staying on as backup until he himself succeeded Stanley as coach. The Hawks won only seven games in 1927-28, and managed another seven wins the next season. As an expansion team, they had gone for experienced players and instant respectability. It was a short-term fix. Now the big names were over the hill, and the Hawks were starting over. But things were looking up, because Chuck Gardiner soon emerged as the finest goalie in the league.

Gardiner was born in Edinburgh, Scotland, on the last day of 1904. Fortunately for the Hawks and their fans, the Gardiner family emigrated to Canada when Chuck was seven. In Winnipeg, naturally, he began to play hockey. But because he had started later than the other kids his age (most of whom had been skating since they could walk), his skating skills were relatively poor. Under the circumstances, Gardiner did the sensible thing. He became a goalie.

Gardiner turned pro in 1926, playing for his hometown Winnipeg Maroons in the Western League. When the Hawks purchased his contract in 1927, Gardiner began a legendary career in the NHL. "Charlie had everything," said the Maple Leafs' great King Clancy, "sure hands, good eyes, quick reflexes, no weak spots, and a fine team spirit." The aggressive Gardiner would stray far from the crease to cut down the

62

angle on shots or break up passing plays. This roving style is standard today, but it was quite unusual in those days (at least in part because protective equipment for the goalie's face and head had yet to be invented). As teammate Johnny Gottselig pointed out, Gardiner "never hesitated to dive in among sharp blades for the puck."

Gardiner played 40 games in his first season, with Lehman handling the other four. For the remainder of his career—despite frequent injury and illness—he played every game but one. In 316 regular-season games, 42 of which were shutouts, he allowed 664 goals for a goals-against-average of 2.10. In 21 playoff games, including five shutouts, he yielded only 35 goals for an incredible average of 1.67.

After the disastrous back-to-back seasons of seven wins each in Gardiner's first two years, the Hawks were about a .500 hockey club for four years, with a total record of 79-74-31 (and six more coaches) from 1929 to 1933. More importantly, these years saw an influx of fine young players: left wing Johnny Gottselig and right wing Harold "Mush" March arrived in 1928, defenseman Taffy Abel in 1929, center Doc Romnes in 1930, and left wing Paul Thompson in 1931. And the Hawks moved into a new home, the magnificent Chicago Stadium, where they played for the first time on December 16, 1929.

The moment of truth for Gardiner and the Blackhawks came in 1933-34. Lionel Conacher, the best defenseman in the league, joined the Hawks before the season, exiled from the Canadiens for that timeless infraction, "breaking training rules." The rugged Conacher was just what the doctor ordered. He anchored the Hawks' backline and also scored 10 goals, an unheard-of output for a defenseman at that time.

Conacher's presence made Chuck Gardiner even better, if that was possible, and Gardiner responded with perhaps the greatest season by any goalie in NHL history. In exactly half of his 48 regular-season games, he allowed one goal or fewer. 10 were shutouts. He yielded a total of 83 goals, for an average of 1.73. He won the Vezina Trophy as the league's outstanding goalie for the second time and was named to the league's all-star team for the fourth straight year. Conacher too was named a first-team all-star.

Under coach Tommy Gorman, the Blackhawks came into the playoffs as legitimate contenders to win their first Stanley Cup. Their middling regular-season record of 20-17-11 was somewhat deceptive because the clubs in the league were evenly matched, the games were tightly contested, and any team—especially one with a great goalie—could catch fire in the playoffs and go all the way. One of the well-worn truisms of hockey is that a goalie at the top of his game can take even a mediocre team to the championship. The Hawks had almost confirmed this point in 1931, when Gardiner carried them to the Stanley Cup Final, where they lost a hard-fought series to the Canadiens three games to two.

In 1934, the Hawks again faced the Canadiens—this time in the opening round. In the first game at Montreal, Gottselig scored twice and Conacher once as the Hawks prevailed 3-2. The second game, played before a raucous crowd of 17,600 at the Stadium, was another nailbiter. The Canadiens' 1-0 margin at the end of regulation tied the series three goals apiece and forced sudden-death (the preliminary playoff rounds then consisted of only two games, with total goals deciding the winner). Gardiner withstood a relentless barrage from the Flying Frenchmen until Mush March, the smallest player in the league and one of the gamest, lit the lamp 10 minutes into overtime to give the Hawks the series four goals to three.

The Hawks then faced the Montreal Maroons. Gardiner's 3-0 shutout in the first game put the Hawks in a commanding position. "The Maroons hammered shots at him from the opening faceoff," the *Tribune* reported, "but Gardiner kicked them out as fast as they came and many times dashed out of the net to smother plays." The Hawks could have lost the second game by two goals and still wrapped up the series. Instead they beat the dispirited Maroons 3-2 to take the series six goals to two.

The Stanley Cup Final against the Red Wings would be the real test. Not only had the Blackhawks finished second to the Wings in the regular season, but they hadn't won a game in Detroit in more than four years—and the first two games of the best-of-five series were to be played in Detroit's Olympia Stadium.

In the first game, Gardiner and Wings goalie Wilf Cude both performed brilliantly. The game was deadlocked 1-1 after regulation play and remained so through an entire sudden-death period. Had Gardiner allowed another goal, the Wings would have had all the momentum—as well as further proof that the Hawks couldn't win at Detroit. But at 1:05 of double overtime, Paul Thompson scored the game-winner for the Hawks. In the second game, Gardiner completely stymied Detroit as the Hawks gained a 4-1 victory. The Hawks needed to win just one more game to secure the Stanley Cup.

Showing some grit of their own, however, the Red Wings won the third game 5-2 at the Stadium. Another heroic effort by Wilf Cude made the difference. Cude turned aside 42 shots, despite sustaining a broken nose in a nasty collision with the Hawks' Rosario Couture midway through the second period. Although they outshot the Wings 44-36, the Hawks were beaten convincingly. Gardiner and Gottselig, close friends off the ice, almost came to blows late in the game. "Everything was breaking against us in those last few minutes and their nerves blew up," Gorman explained to the press. "After the game was over they shook hands, and the incident is completely forgotten."

"We simply were not clicking," McLaughlin told reporters, "and I wasn't surprised. We have that defeat out of our system, we are still one game ahead of the Wings, and our confidence is not shaken." Privately, though, the Hawks were concerned. Gardiner had played his worst game in weeks, and he appeared to be completely spent. McLaughlin deduced that Gardiner was suffering from "nervous exhaustion" and packed him off to Wisconsin for two days of rest and relaxation. Gardiner returned in time for the fourth game of the series, but teammates wondered if he would be able to play effectively—if at all.

He played. It was April 10, 1934, and a throng of almost 18,000 at the Stadium was treated to one of the most dramatic, tension-filled contests imaginable. Again Gardiner and Cude were superb under the most intense pressure. While the crowd grew progressively more anxious, the game remained scoreless for three periods. Then the first 20-minute overtime session came and went.

The big break came halfway through the second overtime when Detroit defenseman Ebbie Goodfellow was sent off for tripping. The Hawks' top forward line of Romnes, Thompson, and March had peppered Cude all night to no avail, but now they had a man advantage. Their first two rushes up ice were thwarted by the Red Wings. On the third try Romnes surged over the blue line and slid the puck to March.

Though he was knocked offstride by a Detroit defender, March still managed to fire a low wrist shot from about 20 feet out. Cude got a piece of it with his right leg, but the puck spun into the net behind him. The Stadium erupted. March—all five-foot-five and 140 pounds of him—dove into the net to retrieve the puck for a souvenir. The Hawks were Stanley Cup champions.

Gardiner had played his best game when it counted most, stopping 40 shots in 90 minutes of play. In eight playoff games, he had lost only once. In the seven winning games, he had allowed a *total* of seven goals. He had recorded two shutouts. "He won the title for the Blackhawks," said Gorman. "Without him, we wouldn't have made it."

The next day, Gardiner collected on an early-season bet he had made with defenseman Roger Jenkins. Because the Hawks had won the championship, Jenkins owed Gardiner a wheelbarrow ride around downtown Chicago. Flourishing a bouquet of roses presented by Lionel Conacher, Gardiner was carted through the streets of the Loop while teammates and bystanders cheered.

Only two months after his greatest triumph, Gardiner was dead. On June 10, 1934, he collapsed in Winnipeg and fell into a coma. As was not uncommon at the time, Gardiner was initially treated at home, but when his condition worsened he was moved to a hospital. Blackhawks general manager Bill Tobin wired Mrs. Gardiner offering to send specialists from Chicago, but it was too late. On June 13, only a few hours after entering the hospital, Gardiner died. He was 29 years old.

An autopsy determined that a brain tumor was the cause of Gardiner's death. Only now did Tommy Gorman and others reveal that Gardiner had experienced severe headaches and nausea during the latter part of the regular season and throughout the playoffs. It turned out that he had been ill for months, yet he had not missed a single minute of play. He had, in fact, played more determinedly even as his symptoms became more ominous.

"Gardiner was loved by everybody who knew him," said Tobin. "He was hockey's greatest goaltender. His loss is going to be a terrible hardship to the team."

Gardiner remains the only goalie to captain the Hawks and the only goalie to captain a Stanley Cup championship club.

CHAPTER 10

Moments, 1932-1938

October 1, 1932
The "Called Shot"

In Game 3 of the 1932 World Series at Wrigley Field, Babe Ruth of the New York Yankees strode to the plate in the fifth inning under a barrage of lemons and other objects thrown from the stands and a hail of verbal abuse from the Cubs' dugout. Bad blood had been stirred up between the two clubs over the Cubs' decision to award shortstop Mark Koenig, a former Yankee, only a partial share of their World Series money because he had not played the entire season for the Cubs. Koenig had made key contributions to Chicago's pennant drive, and Ruth, among others, was outspoken in his belief that the decision was petty and unjust—although those weren't the exact words he used.

The mighty Yankees had a 2-0 lead in the Series. The game was tied 4-4. Homers by Ruth and Lou Gehrig off Cubs ace Charlie Root had given New York an early 4-0 lead, but the Cubs had come back to knot it up in the fourth. When Ruth came up again in the fifth, the crowd and the Cubs' bench were in an uproar.

Root threw the first pitch for a called strike, then threw two balls. His next pitch was another called strike, and the jeering from the crowd grew louder. At this point Ruth made an ambiguous gesture with his index finger (or was it his middle finger?). Was he pointing toward the Cubs' dugout, toward Root, or toward the center-field bleachers? Catcher Gabby Hartnett thought he heard Ruth say, "It only takes one to hit it." Gehrig, who was in the on-deck circle, remembered it this way: "Babe was jawing with Root and what he said was, 'I'm going to knock the next pitch down your goddamned throat.'"

The next pitch was low and away. Ruth swung and hit a tremendous home run into the center-field stands. Some in the crowd sat in stunned silence, while others (including presidential candidate Franklin D. Roosevelt) cheered. Gehrig followed with another home run of his own, and the Yankees went on to sweep the Cubs, four games to none.

Had Ruth really called his shot? Most newspaper accounts of the game made no mention of it, and Ruth himself neither confirmed nor denied it until much later, by which time the event had become so ingrained in baseball mythology that there was no turning back. Then he said, "Well, I guess the good Lord was with me."

For his part, Charlie Root swore until his dying day that Ruth had never pointed to the seats. If he had, said Root, "I'd have put one in his ear and knocked him on his ass."

July 6, 1933
The Dream Game

Arch Ward, sports editor of the *Tribune*, dreamed up what he called the Dream Game—better known as Major League Baseball's All-Star Game—as an added attraction for Chicago's Century of Progress Exposition in 1933. A capacity crowd of 47,595 turned out for the inaugural All-Star Game at Comiskey Park. A nationwide poll of fans had selected the American and National League rosters, and the league presidents appointed Connie Mack and John McGraw, respectively, as managers. These choices had sentimental appeal: Mack was in his 33rd year at the helm of the Philadelphia A's, and McGraw had recently retired due to ill health after three decades with the New York Giants.

The American Leaguers wore their regular home uniforms, while the National Leaguers were decked out in steel-gray flannels with NATIONAL LEAGUE in blue block letters across their chests. With the home folks cheering him on, the White Sox' popular third baseman Jimmie Dykes scored the first run in All-Star history. He coaxed a walk in the second inning and came around to score on a single by Yankee pitcher Lefty Gomez. Dykes played the entire game for the A.L., going two-for-three and fielding his position flawlessly.

Appropriately, the first home run in All-Star competition came off the bat of Babe Ruth; it was a two-run shot in the third off Bill Hallahan of the Cardinals. Ruth was 38 and growing more rotund all the time. Yet he showed that he could still rise to the occasion. In the eighth, he made a fine running catch of Chick Hafey's sinking line drive to end a National League threat.

The American Leaguers held on to win 4-2. Gomez was the winning pitcher, while Hallahan took the loss. Al Simmons of the White Sox had one hit in four at-bats. For the Cubs, catcher Gabby Hartnett and shortstop Woody English each went 0-for-1, and pitcher Lon Warneke surrendered one run in four innings of work (he also rapped a triple and scored a run). Of the 30 players who appeared in the game, 17 were destined for the Hall of Fame.

When this first All-Star Game captured the public's imagination to an extent that hadn't been anticipated, the midsummer classic became an annual event. It became an immensely popular fixture over the years, fueling the genuine rivalry between the two leagues. The next year, Ward inaugurated football's College All-Star Game, which was played at Soldier Field every summer from 1934 through 1976.

September 27, 1935
Stretch Drive

On the morning of September 4, 1935, the Cubs had a record of 79-52 and were in third place in the National League, two and a half games behind the St. Louis Cardinals and half a game behind the New York Giants. That afternoon, the Cubs began the most sensational stretch drive in baseball history. "We suddenly got hot," said second baseman Billy Herman. "I don't mean just hot—we sizzled! All of a sudden we got the notion that we couldn't lose."

The Cubs won every game of an 18-game homestand. "You ever go 75 miles an hour on the highway when everybody else is doing 50?" first baseman Phil Cavarretta said. "That's how we felt. We passed the Giants and caught up to the Cardinals right at the end of the season. With everything up for grabs, we went into St. Louis for a five-game series."

The Cubs needed to win just two of the five games to sew up the pennant. On September 26, an eighth-inning home run by the 19-year-old Cavarretta was all that Lon Warneke needed as he blanked the defending world champions 1-0 for his 20th victory of the year. In the first game of the next day's doubleheader, Bill Lee bested St. Louis ace Dizzy Dean 6-2 for *his* 20th victory of the year. Although the pennant was already clinched, the Cubs also took the second game for good measure.

On the morning of September 28, the Cubs had a record of 100-52. They had won 21 games in a row and were National League champions.

The Cubs led the league in runs scored, batting average, and earned-run average. Five regulars hit better than .300: catcher Gabby Hartnett (.344 with 91 RBIs), Herman (.341 with a league-leading 227 hits and 57 doubles), right fielder Frank Demaree (.325), left fielder Augie Galan (.314 with a league-leading 133 runs scored and 22 stolen bases), and third baseman Stan Hack (.311). But it was pitching that really made the difference down the stretch. Lee won five games, Larry French five, Warneke four, Charlie Root four, Roy Henshaw two, and Tex Carleton one during the streak. The Cubs allowed three or fewer runs in all but one of the 21 games, and in all but three of those games the starting pitcher also finished.

June 22, 1937
Louis vs. Braddock

When Joe Louis stepped into the ring to challenge heavyweight champion Jim Braddock on a pleasant summer evening in 1937, he carried more than his 197 pounds. He also carried the hopes and dreams of his fellow African Americans, the majority of whom were still being denied the most basic civil rights. It was a sign of the times that Louis was described by the *Tribune* before the bout as the "sleepy-eyed son of an Alabama cotton picker" who was "no more excited about tonight's encounter than if he was going a-huntin' or a-fishin'."

The unassuming 23-year-old Louis was seeking to become only the second black man to win the heavyweight title. The first, Jack Johnson, had been anything but unassuming, and when his controversial reign ended it was widely suggested that no other black man ever would, or should, be given a title shot. But now, after two decades, a black man did have the opportunity. Millions prayed that the man in question, Louis, would make the most of it.

Braddock had wrested the title from Max Baer—who, the *Tribune's* Arch Ward claimed, "would have been a setup for any well-conditioned plumber in an informal bust-as-bust-can street corner brawl." Now, two years later, he was making just his first title defense. Like Louis, Braddock weighed in at 197. He was a mediocre 50-21-5, with 26 knockouts, and thus a decided underdog against Louis, who was 33-1 with 28 knockouts. Nonetheless he put on a brave face, professing to be unconcerned about the awesome punching power of the man known as the Brown Bomber. "There will be a knockout tonight," Braddock said, "but it will be Louis, not I, who will be counted out."

An estimated 50,000 spectators filled Comiskey Park for the bout. Among them were Jack Dempsey and Gene Tunney, who had met at Soldier Field nine years before in the famous "long count" title fight.

Louis and Braddock electrified the crowd in the first round, as they charged out of their corners and slugged it out in the center of the ring. A wild haymaker by Braddock missed, and Louis responded with a left-right combination that dazed the champion. Then, out of nowhere, Braddock landed a right uppercut that floored Louis. Joe was back on his feet in an instant. The two fighters traded hard rights to the head at the bell.

In the second round, Braddock was the aggressor. He pounded Louis's body, then scored with a right to the head followed quickly by a left to the midsection. Just before the bell, Louis delivered a pair of solid rights to the side of Braddock's face.

The third through sixth rounds were fairly uneventful, but Louis had more spring in his step and began to wear Braddock down with well-aimed jabs and crosses. By the seventh, a cut over Braddock's left eye was bleeding freely. Early in that round, Louis rocked Braddock with two short lefts to the face. The champion was game, and he kept battling—but even his better blows failed to faze the challenger. Braddock was fading fast by the end of the round.

In the eighth, Braddock presented a stationary target for Louis's volleys. Louis deftly stepped out of the way of a right and responded with a stinging left to the forehead. Braddock flailed in vain with his right, and Louis sent a left hook into his breadbasket. Then Louis planted his feet and delivered a smashing right to the jaw. "Braddock's knees sagged," Ward wrote. "He did not stagger back as he might have from a less deadly wallop. He started to sink slowly but certainly." Braddock toppled over onto his right side, and he was out cold as the 10-count was administered. It took two minutes more for him to regain his senses.

Braddock had done his best, but after all he was merely a good fighter who found himself confronted by a great one. Less than eight rounds into his first title defense, his tenure as champion was over. The reign of his successor would last almost 12 years and include 25 successful defenses, both all-time records.

The people throughout the nation who had huddled anxiously around their radios and then erupted in celebration may not have realized it fully, but a corner had indeed been turned. Joe Louis had taken the first step in what would eventually become a parade of great African-American athletes destined to dominate the world of sports.

April 5, 1938
The Best Seat in the House

The Blackhawks went into the 1938 Stanley Cup playoffs with an uninspiring record of 14-25-9. They dropped the opener in their first best-of-three series, against the Montreal Canadiens, before rebounding to take the next two games. They lost their first game against the New York Americans, then came back with a pair of do-or-die wins to claim that series as well. In each series, a shutout by goalie Mike Karakas staved off elimination and swung the momentum to the Hawks' favor.

The Cinderella Hawks advanced to the finals against Toronto as decided underdogs; they had managed only one win in six tries against the Maple Leafs during the regular season. Worse yet, Karakas was diagnosed with a broken toe (suffered in the last game with the Americans) only hours before the series opener on April 5. "We had sent Paul Goodman, our spare goalie, home before the playoffs started," recalled Hawks captain Johnny Gottselig. "There was no way of getting him to Toronto before the game that night."

Coach Bill Stewart tried to engineer a hasty trade with the New York Rangers, who had already been eliminated, for their outstanding goalie Dave Kerr. But Toronto general manager Conn Smythe threatened to have any such deal vetoed by the league office. He recommended Alfie Moore, a journeyman who was property of the Maple Leafs but had played the entire season with Pittsburgh (then a minor-league club). After briefly scuffling with Smythe in a corridor of Maple Leaf Gardens, Stewart recognized that he had little choice but to give Moore a try. He sent Gottselig and Paul Thompson to fetch him.

The two went to Moore's house, not far from the arena, and were told by his wife that he was at a local tavern. When they got there, the bartender informed them that Moore had left an hour earlier for another tavern up the street. Sure enough, Gottselig and Thompson found Moore on a barstool, seeming a bit worse for wear. "He turned around and when he saw me his face lit up," Gottselig remembered. "'Geez, I'm glad to see you. How about a couple tickets to the game tonight?' he said. 'I'm glad to see *you*, Alfie,' I said. 'You're going to get the best seat in the house.'"

Moore was hustled to the arena and given a shower and several cups of coffee to sober him up, then he took the ice. "When we were warming up," Gottselig said, "Stewart said, 'Take it easy—don't shoot too hard. I don't want him hurt.' But Alfie was stopping everything, laughing and waving at his friends. He was mad at Smythe for sending him to Pittsburgh and said, 'I'll show him.'"

When the Maple Leafs' first shot on Moore ended up in the net, the Hawks figured they were in for a long night. But nothing else got past him. "We threw everything at him but the house," said Toronto goalie Turk Broda. Moore's heroics and two tallies by Gottselig carried the Hawks to a 3-1 win.

Smythe had technically loaned Moore to the Blackhawks, and he promptly unloaned him prior to Game 2 of the series. Goodman, pressed into service after two weeks of inactivity, proved no match for the Leafs in a 5-1 Toronto victory. But when the series shifted to Chicago Stadium, Karakas—outfitted with a special skate that protected his broken foot—was ready to go. A then-record crowd of 18,497 saw the Hawks win 2-1 in Game 3. Then, before another overflow throng of

17,204, the Hawks wrapped up their second Stanley Cup championship with a 4-1 triumph in Game 4.

Alfie Moore received $300 and a gold watch from the grateful Blackhawks for what proved to be the only playoff victory of his career. He ultimately played only 21 games (14 of them losses) in the NHL. In 1961, on the occasion of the Hawks' third Stanley Cup, Moore was asked if he had really been drunk that night in Toronto. "I've always been sort of hazy about that," he replied. "I had quite a few beers that day and I just can't remember."

CHAPTER 11

The Homer in the Gloamin'

"Well, there's a lot of happiness and a lot of sadness in playing baseball."
-- Paul Waner, Pittsburgh Pirates right fielder, 1926-1940

Gabby Hartnett had a front-row seat for two of the most celebrated events in baseball history. He was the catcher when Babe Ruth hit his notorious "called shot" in the 1932 World Series and when Carl Hubbell struck out five future Hall of Famers in succession in the 1934 All-Star Game. Hartnett had plenty of unforgettable moments behind the plate during his splendid 20-year career. But it was what he did *at* the plate one afternoon with darkness falling that ranked as the greatest thrill of his life.

The unlikely tale begins on July 20, 1938. The Cubs are in fourth place with a record of 45-36. They trail the league-leading Pittsburgh Pirates by five and a half games, the New York Giants by five games, and the Cincinnati Reds by a percentage point. Cubs owner Phil Wrigley removes manager Charlie Grimm and names Hartnett to replace him. "Grimm has done a swell job," Wrigley says, "but the club has not done as well as we felt it should."

"What the hell," says Grimm. "That's baseball." The man known as Jolly Cholly has been the Cubs' skipper since succeeding Rogers Hornsby under similar circumstances in August 1932. Wrigley is hoping for lightning to strike a second time in the same place—the managerial change in 1932 sparked the Cubs to the pennant. But the Pirates, led by the future Hall-of-Famers Paul and Lloyd Waner ("Big Poison" and "Little Poison"), will be tough to catch.

75

Hartnett, 37, has been the Cubs' catcher for 17 years, an all-star six times (the All-Star Game itself is only six years old), and the National League's Most Valuable Player in 1935. With Gabby as player-manager, the Cubs embark on a sensational roller-coaster ride through the latter part of the season.

July 21. Both the Cubs and Dodgers participate in a pregame ceremony honoring Hartnett. Photographers have a field day when Babe Ruth, now coaching for Brooklyn, comes over to wish him well. After the pleasantries are concluded, the teams split a doubleheader.

July 30. Cubs starter Dizzy Dean is knocked out in the fifth inning of a 5-4 loss at Philadelphia. Meanwhile, Pittsburgh and New York both win. The Cubs trail the Pirates by eight games and the Giants by three.

August 20. A new low. The Cubs commit six errors and hit into five double plays in an embarrassing 5-2 loss to Pittsburgh. It is their sixth defeat in the last seven games, and makes them only 14-15 under Hartnett. They are nine games behind the Pirates, who now appear to be home free.

August 21. The plot thickens. In the first game of a doubleheader, Cubs ace Bill Lee comes through with his bat as well as his arm. He drives in three runs with a single and a double while holding the Pirates at bay until Jack Russell relieves him in the ninth. The Cubs hang on to win 6-4. Then Tex Carleton stifles Pittsburgh 6-1 in the second game. An appreciative crowd of 40,402 at Wrigley Field sees the Pirates' lead reduced to a still-formidable seven games.

September 5. A Labor Day throng of 42,545 at Pittsburgh's Forbes Field goes home disappointed as the Cubs sweep a doubleheader 3-0 and 4-3. Lee pitches a shutout in the opener despite yielding 10 hits. In the nightcap, Clay Bryant goes the distance as the Cubs overcome a 3-1 deficit with runs in the sixth, eighth, and ninth. The Cubs are five games behind the Pirates, one game behind Cincinnati.

September 11. Lee does it again, outdueling Cincinnati ace Paul Derringer 2-0 to break the Cubs' second-place tie with the Reds. Pittsburgh loses to St. Louis; the Pirates' margin is down to three and a half games.

September 14. Hartnett, who has been a part-time player since assuming managerial duties, contributes his first base hit in a month—a three-run homer that propels the Cubs to a 6-3 win at Boston. The streaking Giants take two from Pittsburgh. The Pirates lead the Cubs by two and a half games, New York and Cincinnati by three and a half each.

September 22. The Cubs sweep a doubleheader from the Phillies, 4-0 and 2-1, in Philadelphia. In the first game, Bill Lee tosses his fourth consecutive shutout for his 20th victory of the season. Clay Bryant wins the nightcap. But the Pirates also sweep a doubleheader, from Brooklyn, to remain three and a half games in front.

September 23. The Cubs sweep *another* doubleheader from the Phillies; they have won four games in less than 30 hours. A bases-loaded double in the ninth by Rip Collins makes the difference in the second game. The Pirates lose to Cincinnati, and their lead is down to two games.

September 26. Although he fails in his bid pitch a record-breaking fifth straight shutout, Bill Lee beats the Cardinals 6-3 at Wrigley Field. The Cubs have won seven in a row and 17 of their last 20. They have moved to within a game and a half of the Pirates, who are also surging, having won eight of their last 10. "If we win five of our remaining seven games," says Pittsburgh manager Pie Traynor, "it doesn't matter how many the Cubs win." While the Cubs are beating the Cardinals, the Pirates are in the stands at Wrigley Field, having arrived in Chicago a day early for the three-game series that will decide the pennant.

On September 27, the papers and the radio were full of news about the Munich Conference, where Great Britain and France were in the process of handing Czechoslovakia over to Nazi Germany. A second world war was not yet regarded as inevitable.

At Wrigley Field, where only the National League pennant hung in the balance, the Cubs turned to Dizzy Dean. Several years earlier, Dean had said, "Anybody who's had the pleasure of seeing me play knows that I am the greatest pitcher in the world." Indeed, he *averaged* 24 wins a year for five years beginning in 1932. But the Dizzy Dean who was acquired from St. Louis before the 1938 season was just a shadow of his former self. In the previous summer's All-Star Game, a line drive had shattered the little toe on his left foot. Because the Cardinals were in a tight pennant race, Dean had continued to pitch, altering his delivery to favor the broken toe. He had ruined his arm in the process.

For the Cubs, Dean was able to pitch only occasionally, but he always gave his team an honest effort—and a full house. He had not started in five weeks when Hartnett gave him the ball for this "must" game. "In a spot such as this," Warren Brown wrote, "Dizzy Dean was perfectly at home. Here was a park packed with popeyed fans. Here was a game on which the entire season might depend. If you had asked Dean—and many did—what he thought about being put on such a spot, Diz had but one answer: 'Gabby's getting smarter every day. Who else would he pick to beat these guys but old Diz?'"

"His arm was hurting him badly," teammate Phil Cavarretta recalled. "The thing I remember best watching this man pitch, his presence on that mound encouraged us to go out there and play hard. Watching him pitch was an inspiration. You could see the man was suffering out there. You'd say, 'My God, let's go out and win it for Diz.'"

Getting by on guts and guile, Dean held the Pirates scoreless for eight and two-thirds innings before running out of gas. As he left the field, a tumult of cheers rang down from the standing-room-only crowd of 42,238. "It was an incredible performance," said Cavarretta. Dean's teammates congratulated him in the dugout, but he was disgusted that he hadn't been able to finish.

With the Cubs clinging to a 2-0 lead and the tying runs on second and third, the ubiquitous Bill Lee relieved Dean. Pirate catcher Al Todd was up to bat. Lee promptly threw a wild pitch, scoring one run and moving the tying run to third. Then, with the crowd roaring its approval, he struck out Todd—the only strikeout of the game on either side—to narrowly preserve a 2-1 victory. It was Dean's seventh win of the year against only one loss.

The Cubs were now only a half game behind the Pirates, and the stage was set for perhaps the most dramatic game ever played at Wrigley Field.

On the gloomy afternoon of September 28, the Cubs trailed 3-1 when Hartnett opened the bottom of the sixth with a double to center. Rip Collins followed with a double off the right-field wall to score Hartnett. Collins advanced to third on a single by Bill Jurges and scored the tying run on a forceout. The Cubs missed a chance to go ahead when Jurges, trying to score from second on a single to left-center, was thrown out at the plate by shortstop Arky Vaughan.

The skies continued to darken as the game remained tied through the seventh. In the eighth, the Pirates scored twice, and only an inning-ending double play prevented further damage.

Leading 5-3, the Pirates needed only six more outs to all but knock the Cubs out of the pennant race. But the Cubs came right back in their half of the eighth. Collins led off with a single. Bill Swift relieved Pirates starter Bob Klinger and walked Jurges. Tony Lazzeri was sent up to bunt the runners to second and third. His first attempt was foul. He missed the second pitch altogether, but the ball got away from catcher Al Todd, and Collins went sliding into third. Lazzeri, having failed to sacrifice, then swung away and delivered a double to right, scoring Collins and sending Jurges to third.

The tying and lead runs were now in scoring position for the Cubs. After Stan Hack drew an intentional walk to load the bases, Billy Herman singled to right. The fans were delirious—for an instant. Herman's hit scored Jurges with the tying run, but Joe Marty (pinch running for Lazzeri) was out at the plate on a perfect throw by right fielder Paul Waner. Now Hack was on second with the go-ahead run, and Herman on first. But Mace Brown came on to pitch for the Pirates and induced Frank Demaree to tap into a double play to end the inning.

By now it was very dark (it would be 50 more years before lights were installed at Wrigley Field). The umpires conferred and decided to let the teams play one more inning, after which it would certainly be impossible to continue.

Charlie Root, the Cubs' sixth pitcher of the day, got through the ninth unscathed, thanks in part to Hartnett, who nailed Paul Waner trying to steal second for the third out. In the bottom half of the inning, Cavarretta hit a long drive to center that was caught by Lloyd Waner. Then Carl Reynolds grounded out to the second baseman. One more out and the game would go into the books as a tie, and the Pirates would still be in first place. The teams would have to play a double-header the next day, with the Cubs needing a sweep to move into first place.

Up to the plate strode Gabby Hartnett. "I swung once and missed," he later recalled. "I swung again, and got a piece of it, but that was all. A

79

foul and strike two. I had one more chance. Mace Brown wound up and let fly; I swung with everything I had and then I got that feeling you get when the blood rushes out of your head and you get dizzy."

"Hartnett swung," Paul Waner remembered, "and the damn ball landed in the left-field seats! I could hardly believe my eyes. The game was over, and I should have run into the clubhouse. But I didn't. I just stood out there in right field and watched Hartnett circle the bases, and take the lousy pennant with him. I just watched and wondered, sort of objectively, you know, how the devil he could ever get all the way around to touch home plate."

Hartnett's home run gave the Cubs a 6-5 victory. There was pandemonium in the stands and on the field. "When I got to second base I couldn't see third for the players and fans there," Hartnett said. "I don't think I walked a step to the plate—I was carried in. But when I got there I saw [umpire] George Barr taking a good look. He was going to make sure I touched that platter."

"The crowd was in an uproar," said Waner, "absolutely gone wild. They ran onto the field like a bunch of maniacs, and his teammates and the crowd and all were mobbing Hartnett, and piling on top of him, and throwing him up in the air, and everything you could think of. I've never seen anything like it."

It took dozens of Andy Frain ushers, as well as the entire complement of Cub players, to protect Hartnett from the hundreds of fans who had swarmed onto the field. The ushers and the other players tugged and shoved and elbowed their way through the mob to the Cubs' clubhouse. A mailman who had caught the home run came and presented the ball to Hartnett, who gratefully gave him an autographed ball in return.

For the first time since July 12, Pittsburgh was out of first place. The next day, the Cubs routed the demoralized Pirates 10-1 for their 10th straight win and their 20th in the last 23 games. Appearing on the mound for the fifth time in a week (including three complete-game victories and two relief stints), Bill Lee had an easy time of it as he went the distance. "The heart was gone out of Pittsburgh," Hartnett said. Two days later, the Cubs clinched the pennant with a victory at St. Louis. It was their fourth flag in the past 10 seasons, each coming at three-year intervals.

On the evening of October 3, thousands of fans greeted the Cubs when their train pulled into the Illinois Central station. The following day, a ticker-tape parade down LaSalle Street drew tens of thousands.

Unfortunately, the Cubs succumbed to the New York Yankees' juggernaut four games to none in the World Series—which proved to be Lou Gehrig's last. But that took only a little of the luster from the Cubs' electrifying charge down the stretch, and none from Hartnett's heroics. His pennant-winning blow went down in baseball lore as the "homer in the gloamin'." Until the day he died, in 1972 (on his 72nd birthday), Hartnett himself called it by another name: "The greatest thrill of my life."

CHAPTER 12

Monsters of the Midway

We'll never forget the way you thrilled the nation
With your T-formation.
  -- *Jerry Downs [pseudonym for Al Hoffmann], "Bear Down, Chicago Bears"*

As the two men left the field after the 1940 National Football League championship game, Bill Osmanski of the Bears tried to console Washington quarterback Sammy Baugh. "Don't feel bad, Sam," Osmanski said. "Think what would have happened if Charlie Malone had caught that first long pass." With the Redskins trailing 7-0 on their first possession, Baugh had fired a perfect strike to Malone, who was wide open at the Bears' four-yard line, for an apparent game-tying touchdown. But the ball had gone right through Malone's hands.

"If Malone had caught that pass," Baugh replied to Osmanski, "the score would have been 73-7."

Indeed, the Bears had annihilated the Redskins 73-0. "The weather was perfect," wrote Arthur Daley of *The New York Times*. "So were the Bears." It remains the most lopsided game in NFL history, and it started the Bears on a run in which they'd win three championships in four years.

It was December 8, 1940. The Redskins were champions of the East at 9-2, the Bears champions of the West at 8-3. The Bears were back in Washington's Griffith Stadium just three weeks after a hard-fought and disputed loss to the Redskins, in the ninth game of the regular season, which had made the difference in the teams' records.

In that game, the Bears trailed 7-3 with time running out when quarterback Sid Luckman found George McAfee deep in Washington territory. After McAfee was brought down at the one-yard line, he feigned injury to stop the clock with 10 seconds left (the Bears were out of timeouts), and was flagged for delay of game. Pushed back to the six-yard line by the penalty, Luckman had time enough to attempt two passes. The first fell incomplete. The second appeared to find Osmanski clear in the end zone. "Frank Filchock grabbed me from behind," Osmanski later recalled, "and pulled my arms against my sides. The ball hit my chest and flopped to the ground. The gun went off."

The Redskins escaped with the win. The officials escaped into one of the stadium's baseball dugouts and down the tunnel to the sanctuary of their locker room with Bears coach George Halas in hot pursuit, spewing all the profanities he could think of—and he had a considerable repertoire from which to draw.

The Bears blamed their defeat on favorable home-field officiating for Washington. This was music to the ears of George Preston Marshall, the Redskins' colorful owner, who never missed an opportunity to stir the pot where Halas was concerned. "The Bears are a bunch of crybabies," Marshall pronounced. "They are quitters. They fold up when the going gets tough."

When it became clear that the two teams would play again in the championship game, Marshall stepped up his verbal assaults on the Bears. "They are the world's greatest crybabies," he repeated. "We have whipped them before and we will whip them again."

Marshall surely realized that he was providing bulletin-board fodder for Halas and the Bears, but there was a method to his madness. Early in the week before the rematch, he sent Halas a telegram. "Congratulations," he wrote. "Game will be sold out by Tuesday night. We should play for the championship every year."

Game day was clear and crisp, with a temperature of 39 degrees. "A perfect day for football!" Marshall exclaimed to reporters and fans from his box behind the Redskins' bench. The overflow crowd at Griffith Stadium was joined by a nationwide radio audience; this was the first NFL game to be broadcast coast-to-coast.

The Redskins' hopes were carried by Sammy Baugh, pro football's first great passer, who had led the league that year for the second time (he led the league in passing six times all told). Baugh was also the

NFL's finest punter—his career average of 45.1 yards per kick is still the best ever—and an outstanding defensive back who was perennially among the league leaders in interceptions.

The Bears were led by their second-year quarterback Sid Luckman, who, like Baugh, also played defensive back and was his team's regular punter. Though not as accomplished a passer as Slingin' Sammy, Luckman was the ideal man for the Bears' modified T-formation offense, which put a variety of options at his disposal and required him to mix them up in response to what the defense was doing.

The game pitted the NFL's best passing team, the Redskins, against its best running team, the Bears. The Redskins had stopped the Bears in the regular-season game and saw no reason why they wouldn't do so again. But Halas had spent hour after hour studying films of the 7-3 loss, and he had returned to Washington convinced that if the Redskins came back with their customary 5-3-3 defensive alignment, Luckman and the Bears would have a field day.

As the Bears left the locker room, Halas gave Luckman three plays he had scripted; each was designed to exploit a specific weakness that Halas had identified in the Redskin defense. The Bears would use these plays on their first possession to test Washington's responses to their man-in-motion schemes.

The Bears began from their own 24-yard line after the opening kickoff. The first of the scripted plays was a fake reverse with man-in-motion. Luckman handed off to George McAfee, who gained eight yards. Halas was elated. He now knew that the Redskins were not prepared to make the adjustments necessary to stop his offense.

On the second play, McAfee went in motion to the right, and Luckman pitched left to Osmanski, who found a hole through the line, stiff-armed a linebacker out of the way, swung to the outside, and raced 68 yards for a touchdown. A flying body block by George Wilson obliterated the last two Redskin defenders about 35 yards from the goal line.

Luckman didn't need to call the third of the scripted plays. "I signaled the coach that the Redskins were in the old defense and he could sit back and relax," he said. Jack Manders kicked the extra point to put the Bears ahead 7-0. The game was less than a minute old. "I was delighted," Halas wrote in his autobiography. "I knew we could collect enough points to win the championship. Our adjusted plays could go time and again through the weaknesses we had detected in the Washington defense."

Max Krause of the Redskins returned the ensuing kickoff to the Bears' 32, and might have gone all the way but for a fine open-field tackle by Osmanski. A few plays later, from the 19, Baugh went to the air and found Charlie Malone all alone for an apparent touchdown. Malone dropped the ball. Washington then attempted and missed a 32-yard field goal.

The Redskins were never in the game after Malone's miscue. The Bears' next drive took them 80 yards in 18 plays, all on the ground, with Luckman scoring on a quarterback sneak. The kick by Bob Snyder made it 14-0.

Baugh was unable to move the Redskins on their second possession, and his punt was partially blocked, giving the Bears the ball in Washington territory. The Bears' subsequent "drive" consisted of one play: a Luckman lateral to Joe Maniaci, who went around left end and scampered 42 yards for a touchdown. Phil Martinovich's extra point gave the Bears a 21-0 lead.

Baugh was replaced at quarterback by Frank Filchock, who fared little better. An interception by Ray Nolting set up the Bears' fourth touchdown, a 30-yard pass from Luckman to Ken Kavanaugh.

It was 28-0 at halftime. Unbelievably, things only got worse for Washington in the second half. On just the second play of the third quarter, Hampton Pool picked off a pass by Baugh and returned it 15 yards for the Bears' fifth touchdown. The Bears would go on to score three more touchdowns in the third quarter and another three in the fourth—even with Luckman sitting out the entire time. Early in the third quarter, the fans stopped cheering. A little later, the Redskin marching band—George Preston Marshall's pride and joy—quit playing, and Marshall himself sat in stunned silence. The fans were roused from their torpor only when an announcement came over the public-address system promoting 1941 season tickets. They booed themselves hoarse, then sat back down to watch the disaster play itself out. By the fourth quarter, the stands were largely empty, and the fans still remaining had taken to cheering for the Bears.

One phrase became so familiar over the course of the afternoon that each time the stadium announcer started to say it, the fans chanted along in unison: "[Lee] Artoe will kick off for the Bears."

10 different players scored the Bears' 11 touchdowns, and six Bears were responsible for the seven successful extra points. In all, 15 different Bears scored in the game. After the 10th touchdown, the officials asked Halas not to kick any more extra points, as they were running out of footballs. Accordingly, the Bears passed on the last two extra-point attempts.

When it was over, the Bears had gained an amazing 382 yards on the ground to Washington's 22. They had attempted only eight passes and completed six, for 119 yards. The Redskins had passed 51 times, completing just 20 for 223 yards. Baugh, Filchock, and Roy Zimmerman had thrown *eight* interceptions, with the Bears returning three of them for touchdowns.

"It was one of those days," Halas said. "Everything we did, we did right. Everything they did, they did wrong."

This is how the Bears scored:

First quarter. Osmanski, 68-yard run (Manders kick). Luckman, one-yard run (Snyder kick). Maniaci, 42-yard run (Martinovich kick). 21-0.

Second quarter. Kavanaugh, 30-yard pass from Luckman (Snyder kick). 28-0.

Third quarter. Pool, 15-yard interception return (Dick Plasman kick). Nolting, 23-yard run (Plasman's kick missed). McAfee, 34-yard interception return (Joe Stydahar kick). Bulldog Turner, 21-yard interception return (Maniaci's kick blocked). 54-0.

Fourth quarter. Harry Clark, 44-yard run (Gary Famiglietti's kick missed). Famiglietti, one-yard run (Maniaci, pass from Solly Sherman). Clark, one-yard run (Sherman's pass to Maniaci failed). 73-0.

"From the moment Bill Osmanski broke away for 68 yards and a touchdown on the third play of the game," George Strickler wrote in the *Tribune*, "until little Harry Clark popped through a hole as wide as a bleacher exit for his second and the Bears' last touchdown late in the fourth period, there was no question in the minds of the 36,034 jammed into Griffith Stadium that the colossus from the west, this day at least, was a superteam."

After he and Redskin coach Ray Flaherty visited the Bears' locker room to congratulate Halas, George Preston Marshall gave his own assessment of the game. "We had the greatest crowd in Washington history, and we played our poorest game," he told reporters. "It looked as if some of our lads had their fountain pens in their pockets trying to figure out who was going to get what share of the playoff money."

The victory party in Halas's suite at the Mayflower Hotel attracted a good many senators, congressmen, and other celebrities, including Marshall himself. When he arrived late in the evening, Marshall had evidently made several previous stops on his way from the stadium. By this time, he had an easy answer for all questions about the game: "I don't remember a thing."

What Halas and the Bears had done would revolutionize football. Their stunning success against the Redskins loosed a stampede to the T-formation by virtually every pro, college, and high-school team in the country.

The formation was not new. "From time immemorial," Halas wrote in his autobiography, "the backfield had lined up in a T, the quarterback directly behind the center, the fullback directly behind him four or five yards with a halfback on each side. The ball went to the quarterback who pivoted and handed or pitched to one of the backs. The other backs became blockers or receivers. The formation made sense for driving straight ahead. The objective then was power, power, power."

By the late twenties, coaches were experimenting with ways to free their linemen and backs from plowing straight into the defense's strength. They shifted players around before the snap, forcing defenders to adjust their own positions at the last second. But something was still missing until Ralph Jones, head coach of the Bears from 1930 to 1932, began to exploit the previously obscure rule by which one man could shift his position and continue moving behind the line of scrimmage right up until the time the ball was snapped.

The man-in-motion feature became the key to the Bears' modern T-formation. In Halas's words, "It broke the game wide open." The man in motion "could take a lateral and run straight ahead," Halas explained, "or he could run downfield to take a long pass, or he could come in behind the defensive line to take a short pass, or he could join the end in blocking for another back coming around with the ball." The man in motion could also be used as a decoy; if a linebacker or defensive back followed him downfield, other areas would be left open and vulnerable.

Throughout the thirties, Halas and his colleague Clark Shaughnessy worked at refining Jones's innovations. They were aided by several new rules. One permitted a forward pass from anywhere behind the line (replacing the earlier limit of at least five yards). Another called for the ball to be placed 10 yards from the sideline after being carried out of bounds, so the offense didn't have to spend a down in order to gain room to maneuver. Still another made the ball less round, more streamlined and thus easier to throw. Halas and Shaughnessy devised myriad plays and blocking schemes to capitalize on these changes. When Sid Luckman arrived in 1939, everything fell into place. Halas now had the quarterback he needed to run his modern T with devastating effectiveness.

With Luckman at the controls, the Bears were close to perfect. The unforgettable championship game of 1940 was just the beginning for the team that became known as the Monsters of the Midway. For the next three years, the Bears dominated the league like no other team before or since.

In 1941, the Bears defeated the Packers 25-17 in the season opener at Green Bay. The Packers—led by the great tandem of Cecil Isbell and Don Hutson—beat the Bears 16-14 at Wrigley Field in the sixth game. Neither team lost another game, and both finished the regular season 10-1-0. A week after Pearl Harbor, they played off for the Western Division championship. Sensing that the game would for all practical purposes decide the world championship as well, more than 43,000 fans packed into Wrigley Field despite the temperature of 16 degrees. After spotting the Packers a 7-0 lead early, the Bears scored 30 unanswered points before halftime and coasted to a 33-14 victory.

The title game was a bit of an anticlimax, as fewer than 14,000 showed up to see the Bears dispatch the Giants 37-9 for their second straight world championship. In 13 games (including the postseason), the Bears scored 30 or more points 10 times. In four games, they scored 48 or more. In no game did they allow more than 24.

In 1942, the Bears had the greatest regular season in NFL history. They won all 11 games, amassing 376 points to their opponents' 84. In their *closest* game, they won by two touchdowns. They scored 35 or more points seven times. In the final six games, they recorded four shutouts and allowed but seven points in each of the other two. Riding an incredible 18-game winning streak, the Bears rolled into Washington for the championship game favored by more than 20 points. Redskin coach Ray Flaherty said nothing to his players before the game; he simply went over to the blackboard and wrote *73-0.* The inspired Redskins pulled off a 14-6 upset to give George Preston Marshall his revenge for 1940.

In 1943, many key players were in the armed forces—as was Halas, who'd joined the Navy. Fortunately for the Bears' temporary co-coaches Hunk Anderson and Luke Johnsos, Sid Luckman remained. The league's Most Valuable Player that season, Luckman was joined by the legendary Bronko Nagurski, who returned to help out after five years in retirement. Nagurski, 34, had initially declined the Bears' entreaties that he come back, saying he was "just a little too old for this type of activity." When Johnsos promised that he could play tackle exclusively and not have to worry about running the ball, Bronko agreed.

The promise was broken in the last game of the regular season. Needing a win to earn the Western Division title and another shot at Washington for the league title, the Bears found themselves trailing the winless Cardinals 24-14 after three quarters in the snow at Comiskey Park. Then Bronko took over. "What a great spot for a legend to be in," William Goldman wrote, "coming back after so many years, one quarter to play, the title on the line, and 10 points behind." Nagurski lined up at his old fullback position, and Luckman gave him the ball time and time again. "He was like an ax hitting a tree," Goldman wrote. "It doesn't matter how big the tree is, when the ax starts coming, you better look out."

Nagurski kept hammering away behind center Bulldog Turner, and the Cardinals found it harder and harder to bring him down. He rushed 16 times for 84 yards in the fourth quarter, carrying the Bears to three touchdown drives for a 35-24 win and the division crown.

In the championship game, Luckman threw for five touchdowns and also intercepted three Redskin passes as the Bears triumphed 41-21—thus avenging their only loss of the regular season and their defeat in the previous year's title game. A reporter asked Nagurski why he had returned after such a long time away from the game. He simply said, "Halas wanted me to." Since the comeback had gone so well, the reporter inquired, would he stay on for another season? "Hell no," Nagurski said, smiling. "I can't go on taking care of Halas all my life."

The Bears of 1941, 1942, and 1943 ran up an unbelievable regular-season record of 29-2-1, averaging almost 34 points a game while holding their opponents to just over 12. Including postseason, their total record was 32-3-1. In addition to Nagurski (whose earlier career had already qualified him), six members of this superteam were destined for the Pro Football Hall of Fame: center Turner, right guard George Musso, left guard Danny Fortmann, left tackle Joe Stydahar, halfback McAfee, and quarterback Luckman.

Only Green Bay and Washington stood between the Bears and absolute perfection during this period. The Packers beat the Bears once and tied them once, while the Redskins beat them twice. Against the rest of the league, the Bears were 25-0-0.

CHAPTER 13

Greetings from the 4-F League

"In 1945, we were fortunate that many of our regulars were not acceptable for military service."
-- *Charlie Grimm, Cubs manager, 1932-1938, 1944-1949, 1960*

By 1945, the final year of World War II, most of the best players throughout Major League Baseball were serving in the armed forces. The players who were left did the best they could. "It was just a matter of playing anyone who was breathing," said broadcaster Red Barber. "Nobody asked too much. It was interesting and it gave people something to do."

Earlier in the war, a man who was supporting a wife and children would be likely to receive a deferment from the draft. But later on, even family men were marching off to answer Uncle Sam's call. Therefore, the major-league rosters were stocked with fuzzy-cheeked teenagers who were too young to be drafted, rickety old-timers who were well past their prime, and, most significantly, men who were classified as 4-F—"physically, mentally, or morally unfit for service." In 1944, there was an average of 10 4-F's on each major-league club; in 1945, it was 16.

Physical reasons for 4-F status included poor eyesight, punctured eardrums, slipped disks, arthritic hips, torn cartilage in knees, bone chips in ankles, flat feet, asthma, diabetes, stomach ulcers, high blood pressure, irregular heartbeats, and being taller than six-foot-six. St. Louis Browns outfielder Pete Gray had the most obvious handicap, having lost his right arm in a childhood accident.

If the 4-F's were too lame to serve in the military, many people asked, how could they be well enough to play baseball? Arthur Daley of the *New York Times* explained. "These lads appear physically fit," Daley wrote, "because their dressing rooms are equipped with whirlpool baths, baking machines, massage tables, and adhesive tape. Some of them have to wear special braces and the majority of them are the most artificially 'physically fit' athletes imaginable. They require persistent attention in order to continue for the brief spurts in which they operate."

The poor standard of play offered up in 1945 can be deduced from the fact that of the 128 non-pitchers who had starting jobs in the majors in 1945, only 32 remained full-time players the next year.

The St. Louis Cardinals were by far the class of the league in these years. They hoisted the pennant in 1942, 1943, and 1944; their 316 wins and .684 winning percentage over the three-year span were the second best of all time (to the Cubs of 1906, 1907, and 1908). Their incredibly rich farm system made them apparently immune to the manpower shortages afflicting other clubs. In 1945, though, their magnificent star Stan Musial was inducted into the Navy.

Musial, who by now was already nicknamed "The Man," had joined the Cardinals late in the 1941 season, when he was 20, and batted .426 in 47 at-bats. In 1942, his first full season, he'd hit .315. He would have won the Rookie of the Year award if it had existed (it wasn't introduced until five years later). In 1943, he'd batted a league-high .357 and been selected Most Valuable Player. In 1944, his average had declined—to .347—while his runs scored and runs batted in had increased.

Musial's absence convinced Cubs general manager Jim Gallagher that the Cardinals were vulnerable. Gallagher "allowed that he would not be surprised if the Cubs won the pennant," Warren Brown wrote in his 1946 history of the Cubs. "He was promptly told that he was nuts. Since he had been told that before, he refrained from further comment. This was not hard to do, for the sportswriters of Chicago were then divided into two general classes: a) those who were not speaking to Gallagher, and b) those to whom Gallagher was not speaking."

As luck would have it, the Cubs opened the season against St. Louis. Chicago's lineup consisted of Stan Hack, third base; Len Merullo, shortstop; Phil Cavarretta, first base; Bill Nicholson, right field; Ed Sauer, left field; Andy Pafko, center field; Don Johnson, second base; Mickey Livingston, catcher; and Paul Derringer, pitcher.

Of the eight position players, only Sauer did not retain his spot for the entire season; he soon surrendered left field to Harry "Peanuts" Lowrey, who'd returned from the service. Derringer, 38, had been around for 15 years and had been a mainstay for the pennant-winning Cardinals of 1931 and Cincinnati Reds of 1939 and 1940. He proved a solid performer for the Cubs, but as the campaign wore on he was overshadowed by Hank Wyse, Claude Passeau, and another pitcher, Hank Borowy, who didn't join the club until July 27.

Despite the presence of the Cardinals, the opener at Wrigley Field on April 17 drew only 11,788 frigid spectators. Nicholson, a great fan favorite, gave the faithful a thrill by smacking a home run in his first at-bat, leading off the second inning. "He could hit a ball a long ways," Johnson recalled. "If he'd swing and miss on a ball, all the audience would go, 'Swish!' That was his nickname, Swish."

After Nicholson's round tripper, the teams traded single runs. St. Louis tied it up 1-1 in the fifth, the Cubs went back in front 2-1, St. Louis tied it again in the eighth. The Cubs finally won 3-2 in the ninth on a walk by Nicholson, a sacrifice by Sauer, and (after an intentional pass to Pafko) a single by Johnson.

The Cubs had made a good start against the team to beat, but they would defeat the Cardinals just five more times in 21 tries for the remainder of the season. Nicholson, who had led the league with 29 and 33 homers, respectively, in the previous two years, would manage only 12 more for the rest of the season. If the Cubs and their fans had been aware of these unpleasant facts, they would have been hard pressed indeed to foresee a pennant waving over Wrigley Field in 1945.

The Cubs were managed by the affable Charlie Grimm, who was in the second of his three stints at the helm. He had guided the club to pennants in 1932 and 1935. "Jolly Cholly" was not considered a particularly strong tactician, but he had played in the majors for two decades and he empathized with his men. "Under Charlie we all enjoyed each other, had a lot of fun with each other," said Merullo. "When you played for Charlie Grimm, that's the type of ball club he had. He did his best to keep you loose."

Don Johnson had played for Grimm in the minor leagues. "Charlie was really funny," he recalled. "In Indianapolis one ball game, it started to rain about the seventh inning. It just rained, rained, rained. All through the seventh and part of the eighth. And the umpire wouldn't stop the game.

"Grimm found a great big beach umbrella someplace. Where in the hell he ever got it, I don't know. He walked out to protest to the umpire, and subconsciously the umpire got under the umbrella with him! When he realized what he had done, he kicked Grimm out of the ball game.

"Where he came up with these things, I don't know. Another time we were playing, and it was so darn dark you could hardly see. The clouds were coming in. Grimm had one of these lanterns the railroad people carry. He walked out there and held it up over the umpire's head and got kicked out again!"

May 8 was V-E (Victory in Europe) Day. The Cubs were en route to the East Coast for their first extended road trip of the season. They had left St. Louis the day before after dropping both ends of a doubleheader. Edward Burns of the *Tribune* noted that "they looked rather ridiculous as they absorbed two severe whippings from a patchwork combination playing under the banner of the world champion Cardinals." The Cubs and Cardinals were tied for fourth place at 8-6.

When the weather heated up, so did the Cubs. On July 4, they took two from the Boston Braves to move into second place, three and a half games behind the Brooklyn Dodgers and percentage points ahead of the Cardinals. Just four days later, the Cubs were in first place after sweeping a doubleheader from the hapless Philadelphia Phillies, 12-6 and 9-2. In the first game, Cavarretta pounded out a triple, a double, and two bases-loaded singles. In the second game, Lowrey rapped a double and a homer. The Cubs had won 13 of the 16 games on their second East Coast swing of the season, including the last 10 in succession. They were 42-28, one game ahead of Brooklyn and a game and a half in front of St. Louis.

On a day off in late July, Grimm and Gallagher went fishing. When they returned in the wee hours "full of beer" by Gallagher's own admission, Gallagher's wife told him that someone from New York had been trying to reach him by phone all afternoon and evening. He dialed the number given and found Larry MacPhail, general manager of the Yankees, on the other end of the line.

"What will you give us for Borowy?" MacPhail demanded.

Gallagher could not believe his ears. Hank Borowy, 29, was a mainstay of the Yankee staff, compiling a record of 56-30 since 1942. Then, as now, quality starting pitchers were a precious commodity. This was all the more true given the wartime talent pool.

"How the hell can you ever get waivers on him?" Gallagher asked.

"I've got the waivers," MacPhail replied. "Do you want him, or don't you?"

By asking for waivers, MacPhail had theoretically made Borowy available to any American League club that was willing to fork over $7,500. But, no doubt suspecting that MacPhail would withdraw Borowy's name as soon as someone filed a claim on him, the other American League general managers all passed. MacPhail was now free to deal Borowy to a National League club for any mutually agreed-upon price.

The startled Gallagher acquired Borowy for $97,000 and two minor-league players who were never heard of again. MacPhail's apparent beneficence has been wondered at ever since. One theory holds that he believed Borowy was about to be drafted into the service, another that he assumed recurring blisters on Borowy's pitching fingers would soon end Hank's career. Grimm had perhaps the most interesting explanation. "A few years before, when Larry was with the Brooklyn Dodgers," Grimm said, "he had made a slick deal with the Cubs for [second baseman] Billy Herman. I've often thought he showed his appreciation by clearing the way for us to land Borowy." The acquisition would prove to be a godsend for Gallagher and the Cubs.

September 2 was V-J (Victory over Japan) Day. The Cubs were in St. Louis for a holiday doubleheader that could have dropped them into a tie for first place. The Cardinals had won five in a row from the Cubs over the past two weekends, and it was up to Borowy to stem the tide. He succeeded admirably, limiting the Cardinals to one run and finally winning 4-1 in 10 innings for the Cubs' most important victory of the season so far. St. Louis won the second game, but the Cubs escaped town with a two-game edge in the standings.

As the season entered its final week, the Cubs continued to maintain a tenuous lead over the Cardinals. "I had a good feeling we were not going to lose," said Johnson. "'Cause when you're losing, you feel you're going to lose. But I had that feeling we were going to win. Later I got to thinking, 'Gee, we *are* going to win!' There's no doubt about it, is there?"

September 23 was Andy Pafko Day at Wrigley Field. The Cubs' center fielder was honored by Chicago's Slovak community before the game and presented with, among other gifts, a nice set of luggage. Then Pafko gave the capacity crowd of 43,755 a gift; his grand slam erased a 3-0 deficit and propelled the Cubs to a much-needed 7-3 win over the Pittsburgh Pirates.

On September 25, the Cardinals came calling; they trailed the Cubs by only a game and a half. Again the Cubs turned to Borowy. Though not at his best, he kept his team in the game. Behind 3-2, the Cubs tallied four times in the bottom of the seventh, with Cavarretta and Pafko each knocking in two teammates. Borowy ran out of gas in the eighth. Lefty Ray Prim replaced him with one out, two runs already in, and the tying run aboard. After an error by Cavarretta put the tying run on second and the go-ahead run on first, Prim pitched out of the jam. He yielded a single with two out in the ninth, then retired St. Louis shortstop Marty Marion to preserve the 6-5 victory. The *Tribune* called the game "the thriller of the decade."

The Cardinals beat the Cubs 11-6 the next day, but they were still a game and a half out with five to play. Next the Cubs traveled to their home away from home, Cincinnati, for a doubleheader with the Reds. They won 3-1 and 7-4, then gathered around the radio to listen to the Cardinals' game at Pittsburgh. The Pirates prevailed 5-2, assuring the Cubs at least a tie for the pennant.

On September 28, Borowy and the Cubs carried a 4-3 advantage into the bottom of the ninth at Pittsburgh. Borowy got the first man out, then gave up a double and a walk. After Paul Erickson came on to relieve the Cubs' ace, a groundout moved the runners to second and third. Then Erickson struck out pinch hitter Tommy O'Brien. The Cubs had won the pennant. It happened to be the 23rd wedding anniversary for Grimm and his wife. "As far as wedding anniversary presents go," Grimm remarked, "I don't believe a finer one could be manufactured."

The Cubs had struggled against St. Louis, winning six and losing 16, but racked up a mark of 90-40 against their other six opponents. Amazingly, they lost only once all season to Cincinnati, while beating the Reds 21 times. They swept 20 doubleheaders, still a record. They led the league in hitting, pitching, and fielding.

Cavarretta won the batting title with a .355 average, drove in 97 runs, and captured MVP honors. Hack batted .323 and scored 110 runs. Johnson hit .302, Pafko .298 with 110 runs batted in. Wyse was 22-10 with a 2.69 earned-run average, Passeau 17-9 and 2.46, Derringer 16-11 and 3.45. Prim, who split his time between starting and relieving, was 13-8 with a 2.40 ERA.

But it was Borowy who put the Cubs over the top. He went 11-2 for the Cubs, leading the league with a 2.14 ERA. He was 3-1 against St. Louis (after losing to the Cardinals 1-0 on August 24, he defeated them three times during the September stretch drive). "Without Borowy," Johnson said, "we could not have beaten the Cardinals. I think everybody felt that way."

Going into the World Series, the Cubs and Detroit Tigers didn't get the respect usually accorded pennant-winning teams. When sportswriters were polled as to the outcome of the Series, Warren Brown abstained. "I don't think either team can win it," he quipped. "I've seen them both play."

The first three games were played in Detroit's Briggs Stadium (later renamed Tiger Stadium). In Game 1, the Cubs knocked American League MVP Hal Newhouser out of the box in the third inning and cruised to a 9-0 triumph behind Borowy's six-hit pitching. "In that first game," Brown wrote, "the Cubs looked and acted like champions. As a team it was the only time in the Series that either side even approximated prewar skill in demonstrating before all those people that this was the major leagues and not an annual Elks' picnic game between the married men and the single men with a barrel of beer on third base."

Detroit's Virgil Trucks, who had returned from the Navy only in the waning days of the regular season, stifled Wyse and the Cubs 4-1 in Game 2. Then Passeau twirled a one-hitter as the Cubs won the next game 3-0. The Cubs thus led the Series two games to one as the action shifted to Wrigley Field for the last four games. But home cooking didn't help—Game 4 went to Dizzy Trout and the Tigers 4-1, and Newhouser topped Borowy and four other Cub pitchers 8-4 the next day.

Sportswriter Charles Einstein described Game 6 as "the worst game of baseball ever played in this country." Routine fly balls fell to the ground untouched, base runners fell flat on their faces, and the teams committed four errors between them. Passeau was sailing along with a 4-1 lead in the sixth inning when a line drive struck him in the pitching hand, tearing the nail off his middle finger. After Wyse and Prim allowed Detroit back into the game, Grimm turned, inevitably, to Borowy with the score tied 7-7 in the ninth. The contest went into extra innings, and the Cubs finally prevailed 8-7 in the 12th to force a seventh game.

Passeau's mishap proved to have drastic consequences for the Cubs. Borowy was slated to pitch Game 7, but he had been forced to go four innings in Game 6. Consequently, all of the Cubs expected Grimm to start Hy Vandenberg in place of Borowy for the deciding game; the 39-year-old was well rested and had been reliable throughout the regular season. But Grimm elected to come back with Borowy. "Asking Borowy to pitch the seventh game was asking an awful lot from him," said Wyse. "But then he wanted to pitch that last game. You have to admire a guy for wanting to do it."

The exhausted Borowy faced just three batters, all of whom reached base. Detroit scored five runs in the first inning, and the Cubs were history. The Tigers won 9-3 to claim the world championship.

It was the seventh straight World Series the Cubs had dropped since their most recent world title in 1908. The next year, Stan Musial returned and led St. Louis to another pennant, while the Cubs fell to third place. In 1947, the Cubs suffered through the first of 16 consecutive seasons in which they would be at or below the .500 level.

CHAPTER 14

Pride of the South Side

"Just a minute, boys. Don't take any pictures unless I'm in 'em."
-- *Marshall Goldberg, Cardinals halfback, after the*
1947 NFL championship game

In 1920, Chicago had two professional football franchises. The Bears were not one of them. It was the inaugural season of the American Professional Football Association (which changed its name to the National Football League two years later), and the Cardinals and the Tigers were Chicago's teams. When they met on November 7, they agreed that the losers would leave town. The Cardinals won 6-3 on a touchdown by quarterback Paddy Driscoll, and the Tigers soon disbanded.

George Halas and *his* team were in downstate Decatur, playing for the A.E. Staley Company. They compiled an outstanding record of 10-1-2, suffering their only defeat at the hands of the Cardinals, 7-6. According to Halas, the Cardinals scored the game-winning touchdown when a group of their fans ran onto the field prematurely as time was about to expire—and as a Cardinal ball carrier was zigzagging toward the goal line. "The guy used [the fans] for blockers," Halas said later, "and went in for a touchdown." It was a good story, and it has been repeated in various sources for years—but it wasn't quite true. Contemporary newspaper reports indicate that the Cardinals scored their touchdown on a fumble recovery by Lenny Sachs early in the third quarter.

Halas and the Staleys moved to Chicago in 1921; they changed their name to the Bears in 1922. By this time, the Cardinals had been around since 1898, when a local contractor named Chris O'Brien founded the Morgan Athletic Club on the South Side. He'd outfitted the club's football squad in some secondhand jerseys from the University of Chicago, describing the faded maroon color as "cardinal red." The team played its games at Normal Field at 61st and Racine and eventually became known as the Racine Cardinals. That name died out after the Cardinals moved to Comiskey Park in 1922.

The Cardinals' first stars included tackle Duke Slater and tailback Joe Lillard, both of whom were African American. A notable feature of the Cardinals' early years was the club's willingness to employ black players in an era in which the practice was almost unheard of.

Red Grange, the most famous college football star of all time, made his professional debut for the Bears against the Cardinals at Wrigley Field on Thanksgiving Day, 1925. There had been some suggestions that the game would be fixed in order to ensure a spectacular performance by Grange, but the Cardinals' rugged play quickly proved these to be unfounded.

The Bears never seriously threatened, and the Cardinals' best scoring chance resulted in a missed field goal by Driscoll, the NFL's dropkicker *par excellence*. The game ended in a 0-0 tie. Although the Cardinals naturally would have preferred to win, they were pleased that Grange hadn't had a field day at their expense. And the tie kept the Cardinals half a game ahead of the Pottsville (Pennsylvania) Maroons in the league standings.

10 days after tying the Bears, the Cardinals lost to Pottsville 21-7 in the snow at Comiskey Park. The game was the last scheduled contest for either club, and it left Pottsville with a record of 10-2-0, compared to the Cardinals' 9-2-1—thus Pottsville had apparently won the NFL championship. But the resourceful O'Brien hastily added two games to the Cardinals' schedule (at the time, the schedules were not imposed by the league but were arranged by the clubs themselves). On Thursday, December 10, a mere four days after the loss to Pottsville, the Cardinals hosted the Milwaukee Badgers. Admission was free, and the few fans just about got their money's worth—the Cardinals blasted the hapless Badgers 59-0. It was later discovered that four high school boys had played for Milwaukee, whose franchise was then promptly revoked.

Just 48 hours after their farcical victory over Milwaukee, the Cardinals beat the Hammond Pros 13-0. Their record now stood at 11-2-1 and was adjudged superior to Pottsville's. We'll never know whether the Maroons planned some scheduling chicanery of their own to add another win or two to their log, because they were suspended from the league for playing an exhibition game in Philadelphia on December 12 in violation of the Frankford Yellow Jackets' "territorial rights." Pottsville's league record was frozen at 10-2-0, and the Cardinals were declared world champions of 1925.

In 1926, Chris O'Brien sold Driscoll to the Bears; Paddy remained with the Bears in one capacity or another until his death in 1968. In 1929, O'Brien sold the Cardinals to Dr. David J. Jones, who in turn sold the franchise to Charles W. Bidwill, Sr., in 1933. Bidwill was a Chicago native, a graduate of Loyola University, and a friend of George Halas's who had recently helped Papa Bear buy out his former partner Dutch Sternaman to become sole owner of the Bears. Halas never forgot the favor, and though the Bears-Cardinals rivalry was often bitter, the two men remained close for the rest of Bidwill's life. When Bidwill passed away, the *Tribune* asserted, "Close associates said he felt greater pleasure at seeing victories by the Bears, his first love, than at seeing the Cardinals win."

On November 28, 1929, at Comiskey Park, Cardinals fullback Ernie Nevers ran for six touchdowns and kicked four extra points as the Cardinals destroyed the Bears 40-6. He was personally responsible for every point the Cardinals scored; the total of 40 remains the NFL single-game record. The Bears' only score came on a 60-yard pass reception by Garland Grange, Red's younger brother.

Nevers was a tremendous all-around athlete. He earned a total of 11 varsity letters in football, baseball, basketball, and track at Stanford; he also played professional baseball and basketball as well as football. He was All-Pro in every year of his five-year career. Nevers retired at the age of 28 to become an assistant coach at his alma mater, and he became a charter member of the Pro Football Hall of Fame in 1963.

After Nevers's single-handed demolition of the Bears in 1929, the Cardinals lost 27 and tied two of the next 31 games between the two clubs. The Bears beat them by such lopsided scores as 32-6, 34-0, 44-7,

48-7, 53-7, and 41-14 in the thirties and early forties. During this time the Cardinals became second-class citizens in Chicago; they played more than 65 percent of their games on the road and sold out Comiskey Park only when entertaining the Bears.

The Cardinals reached their nadir during the war years. In 1943, they lost all 10 of their games, scoring only 95 points while allowing 238. In 1944, the NFL asked the undermanned Cardinals and Pittsburgh Steelers to merge for one season. The two clubs joined forces under the name Card-Pitt—which fans soon changed to "Carpets" because, as Richard Whittingham wrote, "opponents walked all over them." The team went 0-10, scoring 108 points and yielding a then-record 328. The Bears beat the "Carpets" 34-7 and 49-7. In 1945, the Cardinals and Steelers were just slightly more successful separately than they had been together: the Cardinals went 1-9 and the Steelers 2-8. The Cardinals' only win came against the Bears at Wrigley Field in the season's third week.

With a 1-29 record over three years, the Cardinals were in dire straits to say the least, but they were about to pull off one of the most sudden and complete turnarounds ever. Their dismal performance earned them the first selection in the 1944 NFL draft and again in 1945—and they made the most of both opportunities. They chose fullback Pat Harder of Wisconsin and halfback Charley Trippi of Georgia; the duo became half of the Cardinals' legendary "Dream Backfield" that also featured quarterback Paul Christman and halfback Marshall Goldberg (and, later, after Goldberg switched to defense, halfback Elmer Angsman).

In 1946, Bidwill hired Jimmy Conzelman as head coach. A member of the original Decatur Staleys, Conzelman had served as player-coach of four other clubs in the twenties, including the NFL champion Providence Steam Roller in 1928. "Gentleman Jim" was a Renaissance man— a talented writer, editor, orator, songwriter, and businessman as well as an athlete and coach.

Under Conzelman, the Cardinals went 6-5 in 1946 for their first winning season in 11 years and just the second since their championship of 1925. Their late-season win at Wrigley Field was one of only two losses the Bears sustained en route to their fourth world championship in seven years. It proved to be the last time for a long while that the Bears were able to shrug off a defeat by the South Siders.

Charley Trippi, drafted as a "future" in 1945 under the rules which then applied, joined the Cardinals in 1947 after Bidwill outbid the rival All-America Football Conference, offering Trippi $100,000 for four years. (When the bidding wars finally killed the AAFC two years later, three of its teams—the Baltimore Colts, Cleveland Browns, and San Francisco 49ers—joined the NFL.)

Bidwill's Dream Backfield was now complete, but he never saw it in action. He died of pneumonia on April 19, at the age of 51. He was survived by his wife Violet and two sons, Bill and Charles, Jr. Bill would eventually take over the Cardinals and Charles (a.k.a. "Stormy") the family's other business, Sportsman's Park race track in Cicero, but at the time they were only 16 and 18 years old, respectively. For now, control of the enterprises fell to Ray Bennigsen, the late Bidwill's former right-hand man.

The revamped Cardinals won eight of their first 11 games in 1947, and they were tied for the Western Division lead with one game remaining. The team with whom they were deadlocked was the Bears, their opponents in the season finale on December 14. The Cardinals had easily subdued the Bears, 31-7, in the season's second week, and they believed they could do it again.

A crowd of 48,632 packed Wrigley Field; it was the largest turnout ever for a pro football game in Chicago to that time. The Cardinals won the coin toss and elected to receive. The Bears' kickoff was downed in the end zone for a touchback. Then, on the very first play from scrimmage, the Cardinals went for broke. They sent Mal Kutner and Babe Dimancheff wide to the left, and on the snap both went streaking down the sideline. Kutner kept right on going downfield, bringing several Bear defenders with him. Dimancheff, meanwhile, slanted underneath the coverage, caught a perfect strike from quarterback Christman in stride at about midfield, and galloped all the way. The 80-yard touchdown stunned the Bears. Three more Cardinal touchdowns—two by Elmer Angsman and one by Kutner—followed in quick succession, and the score was 27-0 before the Bears knew what had hit them.

The Bears' comeback was too little, too late. They rallied to within 27-21 in the fourth quarter before Pat Harder's field goal provided the final margin of 30-21. The victory was only the Cardinals' 12th over the Bears, against 38 losses, and it marked just the second time they had beaten the Bears twice in the same year. But it propelled the Cardinals into the NFL title game against the Philadelphia Eagles.

The 30,759 diehards who braved the frigid weather at Comiskey Park on December 28 got their money's worth. Christman, relentlessly harassed by the Eagles' eight-man defensive front, completed just three of 14 passes for 54 yards and was intercepted three times. But the Cardinals' running game more than made up for their dismal aerial attack. Trippi's 44-yard touchdown jaunt in the first quarter proved to be the Cardinals' *shortest* scoring play of the day. He later ripped off a 75-yarder, while Angsman added a pair of 70-yard runs. The Cardinals won 28-21.

Bears fans hadn't much minded the Cardinals when they were perennial cellar dwellers, but it was a different story when the resurgent South Siders became world champions. Then Cardinals fans began to chirp, and the rivalry became as heated in Chicago's factories, offices, and taverns as it was on the field.

Both teams were superb in 1948; each won 10 of its first 11 games. The Cardinals lost to the Bears 28-17 at Comiskey Park in the season's second week, and the Bears lost at Philadelphia 12-7 in the fifth week (it was the Eagles' first win ever against the Bears after 11 losses and a tie). Again the Cardinals and Bears met in the final game of the season to decide which would go to the NFL championship game.

This time, a throng of 51,283 filled Wrigley Field, breaking the one-year-old Chicago record. The game matched the league's most prolific offense (the Cardinals had scored 395 points) against its stingiest defense (the Bears had allowed only 151 points). "Here was one of the great games of professional football," wrote the *Tribune*'s Wilfrid Smith, himself a member of the Cardinals' 1925 champions. "Here was a battle of linemen whose fierce, reckless tackling was shudderingly effective. Here was a duel between magnificently accurate forward passers whose skill had to be seen to be believed."

With rookie quarterback Johnny Lujack connecting on seven consecutive pass attempts, the Bears forged a 14-3 halftime lead. It was 14-10 after three quarters, and 21-10 after George Gulyanics plunged into the end zone from one yard out on the first play of the fourth quarter. Then Ray Mallouf replaced Christman and led the Cardinals on an 85-yard drive that culminated in a four-yard run by Trippi. Harder's kick made it 21-17.

The turning point came on the third play after the ensuing kickoff. Vince Banonis picked off a Lujack pass and returned it 22 yards to the Bears' 19-yard line. Trippi banged into the line for one yard, then gained six on a pass from Mallouf. On third down and three at the Bears' 12, Mallouf handed off to Angsman, who slanted off tackle and churned all the way into the end zone. Harder kicked the extra point.

The Cardinals led 24-21 with eight minutes remaining. After the kickoff, Sid Luckman trotted onto the turf to replace Lujack, triggering a riotous ovation. The legendary quarterback quickly completed four successive passes to push the Bears 63 yards downfield. On second down at the Cardinals' 14-yard line, Luckman went for the win. He threw into the end zone—right into the arms of the Cardinals' Red Cochrane. The Cardinals were Western Division champions again.

For the Cardinals' title rematch with the Eagles, the weather in Philadelphia was atrocious; the game went down in NFL lore as "the Blizzard Bowl." The conditions helped stall the Dream Backfield, and the Eagles won 7-0. It was not the first time that Philadelphia coach Greasy Neale had bested a Chicago team to claim a world championship; he had been the Cincinnati Reds' right fielder in the 1919 World Series against the White Sox.

Cardinal rooters claimed that their players had tired themselves out helping the grounds crew clear knee-deep snow from the field before the game, while the Eagles had played cards in the comfort of their locker room. In any event, the Cardinals' brief reign atop the NFL was over. Conzelman resigned, purportedly because of friction with Bennigsen. The Cardinals would not win another postseason game until 1998, by which time the franchise was in Arizona after relocating twice.

Although they did not challenge for another title themselves after 1948, the Cardinals continued to wreak havoc on the Bears' championship aspirations for several more years.

In 1950, the Cardinals defeated the Bears 20-10 in the second-to-last game of the season. Had they won, the Bears would have qualified for the NFL championship game; instead, they finished the regular season tied for first place in the Western Division with the Los Angeles Rams at 9-3. Then they lost a special playoff game to the Rams, 20-10.

In 1951, the Cardinals managed only three wins, but two of them were over the Bears. The Bears finished one game behind the Rams for the division crown, and the Rams went on to take the championship.

In 1955, the Cardinals blistered the Bears 53-14 in the season's 10th week (it was the most points ever scored against the Bears to that time). The Bears rebounded to win their final two games, but at 8-4 they ended up half a game behind the Rams' 8-3-1.

While the Cardinals were not particularly successful in the late fifties, they were never boring. Their battles with the Bears remained fierce and compelling, and not always within the rules. A 1956 game, for example, featured a wild brawl in which the Cardinals' Pat Summerall found himself under attack by four Bears (George Blanda, Harlon Hill, Dick Klawitter, and Bill McColl) while other skirmishes went on all over the field.

These years were also enlivened by the exploits of two future Hall of Famers, Dick "Night Train" Lane and Ollie Matson.

Lane was a tall, rangy cornerback with the guts of a tightrope walker. He worked without a net, as it were, gambling for interceptions and diving for open-field tackles regardless of whether he had any help behind him. It paid off more often than not. Night Train picked off 14 passes (still the single-season record) for the Rams in 1952, his rookie year. He joined the Cardinals in 1954 and kept chugging along; by the end of his career, he'd grabbed 68 interceptions and returned five of them for touchdowns. In 1969, Lane was named the greatest cornerback of the NFL's first 50 years.

Matson was sensational; he was not only big for a running back in those days (six-foot-two and 220 pounds), but he was probably the fastest man in the league as well. Matson was drafted by the Cardinals in

1952 after winning a bronze medal in the 400 meters at that summer's Olympic Games. An excellent running back and an absolutely devastating returner of punts and kickoffs, Matson was All-Pro every year between 1954 and 1957.

By the end of the decade, the Cardinals were sinking in the standings and at the box office. They were 3-9 in 1957 and 2-9-1 in 1958, and their attendance woes became critical. In 1959, the Cardinals moved from Comiskey Park to Soldier Field, but it didn't help. Neither did the trade of Matson to the Rams for *nine* players—"none of whom," a teammate later said, "was worth a damn." The Cardinals went 2-10 and were hard pressed to come up with the $20,000 per game that was the minimum guaranteed to visiting teams according to NFL rules.

Several factors threatened the Cardinals' continued survival in Chicago. The league's other clubs resented getting just the flat $20,000 to play before sparse crowds at Soldier Field while they paid the Cardinals two or three times as much for sold-out games in their own stadiums. The owners were also chagrined by the effect of Chicago's two teams on television revenues: Bears' away games were blacked out in the area if the Cardinals were playing at home, and vice versa. To make matters worse, the Cardinals owed the Park District some $125,000 for renovations to Soldier Field.

When the league ratcheted the visiting teams' guarantee up to $30,000 per game in January 1960, the writing was on the wall. The former Violet Bidwill and her husband, Walter Wolfner, negotiated a stadium lease in St. Louis, then presented the franchise's move as a *fait accompli.* NFL commissioner Pete Rozelle announced the transfer of the Cardinals franchise to St. Louis on March 13, 1960. The other owners were so delighted that they agreed to pay the Wolfners $500,000 for "expenses attendant to moving."

For 40 years, the Cardinals and Bears had engaged in a spirited struggle in the standings and at the cash register. The Bears emerged victorious on both counts. They won 47, lost 19, and tied 6 of the games between the clubs, and their popularity and prosperity eventually overwhelmed the Cardinals.

In the unlikely event that another NFL franchise ever came to Chicago, one thing would be certain: a new crosstown rivalry, like most sequels, wouldn't be as much fun as the original. The rough-and-tumble era to which the Chicago Cardinals belonged was gone for good. So, too, were the men like Chris O'Brien, George Halas, and Charles Bidwill, Sr., who had embodied it.

CHAPTER 15

Fight Nights

"Boxing was a mystery to me. When I look back and see what I had to go through to get to the top, I find it hard to believe."
        -- *Jersey Joe Walcott, world heavyweight champion, 1951-1952*

Jim Norris, a bluff, bushy-browed Irishman, was co-owner with Arthur Wirtz of the Blackhawks and Chicago Stadium, owner of numerous thoroughbreds, and, for more than a decade, the de facto czar of boxing. As president of the International Boxing Club (IBC), Norris arranged and promoted 47 of the 51 championship bouts held in the United States between 1949 and 1955. He was also creator of "Friday Night Fights," which was broadcast live from the Stadium and became one of the most popular television shows of the fifties.

Boxing matches at the Stadium were to Chicagoans of those days what Bulls games at the United Center were 40 years later—the place to see and be seen. Politicians, captains of industry, and other celebrities of all sorts filled the ringside seats and were gawked at by the multitudes in the cheaper sections, who probably had difficulty seeing at all through the haze of cigar smoke wafting to the rafters.

By the end of the fifties, the Stadium's heyday as the nation's foremost boxing venue was over. After a series of investigations into alleged antitrust violations, connections to organized crime, etc., the Supreme Court ordered the IBC's "divestment, dissolution and divorcement" from the sport, and two of Norris's cronies were shipped off to prison.

It had been fun while it lasted. Of the myriad fight nights at the Stadium that added spice to life in Chicago during these years, a handful stood out as both social and sporting events, becoming classics among ring aficionados. They are described below.

109

Rocky Graziano vs. Tony Zale
July 16, 1947

Rocky Graziano and Tony Zale were among the greatest middleweights of all time, and the sport was fortunate that their careers overlapped. They were about as evenly matched as two fighters could be, and they fought three epic battles in a rivalry that became legendary. Graziano and Zale were virtually identical in the categories of boxing's traditional "tale of the tape"—height, weight, reach, chest, waist, biceps, neck, wrist, calf, ankle, thigh, fist, and forearm. There was a notable disparity only in age, as Zale was Graziano's senior by nine years.

When the two met for the title at the Stadium on July 16, 1947, gate receipts of more than $420,000 approximately doubled the previous world record for an indoor bout. Zale, a Gary native known as "the Man of Steel," had been champion since 1940 and numbered among his triumphs a sixth-round knockout of Graziano 10 months before. Graziano was a reform-school alumnus who had been dishonorably discharged from the Army after assaulting an officer and going AWOL. He'd been stripped of his license to fight in New York amid charges of fight fixing, but Jim Norris and the Illinois officials were more forgiving.

Both Zale and Graziano were inclined to slug it out rather than dance around, and they both agreed that the match would never go the scheduled 15 rounds. Zale, a 13-10 favorite among bettors, was the aggressor in the early going. In the first round, he attacked with left jabs accompanied by rights to the body, then delivered a crushing right to the midsection—this was the same punch that had put Graziano away in their earlier contest, and it almost did the trick this time as well. Graziano winced, but was able to wrap up Zale's arms in time to weather the crisis.

In the second round, Zale continued to pepper Graziano with left jabs, opening a cut above Rocky's left eye. By the third, he appeared on the verge of putting Graziano away. He floored Rocky with a short right to the jaw, but the challenger was back on his feet almost immediately. Zale retained the edge in the fourth round, but he never had Graziano in trouble.

In the fifth, Zale again tried to carry the fight to Graziano, but by now his punches were having little effect. Zale was faltering. At the bell, he appeared disoriented and had to be beckoned to the proper corner.

According to referee John Behr and the two judges, Zale was substantially ahead on points through five rounds. But the champ never made it through the sixth. Early in that round, Zale trapped Graziano in Rocky's own corner. "As Zale moved in," Wilfrid Smith wrote in the *Tribune*, "Graziano's countering right, thrown with all the power of youth, smashed into Tony's jaw. Zale reeled back, dropped his hands momentarily, and by that gesture the thousands sensed that Zale was badly hurt."

Now the pursuer, Graziano landed a left hook and a short right in quick succession. Zale staggered backward. Graziano unleashed a torrent of blows that rendered Zale all but defenseless; the champion gamely but ineffectually stabbed at Graziano with his left while Rocky hit him with several bruising rights. Finally, a right to the jaw sent Zale partially through the ropes; he sagged against the middle strand as Behr shooed Graziano toward a neutral corner. After counting only to three, Behr signaled that the fight was over. It was 2:10 of the sixth round.

When the new champion met the press after the fight, he presented quite a sight—his left eye was still bleeding, his right eye was swollen completely shut, and the bridge of his nose was also bloodied. Nonetheless, the garrulous Brooklyn native was cocky as could be. "Zale couldn't hurt me tonight," Graziano said. "He couldn't hurt me with a hammer. I knew I had him in the fifth. He hit me in the belly and I didn't even feel it."

Fight fans who believed that the 34-year-old Zale had reached the end of the line were in for a surprise. So was Graziano. The following year, Zale recaptured the title by knocking Rocky out in the third and rubber match between the two men.

Sugar Ray Robinson vs. Jake LaMotta
February 14, 1951

The sensational middleweight title bout between Sugar Ray Robinson and Jake LaMotta on February 14, 1951, went down in Chicago boxing lore as "the second St. Valentine's Day Massacre."

When Robinson stepped into the Stadium ring that night, his record as a professional was a stupendous 122-1. LaMotta was responsible for the "1"—he had defeated Sugar Ray in the second of their eventual *five* meetings in the early forties. Now, after six years, their paths crossed again because Robinson had outgrown the welterweight class, of which he was world champion, in two ways—it was difficult for him to stay under the 147-pound weight limit, and it was impossible for him to find worthy challengers.

Both fighters were 29 years old, but that was all they had in common. Robinson was tall, lean, lithe, and even elegant; he was now carrying 154 pounds on his five-foot-11 frame, but his chest was only 36½ inches and his waist 28½. LaMotta was built like a fireplug; though only five-foot-eight, he sported a 42-inch chest and 33-inch waist. After strenuously reducing for several weeks, he came into the fight just half a pound below the middleweight maximum of 160.

The fight drew a crowd of 14,802 and a national television audience of millions. From the opening bell, LaMotta forced the issue. The man later portrayed by Robert DeNiro in *Raging Bull* stalked Robinson, battering him with body blows and forcing him to retreat from lefts to the head. LaMotta dominated for the first eight rounds.

The tide turned in the ninth. Now LaMotta's spirit was willing, but not his body. All of a sudden he was a stationary target for Robinson's harassing jabs and punishing shots to the midsection throughout the ninth and 10th rounds. LaMotta flashed back to life in the 11th, briefly backing Robinson into a corner and flailing at him with both hands. When Sugar Ray broke free, he took command for good. "I came out fast and got going after that," he said.

"LaMotta was finished," Wilfrid Smith wrote, "but he would not quit. Throughout the 12th round Robinson hit the fading champion with either hand. He jabbed and hooked and all that saved LaMotta was an ingrained desire to walk toward the man who dealt him punishment." LaMotta did not land a meaningful punch in the 12th, but he absorbed plenty. Late in the round, Robinson was hammering him so savagely that even George Gainford, Robinson's manager, yelled, "Stop the fight! Stop the fight!" Referee Frank Sikora, however, did not act.

LaMotta had never been knocked down in his career, and against Robinson he retained this distinction by sheer stubbornness. By the 13th round he was completely defenseless. For two minutes Sikora glanced nervously at the Illinois boxing commissioners sitting ringside, as if looking for advice, while Robinson continued to pound LaMotta. Jake was bleeding from the mouth and from the left eye when he staggered back against the ropes with his arms at his sides. Finally, Sikora moved in and stopped the contest.

Robinson was awarded a technical knockout. It was later suggested that LaMotta's reputation for occasional brutality in the ring had led Sikora and the other officials, perhaps unconsciously, to allow him a taste of his own medicine before calling a halt to the carnage.

LaMotta admitted that this had been the toughest of his six fights with Sugar Ray. "I just ran out of gas," he said. He had lost 17 pounds in the past few weeks, including four pounds the day before the bout. The drastic weight loss had sapped his strength, and no fighter could hope to beat Sugar Ray Robinson at less than a hundred percent.

It took more than two hours for the exhausted LaMotta to summon the energy to get dressed and leave the Stadium. Robinson spent a portion of that time soaking his left hand in a bucket of ice. "No bones broken," Dr. Vincent Nardiello assured reporters. "He just hit Jake so hard and so often with it that it's thoroughly bruised."

Rocky Marciano vs. Jersey Joe Walcott
May 15, 1953

Jersey Joe Walcott fought for the heavyweight championship eight times between 1947 and 1953. He lost gamely in the immortal Joe Louis's final two title defenses. He split four remarkable bouts with Ezzard Charles—losing twice, then winning once to claim the title and once more to defend it. Then he was defeated in a spirited battle with Rocky Marciano.

Walcott's performance against Marciano earned him a rematch eight months later, in the latter's first title defense. Marciano, 29, had enjoyed a relentless climb through the ranks of pretenders and contenders since donning the gloves only five years before. Though he was small for a heavyweight at 184½ pounds, the son of a Brockton, Massachusetts, shoemaker was a devastating puncher who had won all 43 of his fights, 38 by knockout. He had knocked Louis out of the ring altogether in one of the great man's unfortunate comeback attempts.

Walcott came into the rematch at 197¾ pounds. Officially he was 39 years old, but he had confessed to more than that two years earlier. Briefly considering retirement after his second loss to Charles, Walcott had said, "You can tell them the truth; I am 41." So he might have been 43 when he clambered into the ring to face Marciano. Either way, he was the oldest man to hold the heavyweight title until 45-year-old George Foreman in 1994.

For the first two minutes, Walcott appeared a bit gun shy. He well remembered the straight right to the jaw with which Marciano had knocked him out in the 13th round of their previous fight. This time, Marciano tried a different tack. He threw a roundhouse left hook that dazed Walcott, then followed with a withering right uppercut before Jersey Joe knew what hit him. "It wasn't a crushing knockdown," A.J. Liebling wrote, "the kind that leaves the recipient limp, like a wet hat, or jerky, like a new-caught flatfish. This appeared to be a sit-down-and-think-it-over knockdown, such as you might see in any barroom on a night of full moon."

With hundreds of late-arriving fans still searching for their seats and television viewers rummaging through their refrigerators, ring announcer Ben Bentley hoisted Marciano's hand in the air at 2:25 of the first round.

Walcott and his manager, Felix Bocchicchio, maintained that referee Frank Sikora had quick counted. "Gentlemen," Bocchicchio said, "I never saw no robbery equal to this tonight."

"I could've gotten up at two," said Walcott, "but I was looking at Felix and he told me to stay down. I never heard the referee count past seven. It's the most ridiculous thing I ever seen." Many fans agreed that they hadn't heard Sikora count to 10, but that was not unusual considering the terrific din inside the Stadium. Moreover, Walcott had remained on the seat of his pants, making no move to get up even after Sikora finished counting him out. "I was surprised he didn't get up," Marciano commented matter-of-factly.

Actually, few did get up after Rocky tagged them. He defended his title five more times, winning four by knockout, then retired undefeated in 1956 at the age of 32. There was no one left for him to fight.

Sugar Ray Robinson vs. Carmen Basilio
March 25, 1958

"They may fight again, but they'll never fight any better." So said a sportswriter after Carmen Basilio narrowly defeated Sugar Ray Robinson for the middleweight crown at Yankee Stadium on September 23, 1957. This prophecy was proven wrong just half a year later.

Their electrifying first fight, a split decision, had made Basilio only the second man in the history of boxing to win both the welterweight and middleweight titles (Robinson was the first). It had also made a rematch inevitable. Norris and the two principals obliged on March 25, 1958. An overflow crowd *announced* at 17,976—including Joe DiMaggio and Mayor Richard J. Daley—turned out at the Stadium. Every seat was filled, and the aisles were jammed with customers who had paid $10 for "general admission" tickets. Some 375,000 additional fans tuned in via closed-circuit television from 300 arenas and theaters across the country. It was the largest paid audience for any bout to that time.

Basilio, a week short of his 31st birthday, was the smallest middleweight champion ever at five-foot-eight and a shade over 150 pounds. Nonetheless the upstate New York onion farmer was made a slight favorite over Robinson, who was nearly 37, had fought 149 professional bouts, had to starve himself to make weight, and was in perpetual trouble with the Internal Revenue Service. It seemed that age and adversity had finally caught up to the man who was widely regarded as the greatest fighter, pound-for-pound, of all time.

The match began with both men using rabbit punches and low blows to augment their lawful sallies. Late in the first round, Basilio stung Robinson with a smashing right to the body, then the pair slugged it out toe-to-toe as the crowd roared. They continued even after the bell, with referee Frank Sikora struggling to separate them.

Basilio had the better of it for the first two rounds, while the third and fourth were Robinson's. In the third, a left hook by Sugar Ray opened a cut on the right side of Basilio's nose. In the fourth, Robinson deftly jabbed while evading a series of threatening rights by Basilio. The fifth round featured a stirring exchange, which ended with Robinson delivering an overhand right that landed squarely on Basilio's left eye.

Soon the eye was completely closed. Basilio fought on, unable to follow Robinson's movements or to judge distance. "That threw me off balance," he later needlessly explained. Robinson, who hadn't survived 15 years in the ring by being sentimental or squeamish, knew what he had to do. He remorselessly attacked Basilio's bad eye for the rest of the fight. Although the eye continued to swell and gradually turned from red to progressively deeper shades of purple, Basilio neither gave up nor gave in.

"They called Carmen Basilio a little guy," David Condon wrote, "but they hadn't measured his heart." Try as he might, Robinson could not finish him off. Basilio tried to protect the eye as best he could, leaving himself vulnerable at other points on the head and body. He kept on the offensive—but each time he advanced, half blind, toward Robinson he subjected himself to more punishment. In the 10th round, Basilio waded in and rocked Robinson with a combination that had the crowd on its feet cheering. In the 11th, he staggered Sugar Ray with a straight right to the head.

While Basilio desperately stalked Robinson throughout the later rounds, there was now little to fear from what few blows he managed to land. Badly tiring himself by now, Robinson took to grabbing Basilio and leaning on him for seconds at a time. As the final bell sounded, Sugar Ray had Carmen in an embrace signifying only exhaustion.

Referee Sikora gave nine rounds to Basilio, five to Robinson, and called one even. Judge John Bray had it 11-4 in favor of Robinson, and judge Frank McAdam had it 11-3-1 for Robinson. The victory marked the fifth and last time that Robinson captured the middleweight championship. After the decision was announced, Basilio stalked sadly out of the ring. "Basilio's only consolations," wrote George Strickler, "were his remarkable record of having stayed 30 rounds in two title bouts against

Robinson without hitting the floor, and the most lucrative payday of his career." Each fighter took home approximately $175,000—big money in those days.

Robinson was unable to leave the ring under his own steam; he was assisted by his cornermen. Later, while family and friends celebrated in his suite at the Conrad Hilton Hotel, he lay in bed and told reporters, "I'm *so* tired."

Basilio, meanwhile, had a hemorrhage inside his eye that would require a nine-day hospital stay and almost cost him the eye. Reporters asked his handlers if anyone had considered tossing in the towel as Basilio's eye had gotten worse and worse for the last 10 rounds of the fight. The answer was no. "He never complained," said manager John DeJohn, as if that was all there was to it. Trainer Angelo Dundee concurred. "All he said," Dundee added, "was that he couldn't see."

"I could've gone another 15 rounds," said Basilio.

"Well," replied Robinson, "maybe *he* could have went another 15, but he wouldn't have went them with me."

CHAPTER 16

Moments, 1947-1956

May 18, 1947
"Record 46,572 See Dodgers Beat Cubs, 4-2"

A cursory glance at the front page of the *Tribune* sports section for May 19, 1947, would have revealed the headline above, followed by a subhead reading "Brooklyn Bats Rout Schmitz in 4-Run 7th," and finally by a sub-subhead reading "It's Fifth Defeat in Row for Chicago."

One would have needed to delve into the small type to discover that the largest paid crowd in Cubs history had turned out not to root, root, root for the home team, but to witness the Chicago debut of Jackie Robinson, who was a month into his career as the first African-American player in the major leagues.

Dodgers general manager Branch Rickey had been itching to sign African-American players for some time, and he had finally settled on Robinson as the man who best combined the playing ability and intestinal fortitude that would be required of the first one.

Robinson was no kid at 28 years old, and he was both a college graduate and a former Army officer. He had promised Rickey that he would turn the other cheek in response to the abuse he was sure to face from fans, opponents, and even certain teammates.

Robinson's first game in Chicago was nothing special, at least in the box score. He went 0-for-4 with two strikeouts (thus ending his 14-game hitting streak), and he also made an error playing first base. Even so, the huge crowd cheered his every move.

The Dodgers' win and Cubs' loss left the two clubs tied at 14-12 for the young season, but they were headed in opposite directions. The Cubs were in the first of 16 consecutive seasons in which they'd finish at or below the .500 level. The Dodgers were destined to win the National League pennant in 1947 and five more times in the next nine years.

For the season, Robinson batted .297, led the league with 29 stolen bases, scored 125 runs, and won the Rookie of the Year award (which has since been named for him). Two years later, he was elected Most Valuable Player. Robinson's success on the field and his deportment off it paved the way for a parade of African-American players who soon followed, enriching the game immeasurably.

To this day, no larger crowd has spun the Wrigley Field turnstiles than the 46,572 who showed up to see the first integrated major-league game in Chicago.

July 18, 1948
Lightning in a Bottle

In the summer of 1948, White Sox fans could hardly savor the misfortunes of the last-place Cubs, for the Pale Hose were even worse. But on July 18, an obscure outfielder by the name of Pat Seerey gave them something to shout about, if only for one game.

The five-foot-ten, 200-pound Seerey had been acquired early in the season after five years with the Cleveland Indians, during which time he had hit 68 home runs while struggling to keep his batting average over .225. He'd also struck out about twice for every seven at-bats. Seerey was a player of limited talents to say the least—just the sort of fellow who would be rendered obsolete when the doors were opened to more than a handful of African Americans. On this one day, though, he accomplished something that Babe Ruth, for one, never did.

The White Sox, visiting the Philadelphia A's for a Sunday doubleheader, were behind 5-1 in the first game when Seerey came to bat in the fourth inning. He blasted a solo home run that cleared the roof of the left-field pavilion. In the fifth, with a teammate on base, he landed one on top of the roof. In the sixth, he again hit the roof, this time with two teammates aboard.

Seerey had hit three home runs and knocked in six runs in a little less than an hour, but his production was not sufficient to keep the game from going into extra innings after the Sox blew a four-run lead in the seventh. He came up again with two outs in the top of the 11th. This time his drive fell short of the roof, landing in the left-field stands instead. Seerey's fourth home run of the game provided the margin of victory as the Sox prevailed 12-11 for their 26th win of the year against 50 losses.

The unknown Seerey was only the third player in the modern era to hit four homers in a single game, equaling the feats of Lou Gehrig in 1932 and Chuck Klein in 1936. He and the Sox immediately reverted to form in the second game of the doubleheader, losing 6-1. For the season, the Sox lost 101 games and finished 44½ games behind Cleveland. (The Cubs also finished last, marking the first time that both Chicago clubs had achieved that dubious distinction in the same year.) Seerey ended up just about where he always did—18 homers, 64 RBIs, a .229 average, and 94 strikeouts in 340 at-bats. The next year, after going hitless in four at-bats, he disappeared from the major leagues for good.

March 23, 1952
Hat Trick

The end of the 1951-52 campaign couldn't come soon enough for the lowly Blackhawks, who were headed for their third consecutive last-place finish and the sixth straight year in which they missed the playoffs. Only 3,254 fans showed up at the old Madison Square Garden expecting to see the New York Rangers and the Hawks go through the motions in the season finale. Thousands more would later claim to have been there, for the game featured one of the most incredible sequences ever witnessed in the NHL. It began at 6:09 of the third period, when Hawks right wing Bill Mosienko took a pass from center Gus Bodnar, faked a shot to the left of goalie Lorne Anderson, then beat Anderson with a low wrist shot to the goalie's right.

Mosienko, the Hawks' leading scorer, raised his stick in the time-honored fashion of celebrating a goal, then skated back to center ice for the ensuing faceoff. Again Bodnar controlled the puck and got it to

Mosienko, who sped in on Anderson and fired the puck past him for a second goal in 11 seconds. The time was 6:20.

Mosienko accepted congratulations from his linemates, then returned to center ice for another faceoff. Bodnar won the draw yet again, and this time he flipped the puck to left wing George Gee. Anderson, a rookie who was understandably rattled by now, committed himself to Gee too soon—and when he did, Gee slid the puck over to Mosienko, who deposited it into a wide-open net.

The time was 6:30. Mosienko had scored three goals in 21 seconds—a record that will probably never be broken. "Anderson might have stopped Mosienko's first shot," according to the *New York Times*. "But the second and third goals were neatly executed and could have fooled any goalie in the league." While Mosienko collected the puck for a souvenir, Ranger fans saluted him by showering the ice with their hats. The *Times* also reported that "the crowd of 3,254 cheered Mosienko with a volume that seemed to come from twice that number when the record-breaking accomplishment was announced."

It was typical of Mosienko to provide a bright spot in this dismal era for the Blackhawks, who qualified for the postseason only four times in his brilliant 14-year career. Mosienko was inducted into the Hall of Fame in 1965.

December 16, 1956
"We Played Rough"

The Detroit Lions came into Wrigley Field for the regular-season finale of 1956 needing a win or a tie to wrap up the NFL's Western Division championship. They sported a 9-2-0 record, half a game better than the Bears' 8-2-1. The two teams had met just two weeks before. In that game, former Bears quarterback Bobby Layne threw for two touchdowns, ran for a third, and kicked six extra points in a 42-10 blowout. Despite this, the Bears professed confidence. "The Lions have a good ballclub," said defensive back J.C. Caroline, "but they're not *that* good."

The game in Detroit had been fight-filled, and there was reason to believe that the rematch would offer more of the same. Players from both teams had virtually promised as much. The Lions even brought off-duty Detroit policemen along to guard their bench.

From the outset, the Bears' front seven ferociously smothered running plays and relentlessly harassed Layne on passing plays. Early in the second quarter, with the Bears ahead 3-0, Layne turned to hand off to Gene Gedman, and, as he did so, he was leveled from behind by defensive end Ed Meadows. "I didn't see Meadows before or after he hit me," Layne said after the game. "I never heard anything. The lights just went out, that's all."

Layne was carried off the field suffering from a concussion, and he did not return. Detroit coach Buddy Parker was livid. "We heard rumors all week that the Bears would be out to get Layne," he said, "but we didn't think they would be so open about it."

Meadows was unrepentant. "[Layne] has his back to the line every time with the ball," he said, "and I didn't know if he still had the ball or not. Believe me, there was nothing deliberate about it. Sure I was trying to tackle him, and I always try to tackle hard. But as for me being out to get him, there's nothing to that at all."

Shortly after the incident, backup quarterback Harry Gilmer tossed an 18-yard touchdown pass to Bill Bowman to put the Lions ahead 7-3. On the third play of the Bears' next possession, fullback Rick Casares took a pitchout from Ed Brown, wheeled around right end, and took off down the sideline 68 yards for a touchdown.

The Bears never trailed after Casares's electrifying run. Late in the half, Caroline, a star cornerback, took a turn in the offensive backfield and scored on a sweep from nine yards out. The Bears led 17-7 at halftime. From then on, it was all Casares. He finished with 190 yards on 17 carries. Sustaining a pinched nerve late in the fourth quarter, with the Bears leading 31-14, Casares left the game to a tremendous ovation. The injury might have prevented him from breaking the NFL record for rushing yards in a season; with 1,126, he fell short of the existing record by only 20 yards.

The Lions' frustration bubbled over after Joe Fortunato's 27-yard interception return for a touchdown gave the Bears an insurmountable 38-14 advantage. "On the ensuing kickoff," George Strickler wrote in the *Tribune*, "fights broke out in two places on the field and in a twinkling both squads came off the bench followed by several hundred fans, mostly irresponsible juveniles who could not fight their way out of a bad dream."

After order was restored, the Lions scored a late touchdown to make the final score 38-21. The Bears had pulled out the division title. When asked how they had done it, Caroline said simply, "We played rough."

CHAPTER 17

Nashua vs. Swaps

"Nashua was the strongest, soundest horse this writer has ever seen."
-- Joe Hirsch, Daily Racing Form *columnist, 1954-2003*

Before falling out of favor in the wake of the ill-starred contest between Foolish Pleasure and Ruffian in 1975, match races were a popular staple of the Sport of Kings. When a pair of truly outstanding horses reigned at the same time, they would almost inevitably be brought together for a much-hyped and very lucrative showdown. One of the most famous of these took place on August 31, 1955, at Washington Park in Homewood. It featured the two most illustrious three-year-olds of the day, Nashua and Swaps.

The two had competed once before, in the Kentucky Derby of that same year. On that occasion, Swaps took command from the outset, then held off Nashua by a length and a half in a stirring stretch duel. Swaps returned to California after the Derby, leaving the Preakness and Belmont Stakes to Nashua, who won both races impressively. In July, Nashua came to Arlington Park and triumphed in the Arlington Classic—his eighth victory of the year in nine starts. Swaps, meanwhile, was still undefeated for the year. The public and the media clamored for a rematch. As soon as Nashua crossed the finish line in the Classic, Ben Lindheimer (executive director of the Arlington and Washington tracks) turned to Nashua's owner William Woodward, Jr., who was sitting beside him, and proposed the match race. Several days later, Lindheimer announced that Nashua and Swaps would meet at Washington Park on the last day of August for $100,000, winner-take-all.

At this time, thoroughbred racing was in the midst of its golden age. The forties and fifties were a period of unparalleled popularity and profitability for the racetracks. Media coverage of horse racing was considerably more extensive than that accorded hockey, pro basketball, or even pro football. An event like the Washington Park Match Race was a very big deal indeed.

Nashua was the best in the East, Swaps the best in the West. They met in the middle for the great match race.

Swaps arrived in Chicago first and prepared for the match race by running in the American Derby, also at Washington Park, on August 20. Trying the grass for the first time in his career, he beat Traffic Judge (runner-up to Nashua in the Classic) by one length at a mile and three-sixteenths. Nashua warmed up for the race at Saratoga, where trainer Jim Fitzsimmons kept the rest of his stable and where jockey Eddie Arcaro was available for morning workouts.

In Fitzsimmons and Arcaro, Nashua had two of the greatest names in the history of racing on his side. Fitzsimmons, a living legend, was 81 years old and had been in the game as a stablehand, jockey, and trainer since 1885. Though severely stooped by arthritis in his spine, he was invariably cheerful—hence his nickname, Sunny Jim. He had trained two Triple Crown winners, Gallant Fox and Omaha, and countless other stakes winners. He was also known for the many pearls of wisdom that he freely dispensed: "What you can learn from fixing up a cheap horse will come in handy on an expensive one"; "No trainer has ever made a bad horse good, but some trainers have made good horses bad"; "Keep regular hours, eat simple food, get plenty of fresh air, and always remember that human beings are inconsistent."

Arcaro had piloted two Triple Crown winners, Whirlaway and Citation (he remains the only jockey to have swept the series twice). His five wins in the Kentucky Derby, five in the Preakness, and six in the Belmont Stakes were all records. Horseplayers called him Steady Eddie, Heady Eddie, or, simply, The Master. The less charitable called him Old Banana Nose. Arcaro's career had almost come to an untimely end in September 1942, when he was suspended indefinitely for a flagrant bumping incident that sent a fellow jockey somersaulting over the inner rail. William Woodward, Sr., chairman of the Jockey Club, was inclined to make the suspension permanent, but he finally relented after an entreaty from the influential and elderly owner Helen Whitney, who explained that she wanted to see Arcaro ride in her colors at least once more before she died. Arcaro returned to the races after 51 weeks on the shelf. In the great match race, he would be riding for the son of the man who had suspended him.

Interestingly, though they were a nearly invincible team, Arcaro hated Nashua, whom he called "one mean bastard," and the feeling seemed to be mutual. "He'd bite me," said Arcaro, "if I let him."

While Nashua was a regally bred standard bearer of the Eastern racing aristocracy, Swaps was the product of humbler origins. The first California-bred to win the Derby since 1922 was owned by a rough-hewn cowboy, Rex Ellsworth, and trained by another, Mesh Tenney. His jockey was a 24-year-old Texan, Bill Shoemaker, who before long would succeed Arcaro as the rider everyone wanted for a big race.

Nashua arrived at Washington Park less than a week before the race and was stabled in the same barn as Swaps, at the opposite end of a long shedrow. One morning, photographers asked Fitzsimmons if they could bring Tenney over to pose with him. "Don't bother that man, boys," said Fitzsimmons. "He's got enough on his mind. He's not only got Swaps to care for, but a stable full of other horses. I've only got one horse here. I'll walk down to his end of the barn." So, leaning heavily on his crutch, the crippled old man struggled over to the other end of the shedrow to greet Tenney. It was a typical gesture by the classy Fitzsimmons.

Although it did not become widely known until later, Swaps had a chronic foot problem that flared up in the days just before the race. Ellsworth and Tenney even went to Lindheimer to see about postponing the event. But time had been set aside for a national telecast on CBS, and thousands were on their way to Chicago to witness what had been billed as the race of the century. Race day was also the closing day of Washington Park's season. A postponement or cancellation would be a financial and public-relations disaster. Ellsworth agreed to go ahead.

Both camps did their best to keep cranking the hype machine. "Swaps can beat Nashua," Tenney asserted, "at any distance from a half-mile to two miles." Fitzsimmons had a ready rejoinder. "Nashua can beat Swaps," he said, "doing anything."

The crowd of 35,262—amazing for a Wednesday afternoon—was augmented by millions tuned in on radio or television. The race was carded for a mile and a quarter, with each horse carrying 126 pounds—the same conditions as their earlier meeting in the Derby. Heavy rains the night before had made the track soggy, but there was no standing water, and the racing surface was officially labeled "good." In the fourth race of the day (the match race was to be the seventh), Arcaro went out to assess the track's condition for himself. He took the mount on a cheap claimer named Mighty Moment and rode all the way around the track looking down, studying the ground. Mighty Moment finished sixth, but Arcaro succeeded in mapping out the route that he and Nashua would take in the match race.

In the Derby, Shoemaker and Swaps had gotten the jump on Arcaro and Nashua. Arcaro had bided his time in the early stages, waiting for another contender named Summer Tan to make a move. By the time Nashua raced Summer Tan into submission, Swaps had gotten away to a clear lead, and he was able to withstand a determined drive by Nashua in the last quarter mile. Arcaro vowed that he and Nashua would dictate the pace this time.

Both horses appeared to be in peak form as they paraded to the post. No one in the crowd would have guessed that Swaps was less than a hundred percent; even Tenney wasn't sure *how much* less than his best he was that day. Swaps was favored at 1-3; Nashua was 6-5. They entered the starting gate, Nashua in the No. 2 stall and Swaps in No. 4, and were off.

"There was nothing complicated about it," Evan Shipman wrote in *Daily Racing Form*. "As the doors opened, Arcaro, yelling like a banshee and wielding his whip with all his strength, shot Nashua to the front, while Swaps, away on the outside, veered farther out toward the outside rail." Arcaro pushed Nashua from the bell and kept pushing him; he also forced Swaps away from the best footing on the inside part of the track. Nashua led as they passed the grandstand for the first time, and it was clear that Arcaro intended for him to lead all the way to the wire.

Time is of little importance in a match race, of course, because all that matters is beating the other horse. But Arcaro put Nashua through the early stages of the race at a murderous pace, playing "catch us if you can." Nashua went half a mile in 46 seconds, and six furlongs in 1:10.4 (a full second faster than excellent sprinters had managed in six-furlong races earlier in the day). He was going to make it very difficult for Swaps, racing outside in the heavier going, to get around him.

Swaps was game, and several times Shoemaker brought him almost abreast of his rival. But Nashua refused to yield. Each time Swaps ranged up to contest the lead, Nashua dug in and extended his advantage. Even in the home stretch, Arcaro kept his whip busy to make sure that Nashua continued driving. Only in the final furlong, by which time the outcome had been decided, did he permit Nashua to coast.

Nashua came to the wire six and a half lengths in front.

"It was a great race and, naturally, the thrill of my life," said Fitzsimmons. He went on to explain that he had instructed Arcaro simply to "Get out and go." Then, smiling, Sunny Jim said, "And Eddie did." The race catapulted Nashua to Horse of the Year honors. (Two years later, at the age of 83, Fitzsimmons trained another Horse of the Year, Nashua's half brother Bold Ruler—who went on to even greater renown as the sire of Secretariat.)

Tenney was gracious in defeat. "It was a great race and a mighty tough one to lose," he said, "but I'll definitely say the better colt won this afternoon." He didn't make any excuses, declining even to mention Swaps's injury—but he did give the colt the rest of the year off. When Swaps came back in 1956 and won eight of his 10 starts, it was his turn to be Horse of the Year.

Nashua raced from May 1954 to October 1956, Swaps from May 1954 to September 1956. But even though their careers overlapped almost exactly, they met only twice. Of Nashua's 30 starts, 21 were in New York or New Jersey. Of Swaps's 25 starts, 18 were in California. We'll never know what might have happened had they come together for a third contest to settle their rivalry. Regardless, each did quite well going his own way. Nashua was champion two-year-old of 1954, champion three-year-old and Horse of the Year in 1955. Swaps was champion older horse and Horse of the Year in 1956. He closed out his career in Chicago with a victory in the Washington Park Handicap.

The Washington Park Match Race was a memorable Chapter, but far from the only one, in the careers of its principle protagonists: both horses, both jockeys, and both trainers had many triumphs ahead, and all six were destined for the National Racing Hall of Fame. But for William Woodward, Jr., Nashua's owner, the match race was the last great victory. Less than two months later, he was shot to death in a bedroom of his Long Island estate—by his wife, who evidently mistook him for a burglar. When his executors liquidated Woodward's assets, his many thoroughbreds included, Nashua fetched a price of $1,251,200. It was the first time that a horse had ever been sold for more than a million dollars.

CHAPTER 18

Go-Go Sox

"Luis Aparicio brought the stolen base back into baseball, and whenever he would get on base the chant would arise, spontaneously, from every corner of the park: '*Go... Go... Go....*'"

-- *Bill Veeck, Jr., White Sox owner, 1959-1961, 1976-1980*

Picture a cramped, dimly lit room in Cleveland. A 39-year-old man sits on a folding chair in his underwear, listening to a transistor radio and nervously dragging on a cigarette. Suddenly he springs to his feet, claps his hands, and shouts, "One pitch!" Several minutes later and 300 miles away, residents of Chicago who haven't been tuned to *their* radios are jolted by the sound of air-raid sirens in the night.

The two events are related. It is September 22, 1959, and—to the infinite relief of thousands of panicked Chicagoans—World War III has *not* commenced. The White Sox have won the pennant.

The man with the cigarette was Early Wynn, a beefy righthanded pitcher who was as fearsome on the mound as he was genial everywhere else. White Sox owner Bill Veeck, Jr., once jokingly told him, "You'd knock your own poor mother down." Wynn replied, "Only if she were digging in." The glowering hurler was one of three players who were disproportionately responsible for the White Sox' success in 1959. The others were a pair of wispy infielders, neither of whom exceeded 160 pounds soaking wet. At shortstop and second base, respectively, the electrifying Luis Aparicio and the gritty Nellie Fox formed the niftiest double-play duo in the league; they were also the Sox' catalysts on offense, batting first and second in the lineup.

The Sox had entered the season as clearly a team on the rise. After five straight third-place finishes from 1952 through 1956, they'd moved up to second in 1957 and 1958. But standing between the Sox and their first American League championship since 1919 were the mighty New York Yankees, winners of four pennants in a row and nine in the past 10 years. The Yankees were managed by the legendary Casey Stengel, and their roster included future Hall-of-Famers Yogi Berra, Whitey Ford, and Mickey Mantle. People said that rooting for them was like rooting for that other fifties powerhouse, U.S. Steel.

The U.S. Steel analogy was apt, for the Yankees and most teams played baseball with all the subtlety of a sledgehammer. The White Sox were the exception that proved the rule. In an era dominated by lead-footed sluggers who launched tape-measure home runs, the Sox excelled at "small ball"—they had solid pitching, played airtight defense, and led the league in stolen bases every year. They were a throwback to teams of 40 and 50 years earlier. "In modern baseball," Veeck wrote, "the winning equation is Power + Pitching = Pennant. Teams like the White Sox which depend upon speed and defense delight the hearts of all old-timers and generally finish in the second division."

But Veeck's manager was convinced that his club could beat the Yankees, and he said so. "I should have listened to Al Lopez," wrote Veeck. "Al told me from the beginning that we were going to win it. 'This,' he kept telling me, 'is my kind of team.'" Lopez's opinion carried some weight. In eight seasons of managing, first with Cleveland and then with the Sox, he had never finished lower than second place, and he had guided the Indians to the flag in 1954 for the lone interruption in the Yankees' decade of dominance.

Throughout the first half of the season, Cleveland set a rather leisurely pace with the White Sox close behind. Even the lowly Kansas City A's and Washington Senators remained within 10 games of the front. It was a case of "man bites dog" on May 20, when the Yankees found themselves in last place. They soon climbed out of the cellar but continued to flirt with the .500 mark. Nonetheless, many fans assumed that it was just a matter of time before the Yankees took up residence at the top of the standings.

When New York invaded Comiskey Park for a four-game series on the last weekend of June, the race was starting to take shape. The Indians clung to a one-game lead over the White Sox, with the surprising Baltimore Orioles a game and a half out, and the resurgent Yankees only two games back. On Friday night, June 26, Sox center fielder Jim Landis went four-for-four to no avail, as New York won 8-4 to draw even with Chicago at 36-32.

On Saturday, though, the Sox bounced back in dramatic fashion. They trailed 2-1 in the bottom of the eighth when Nellie Fox walked with two outs and nobody on. First baseman Earl Torgeson followed with a single, and catcher Sherm Lollar walked to load the bases. Then Harry "Suitcase" Simpson, a seldom-used outfielder, lofted a wind-aided grand slam off the upper-deck railing in right field. New York's Norm Siebern and Bill "Moose" Skowron clouted back-to-back homers to open the ninth, but the Sox held on for a nerve-wracking 5-4 win that moved them into a second-place tie with Baltimore.

Sunday belonged to the White Sox, who swept the doubleheader by scores of 9-2 and 4-2. In the first game, Wynn bested Whitey Ford. "If I had to win one game," Stengel remarked, "I'd have to say I'd want Wynn to go. He knows just about all there is to know about pitching." In the second game, Dick Donovan surrendered only one hit through the first seven innings and only five altogether before he began to falter in the ninth. Turk Lown retired the last two Yankees to preserve the win.

The White Sox' three-out-of-four weekend left them a game out of first place and dropped New York to four games out. More importantly, it damaged the Yankees' aura of invincibility in the minds of the Sox players.

By now, Sox fans had the Comiskey Park turnstiles clicking at an unprecedented rate. This was testament both to the club's play on the field and to the promotional genius of Veeck, who had wrested controlling interest in the franchise away from the Comiskey family just prior to the season. Veeck was a baseball lifer who had literally grown up in Wrigley Field, where his father served as president of the Cubs from 1919 to 1933. After his father passed away, Veeck continued working for the Cubs for several years, then went out on his own. He had run the Milwaukee Brewers (then a minor-league club), the Indians (who won the 1948 World Series on his watch), and the St. Louis Browns (who gave new meaning to the word "lowly") before taking over the White Sox. At Comiskey Park, he introduced the exploding scoreboard that shot off fireworks after each White Sox home run.

Though no stunt or gimmick was too outlandish for Veeck, he was not a buffoon but a savvy businessman whose objective was simply to attract as many customers as possible. It was the means, not the end, which set Veeck apart from the staid owners of other teams. The press nicknamed him "baseball's Barnum," a label he hated. P.T. Barnum had said, "There's a sucker born every minute," implying contempt for his customers. Although Veeck was a born salesman himself (a "hustler," in his own words), he always laughed with, not at, the people to whom he owed his livelihood.

"You know what's gonna be fun tonight?" Veeck asked before a game in May. "Some guy is going to win 1,000 tickets to Saturday's game with the Red Sox." The very idea tickled Veeck. "What would you do if somebody suddenly handed you a thousand tickets to a ball game? You'd be a big guy in your block, but what would you do with the rest?" Such questions were endlessly amusing to Veeck, who always seemed to be having at least as much fun as the fans he attempted to entertain.

Attendance at Comiskey Park increased 78 percent over the previous year, and Sox fans were galvanized. "We'd come into the ninth inning, three runs behind," Veeck wrote, "and [the fans] would fill the park with a sort of electric excitement that told us they *knew* that one way or another we were going to pull it out. So there'd be a base on balls and an error and a squibbling hit and a wild pitch and a sacrifice fly and we'd win."

On July 12, the White Sox took both ends of a doubleheader from Kansas City, 5-3 and 9-7. Rookie right fielder Jim McAnany rapped a bases-loaded triple in each game and made a sensational game-saving catch in the eighth inning of the nightcap. Thirty-eight-year-old reliever Gerry Staley saved both games. The Sox had now won 14 of their last 20 games but had failed to gain on the Indians, who remained a game in front.

Nine days later, on July 21, the Sox pulled into a virtual tie with Cleveland with a more typical offensive performance against Boston. They amassed a total of nine hits, all singles. The last of these, in the bottom of the seventh inning, squirted off the end of Landis's bat and came to rest not far behind first base, while Aparicio raced around from second to score the tie-breaking run. Donovan went the distance as the Sox won 2-1. The Comiskey Park crowd numbered 28,534 paid and 3,582 guests of the management, all card-carrying bartenders having been admitted for free.

In a bizarre contest the next afternoon, Norm Cash was picked off second, Landis was retired trying to stretch a double into a triple, and McAnany was thrown out at home plate twice. The White Sox trailed 1-0, led 2-1, were tied 2-2, and trailed 4-2 before finally subduing the Red Sox 5-4 on Lollar's third hit of the game, a single which scored Fox from second. When Cleveland lost to New York that evening, Chicago moved into sole possession of first place.

On July 24, an eighth-inning triple by Fox and a ninth-inning home run by left fielder Al Smith turned a 1-0 deficit into a 2-1 triumph over Baltimore.

The next day, Lollar's ninth-inning homer sent the game into extra innings, Lown pitched six shutout innings in relief, and the Sox prevailed on a pinch single by Simpson in the 17th. Better than half of the 25,782 witnesses were freebies because Veeck had thrown the gates open to Pony Leaguers, honor students, and striking steel workers.

The Sox were 22-9 in the past five weeks and 12-4 since the midseason break. They stood half a game ahead of Cleveland.

On Sunday, July 26, the White Sox split a twin bill with the Orioles, and Cleveland took two from Washington to reclaim first place by a half game. There were no games Monday; the Indians spent the off day atop the standings.

A throng of 43,829 packed Comiskey Park on Tuesday night for the opener of a three-game series with the hated Yankees. Smith's two-run homer in the bottom of the eighth gave the Sox a seemingly safe 4-1 edge heading into the ninth. But New York battled back, scoring twice and putting the tying run on base before veteran lefty Billy Pierce fanned Bobby Richardson to end the threat and the game. It was a gutsy effort by Pierce, who allowed 10 hits but walked none and struck out eight. He received a lengthy ovation after the final out. The Sox were back in first place.

Rain terminated the next day's game with the Sox and New York tied 4-4. The day after that, Chicago's popgun offense produced three decidedly unimpressive runs. The first came on a single, stolen base, safe bunt, and infield out; the second on a misjudged fly ball which fell for a double, followed by a single; and the third on a two-base error, an infield out, another error, and an infield single. It was enough, as Wynn limited the Yankees to six hits and one unearned run for a 3-1 decision.

It was Stengel's 69th birthday, and not a very happy one for the "Old Perfessor." White Sox fans mockingly sang "Happy Birthday to You" as Stengel and his charges trudged slowly to the clubhouse entrance. The Yankees left town with a malodorous record of 48-51; they were 10½ games behind the Sox, who led the Indians by one game.

The Yankees were done. By August, there was no question that the pennant would be won by either Chicago or Cleveland—two teams that could hardly have been more different. Cleveland's attack featured sluggers Rocky Colavito, Tito Francona, Woodie Held, and Minnie Minoso (the former Sox star who'd been traded for Wynn and Smith prior to the 1958 season). Cleveland would lead the league in home runs and finish last in stolen bases, Chicago would finish last in home runs and first in stolen bases. If the Indians were a steamroller, the White Sox were a motor scooter. "A typical White Sox rally," Veeck wrote, "consisted of two bloopers, an error, a passed ball, a couple of bases on balls, and, as a final crusher, a hit batsman."

On August 25, the Sox added a potent bat to their lineup when they acquired Ted Kluszewski from the Pittsburgh Pirates. Suitcase Simpson was sent packing to make room for the 34-year-old "Big Klu," who was reputed to be the strongest man in baseball. Several years earlier, when asked about that, Leo Durocher had nominated Gil Hodges. "What about Kluszewski?" someone suggested. "Kluszewski?" Durocher thundered. "Hell, I thought we were talking about human beings!" At six-foot-two and 245 pounds, Kluszewski was indeed imposing; he would cut the sleeves off his uniform to give his massive biceps free reign. He had blasted 171 home runs between 1953 and 1956, but only 12 since then. Although it seemed that his glory days were well behind him, it turned out that Kluszewski still had a few tricks left up his sleeveless jersey.

Throughout August, fans looked forward to the White Sox' four-game showdown with the Indians on the last weekend of the month. Neither team let up in the weeks preceding the fateful series; the Indians went 17-9, while the Sox went 18-9.

The Sox brought a one-and-a-half game lead into Cleveland's colossal Municipal Stadium on the muggy evening of August 28. They were greeted by a hostile crowd of 70,398 and a virtual quagmire in the infield. Several days before, Cleveland groundskeeper Emil Bossard had begun watering the basepaths more than usual; when he was through, he had made them as soft and spongy as possible. The slow track made no difference to the plodding Indians, of course, but it was supposed to hinder the Go-Go Sox. "Chicago won't steal any bases against us this weekend," Bossard chortled.

Bossard's handiwork had little effect on Friday night's game, in which Lollar, a tower of strength all season, cracked a three-run homer in the seventh inning to snap a 3-3 tie and provide the unheralded righthander Bob Shaw his 14th victory against just four defeats. Landis collected three hits, Fox and Kluszewski two each.

Dick Donovan was called to emergency duty when projected starter Ken McBride came down with tonsillitis on Saturday. Donovan responded by tossing a five-hit shutout as the Sox won 2-0. Employing a variety of slow curveballs, sliders, and changeups, he kept the Indians off balance all day.

Lopez remained cautious. "We're still going to keep playing like hell," he said. "Nothing has been easy for us this year. We've won the hard way and we'll have to keep doing it that way." On Sunday, 66,586 Cleveland fans turned out (pushing the total for the series to almost 190,000) to see if the Indians could arrest the White Sox' momentum. Most had long since departed by the end of the doubleheader, in which the Sox captured both games to complete a stunning sweep of the series. In the first game, Chicago trailed 2-0 in the sixth when Wynn's home run triggered a five-run rally that paved the way to a 6-3 win. The second game was effectively over when Turk Lown entered the fray in the sixth. He shut out the Indians for the final four innings, and the Sox triumphed 9-4.

The Indians had come into the series riding an eight-game winning streak. After leading for exactly one half inning of the 36 played, they left as a thoroughly beaten ballclub. For the White Sox, the series had been almost too good to be believed. Their record now stood at 80-49. Their advantage in the standings was five and a half games. When the Sox touched down at Midway Airport that night, they were met by a welcoming committee of thousands.

The raucous reception of August 30 was a dress rehearsal for the celebration that now seemed inevitable—and was. It was both ironic and fitting that the coup de grace was delivered in Cleveland. On September 22, Smith and "Jungle" Jim Rivera smashed back-to-back homers in the sixth inning, putting the Sox ahead 4-1. Wynn was touched for a run in the bottom of the sixth. Bob Shaw relieved him and carried the 4-2 margin into the ninth, when the Indians loaded the bases with one out.

This is where we came in. Wynn was back in the clubhouse, fidgeting with a cigarette and listening to the radio, when Gerry Staley came on to replace Shaw. The tying and winning runs were aboard, and Vic Power was at bat for the Indians. Staley's first offering was a sinker, low and a tad outside. Power swung and pounded a grounder up the middle. Aparicio flashed to his left, speared the ball in his glove, started to flip it to Fox covering second, then glided across the bag himself and fired to Kluszewski to complete the double play. "One pitch!" cried Wynn.

Staley's one pitch had saved the game and wrapped up the pennant. "This was the perfect example of the way we've played all year," said Veeck, "and a typical way to end it." The clincher was Wynn's 21st victory of the season; he wound up with a log of 22-10 and received the Cy Young Award as the finest pitcher in the major leagues (in those days, there was one award covering both leagues). The Sox' five-game margin over the Indians was neatly accounted for by Wynn's 6-1 mark against his former teammates.

Back in Chicago, city officials allowed enthusiasm to overcome their better judgment—they fired up the air-raid sirens. The public had been trained to understand that an alarm heard any time other than

10:30 a.m. on a Tuesday (when the sirens were regularly tested) would indicate a genuine air raid—or at least a tornado. It was the height of the Cold War, after all, and it was not surprising that thousands of Chicagoans believed that they were about to meet their maker. Police, fire, and Civil Defense authorities were inundated with frantic phone calls. Although Mayor Richard J. Daley later pooh-poohed the incident and chided those who had "overreacted," he was careful to quash any suggestion that turning on the sirens had been his idea.

The 1959 White Sox did not do it with mirrors. Their mastery of small ball enabled them to win 35 of 50 one-run games. They led the league in pitching and fielding. Their 113 stolen bases were the most in the league since 1944; Aparicio's 56 were more than all but one *team*. In the balloting for the Most Valuable Player award, the men who were first and second in the batting order switched places, with Fox preceding the man he usually followed. Wynn finished third.

The Sox were back in the World Series after an absence of 40 years, and 48,013 fans packed Comiskey Park for the first game on October 1. The Sox gave them plenty to cheer about, with Kluszewski the ringleader. He drove in the first run with a single in the first inning. He belted a two-run homer in the third. He followed with another two-run homer in the fourth. The Sox led 11-0 after four innings, and that proved to be the final score as Wynn and Staley combined to blank the Los Angeles Dodgers. "This is the greatest thrill I've ever had in baseball," said Kluszewski. "It's absolutely the biggest moment of my career."

Realizing that one game did not the Series make, Lopez said only, "It was a good game." He was wise not to gloat, for Los Angeles won four of the next five games to take the Series. To their credit, the Sox went down battling. They lost Games 2 and 4 by one run each, Game 3 by two runs. In Game 5, Donovan came on with the bases loaded and one out in the eighth; he pitched out of that jam and retired the Dodgers in order in the ninth to preserve a tense 1-0 decision for Shaw. In Game 6, Kluszewski clubbed a three-run homer, but that was all the Sox could muster as they lost 9-3.

Even in a losing effort, Big Klu was the hitting star of the Series. He batted .391, with one double, three home runs, five runs scored, and 10 runs batted in. Fox also distinguished himself, batting .375 in the six games.

The White Sox had eight consecutive winning seasons before 1959 and eight more after, but they didn't return to the fall classic. They *did*, however, provide the blueprint for most of the pennant winners of the next three decades. Small ball was back.

"When I think of that season," Veeck wrote, "I think of a squibbling hit and everybody running."

CHAPTER 19

The Puck Stops Here

"You've got to be a little sick to be a goalie. The more you think about it the more you wonder."

-- Glenn Hall, Blackhawks goalie, 1957-1967

The Blackhawks of the early sixties were blessed with three terrific young forwards (Bobby Hull, Stan Mikita, and Bill Hay) and two rock-solid veteran defensemen (Pierre Pilote and Elmer "Moose" Vasko). But the glue that held the whole enterprise together was goaltender Glenn Hall, who was so respected around the league that both teammates and opponents called him "Mr. Goalie."

For Mr. Goalie, there was a difference between loving to play hockey and actually enjoying it. He was so wracked with anxiety about his job that he vomited before every game, and even *during* many. He was afraid, he said, not of losing itself so much as he was of playing poorly and letting his teammates down. Throughout his long career, instances of the latter were rare indeed.

Hall was entirely fearless in doing whatever it took to stop the puck. He pioneered the "butterfly" style of goaltending, in which the goalie drops to his knees with his shin pads splayed out in either direction. This practice tended to put his face directly in range not only of the puck, which was more or less a given, but of swinging sticks as well. Hall nonetheless disdained the protective masks that many other goalies had taken to wearing.

The Blackhawks had compiled an abysmal record of 117-288-85 from 1950 through 1957 and were rumored to be losing more than $1 million per year. If that kept up, co-owner Jim Norris joked, he'd be broke within a couple hundred years. He and his partner Arthur Wirtz gave their new general manager Tommy Ivan a virtual blank check to get the franchise turned around. Ivan, who had coached the Detroit Red Wings to three Stanley Cup championships in recent years, did not disappoint.

After being the laughingstock of the league for almost two decades, the Hawks compiled a respectable record of 29-24-17 in 1960-61 and were recognized as a team on the rise. But the reward for their first winning season in 15 years was a dubious one: a date with the mighty Montreal Canadiens in the opening round of the playoffs. The Canadiens had won their fourth consecutive Prince of Wales Trophy as regular-season champions, and they were heavy favorites to win their *sixth* successive Stanley Cup. Mr. Goalie would be up against the league's most potent offense, led by Jean Beliveau, Bernie "Boom-Boom" Geoffrion, and Dickie Moore. As if that weren't bad enough, the Canadiens also had Doug Harvey, six-time winner of the Norris Trophy as the league's best defenseman, and Jacques Plante, five-time winner of the Vezina Trophy as outstanding goalie.

The first game of the series, at Montreal's Forum, gave little indication that the Canadiens were vulnerable. Although the hustling, tight-checking Hawks grounded the Flying Frenchmen for two periods (after which the score was tied 2-2), Montreal exploded for four goals in less than seven minutes early in the third, turning the game into a 6-2 rout.

The Hawks continued their tough, physical play in the second game, and their aggressiveness staked them to 2-0 and 3-2 leads. Each time, though, the Canadiens came back. Finally, with 2:55 remaining in the third period, Hawks captain Ed Litzenberger tallied on a tip-in of a drive by Pierre Pilote. The Hawks deftly played "keep away" from the Canadiens in the neutral zone while the clock ticked down, and they escaped with a 4-3 win.

The third game, in Chicago, proved to be the turning point. They were hanging from the rafters in the Stadium; there were at least 18,000 spectators on hand, but because of fire regulations the Hawks announced (as they did at every sold-out game) a crowd of 16,666. The Hawks again emphasized physical—the Canadiens said "dirty"— hockey.

Midway through the second period, Montreal's Phil Goyette was tripped twice in the space of 25 seconds, leaving the Hawks at a two-man disadvantage for a minute and 35 seconds. When Pilote, Vasko, Eric Nesterenko, and Hall killed off the penalty, the Stadium crowd erupted in a standing ovation that seemed to galvanize the Hawks. They launched repeated assaults on the Canadiens' goal before Murray Balfour finally lit the lamp on a rebound with 1:27 left in the period.

As Hall turned aside one challenge after another from the Canadiens, it looked as if Balfour's goal would stand up to give Mr. Goalie the first playoff shutout of his career. After one particularly sensational save by Hall, Bill Hicke became so frustrated that he speared Mikita in the ribs. The two dropped the gloves and had at it, and they were both given five-minute penalties for fighting. As soon as they entered the penalty box, Mikita scaled the barrier between them and resumed the fight with increased vigor. At this point, he and Hicke were given the rest of the night off. With 1:20 left in the game, Bill Hay was whistled for tripping. Several seconds later, the Canadiens pulled goalie Jacques Plante and added a fifth attacker. Goyette won a faceoff in the Hawks' end and got the puck to Henri Richard, who buried it from 15 feet out.

The remaining 36 seconds of regulation play were scoreless, as was the first overtime. So was the second—although it included an apparent goal by Montreal's Doug Harvey that was disallowed because Harvey had batted at the puck with his stick above the shoulder. The Canadiens had the better of the play for the most part, but Hall was equal to everything they threw at him. In the 13th minute of the third overtime, with Dickie Moore off for hooking, Balfour swatted a backhander home in the midst of heavy traffic to give the Hawks a thrilling 2-1 victory. Incensed over the penalty call that had led to the winning goal, Montreal coach Toe Blake clambered onto the ice and punched referee Dalton McArthur in the shoulder (he would be fined $2,000 but not suspended). It was 12:53 in the morning, and no one was more fatigued than Hall, who had faced 54 shots from the Canadiens and stopped 53.

After their grueling triple-overtime loss, the Canadiens could have tossed in the towel, but in the fourth game they showed why they were champions and why they were nicknamed the Flying Frenchmen. Before another announced crowd of 16,666 at the Stadium, the Canadiens flew all over the ice, skating circles around the Hawks and peppering

Hall with 50 shots while the Hawks managed only 21 on Plante. The Canadiens won 5-2, but they would not score another goal in the series.

In the fifth game, at Montreal, Vasko, Ab McDonald, and Mikita dented the twine and Hall turned back 32 shots as the Hawks won 3-0. It was Hall's first shutout in Stanley Cup play, and it was the first time the Canadiens had been shut out all year. "That was a clutch game," said coach Rudy Pilous, "and it was our best game of the series."

The sixth game surpassed it. Again more than 18,000 packed the Stadium. In the 12th minute of the first period, the Canadiens got a big chance when the Hawks were assessed two penalties within 18 seconds. Playing at a two-man disadvantage for a minute and 42 seconds, the Hawks allowed only three shots—all of which were fired from well beyond the blue line. After that, Hall was invincible. Three second-period tallies by the Hawks provided more cushion than he needed, and as the clock ticked down toward a second straight shutout, the crowd gave one of the longest and loudest ovations ever heard in the Stadium. "The appreciative audience stood cheering and applauding Hall's superlative performance," David Condon wrote in the *Tribune*. "The reaction of the crowd was as tingling as the Hawks' performance."

"Did you ever see anything to beat that crowd?" cried the delighted Norris. Reporters assured him that they had not. "We earned it," Norris went on. "We earned it by hustle. No loser could beef about losing to a team that hustled like the Hawks. I'm glad we didn't back into it."

For his part, the laconic Hall admitted that he was thrilled by the two shutouts, "but I would have settled for 3-2."

The Hawks advanced to the Stanley Cup Final for the first time since 1944, when they'd been swept by the Canadiens in four games. This time, their opponents were the Detroit Red Wings, for whom Hall had won the Calder Trophy as NHL rookie of the year in 1956.

Now that the seemingly unbeatable Canadiens had been eliminated, Pilous had to guard against complacency. He went out of his way to remind all who would listen that the Stanley Cup didn't belong to the Hawks just yet. His worst fears were nearly realized in the first game, at the Stadium, when the Hawks narrowly prevailed 3-2 after leading 3-0 in the first period. After goals by Hull, Ken Wharram, and Hull again in the first 14 minutes, the Hawks turned very conservative, abandoning the rugged forechecking that was their trademark. "Another couple of periods like those last two," Pilous said, "and we'll be out of it."

The Hawks were flat in the second game at Detroit's Olympia Stadium. Gordie Howe, the best all-around player in the league, logged over 50 minutes of ice time and accounted for two assists. Hank Bassen, the Wings' backup goalie who was playing because of an injury to Terry Sawchuk, was brilliant. Alex Delvecchio's empty-net goal with 38 seconds left sealed a 3-1 win for the Red Wings.

Back on home ice for the third game, the Hawks looked more like the team that had dispatched the Canadiens, winning 3-1. Mikita, Ron Murphy, and Balfour scored within six and a half minutes in the second period; each goal was scored from within 10 feet of the net after a series of crisply executed passes. Bassen had little chance to stop any of them. Hall was beaten midway through the third period on a fantastic move by Howe, but that was his only lapse as he made 35 saves.

For the fourth game, in Detroit, Sawchuk returned to action for the Wings, who also had their fine defenseman Marcel Pronovost back from an injury suffered prior to the series opener. The game was neatly played on both sides, with only five minor penalties called in the entire contest. One of these, on Bobby Hull, gave Detroit a power-play chance nearly halfway through the second period, and Delvecchio converted to tie the score at one apiece. Neither team scored again until 13:10 of the third period, when Bruce MacGregor, a 19-year-old rookie, got the first goal of his career on a shot that Hall had appeared to smother between his pads. "Both of those kids [MacGregor and Howie Young] were in the crease," Tommy Ivan claimed after the game, "and MacGregor just pushed the puck through Hall's pads." Ivan called referee Frank Udvari "gutless" for failing to disallow the goal. The Hawks' long and loud complaints notwithstanding, the rookie's goal evened the series at two games each.

The fifth game was deadlocked 3-3 early in the third period when the Hawks' line of Hay, Hull, and Balfour made an electrifying rush up ice. Just inside the Detroit blue line, Hull faked a shot and slid the puck across to Balfour, who was streaking in with Howie Young in hot pursuit. As Balfour reached for the pass that might have set up his third goal of the game, Young shoved his stick into Balfour's skates and sent him crashing into the right goalpost. Balfour left the game with a broken left arm, and from then on the Hawks played like men possessed. With Young off for tripping Balfour, Mikita netted the go-ahead goal, assisted by Pilote and Vasko. Five minutes later, Pilote received credit for a goal when his slap shot deflected off a Detroit defenseman and into the net. Another goal by Mikita put the game out of reach with six and a half minutes left, and the Hawks won 6-3.

Hall and the Hawks were at their best in the sixth game. They trailed 1-0 in the second period when Hall made two incredible glove saves of airborne shots that appeared to be past him. Then Reggie Fleming's shorthanded goal for the Hawks turned the tide. With a little over a minute to go in the period, Detroit goalie Bassen sprawled to stop a blast by Hull, only to see the rebound pop right out to Ab McDonald, who shoveled it into the net for a 2-1 lead. The Hawks never looked back after that. They scored three more times in the final period to turn the game into a 5-1 cakewalk.

For the third time, the Hawks were Stanley Cup champions. After the teams lined up for the traditional handshakes and Hawks were presented with the Cup, Mr. Goalie's teammates paid him the ultimate compliment: they lifted him to their shoulders and carried him off the ice. He had allowed just 12 goals in the last eight games of the playoffs.

A year and a half after leading the Hawks to the Stanley Cup, Glenn Hall was forced to leave a game against the Boston Bruins because of a back injury. Denis DeJordy replaced him. It was November 7, 1962, and the date was noteworthy because it marked the first time since the start of the 1955-56 season that Hall had been off the ice during a regular-season or playoff game. He had played—without a mask and without a break—for 552 consecutive games, or more than seven full seasons (the first two were for Detroit, the rest for the Hawks).

"Hall had played the most demanding position in sports," George Vass wrote in his 1970 history of the Blackhawks, "for 31,195 minutes and 33 seconds. He had played despite severe injuries, despite the constant tension that kept his stomach in turmoil and brought him to the bench on occasion to throw up. He explained his unbelievable tenacity as a case of simply doing his job: 'Sure, there have been times in the last seven years when perhaps I wasn't in condition to play, but making that decision is not my job. My job is to stop the puck.'"

CHAPTER 20

Iron Men

"We don't let up."
    -- George Ireland, Loyola University men's basketball coach, 1951-1975

When Loyola University basketball coach George Ireland came into work on Monday, February 4, 1963, he discovered that he had lost two key players. Guard Pablo Robertson and forward Billy Smith, both sophomores, had failed to pass their midterm exams and were therefore ineligible for the remainder of the season. It says something about the academic integrity of the university and its athletic department that Ireland's top two reserves could be booted off a team that was undefeated, ranked No. 2 in the country, and taking aim at a possible national championship. Many other universities would have finagled a way to keep the two players on the team, but at Loyola the term "student-athlete" retained its intended meaning. Loyola's players were students first and athletes second. As if to drive the point home, the Ramblers' five starters went on to earn *11* college degrees among them.

The five were forwards Jerry Harkness and Vic Rouse, center Les Hunter, and guards Ron Miller and John Egan. They were four African Americans and an Irish kid from the South Side, representing a Jesuit school that was virtually unknown outside of Chicago. Their climb to the top of the college basketball world was an inspiring story in itself, which also took on greater significance as a harbinger of changing times.

Segregation was still a fact of life in 1963. In the South, African Americans were expected to pursue their higher education at tradition-ally black institutions such as Alabama A&M, Jackson State, Grambling, Southern, and Tennessee State, or not at all. The more prestigious universities, even state schools funded by taxpayers and theoretically open

146

to any qualified resident, were off-limits. James Meredith's attempt to enroll at the University of Mississippi in September 1962 had triggered rioting that left two people dead and 160 injured. It took the intervention of the federal government to get Meredith admitted, and he could not set foot on campus without an escort of U.S. marshals to ensure his safety.

Even in the rest of the country, where the universities were integrated, most athletic teams featured no more than a few African Americans. Basketball coaches observed an unwritten rule limiting the number of black players on the court at any given time to three for home teams and two for road teams. Ireland defied the quota system with his four African-American starters, regardless of whether the Ramblers were at home or away.

The absence of Robertson and Smith meant that Loyola's five starters were going to be pretty much on their own for the rest of the season. The five "iron men," as they soon came to be called, had been a cohesive and productive unit since the previous year, when they'd carried Loyola to a 23-4 record and a third-place finish in the National Invitational Tournament. Harkness, an All-American in 1962 and destined to repeat in 1963, was the only senior; the other four were juniors. "Harkness leads us," said Ireland, "like the leader of a hungry pack of wolves."

Harkness was a native of the Bronx who had not played high-school basketball until his senior year, after baseball great Jackie Robinson saw him in a pickup game and encouraged him to give it a try. Miller was also from the Bronx. Hunter and Rouse were high-school teammates and best friends from Nashville. They had decided to stick together when it came time to go to college. "I had offers from Massachusetts, Notre Dame, and UCLA," Hunter said, "but Rouse had a knee operation and they weren't interested. Loyola was the only one that would take us both." Egan was the lone Chicagoan, a product of St. Rita High School. As the only white player among Loyola's starters, he'd inadvertently made history by fouling out against Wyoming on December 29, 1962. When Robertson replaced him, it marked the first time that an integrated university's team had five black players on the floor at once.

147

Ireland was an alumnus of Notre Dame, where he'd been a team-mate of DePaul coach Ray Meyer on the 1936 national championship team. He had gone directly into coaching after college, spending 15 years at Marmion Academy in Aurora before coming to Loyola in 1951. Ireland's philosophy was very simple: to run, run, run on offense and to press, press, press on defense. His current group of players was perfectly suited to this approach. "Our whole premise was to get out and run," recalled Hunter. "We pressed regardless of how far we were ahead or behind. A lot of teams tried to freeze the ball and we stole it." Assistant coach Jerry Lyne would file an extensive scouting report on each opponent, which Ireland and the players all but disregarded. "We'd go over everything," said Harkness, "and then at the last minute Ireland would look at us, rip up the report and say, 'They'll never get into their offense. We'll press 'em and throw everything off.'"

Loyola was 20-0 and had throttled its opponents by an average margin of 29 points when Robertson and Smith departed. Ireland was optimistic that his team could overcome the setback. "We can keep going," he said. "We have a group of kids who are thoroughbreds. They don't fold up. They respond when they're asked, just like thoroughbreds."

There were six games left on the schedule. On February 12, the Ramblers squeaked past Marquette 92-90 in overtime. On February 16, top-ranked Cincinnati lost 65-64 at Wichita State (the Bearcats' first defeat after 37 straight wins), but status quo was maintained in the rankings when Loyola also lost that same night, 92-75 at Bowling Green. Two days later, after learning that they'd been invited to the NCAA tournament, the Ramblers routed St. John's 70-47 in New York.

The Ramblers had slipped to No. 3 nationally, behind Cincinnati and Duke, when they visited Houston on February 23. Houston's first black students were to be admitted in the fall; among them would be future NBA stars Elvin Hayes and Don Chaney. This was Houston's last home game as an all-white university, and many in the crowd seemed sorry to see the old era pass into history. "They called us all the 'n' names," Miller recalled. "They said everything." Fans also pelted the Ramblers with coins and ice cubes. After Loyola escaped with a hard-earned 62-58 win, Houston coach Guy Lewis apologized for the fans' behavior.

On February 27, the Ramblers trailed Ohio 54-47 at halftime and were tied 78-78 midway through the second half, but their running and gunning finally wore the Bobcats down. Loyola pulled away in the stretch to win 114-94. Hunter scored 34 points and Harkness 32 in his final game at Loyola's Alumni Gym. Harkness left the court on the shoulders of exultant Rambler fans.

Loyola took on Wichita State in the regular-season finale before a full house at the Stadium. The Shockers were still basking in the notoriety of their upset over Cincinnati 10 days earlier and had climbed to No. 8 in the rankings. Against Loyola, they exploited foul trouble by Hunter and Rouse (both eventually fouled out) to achieve a 52-38 advantage in rebounds which proved decisive. Wichita State won 73-72. Of the three losses that Cincinnati and Loyola had suffered between them, two had come at the hands of the aptly named Shockers.

There were serious questions confronting Ireland and the Ramblers as they entered the NCAA tournament. They had not looked like the same team without Robertson, a lightning-fast point guard, and Smith, a fierce rebounder and inside scoring threat. The previously unbeaten Ramblers had lost two of their last six games and just narrowly averted two more losses. The Wichita State game proved beyond a doubt that Loyola's starters were working without a safety net. Ireland's bench had produced a total of 15 points in the six games, all but two of them in the lopsided wins over St. John's and Ohio. The five iron men had their work cut out for them.

Loyola opened the tournament on March 11 against Tennessee Tech at McGaw Hall in Evanston. The Ramblers were ready. They scored 16 of the game's first 18 points and surged to a 61-20 lead by halftime. Loyola shot 56 percent from the floor and presented an almost perfectly balanced attack—none of the five starters scored more than 21 points or fewer than 17. Ireland called off the dogs when Loyola went over the 100-point mark with five minutes left. He emptied the bench, and all four of his remaining reserves not only played but scored. (None of the backups scored another point in the tournament, and just one of them, Chuck Wood, saw further action.) The final score was 111-42.

Among the awestruck spectators was Babe McCarthy, coach of the Mississippi State team that was due to face Loyola next. "I wish I'd

149

stayed home," McCarthy said. "Nobody can beat a team like that. They are the best fast-break team, the best ball hawks, I've ever seen."

McCarthy, his players, and the Mississippi State administration emerged as heroes of a sort in the following days. Not only was their university all-white, but its athletic teams were forbidden by tradition to even play against integrated teams. Nonetheless, the Maroons intended to keep their date with Loyola on March 15 in East Lansing, Michigan.

The Maroons had accepted an automatic bid to the tournament as champions of the Southeast Conference on March 2, and the question of their participation might have ended there. However, when the brackets were published and the likelihood of a matchup with Loyola became apparent, newspapers and politicians in Mississippi saw a chance to make some hay. A paper in Jackson invited readers "to clip the photo of the Loyola team and mail it today to the board of trustees" of the university. An editor in Meridian was more explicit: "Especially in these times we should make no compromise regarding our Southern way of life; we cannot afford to give a single inch."

After Loyola dispatched Tennessee Tech (itself an all-white team), the issue came to a head. When asked about the controversy, Harkness showed that he was wise beyond his years. "I think that Mississippi State wants to play us," he said. "If they don't, they'll never know how good they are."

Mississippi State did want to play Loyola—and went to great lengths to do so. The Maroons were scheduled to fly from Starkville, Mississippi, to East Lansing on Thursday morning, March 14. On Wednesday, a state legislator obtained an injunction prohibiting the team from leaving the state. That night, coach McCarthy and several other officials drove from Starkville to Memphis, then flew to Nashville. On Thursday morning, the Hinds County sheriff showed up at the Starkville airport to enforce the injunction. The injunction was duly served—to the Maroons' freshman team, which had been sent to the airport as a decoy. The varsity team had already left from a small private airport. They met up with McCarthy and the others in Nashville, then continued on to East Lansing.

The game attracted an overflow crowd of 12,143 at Michigan State's Jenison Fieldhouse. Flashbulbs popped all over the arena when Loyola captain Harkness shook hands with his counterpart, Leland Mitchell, before the game. Mississippi State came in with a record of 21-5. The Maroons were a methodical, disciplined team whose tallest starter was only six-foot-five. The Ramblers also were under-sized (the lithe, six-foot-seven Hunter was their tallest starter), but their athleticism made up for what they lacked in height and heft.

From the opening tip, Mississippi State did everything but deflate the basketball in order to slow the pace. The Maroons held Loyola off the scoreboard for almost six minutes as they crept out to a 7-0 lead. A pair of three-point plays by Harkness jump-started the Ramblers, and strong rebounding by Hunter and Rouse carried them to a 26-19 edge at halftime. In the second half, the Maroons patiently stuck to their plan on offense, allowing 90 seconds or so to elapse in each possession before taking a shot (there was no shot clock in those days) and not attempting any shot that was closely contested.

Mississippi State was poised and determined throughout, but ultimately Loyola's superiority on the boards proved too much to overcome. Loyola won 61-51. Harkness tallied 20 points, Rouse 16 points and 19 rebounds, and Hunter 12 points and 10 rebounds.

Less than 24 hours after their physically and emotionally draining victory over Mississippi State, the Ramblers were back on the court facing Illinois in the regional championship game. Far from being exhausted, the Ramblers seemed to be gathering strength as the tournament progressed.

The Illini had arrived by defeating Bowling Green, thus denying Loyola a chance to avenge one of its two losses. They were 20-5 and had shared the Big Ten championship. But they were no match for the Ramblers, whose swarming full-court press forced a succession of Illini turnovers and turned the game into a blowout shortly after halftime. Loyola led 40-34 two minutes into the second half. Three minutes later, the score was 53-34, and the rout was on. Loyola piled up a 28-point lead late in the second half and coasted to the finish. The final score was 79-64. In a sensational performance, Harkness scored 33 points. Rouse grabbed 19 rebounds and Hunter 15. "Loyola is the greatest offensive rebounding team I've ever seen," said Illini coach Harry Combes.

Cincinnati, Duke, and Oregon State joined Loyola in the Final Four at Freedom Hall in Louisville. Cincinnati, ranked No. 1 since the first preseason poll, was appearing in its fifth consecutive Final Four and was seeking its third straight national championship. Before worrying about the Bearcats, however, the Ramblers had to contend with Duke, which was riding a 20-game winning streak and sported a record of 27-2 (identical to Loyola's).

Duke came out in a zone defense which caused no trouble for Loyola. Time and again in the early going, Duke defenders strayed too far from the basket chasing Harkness and Miller, leaving the lane wide open for Hunter, who had a field day inside. Loyola's offensive rebounding was devastating as well. "We just went out and jumped higher," Ireland explained succinctly. The Ramblers built a 13-point lead by halftime. Led by their All-American forward Art Heyman, Duke played better in the second half and closed the gap to just 74-71 with 4:19 remaining. "Then," Roy Damer wrote in the *Tribune*, "the Ramblers took off in their usual breathtaking manner, pouring in 20 points in four minutes and leaving the Atlantic Coast Conference champions crushed." Loyola won 94-75, with Hunter matching Heyman's game-high 29 points and also snatching 18 rebounds. Again the Ramblers spread the scoring around, with Harkness contributing 20 points, Miller 18, Egan 14, and Rouse 13.

So it was that the iron men took the floor for the national championship game on Saturday, March 23. The standing-room only crowd was announced at 19,153—the same as the night before and the maximum allowed per fire regulations. The contest was televised nationally and carried in Chicago by WGN Channel 9; it was the very first Loyola game to be televised all season, which would have been inconceivable in later years when college basketball in general and the NCAA tournament in particular generated far more hoopla (not to mention revenue).

Not surprisingly, the Cincinnati Bearcats also were there, having drubbed Oregon State 80-46. The Bearcats were now 29-1 for the season and 11-0 in the tournament since 1961. There was no question by this time that Loyola was for real, but many wondered whether *any* team could stand up to the Cincinnati juggernaut. The game presented two extremes in style and approach: Loyola was the top scoring team in the nation, at 93 points per game, while Cincinnati was the stingiest defensive team, with 53 points per game allowed. Something had to give.

For most of the game, it looked as though the Ramblers were finally giving out. Cincinnati's vaunted defense was airtight early on, forcing Loyola to miss 13 of its first 14 shots. As the Ramblers grew increasingly frustrated on offense, they began to let down at the defensive end. Cincinnati ran its plodding half-court offense nearly to perfection, setting screens, cutting to the basket, getting rebounds and tip-ins, and making numerous trips to the foul line. The Bearcats led 29-21 at the intermission, and it could have been worse. Most of Loyola's field-goal attempts had been launched from the outskirts, and on the rare occasions when they'd gotten the ball down low, the Ramblers found a wall of defenders waiting. Harkness had been shut out entirely; he had not made a single field goal.

The Ramblers were down by six points early in the second half when Hunter missed a bank shot that would have trimmed the deficit to four. Then Cincinnati tallied three times in short order to extend its lead to 37-25. A few minutes later it was 45-30. "We knew we didn't have a chance to catch up," Ireland said later, "unless we put the press on."

Less than 12 minutes remained on the clock. Loyola's full-court press caused a turnover that resulted in a three-point play and gave Cincinnati center George Wilson his fourth foul. Wilson went to the bench for four minutes, and in the meantime forward Tom Thacker and guard Tony Yates each committed his fourth foul. The foul trouble forced the Bearcats to play even more conservatively than they always did. Loyola still trailed 48-37 with 7:38 left, but a jumper by Rouse and two free throws by Hunter made it 48-41 with just over six minutes to go. After Yates missed a free throw, Hunter secured the rebound and Harkness bagged a turnaround jumper from the foul line.

Harkness's first basket had come more than 35 minutes into the game. His second came a mere six seconds later, as he picked off an errant pass and glided in for an easy lay-up. Now it was 48-45 with 4:24 remaining, and the Bearcats were clearly rattled. They continued trying to stall, but the Ramblers fouled them each time to stop the clock. With the score 50-45, Harkness made one free throw and missed the second.

Luckily, Cincinnati tipped the ball out of bounds under the basket. Loyola's in-bounds pass went to Harkness, whose jumper made it 50-48 with 2:42 left.

Hunter's clutch tip-in of a missed jumper by Harkness kept Loyola's hopes alive as the end of regulation play loomed. The Ramblers now trailed 53-52 with just 15 seconds left. As soon as Cincinnati inbounded the ball, Harkness fouled guard Larry Shingleton. Shingleton made his first free throw and could have all but clinched the game by making the second. But the ball bounced off the rim into the eager hands of Hunter, who hurled an outlet pass to Miller, who in turn fired the ball along to Harkness. Harkness unleashed a 12-foot jumper with five seconds left. It was good. The stunned Bearcats neglected to call timeout, so the horn sounded with the game tied at 54 (it was the first time Loyola had drawn even since the score was 4-4).

When Harkness notched the first two points of overtime, the Ramblers had their first lead of the game. Wilson tallied on a layup for Cincinnati, then Miller canned a high-arcing 20-footer for Loyola. Shingleton got behind the Ramblers for a layup that tied the score at 58 with 2:15 remaining. Now, strangely, the Ramblers decided to hold onto the ball and go for the final shot. Almost a minute had elapsed when Miller tossed an errant bounce pass that hit Egan in the foot and rolled away. Shingleton dove after the ball for Cincinnati, followed closely by Egan, resulting in a jump ball between the two shortest men on the court. "Shingleton wasn't much taller than me," said Egan, "only about six feet. But I didn't really question whether or not I could get the jump ball. The idea was to tip the ball between two of our guys to control it."

Egan did tip the ball first, and Miller caught it. There was just about a minute left to play. Miller got the ball to Harkness, who dribbled up court. Harkness, Egan, and Miller played keep-away from the Bearcats while Harkness looked for an opening. Finally, inside the final 10 seconds, Harkness made a move along the left side. Finding his path to the basket blocked by Ron Bonham, Harkness slid the ball across to Hunter. Hunter's short jumper rolled around the rim and fell out. Rouse, slicing in from the right side, got both hands around the ball and guided it into the basket as time expired.

The Ramblers were national champions.

The five iron men had played the entire game, including overtime, without relief. They had shot just 27 percent and scored their lowest total of the season but had prevailed nonetheless. "I never thought we'd lose it," said Rouse. "We came too far to lose it." Ireland, among others, admitted that he hadn't been quite so sure. "Man," Miller said, "that must be the greatest comeback in the history of the tournament."

In later years, as the Ramblers looked back across the decades to their miracle season, their stirring and unlikely victory over Cincinnati was a fond memory, of course. But the earlier game against Mississippi State was perhaps even more meaningful in the final analysis. "In a game like that you have two winners," Harkness said. "Mississippi State made a statement to the community that broke down some of the barriers, and we played a part in it."

CHAPTER 21

Papa Bear's Last Hurrah

"We were getting tired of hearing how great the Packers were."
-- *Joe Fortunato, Bears linebacker, 1955-1966*

On November 24, 1963, the Bears went into Pittsburgh for a crucial game against the Steelers. The Bears held a narrow lead in the Western Division over the NFL's two-time defending champions, the Green Bay Packers, whom they had soundly beaten the week before. At 9-1, they were poised for a run at their first championship in 17 years. What should have been a thrilling time for the Bears and their fans, however, had been marred by a stunning tragedy—the assassination of President John F. Kennedy less than 48 hours before the Bears were scheduled to play Pittsburgh. Despite suggestions that he do so, NFL commissioner Pete Rozelle chose not to postpone that weekend's games. "Everyone has a different way of paying respects," he said on Sunday. "I went to church today, and I imagine many of the people at the games did, too. I cannot feel that playing the games was disrespectful nor can I feel that I have made a mistake." Later, though, Rozelle called the decision the worst mistake of his life.

The Bears-Steelers game, like all those in the league that day, would be played in a virtual vacuum, since all television and radio coverage was focused on the nation's mourning of the late President. The Bears were tuned in along with millions of their fellow citizens when news came that the President's alleged assassin, Lee Harvey Oswald, had himself been shot to death in the Dallas police headquarters. In the locker room at Forbes Field, coach George Halas ordered the radio switched off and implored his players to concentrate on the game at hand.

The Steelers came into the game 6-3-1, and still had a slim chance to win the Eastern Division and with it a berth in the NFL championship game. It was a must game for both teams, and they played like it. The sellout crowd of 36,465 was treated to a tough, seesaw battle. The teams traded touchdowns in the first half and went into halftime tied 14-14. The third quarter was scoreless, thanks to two missed field-goal attempts by Pittsburgh's Lou Michaels. Finally, Michaels connected from 11 yards out to give the Steelers a 17-14 lead early in the fourth quarter. Charlie Bivins's fumble of the ensuing kickoff was recovered by Pittsburgh on the Chicago 12-yard line, apparently dooming the Bears—but the Steelers were called for offsides on the play.

The Bears got another chance. With less than five minutes remaining, though, they found themselves with a second-and-36 from their own 22-yard line. By now they knew that the Packers had beaten the 49ers 28-10 in Milwaukee. A loss would drop the Bears into a first-place tie with the defending champs.

The Bears' leading ground gainers, Joe Marconi and Willie Galimore, were being shut down; they would combine for fewer than 90 yards all day. Quarterback Bill Wade was thus forced to go to the air, and he had been intercepted three times already. "Throw the ball to me," Mike Ditka told Wade in the huddle, "and I'll try to run with it." The Bears' tight end ran a hook pattern, and Wade hit him about five yards beyond the line of scrimmage. The first Steeler to hit Ditka, defensive back Clendon Thomas, was also the one who brought him down—63 yards downfield from their initial contact. In between, Ditka literally ran over almost every defender on the field. At midfield, three Steelers converged from different angles, all hitting Ditka simultaneously. Only Ditka was on his feet after the collision, still charging toward the goal line. Thomas eventually wrestled him down at the Pittsburgh 15. "I lost my legs," Ditka said after the game, unhappy that he hadn't gone all the way. "They were completely dead. I had just run pass patterns on the three previous plays, and suddenly I found myself in the clear with the ball. I kept looking for somebody to lateral to, but nobody showed up."

Ditka needn't have apologized. "One of the greatest individual efforts I have seen in 40 years of football," said Halas. "They had him stopped a half dozen times, but his feet never stopped churning." The play, which became a staple of NFL Films highlight reels, set up the field goal by Roger Leclerc that gave the Bears a hard-earned 17-17 tie and kept them in first place.

The Bears had won five of their last six games in 1962 to finish 9-5, and they came into 1963 with high hopes for continued improvement. But their road to a possible championship would have to go through Green Bay. "If we're going to win this thing," Halas said before the season, "we're going to have to beat Green Bay twice." It was a tall order: the Packers had demolished the Bears by scores of 49-0 and 38-7 the year before en route to an almost-perfect 14-1 record and a second straight championship.

The litmus test came soon enough, as the Bears and Packers squared off in the very first game of the 1963 season. Green Bay had suffered a setback in April when its star running back Paul Hornung was suspended for having wagered on NFL games. Nonetheless, the champs came into the opener with 26 wins in their last 30 games and with all their key players except Hornung back for another year. A record crowd of 42,327 jammed into the newly expanded Lambeau Field expecting to see the Packers win their sixth in a row over Chicago and take their first step toward a third successive title.

Instead, it was the Bears who stepped up. Displaying the ferocious defense that would be their trademark all year, they held Green Bay to just 150 yards in total offense and forced five turnovers. Each of the Bears' 11 defensive starters played the entire game. In the first quarter, Richie Petitbon's recovery of a Jim Taylor fumble set up the Bears' first score, a 32-yard field goal by Bob Jencks. In the third quarter, Roosevelt Taylor's interception led to a 68-yard drive that was capped by the game's only touchdown, a one-yard plunge by Joe Marconi. When it was over, the Packers had ventured into Bear territory only three times, never getting within 30 yards of the goal line. "When you give up four interceptions," said Packer quarterback Bart Starr, who had done just that, "you don't deserve to win."

The Bears won 10-3. "This effort today culminates months of planning," Halas said. "The coaches have worked hundreds of hours toward this one game. But the victory belongs to the players. They were ready physically, and they were ready mentally. Gentlemen, this was the greatest team effort in the history of the Chicago Bears."

Proving that they were for real, the Bears ran off four more wins after the Green Bay game. Then, inexplicably, they suffered a 20-14 defeat at the hands of the worst team in the league, San Francisco (it was the first of only two wins for the 49ers that year). The loss dropped the Bears into a first-place tie with the Packers, who had gone unbeaten since the opener. Both teams took care of business for three more weeks, so they came into their rematch in Chicago with identical 8-1 records.

The Bears-Packers game on November 17 was perhaps the most highly anticipated regular-season contest in NFL history up to that time. Over 49,000 fans turned out at Wrigley Field—some of whom paid scalpers $100 for the privilege. As was true of all home games in those days, even sellouts, the game was not televised within a 75-mile radius of the city, so fans drove to taverns, bowling alleys, and American Legion halls in outlying areas of Illinois, Indiana, and Wisconsin. One group of 400 chartered an entire train, which they christened the Victory Special, for the 180-mile trip to a Galesburg hotel. Well supplied with liquid refreshments, these fans spent six hours on the train there and back for the chance to watch the game on television.

They were not disappointed.

The Bears' J.C. Caroline set the tone on the game's opening kickoff when he obliterated Herb Adderley after a return of just several steps. Thereafter, as George Strickler wrote in the *Tribune*, "the underdog Bears relentlessly carried the fight to the foe, on offense as well as defense." The Packers were never in the game. They didn't score until late in the fourth quarter, when they were already trailing 26-0. Only one other time, on a pass-interference penalty in the second quarter, did they advance inside the Bears' 38-yard line. The Bears intercepted five passes and recovered two Packer fumbles. They limited Jim Taylor, the league's reigning rushing champ, to 23 yards.

"The Bear defense met every expectation," Strickler wrote. "The offense exceeded even the wildest hopes of the most rabid Bears followers." All season, the defense had been disproportionately responsible for the team's success; when the two groups passed each other going on and off the field, Ed O'Bradovich remembered, he and his defensive mates would say to the offensive unit, "Just hold 'em." But on this day, the offense more than held its own. With superb blocking up front and a balanced distribution of carries among Galimore, Marconi, Rick Casares, and Ronnie Bull, the Bears churned out 248 yards on the ground. They scored the first three times they had the ball, on two field goals by Roger Leclerc and a spectacular 27-yard gallop by Galimore. Leclerc added a field goal in the third quarter and another in the fourth before Bennie McRae's 44-yard interception return set up a touchdown run by Wade from five yards out. The final score of 26-7 could have been even more one-sided, but Leclerc missed four field goals in addition to the four he made.

The Bears presented the game ball to offensive line coach Phil Handler, whose charges had completely dominated the line of scrimmage. Although the Packers were without Bart Starr, who'd been out three weeks with an injury, Green Bay coach Vince Lombardi offered no excuses. "The Bears were terrific," he said. "They beat us up front where it counts—and both ways. I'm happy for Papa George; he's a hell of a guy."

Halas himself was virtually speechless after the game. "Thank you, fellows," was all he managed to tell his team before being overcome with emotion.

"Somebody may still beat the Bears," Lombardi said wistfully. "I'm making no predictions. But they have four games left to play. So do we."

Chicago's tie with the Steelers on November 24, coupled with Green Bay's win over the 49ers, sliced the Bears' advantage to half a game. For the final weeks of the regular season, the Bears would take the field on Sunday knowing what the Packers had already done— Green Bay's last three games were scheduled for Thanksgiving Thursday and the following two Saturdays. The Packers' remaining games were all on the road, the Bears' all at home. On Thanksgiving Day in Detroit, the Packers struggled to a 13-13 deadlock that might have eliminated them from the race, but three days later the Bears could only manage a tie of their own with Minnesota, 17-17. Both teams looked more like themselves the next weekend: Green Bay dispatched the

Rams 31-14 on December 7, and the Bears handled the 49ers 27-7 the next day.

On December 14, the Packers won 21-17 at San Francisco to finish the season with a record of 11-2-1. If the Bears lost to the Lions, they would be 10-2-2, and Green Bay would have its fourth consecutive Western Division crown.

An overflow crowd of more than 46,000 at Wrigley Field saw the Bears squander several opportunities in the first half, and Detroit led 7-3 at halftime. In the third quarter, Wade dropped back from his own 49-yard line and spotted flanker Johnny Morris at the Lions' 40. Detroit's nearest defender slipped just as Morris caught Wade's pass, and from there it was a footrace to the goal line. Morris, one of the fastest men in the league, went all the way for a 51-yard touchdown. The extra point gave the Bears a 10-7 lead. A Lion fumble on the next possession gave the Bears the ball right back, and several minutes later Wade connected with Ditka on a touchdown pass from 22 yards out.

The Bears led 17-7 entering the fourth quarter. The Lions scored early in the quarter to make it 17-14. Finally, with less than two minutes remaining, Detroit got the ball again for one last drive. Now the Bears entrusted the game and the season to their tremendous defense and its five All-Pros: linebackers Joe Fortunato and Bill George, right end Doug Atkins, and safeties Richie Petitbon and Roosevelt Taylor. It was a lesser light, though, who made the play that saved the day. With only 35 seconds left and 65 yards to go, the Lions had to pass. Quarterback Earl Morrall looked for Gail Cogdill on a short out pattern. As Cogdill reached for the ball, Bears cornerback Dave Whitsell risked everything. He went for the interception. If he missed it, Cogdill would have smooth sailing down the sideline deep into Bear territory— perhaps even into the end zone. But Whitsell didn't miss. Timing his move perfectly, he picked off the pass and returned it for a touchdown. The Bears were headed to the championship game.

For the third year in a row and the fifth in the past six, the New York Giants were champions of the East. At age 37, quarterback Y.A. Tittle was phenomenal, setting new NFL records for passes attempted (367), completions (221), yards (3,145), and touchdowns (36) in a season, while throwing just 14 interceptions. In addition to Tittle, the Giant roster included several holdovers from the team that had routed the Bears 47-7 in the 1956 title game at Yankee Stadium: running back Frank Gifford, linebacker Sam Huff, offensive tackle Rosey Brown, and defensive end Andy Robustelli. Each was destined for the Hall of Fame.

It was a classic matchup. New York had scored an all-time record 448 points; the Bears had allowed only 144. Though a bit long in the tooth, the Giants were still formidable—and hungry, for they had suffered losses in their last four championship games. New York was installed as a 10-point favorite, but Bart Starr, for one, thought the Bears would prevail.

Several days before the game on December 29, the Bears covered the Wrigley Field grass with a layer of hay and a heavy tarpaulin, then surrounded the tarp with huge heaters. All this care proved too effective: when the tarp was pulled aside and the hay removed on game day, it was discovered that the field had thawed completely and was very damp and spongy. The temperature that day was nine degrees above zero and there was a stiff breeze blowing off the lake, so it didn't take long for the moisture in the grass to freeze solid, turning the field into a sheet of ice.

Almost 46,000 fans shoehorned their way into Wrigley Field, bundled up like arctic explorers. The NFL's 75-mile television blackout included even this game, so thousands of Chicagoans paid to watch the contest on closed-circuit TV at McCormick Place, the Amphitheatre, and other venues.

The game started ominously, as the Giants marched down the field for a touchdown on their first possession, following a fumble by Bill Wade. Tittle capped the drive with a 14-yard pass to Gifford. Still in the first quarter, the Giants had a chance to go up by two touchdowns, but wide receiver Del Shofner lost Tittle's pass in the sun and dropped the ball. He was all alone in the Bears' end zone at the time. "Miserable," Shofner said after the game. "Just miserable."

On the very next play after the miscue, linebacker Larry Morris intercepted Tittle and ran 61 yards down to the Giants' five-yard line. Ronnie Bull plunged ahead for three yards, and Wade got the touchdown on a quarterback sneak. Bob Jencks's extra point tied it up. A 13-yard field goal by Don Chandler late in the second quarter gave the Giants a 10-7 lead at halftime.

In the second half, the Bear defense performed in the manner to which fans had grown accustomed. O'Bradovich, the hulking defensive end, anticipated a screen pass and picked it off at New York's 24-yard line. He returned it to the 14. Wade connected with Mike Ditka over the middle, and Ditka bulled his way down to the one. After a sneak through the line failed, Wade vaulted over for the score. Jencks converted the point after to put the Bears up 14-10. For the rest of the third quarter and well into the fourth, Tittle and the Giants could not move the ball. But the Chicago offense was no better, so the Bears continued to cling to their tenuous four-point lead. After a field-goal attempt by Roger Leclerc went awry, New York advanced to the Bears' 36. Bennie McRae batted down a pass in the end zone to halt the drive.

The Bears gained possession. A first down would have all but clinched the win. The Bears played it safe. Guarding against any possibility of a fumble, they plunged into the line three times. On fourth and one at midfield, their excellent punter Bobby Joe Green booted one into the New York end zone for a touchback. The Giants took over at their own 20, and they marched into Bear territory with less than a minute remaining. Tittle called his last timeout. Now the ball was on the Bears' 39-yard line with 10 seconds left—time enough to throw once, maybe twice.

"Hail Mary" was not used as a football term in those days, but that is precisely what the Giants attempted. Shofner, their swiftest receiver, raced all the way into the end zone. Tittle threw. "I can still see my old roommate Richie Petitbon jumping for the ball with outstretched arms," tackle Bob Wetoska remembered. "All I could think was, 'My God, if he catches it, we win!' And he did catch it, and we did win." Petitbon's interception wrapped up the championship for the Bears.

"The day belonged to the Chicago Bear defense," Richard Whittingham wrote. "Five crucial times the Bear defenders came up with pass interceptions. Two of these set up the Bears' only touchdowns of the afternoon, and one ended the Giants' last-ditch chance as time ran out." Defensive coordinator George Allen was given the game ball.

"14 points and they win a championship," Sam Huff said bitterly. It was a crushing loss for the Giants, whose veterans recognized that this had been their last chance. In fact, neither team would appear in another championship game for over two decades. Lombardi and the Packers, on the other hand, rebounded to win three more championships in the next four years, cementing their place in history.

It had been 17 years since the Bears' last title, and many people had doubted that they'd ever win another one with Halas as their coach. "I have waited a long time," said Papa Bear. "I guess today's game proves that if you live long enough, everything nice you want to happen, will happen."

Halas was asked if, now that the monkey was off his back, he planned to retire. "I guess I will have to hang on," he replied. "Where could a 68-year-old find another job?"

Halas finally did retire on May 27, 1968. He had played with the Bears for 10 years (1920-1929). He had been their head coach for 40 years (four periods of 10 years each, beginning in 1920, 1933, 1946, and 1958). He had won 324 games—95 more than Curly Lambeau, who ranked second at the time—and compiled a winning percentage of .671. He had won eight championships.

If there were a Mount Rushmore representing the towering figures in the history of pro football, Halas would occupy George Washington's position. Even Lombardi, a legend in his own right, treated him with deference. "There is only one man I embrace when we meet," Lombardi said, "and only one I call 'Coach'—George Halas."

CHAPTER 22

Moments, 1960-1969

April 19, 1960
Homecoming

On May 1, 1951, Orestes "Minnie" Minoso made his debut with the White Sox, thus becoming the first black player to appear in a major-league game for a Chicago team.

"I'm the first guy to bat," Minoso recalled many years later. "First pitch comes right over the plate and I hit a home run to center field. The people who wanted to boo me didn't get a chance. But later they got a chance. The bases were loaded and I was playing third base. A hit bounced off the bag and hit my ankle, then went through my legs. I was charged with an error, and two runs scored. My first game on the White Sox I was at the top and then sunk to the bottom. Same day, good and bad."

As time went on, there was a lot more good than bad. In his first seven years, Minoso hit over .300 five times, knocked in 100 or more runs three times, and led the league in stolen bases three times. His aggressive style ignited the Go-Go White Sox, and he became the most popular player on the South Side. But then he was traded to Cleveland, and he missed the pennant year of 1959.

Minoso returned to the White Sox in 1960, at the age of 37. A record opening-day crowd of 41,661 at Comiskey Park gave him a hero's welcome, and he gave them their money's worth. A more eventful day would have been difficult to imagine.

In the first inning, Minoso beat out a bunt for an apparent base hit but was called out for running outside the baseline. A lengthy rhubarb ensued.

In the second, he hit a screaming liner and was robbed on a circus catch by Kansas City center fielder Bill Tuttle; he was credited with a sacrifice fly when Luis Aparicio scored on the play.

In the fourth, Minoso hit a grand slam. In the fifth, he narrowly missed colliding with Aparicio as both men chased a pop fly; he dropped the ball for an error.

In the seventh, he raced into the gap to spear a line drive that would have scored two runs.

In the top of the ninth, with the score tied 9-9, he threw out a runner at the plate. In the bottom of the ninth, he hit another home run to win the game.

Minnie was back, as his two home runs, six runs batted in, two sensational defensive plays, and countless ovations from the crowd amply demonstrated. "I'm comfortable here," he said after the game. "I was here before and I feel like this is my home."

July 29, 1963
Once and Future Kings

The man who had dominated professional golf for the past five years and the man who would dominate the game for the next two decades were already well acquainted when they met in the 1963 Western Open at Beverly Country Club on the South Side. In Arnold Palmer's 1960 U.S. Open victory, Jack Nicklaus had been runner-up; in Nicklaus's 1962 Open win, he had defeated Palmer in a playoff. The 33-year-old Palmer had won seven major championships. Though he was 10 years younger, Nicklaus had already won five majors, including the Masters three months before and the PGA just a week before the Western.

Nicklaus was poised to surpass Palmer as the best player in the world, but not yet as the most popular. At every tournament Palmer was trailed by huge and demonstrative galleries, known collectively as "Arnie's Army." The crowds at Beverly were no exception; they politely applauded such luminaries as Nicklaus, Sam Snead, and Julius Boros, but they reserved their most effusive responses for Palmer.

They were pleased within the ranks when Palmer shot 67 in the third round to surge into a tie for the lead. Arnie capped his sensational back nine of 31 by sinking a 20-foot putt to birdie the mammoth 596-yard 18th. Nicklaus's 71 left him seven strokes behind.

Sunday belonged to Nicklaus. "I thought I might have a good chance," he said, "if I did a 65 today." He didn't—but his 66 was the best round of the tournament, punctuated by a six-foot birdie putt on 18 that drew him even with Boros at four-under 280 for the 72 holes. Palmer struggled to a 73 for the day, giving *him* 280 for the tournament as well.

For the first time in the Western's 60-year history, three players had tied for the championship. Palmer, Nicklaus, and Boros came back on Monday to settle the issue in an 18-hole playoff.

Much to the delight of his army, Palmer required only 33 strokes to complete the front nine, while Boros and Nicklaus took 36 and 37, respectively. But things tightened up on the back nine. After 15 holes, Palmer and Boros were deadlocked at two-under 57, with Nicklaus at even-par 59. On 16, Nicklaus missed a chance for birdie from six feet out, and the three players went to 17 with the status quo intact.

The 17th hole was a nasty 210-yard par three with a sloping green shielded by an array of bunkers. It had separated the contenders from the pretenders all weekend, and it proved decisive in the playoff as well. Boros's tee shot landed in the rough behind the green, Palmer's in a bunker in front. Nicklaus struck a near-perfect shot that plopped onto the green, then rolled to within five feet of the cup.

Boros's chip from the rough and Palmer's blast from the sand each ended up 35 to 40 feet from the hole. Both putted to within three feet. Now it was Nicklaus's turn to putt. If he made it, he would go to 18 no worse than tied for the lead. But he went for it too aggressively, and the ball skittered past the hole.

Palmer made his next putt. Boros missed, and Nicklaus missed again. They went to 18 with Palmer leading Boros by one and Nicklaus by two. Nicklaus banged his third shot over the green and into the crowd; he took a bogey six. Boros missed his birdie try from 10 feet out, and Palmer tapped in for par to claim the championship.

The win placed Palmer's earnings for the year at $96,955—a new record. Nicklaus, of course, would be heard from again.

December 12, 1965
"When He Gets There He's Gone"

A steady rain turned Wrigley Field into a virtual swamp for the Bears-49ers game of December 12, 1965. Like all of his fellow players, the Bears' sensational rookie Gale Sayers was concerned about the conditions. "It was a rainy, muddy day and I actually didn't like playing in that kind of weather," he recalled. "So many things can happen; you can slip, pull a muscle, tear a hamstring."

It wouldn't have been surprising if the sloppy footing had neutralized Sayers more than anyone else, for speed and agility were his chief weapons. But Sayers ran wild. First he caught a screen pass from Rudy Bukich and romped 80 yards for a touchdown. Then he ran 21 yards from scrimmage for a second touchdown. He scored again on a seven-yard run from scrimmage.

Next, Sayers took a handoff and zigged and zagged his way 50 yards for yet another touchdown. It appeared that he alone was playing on a dry field, while 21 other men slipped and slid around him.

His fifth touchdown came on a straightforward plunge from one yard out.

Sayers saved his most spectacular play of the day for last. Fielding a San Francisco punt at his own 15-yard line, he made a dazzling move against the grain, leaving his would-be tacklers stupefied. He went 85 yards to the end zone, and was all by himself after passing the midfield stripe.

With this sixth touchdown, Sayers equaled the single-game record. It was his 21st of the season, also a record at the time. He might have scored once more, but he slipped (finally) making one of his patented cuts on a punt return—after he'd already gone 32 yards. "The way things were going," Sayers recalled years later, "I probably could have scored eight touchdowns that day. But back then no one cared about records. I didn't even know I'd tied the six-touchdown record until after the ballgame."

The final score was 61-20. The man known as the Kansas Comet amassed 336 total yards for the day—with 113 yards on nine rushes (an average of 12.5 per carry!), 134 yards on punt returns, and 89 yards on two pass receptions. "I never saw such a thing in my life!" said Bears coach George Halas. It was fitting that the greatest single-game performance by a rookie in NFL history had come from the man who was in the midst of the greatest rookie season in NFL history.

San Francisco defensive back George Donnelly offered an apt description of Sayers's elusiveness in the open field: "He looks no different than any other runner when he's coming at you, but when he gets there he's gone."

For the Bears, just two years removed from their most recent championship, the future looked bright with Sayers and another rookie, middle linebacker Dick Butkus, destined to rank among the greatest players of all time. Regrettably, knee injuries drove both players into premature retirement, and a succession of losing seasons followed. It would be 10 years before the Bears found a player of similar stature, Walter Payton, and 10 more before they again wore the crown.

March 12, 1966
The Roar From the Crowd

In the first five decades of the National Hockey League's existence, only three players scored 50 goals in a single season—Maurice "Rocket" Richard of the Canadiens in 1944-45, Bernie "Boom-Boom" Geoffrion of the Canadiens in 1960-61, and Bobby Hull of the Blackhawks in 1961-62. No one had scored 51.

As the 1965-66 season progressed, hockey fans and the media began to consider it a cinch that Hull would go to 51 and beyond that year. He scored his 50th goal on March 5 against the Detroit Red Wings. "I think it took a lot of pressure off me," said Hull. "The monkey is off the back now." Hull was averaging nearly a goal a game for the season, and he was certain that the record-breaker would come in the next game or, at the very latest, the game after that.

But not only was Hull shut out in the next game, so were the Hawks. The same thing happened in the next game. And in the next. It was unbelievable: the league's highest-octane offense failing to score in three straight games. In the fourth game after Hull's record-tying goal, he and the Hawks again struggled. They trailed the New York Rangers 2-1 entering the third period.

When the Hawks went on the power play with a little over five minutes gone in the period, the sellout crowd at the Stadium buzzed in anticipation. But almost immediately, New York's Reggie Fleming picked off an errant pass and started up ice with a chance for a short-handed goal. Lou Angotti of the Hawks was able to disrupt Fleming inside the Chicago blue line. Angotti kicked the puck across to Hull, who gained control and headed out of his own zone.

As Hull crossed the Rangers' blue line, goalie Cesare Maniago braced himself for a slapshot. Hull's was the most wicked in the league, clocked at up to 118 miles per hour. As Maniago tried to get set, the Hawks' Eric Nesterenko cut in front of him. Hull fired. It was a low screamer that, thanks to Nesterenko's screen, Maniago didn't see until it was too late. Before he could react, the puck was in the net. "Nesterenko lifted the blade of my stick," Maniago said after the game, "and the puck went under it."

The Rangers' protests were in vain. It was number 51 of the season for Hull, and it touched off a riotous celebration in the Stadium that delayed the game for several minutes. Hull skated around the ice shaking hands with fans who stuck their arms out over the glass. Galvanized by all the excitement, the Hawks scored twice more in the remaining minutes to pull out a come-from-behind win, 4-2. When reporters asked Hull what the key to the record-breaking goal was, he had an answer that wasn't surprising to anyone who had ever attended a Hawks game in the Stadium. "It was the crowd," he said. "The roar from the crowd."

Hull finished the season with 54 goals; he broke his own record with 58 three years later. After he retired, he said, "When I played in that great building, Chicago Stadium, and I picked up the puck, I could feel every voice. It was like the fans were coming up the ice behind me."

March 12, 1967
The Curse is Lifted

One year to the day after they celebrated Bobby Hull's individual achievement of 54 goals in a single season, the Blackhawks celebrated a team achievement that was also unprecedented. In so doing, they also killed off the legendary "Curse of Muldoon."

The story went like this: when the Hawks fired coach Pete Muldoon after their inaugural season of 1926-27, he raised his hands, rolled his eyes, and solemnly pronounced, "This team will never finish in first place."

In fact, the legend was invented by a Toronto newspaperman on a slow news day in the early forties. Nonetheless, it was also a fact that going into the 1966-67 season, their 41st in the league, the Hawks had never finished first—nor had even come close until the past few seasons.

Though laden with All-Stars like Hull, Stan Mikita, Pierre Pilote, Ken Wharram, and Glenn Hall, the Hawks hadn't been able to get over the hump. They finished third in 1960-61, then stormed through the playoffs to win the Stanley Cup. They finished third twice more and second three times over the next five seasons.

For all practical purposes, 1966-67 would be their last chance to overcome the imaginary curse, because it was the last season before the NHL expanded. If the Hawks were ever to finish first among the "original six" teams, it would have to be this year.

The Hawks ran off a 15-game unbeaten streak early in the new year to build up a substantial lead in the standings. Still, the skeptics could point to 1962-63, when the Hawks led all the way only to collapse in the last three weeks. But the Hawks kept winning, and finally, on the sunny Sunday afternoon of March 12, they had a chance to clinch the Prince of Wales Trophy as regular-season champions. Their game against the Toronto Maple Leafs drew a capacity crowd to the Stadium and was televised throughout the United States and Canada—though not in the Chicago area.

After killing off a two-man disadvantage early in the game, the Hawks drew first blood on a goal by Ken Hodge from Phil Esposito and Hull at 11:54 of the first period. Less than four minutes later, Hodge lit the lamp again, this time assisted by Esposito and Pat "Whitey" Stapleton.

In the final minute of the period, Hodge, Stapleton, and Hull came winging out of their own zone. Hodge, on the right wing, sent the puck across to Stapleton, who carried it over the Toronto blue line and cen-

171

tered to Hull. The Golden Jet fired one of his patented slap shots from about 40 feet out. It sailed over goalie Terry Sawchuk's right shoulder to give the Hawks a 3-0 lead.

The Blackhawks' first-period barrage had given the great Glenn Hall more than he needed. He ended up turning away 39 shots for a shutout. Lou Angotti scored twice in the third period for the final margin of 5-0. When the horn sounded, the fans showered the ice with hats, half-eaten hot dogs, paper cups, and rolled-up programs. The Hawks clomped downstairs to their dressing room for a well-earned revel.

Coach Billy Reay and general manager Tommy Ivan were thrown into the showers in their suits and ties. "I knew we were up for this one," said Hodge as he wiped champagne from his eyes. "You could feel it before the game—everyone was raring to go. You'd have to be blind not to see it."

The 1966-67 Hawks were easily the class of the NHL, scoring a then-record 264 goals while allowing only 170, lowest in the league. Mikita pulled off an extraordinary sweep by winning the Hart Trophy as most valuable player, the Art Ross Trophy as leading scorer, and the Lady Byng Trophy as most gentlemanly player. Hall and Denis DeJordy shared the Vezina Trophy for goaltending excellence.

But when the Maple Leafs bounced the Hawks from the playoffs in the first round, Ivan decided that changes were in order. Hall was left unprotected in the expansion draft, while Esposito, 25, and Hodge, 22, were sent to Boston in one of the most disastrous trades in franchise history. Esposito led the league in goals scored for six straight years, surpassing Hull's previous record several times in the process, and the Bruins won the Stanley Cup in 1970 and 1972.

November 9 and 16, 1969
Brian's Swan Song

On November 9, 1969, at Wrigley Field, the Bears throttled the Pittsburgh Steelers 38-7 for what proved to be their only victory of the worst season in franchise history.

The Bears' defense held Pittsburgh to 31 yards rushing and also recorded eight sacks, including two in the end zone (by Ed O'Bradovich and Dick Butkus). On offense, the great Gale Sayers rushed for 112 yards and two touchdowns, while quarterback Bobby Douglass rushed for 72 yards. Running back Brian Piccolo notched the Bears' first touchdown on a 25-yard pass reception from Douglass.

(The victory turned out to be a mixed blessing for the Bears. When the Steelers also finished 1-13, they got the first pick in the next year's NFL draft by virtue of having lost to the Bears. They selected quarterback Terry Bradshaw, and they won the Super Bowl four times in the next 10 years.)

Sayers and Piccolo had both joined the Bears as rookies in 1965, Sayers as a first-round draft pick (fourth overall) out of Kansas and Piccolo as an undrafted free agent from Wake Forest. They'd been best friends ever since. Sayers had been a superstar all along, while Piccolo was still in the process of establishing himself. His touchdown against the Steelers was just the fourth of his career, whereas Sayers had tallied six *in one game* as a rookie and totaled 52 for his career to this point.

The Bears traveled to Atlanta the next Sunday, November 16, and lost to the Falcons 48-31. Sayers scored the Bears' first touchdown on a 10-yard gallop, and Piccolo scored the last on a one-yard plunge.

Piccolo never played football again. He had not been feeling well for some time and was suffering frequent coughing fits. When the Bears returned to Chicago after the Atlanta game, he was sent to the doctor for tests and soon diagnosed with embryonal cell carcinoma, an aggressive form of lung cancer.

Piccolo died at the tender age of 26 on June 16, 1970, seven months to the day after his final game for the Bears. He was survived by his wife Joy and their three young daughters.

It has been a long time since Piccolo's passing, but he has not been forgotten. Both the Bears and the Atlantic Coast Conference present annual awards named for him, honoring players judged to have been the most courageous. And, of course, his legacy has been preserved by *Brian's Song*, the 1971 made-for-TV film that explores the close relationship between Piccolo (played by James Caan) and Sayers (played by Billy Dee Williams).

Film critic Leonard Maltin called *Brian's Song* "a milestone of excellence." Like all movies that are "based on a true story," it took certain liberties with the facts. For example, George Halas (played by Jack Warden) is depicted as the Bears' head coach in 1969, when in reality he was succeeded by Jim Dooley before the 1968 season. The film is true where it really matters, though. It compellingly represents the remarkable bond between the reserved Sayers and the happy-go-lucky Piccolo. It also captures, word-for-word, the emotional speech that Sayers delivered when presented with an NFL award for courage several weeks before Piccolo's death.

"Brian Piccolo is the man of courage who should receive this award," Sayers said. "It is mine tonight. It is Brian Piccolo's tomorrow. I love Brian Piccolo, and I'd like for all of you to love him. When you hit your knees tonight, please ask God to love him too."

CHAPTER 23

Bullish

"The fans responded to the kind of team we were because the city is a blue-collar city, and the players were much the same way."
                                    -- Jerry Sloan, Bulls guard, 1966-1976

When the Bulls came on the scene in 1966, Chicago had already been home to half a dozen failed and forgotten pro basketball franchises. The Tigers, featuring George Halas as owner and head coach, had survived from 1927 to 1929. They were followed by the Duffy Florals, the Studebakers, the American Gears, and the Stags. As recently as 1963, Chicago had lost its two-year-old NBA franchise, the Zephyrs, to Baltimore. Few doubted that the Bulls would soon go the way of their short-lived and little-lamented forerunners.

Although the city was home to the legendary Harlem Globetrotters and to a number of successful college programs, it was, in the words of *The Sporting News*, "long regarded as the burial grounds of professional basketball." In 1947, the American Gears won the championship of the National Basketball League, while the Stags were runners-up for the Basketball Association of America title. Chicagoans yawned.

Both the Gears and the Stags were defunct by 1950. The National Basketball Association, formed by the merger of the two earlier leagues, did not see fit to grant Chicago another franchise until 1961, when the Packers were born. Their six-foot-11 center Walt Bellamy was Rookie of the Year, but the Packers finished 18-62 and didn't draw flies to their home games at the International Amphitheatre. Owner Dave Trager announced that the franchise would move to Baltimore as soon as the promised new arena there was ready. That turned out to be not as soon as he had thought. The team remained in Chicago for the entire 1962-

175

63 season, changing its name to the Zephyrs and playing its home games in the Coliseum—the ancient building that had been forsaken by the Blackhawks more than 30 years before. The Zephyrs improved slightly, to 25-55, and featured another Rookie of the Year, forward Terry Dischinger, but few people noticed and fewer cared when the team packed its bags after the season.

Along came Dick Klein, a former player for Northwestern University and the Gears who believed that an NBA franchise could not only survive but flourish in Chicago. First, he tried to purchase the Zephyrs to prevent their move to Baltimore. When that effort failed, he began campaigning for an expansion team and rounding up investors. "He was a P.T. Barnum-type guy," said Johnny "Red" Kerr. "He could sell anything to anybody."

Selling the NBA on Chicago was the greatest challenge of Klein's career as a salesman. The league was in a bad way itself. It had no national television contract, NBC having bailed out in 1962, and had little inclination to try another Chicago experiment. The owners of the nine existing clubs informed Klein that he could get a franchise for $600,000, which was at least $400,000 more than he could muster. Klein formally applied for a franchise on April 11, 1963, neglecting to enclose the required $100,000 deposit. "I said the check would be forthcoming," he recalled. "Later, I learned my telegram had been filed in the wastebasket."

Undeterred, Klein resumed the task of accumulating investors. It looked as if he and his group had caught a big break when Maurice Podoloff, the NBA commissioner who had been solidly against expansion into Chicago, resigned in mid-1964. But Podoloff's successor, Walter Kennedy, proved no more agreeable. "Dick," he said when Klein asked him for a meeting, "don't waste my time."

Then, in 1965, ABC expressed interest in carrying the NBA's games. One of its conditions was that the league place a team in Chicago, the nation's second-largest television market. All of a sudden Klein's quest seemed less quixotic, and several big investors signed on. But when Klein reported to Kennedy that he had gathered the $600,000, he found that the franchise fee had risen to $750,000. When he returned with $750,000, he was told the fee was $1 million. By now there were seven or eight other groups competing with Klein's for the expansion franchise, and the NBA was taking full advantage of the situation. The fee was ratcheted up yet again, to $1.25 million.

All of the prospective owners were summoned to the league offices in New York on January 26, 1966. "When I made the presentation," Klein remembered, "they asked me what single thing made my group stand out. I said, 'I have approximately half a dozen partners, and any one of them could buy the whole league.'" Klein got the franchise. Employing a bit of hyperbole to boost its image, the league announced that he had paid $1.6 million.

Klein wanted a nickname for his team that would evoke the stockyards and the brawny, big-shoulders character of Chicago. He almost settled on "Matadors," but he wasn't sure because it had three syllables. "Chicago had the Bears and the Sox and the Cubs and the Hawks," he explained, "all single syllables." When he hit upon "Bulls," Klein knew instantly that he'd found the right name.

He also wanted a strong Chicago connection in his coach. His first choice was Ray Meyer, whom he could not persuade to leave DePaul University. He then received a petition on behalf of Johnny Kerr, a Chicago native and former University of Illinois star who was just finishing up his playing career. "They had something like 1,600 names," Kerr recalled, "but I'm not sure all of them were real. It's a little like how they used to register people for voting in Cook County." Genuine or not, the petition worked. Kerr was hired.

The Bulls drafted two players from each existing club in the 1966 expansion draft. Because Kerr and his intended assistant, Al Bianchi, were technically still active players, both were acquired through the draft. They promptly retired as players and signed on as coaches. The following players were the first to become property of the Bulls: Kerr and Jerry Sloan from Baltimore, Ron Bonham and John Thompson from the Boston Celtics, Nate Bowman and Tom Thacker from the Cincinnati Royals, John Barnhill and Don Kojis from the Detroit Pistons, Bob Boozer and Jim King from the Los Angeles Lakers, Len Chappell and Barry Clemens from the New York Knicks, Bianchi and Gerry Ward from the Philadelphia 76ers, Jeff Mullins and Jim Washington from the

St. Louis Hawks, and Keith Erickson and McCoy McLemore from the San Francisco Warriors.

Of all these players, only Sloan and Boozer would make a lasting impression with the Bulls. Thompson retired to go into coaching and later led Georgetown University to the NCAA championship. King and Mullins were traded to the Warriors for point guard Guy Rodgers.

At the Bulls' first training camp at North Central College in Naperville, Rodgers and the 14 remaining players from the expansion draft were joined by nine rookies picked up in the college draft. The apparent plum of the latter group was Dave Schellhase, who'd led the nation with 32.5 points per game and had signed a contract for the considerable sum of $35,000. Unfortunately, it took only a few workouts to show that Schellhase wouldn't make it. "He had been a nice player at Purdue," Kerr said, "but he didn't have the size to be a pro forward or the quickness to be a guard. He came to training camp about 20 pounds overweight and was eaten up by our veterans."

The 1966-67 Bulls had 179 season ticket holders, each of whom paid four dollars per game for a courtside seat at the Amphitheatre. Their front office "staff" was general manager Klein, marketing director Jerry Colangelo, public-relations man Ben Bentley, and a receptionist. The Bulls organized a parade down State Street to publicize the season opener. It consisted of two trucks and a car. "The press that came to the parade might have been giggling," Klein said, "but at least they were talking about us."

Klein actually put an ad in the papers calling for players, and about 180 showed up for an open tryout. Kerr was not amused. "I told Al [Bianchi] to line them all up against a wall and have them count off by twos," he said, "then have the twos go home. We did that, and later on we sent all the ones home, too."

The Bulls played their first game on October 15 at St. Louis with a starting lineup of Sloan and Rodgers at guards, Boozer and Kojis at forwards, and Chappell at center. They won 104-97 behind Rodgers's 37 points. Three nights later they made their home debut against San Francisco. Newspapers estimated that the announced crowd of 4,200 was padded by about 1,000. In any event, the few fans on hand got their money's worth. The Bulls rallied late to overcome a 13-point deficit and won 119-116. Sloan scored 26 points and Rodgers had 20 assists.

The Bulls were young and quick, and they played an entertaining style built around the fast break. When they won four of their first five games, Chicagoans sat up and took notice. On October 23, the Bulls had their first sellout. "We could have sold 30,000 seats that night in a 7,000-seat arena," Klein asserted. "We let 9,000 in and the fire marshal came to me and said, 'Dick, you gotta close the doors.'" Officially, the crowd was 8,472, the largest crowd ever for an NBA game in Chicago up to that time.

"They got people who can't get into the game," said Sloan. "It's sold out. I thought, 'My goodness, we're not that good, are we?' We certainly found out that night. The Knicks waxed us pretty good, and reality started to set in."

A nine-game losing streak in November and December dropped the Bulls into last place in the West Division at 8-15. "I remember how cold it was that first winter," sportswriter Bob Logan said, "and how small the crowds were." The Great Blizzard of '67 struck in late January, dumping almost 30 inches of snow on the city. On January 29, the Bulls lost to Los Angeles by 20 points before an announced crowd of 1,077. Klein later admitted that the actual attendance, "including security guards, was something like 72 people." Since the Lakers were stranded in Chicago after the game, Klein treated them to a steak dinner.

By the end of February, the Bulls were 25-44 and still mired in last place, three games behind Detroit for the final playoff berth. On March 1, they traveled to Evansville, Indiana, to take on Philadelphia. (Sloan had played his college ball at Evansville, and the Bulls played five "home" games there to capitalize on his popularity.) The 76ers were en route to a 68-13 record and the world championship, but the Bulls upended them 129-122. The game was a turning point for the Bulls—they won eight of their last 12 to qualify for the playoffs.

The Amphitheatre's management did not consider the NBA playoffs as big a happening as the boat show it had already scheduled, so the Bulls' postseason home games were relegated to the decrepit Coliseum. The Bulls were swept by St. Louis in the first round, with the lone home game drawing a mere 3,739.

The Bulls' first season had been more successful on the court than at the ticket windows. Their 33-48 mark was the best ever by a first-year expansion team, and Kerr was selected Coach of the Year. Rodgers led the league in assists; he and his backcourt mate Sloan were all-stars. Center Erwin Mueller was named to the all-rookie team.

The second season was a disaster in every way. Perhaps inevitably, the sense of spontaneity and fun created in that first year vanished. So did many members of the cast of characters. Bianchi left to become the first head coach of the Seattle SuperSonics. Kojis was left unprotected in the expansion draft. Mueller jumped to the new American Basketball Association. Rodgers was traded to Cincinnati for Flynn Robinson, a prolific scorer but not a team player. "It was discouraging to see Guy go," said Boozer. "It was discouraging to see Klein selling and trading players to keep the cash flowing."

Because the original McCormick Place had recently burned to the ground, the Amphitheatre was needed to host Chicago's conventions and expositions. The Bulls, minor tenants, lost their lease and moved to the Stadium. "We'll rattle around in the Stadium like a ping-pong ball on a brick street," Klein told Stadium and Blackhawks owner Arthur Wirtz. Crowds that didn't seem too bad in the cozy 7,000-seat Amphitheatre looked ridiculously small in the 18,000-seat Stadium.

The Bulls' first home game, a two-point loss to the Lakers, drew 2,234 fans. The club lost its first nine games, won one, then lost six more. In desperation, Klein acquired the glowering, six-foot-11 Reggie Harding to play center. Harding was reputed to carry a pistol in his gym bag. Kerr later claimed that Harding regularly threatened to pistol whip Robinson, whom he felt was showing him up in practice. Harding was waived halfway through the season, and he soon took up a life of crime. He was shot to death in Detroit in 1972.

The Bulls' plodding new lineup forced Kerr to abandon the up-tempo style he'd employed effectively the year before. The result was a team that was not only bad, but boring as well. "We were doing nothing at the gate," Bentley recalled. The Bulls staggered to a 29-53 record but made the NBA's expanded playoffs, where they bowed to the Lakers four games to one in the first round.

After the season, Colangelo left to take over as general manager of the expansion Phoenix Suns. The first person he hired was Kerr, as head coach. Kerr had grown increasingly unhappy under Klein. "Klein was the owner and general manager," said Bentley, "and he wanted to be the coach, too. He would always have a little something to say to the coaches if they lost a game."

The departure of the popular Kerr was a serious blow. But when Klein tapped an obscure young coach from Weber State University in Utah to replace him, he probably saved the franchise. The announcement attracted little notice in the press—because Dick Motta's first day as coach of the Bulls was also George Halas's last as coach of the Bears.

The Bulls were still all but invisible in Chicago. "We had four people in the front office," said Motta. "We had a coach and no assistant. There were no newspaper people following us on the road. We didn't do radio on the road. We didn't do TV on the road. They sold, I think, 38 season tickets that year."

The Bulls opened the 1968-69 season with a starting five of Sloan and Robinson at guards, Boozer and Washington at forwards, and rookie Tom Boerwinkle at center. Their new coach was quite a contrast from the easygoing Kerr. He battled ceaselessly with his bosses, the media, referees, and any player who didn't want to do things his way. A month into the season, Motta went home from practice one night and called Klein at home. "If Flynn [Robinson] is there tomorrow," he said, "I'm gone."

Klein resented the ultimatum and told Motta so. Nonetheless, he traded Robinson to the brand-new Milwaukee Bucks for forward Bob Love and guard Bobby Weiss. Then he phoned Motta to "congratulate" him for forcing what he called the worst trade he'd ever made. "Motta had no idea who we were," said Weiss, "and Klein did not like the deal. It was just one of those things that worked out." Motta later described the trade as "the major turning point of the franchise." The wiry, six-foot-eight Love became a force at both ends of the court (he would lead the Bulls in scoring for seven consecutive seasons), and the scrappy Weiss proved a solid sixth man.

The Bulls went 33-49 and missed the playoffs in Motta's first year, but they were starting to jell.

Klein held only 20 percent of the Bulls' stock, so he served as managing partner only at the pleasure of his fellow investors. By 1969, they weren't so pleased. "I rubbed some furs the wrong way," Klein later remarked. The Bulls' first two picks in that year's college draft, Larry Cannon of LaSalle and Simmie Hill of West Texas State, both signed with the ABA when Klein refused to be drawn into a bidding war for either player. Motta was livid, and he began lobbying board members to have Klein ousted as managing partner. He was preaching to the converted, for plans to remove the Bulls' founder had already been percolating for some time by then. Klein was voted out, and Pat Williams was appointed general manager.

Williams's first order of business was to complete a trade with the club he had just left, the 76ers, for forward Chet Walker. The Bulls sent Jim Washington to Philadelphia for Walker and Shaler Halimon. Walker, master of the pump fake and an excellent free-throw shooter, was just what the Bulls needed—a "go-to" guy who could deliver in pressure situations.

Williams's next agenda item was to aggressively market the Bulls. "Boy, I hit every banquet, every circuit, every promotional idea," he recalled. "Anything you could do to whipsaw people in there, we were doing it." Williams introduced a new mascot, Benny the Bull (which was named after Bentley) to attract children. He instituted giveaways of all kinds at virtually every home game. The Bulls' continued improvement on the court and Williams's marketing savvy pushed home attendance to better than 10,000 per game in 1969-70. For Klein, the success he had so long predicted was bittersweet. "Dick was [still] there as the owner," Williams remembered, "he had tickets to the games, but he had no power. It was strange."

On January 17, 1970, the Bulls trailed 115-100 with 3:47 left in a game at Milwaukee. While the fans were gathering up their coats and hats, the Bulls came back. A jumper by Shaler Halimon brought them to within three with eight seconds remaining. The Bulls quickly fouled, and the Bucks made one of two free throws to lead by four. Halimon struck again, this time from 25 feet out. Milwaukee's in-bounds pass clipped the backboard, giving the Bulls one more chance. At the buzzer,

Halimon buried one from the corner to force overtime. The Bulls won 132-130.

While Halimon had eight seconds of glory, the man who came to Chicago with him made a difference for six years. "Chet [Walker] was a great clutch player," said teammate Matt Guokas. "When teams stopped our offense, we needed good one-on-one players to finish it off. Chet was the guy." Walker teamed with Love to give the Bulls a superb forward tandem. Meanwhile, the fiery Sloan thrived under Motta, a kindred spirit, emerging as the most tenacious defender in the league. "It took me about 10 minutes to recognize that he was very special," Motta said. "There weren't many players that had his intensity." And Boerwinkle developed into an outstanding rebounder and passer. "He really set the whole Motta program up," said Sloan, "because of his ability to pass the ball."

The 1969-70 Bulls finished 39-43 and won only one of five games in their first-round playoff series. It was clear, however, that they were on the verge of being one of the elite teams in the league. As Motta left the locker room after the last playoff game, he said, "I wish the season started all over again tomorrow."

The Bulls won 50 or more games in each of the next four seasons. Attendance soared. The Bulls didn't win any championships in those years, but they won over enough Chicagoans to ensure that the franchise was here to stay. "The thing I really feel a little bit of pride in," said Sloan, "is the fact that we kept the franchise here. Otherwise it would have been gone."

CHAPTER 24

Summer of '69

"You don't think pennants in July."
-- *Gil Hodges, New York Mets manager, 1968-1972*

Leo Durocher took over as manager of the Cubs in the wake of the ludicrous College of Coaches era, in which the club had gone five years with a rotating band of "head coaches" instead of a full-time manager. Durocher, a salty old-timer who had played for or managed five pennant winners and had issued the famous quote "Nice guys finish last," immediately promised better days ahead. "This is not an eighth-place club," he said, referring to the Cubs' finish in 1965, and he was proven right, though not in the way he intended—his 1966 team finished 10th. But the Cubs' climb to respectability and beyond was swift and sure thereafter. With relative youngsters like Fergie Jenkins, Bill Hands, Glenn Beckert, Don Kessinger, and Randy Hundley jelling around the veteran nucleus of Ernie Banks, Billy Williams, and Ron Santo, the Cubs rose all the way to third in 1967 (improving by 28½ games) and finished third again in 1968.

At spring training in 1969, Durocher announced, "The Cubs are now ready to go for all the marbles."

The season could hardly have begun more rousingly. On Opening Day, April 8, Banks cracked two home runs before an overflow crowd of 40,796 at Wrigley Field that included his 73-year-old father, Eddie, who was visiting from Dallas. But Philadelphia's rookie shortstop Don Money rapped two homers of his own, including a three-run shot off Jenkins that tied the score in the top of the ninth. The game went into extra innings, and the Phillies took a one-run lead in the top of the

11th. With one out in the bottom of the 11th, Randy Hundley singled. Then Willie Smith stepped out of the dugout to pinch hit for Jim Hickman. Smith took Barry Lersch's first pitch. He lined the second pitch into the right-field bleachers, and just like that the Cubs had won, 7-6.

The Cubs won 11 of their first 12 games, and almost every one produced a different hero. In the Cubs' second win, Williams rapped four doubles; in their third, Santo clubbed two homers. In their fourth, Joe Niekro and Ted Abernathy combined for a 12-inning shutout. The fifth victory featured a three-run rally in the ninth inning, the sixth a shutout by Ken Holtzman, and the seventh outstanding relief work by Hank Aguirre. The Cubs' eighth win was a five-hit shutout by Jenkins, and their ninth was another shutout, by Hands and Phil Regan. In the 10th win, Williams, Banks, and Santo each had three hits, and in the 11th, reserve outfielder Al Spangler knocked in three runs.

The Cubs assumed sole possession of first place in the National League East on April 14. They breezed through April at 16-7 and sailed through May at 16-9. In May, they recorded *nine* shutout victories, including a 19-0 bludgeoning of the San Diego Padres on May 13 in which Banks drove in seven runs. The Cubs' successes in the spring seemed but a prelude to greater victories that would be earned in the summer and fall. After two months of the season, they looked unbeatable.

National League East Division standings—June 1, 1969

	W.	L.	Pct.	G.B.
Chicago	32	16	.667	--
Pittsburgh	24	23	.511	7½
New York	21	23	.477	9
St. Louis	21	25	.457	10
Philadelphia	18	24	.429	11
Montreal	11	32	.256	18½

What an unaccustomed position the Cubs were in, and how they and their fans relished it! "I'm elated at the way this team is playing," Durocher crowed. "They smell the money." The phrase "Cub Power" appeared on T-shirts and bumper stickers. The Cubs' new fight song, "Hey Hey, Holy Mackerel," blared from radios and jukeboxes. Santo marketed his own brand of pizza and took to clicking his heels in a "victory kick" after each win at home. Williams broke the National League record for consecutive games played and was honored with his own "day" at Wrigley Field. A group of bleacherites named themselves the Bleacher Bums and adopted yellow hardhats as their uniform, Ray's Bleachers at Waveland and Sheffield as their official watering hole, and pitcher Dick Selma (who led their cheers and chants from the bullpen) as their honorary chairman.

Ernie Banks, especially, was having the time of his life. He had played brilliantly for a full decade and won the Most Valuable Player award twice before even attaining the plateau of .500 (the 1963 Cubs finished 82-80). "Without Ernie Banks," former White Sox manager Jimmie Dykes had said, "the Cubs would finish in Albuquerque." Now, at the age of 38, in his 17th season, Banks was finally playing with a first-place club. He became a sports commentator on Channel 9 and was given a column in the *Tribune* called "The Wonderful World of Ernie Banks."

Banks's popularity annoyed Durocher, who advised reporters to "cut that 'Mr. Cub' crap," but Ernie didn't seem to mind. "Leo Durocher," he said, "is the greatest manager I've ever seen." Banks also used his column to proclaim how grateful he was to have been a Cub for so many years. "Baseball has meant playing with the greatest team," he wrote, "from the owner, Mr. Phil Wrigley, on down. The 'working' conditions have been wonderful in the good and the bad years. How those players on the other clubs envy us!" Did he really believe all this stuff, or even a portion of it? Only Ernie knew for sure.

National League East Division standings—July 1, 1969

	W.	L.	Pct.	G.B.
Chicago	50	27	.649	--
New York	40	32	.556	7½
Pittsburgh	38	38	.500	11½
St. Louis	35	41	.461	14½
Philadelphia	33	39	.458	14½
Montreal	21	52	.288	27

The Cubs won nine of 12 games on a late June homestand, including four straight from Pittsburgh and three of four from St. Louis. Thus they sent their two most likely challengers spinning out of contention. By July 4, after Jenkins bested the great Bob Gibson in 10 innings, the Cardinals were seven games under .500 and 16 games behind the Cubs. The Pirates, in the throes of a seven-game losing streak, were 14½ games off the pace.

The New York Mets had now emerged as the Cubs' nearest pursuers. It was understandable that the Cubs weren't sweating too hard just yet, for the Mets had been a running joke since entering the league in 1962. They'd lost an unprecedented 120 games their first season and had finished last or second-to-last every year since. Their numerous and inventive ways of losing ballgames had inspired Casey Stengel, their first manager, to call them "those amazin' Mets."

Now, under the fatherly Gil Hodges, the Mets were changing the meaning of their nickname. An 11-game winning streak in late May and early June had put them over the .500 mark for the first time in their history, and they were still rising. There was no question that their pitching was good enough to keep them in the race (they had an outstanding young staff anchored by third-year man Tom Seaver, sophomores Jerry Koosman and Nolan Ryan, and rookie Gary Gentry), but their everyday lineup was adequate at best. "I know the Dodgers won pennants with just pitching," Santo declared, "but this Mets lineup is ridiculous."

On July 8, the Cubs invaded New York's Shea Stadium for a firsthand look at the upstarts. Jenkins carried a 3-1 lead into the bottom of the ninth inning. The first batter, Ken Boswell, lifted a shallow fly ball that looked like an easy out, but the Cubs' rookie center fielder Don Young misjudged it—he broke back, then raced in too late. It fell for a double. Tommie Agee fouled out, then Donn Clendenon drove one deep to left-center. Young sprinted back to the warning track, reached out and made a fine catch—only to have the ball drop out of his glove when he slammed into the wall. Clendenon was credited with a double, and the score was now 3-2. A legitimate double by Cleon Jones tied it up. After an intentional walk and a groundout, Ed Kranepool came to bat. Kranepool's fifth-inning homer had been the only hit off Jenkins prior to the ninth. Jenkins fooled him this time with an off-speed pitch, but Kranepool threw his bat at the ball and looped it into left to score Jones with the winning run. "Somebody said the Cubs weren't taking us seriously," Jones said after the game. "Maybe they'll take us seriously now."

"[Jenkins] pitched his heart out," said Durocher, "and one man can't catch a fly ball. It's a disgrace." Although neither ball that escaped Young had been scored an error, his teammates believed he should certainly have caught the first one, at least. Santo said so within earshot of reporters. "*Everybody* was saying, 'Jesus Christ, the ball's got to be caught,'" Beckert recalled. "Santo's name got associated with it. Not the other 24 guys who were saying the same thing."

Santo called a press conference the next morning to apologize for his remarks. That evening, though, Young was on the bench and another rookie, Jimmy Qualls, was in center field. A delirious crowd of 59,083 saw Seaver retire the first 25 Cubs to face him before Qualls lined a single to left with one out in the ninth. Seaver made short work of the next two batters to complete a one-hit shutout, 4-0, for New York's seventh consecutive win and the Cubs' fifth straight loss.

It looked like more of the same the next day when Jones scaled the fence to rob Santo of a three-run homer in the fourth. But Qualls jump-started a five-run rally when he stretched a single into a double leading off the fifth. The Cubs went on to win 6-2 behind a gritty effort from Hands.

The Cubs' lead was five games when the Mets came calling at Wrigley Field the next week. "People used to laugh and laugh at the Mets," said Banks, "but not anymore." On Monday, July 14, a raucous crowd of 40,252 was treated to an exquisite pitching duel between Hands and Seaver. Kessinger led off the Cubs' sixth with a single, went to second when Beckert grounded to the right side on a hit-and-run play, and scored on a single by Williams. Hands scattered six hits before Regan relieved him with one out in the ninth. The Cubs won 1-0, and Santo did his victory kick again and again for the ecstatic Bleacher Bums. "That," said Durocher, "was a World Series game."

But New York won 5-4 on Tuesday on a three-run homer by journeyman infielder Al Weis; it was Weis's second homer in the past four years and only the fifth of his career. Even more appallingly, the usually light-hitting Mets chased Jenkins to the showers on Wednesday with a six-run barrage in the first two innings en route to a 9-5 triumph. In their clubhouse the jubilant Mets mimicked the antics of Santo and Selma.

The Cubs' lead was still a reasonably secure four games, but the Mets had been emboldened. "These boys have thought all along they were strong contenders," said Hodges, "but it's been tough convincing some others." As Hodges spoke, Santo sat stunned in the opposite clubhouse. "Two out of three in our park," he lamented. "I still don't believe it."

The Cubs went into the All-Star break on a high note, sweeping a doubleheader at Philadelphia on July 20. The second game was halted for several minutes while both teams lined up along the foul lines and a recording of "God Bless America" was played in honor of the Apollo 11 astronauts who had just touched down on the moon. The Cubs were represented in the All-Star Game by their entire infield—first baseman Banks, second baseman Beckert, shortstop Kessinger, third baseman Santo, and catcher Hundley.

National League East Division standings—August 1, 1969

	W.	L.	Pct.	G.B.
Chicago	65	41	.613	--
New York	55	44	.556	6½
St. Louis	55	49	.529	9
Pittsburgh	53	50	.515	10½
Philadelphia	42	60	.412	21
Montreal	33	70	.320	30½

As always, Durocher and controversy were close companions. After calling in sick for two games against Los Angeles in late July, he was spotted at a Wisconsin summer camp enjoying parents' weekend (and his own 64th birthday) with his third wife and her 12-year-old son. The newspapers had a field day. "The Chicago sportswriters," Durocher wrote, "sensing my demise, were sniffing around like the jackals that most of them are." Wrigley decided not to fire Durocher after Leo apologized to him face-to-face. Strangely, the shy, eccentric chewing-gum magnate had great affection for the abrasive, profane Durocher, and the feeling was mutual. In his autobiography, Durocher proclaimed the Cubs' owner "simply the finest man to work for in the world."

Despite the distraction of Durocher's near firing, the Cubs surged in early August. Jenkins and Hands each won twice during a seven-game winning streak that extended the lead to nine games. On August 13, Hands beat San Diego 4-2 for his sixth consecutive win. That same day, St. Louis inched ahead of New York into second place. On August 16, Jenkins subdued San Francisco 3-0 for his second shutout in four days.

On August 19, the Cubs launched an 11-game homestand that they believed would all but put the pennant race to bed. It started swimmingly: Santo's three-run homer in the first was all they needed as Holtzman tossed a no-hitter to beat Atlanta 3-0. Holtzman, who struck out none, benefited from Beckert's two sparkling plays and from a stiff breeze that kept a long drive by Hank Aaron in the park and within Williams's reach in the left-field corner. In addition to thrilling a capacity crowd at Wrigley Field, Holtzman's no-hitter also marked a new high-water mark for the Cubs, who were now 32 games over .500.

Almost a quarter of the season remained. On August 22, President Richard M. Nixon predicted that the Cubs and the Baltimore Orioles would meet in the World Series. That same day, however, the Cubs dropped their third straight game since Holtzman's gem. "We're just not hitting," Durocher said, rejecting any suggestion that his regulars were tired. "If we faulted Leo for one thing," Beckert recalled years later, "it was that he played the same guys every day. He never asked if you were hurt. There was no such thing as being hurt. He just put the lineup out there."

"Everyone's a little tired," said Williams, who had played every game since 1963, "but we've just got to keep battling." The Cubs pounded Houston 11-5 on August 23. But they managed only a split with the Astros in a doubleheader the next day, then lost three in a row to Cincinnati before salvaging the final game of the homestand.

The Cubs had lost seven of the 11 games. Worse yet, the Mets had won 12 of 13 since their brief visit to third place on August 13. The Cubs left town only three games in front.

National League East Division standings—September 1, 1969

	W.	L.	Pct.	G.B.
Chicago	83	52	.615	--
New York	76	54	.585	4½
Pittsburgh	70	60	.538	10½
St. Louis	71	62	.534	11
Philadelphia	52	78	.400	28½
Montreal	41	93	.306	41½

Having flubbed a chance to solidify their lead at home, the Cubs summoned the will to win four of five on a road trip to Atlanta and Cincinnati as August gave way to September. In Atlanta, 60 Bleacher Bums accompanied the team—their airfare, hotel accommodations, and game tickets having been paid for by Phil Wrigley.

The Cubs returned home on Friday, September 5, having stretched their lead back to five games. But then they started to skid in earnest. Pittsburgh came into Wrigley Field and routed Holtzman, then Jenkins. In the third game of the series, Jim Hickman's two-run homer in the eighth put the Cubs ahead 5-4; it was the 11th home run in a month for Hickman, a previously obscure outfielder who'd broken in with those woeful '62 Mets. Alas, Willie Stargell homered with two out in the ninth to tie it up, and the Pirates won on two unearned runs in the 11th to complete a three-game sweep. After the game, Durocher gave his shaken team what it needed least under the circumstances—a gratuitous tongue-lashing in which he implied that many of his key players were quitters.

It was out of the frying pan and into the fire as the Cubs headed to New York with Durocher's tirade ringing in their ears. The Mets were just two and a half games back as the clubs opened a two-game set on Monday night, September 8. Hands had an idea that he hoped would fire up the Cubs and send a message to the Mets. Before Monday's game he told his teammates, "[Tommie] Agee is going on his ass the first pitch." Sure enough, his first delivery was right under Agee's chin. "I have never seen a better knockdown pitch," recalled Gene Oliver, the Cubs' backup catcher. "But Tommie Agee, being the professional that he was, was not intimidated. He did not even make a face at Hands." The young Mets didn't back down. When Santo led off the Cubs' second, Koosman drilled him in the forearm. Then, in the third, Agee smacked a two-run homer that sent the crowd of 48,930 into an uproar.

Singles by Kessinger, Beckert, and Williams and a sacrifice fly by Santo tied the score in the sixth. In the bottom of that frame, Agee was on second when Wayne Garrett singled to right. Hickman fielded the ball on the second hop and fired a perfect strike to Hundley, who swiped at the sliding Agee. "I tagged Agee about six feet up the line," said Hundley, "and I tagged him so hard the ball almost popped out of my mitt. And all of a sudden I heard this tremendous roar go up. I turned, and [umpire] Satch Davidson's giving the 'safe' sign!" Hundley and Durocher argued frantically, to no avail. Koosman, who struck out 13, made the run stand up for a 3-2 decision.

The unlucky "13" theme continued the next night. First a black cat appeared on the field, paused in front of Santo in the on-deck circle, and moseyed into the Cubs' dugout. Then Clendenon and Art Shamsky each hit his 13th home run of the season, sending Jenkins to his 13th loss by a score of 7-1. Seaver held the Cubs to five hits for his 21st victory; he was on his way to the Cy Young award. Late in the game the crowd of 58,436 serenaded Durocher: "Goodbye Leo, goodbye Leo, goodbye Leo, we hate to see you go!"

The lead was now half a game.

On September 10, the Cubs lost to the lowly Phillies. The Mets swept a doubleheader from Montreal. After being alone in first place for 149 consecutive days, the Cubs had fallen to second. Durocher had no comment, but Santo said, "I'm optimistic, very optimistic." The next night, Philadelphia scored three runs in the eighth to hand the Cubs another defeat—their eighth straight—while the Mets shut out Montreal.

The Cubs finally ended the losing streak on September 12, topping St. Louis 5-1 behind Banks's four RBIs and a typically fine performance by Hands. Unbelievably, they still lost ground in the standings when New York beat Pittsburgh *twice* by identical scores of 1-0. The following day, the Cardinals scored four in the eighth off Jenkins and two relievers to erase a 4-3 Cub advantage, and the Mets won their 10th in a row on Ron Swoboda's grand slam.

The Cubs were now three and a half games out. "We just can't put anything together," Durocher said. "Everything has gone wrong."

It was all over but the shouting. Holtzman held his own against Bob Gibson for nine innings the next day before Lou Brock homered in the bottom of the 10th to snap a 1-1 deadlock. Of course, the Cubs' 1964 trade of Brock to St. Louis for pitcher Ernie Broglio was already infamous by this time, and it has continued to live in infamy. "If I'd been in Chicago," Brock later said, "the Cubs would have won the pennant in '68 and '69."

A loss at Montreal put the Cubs four and a half games behind with 14 left to play. "Sure we're pressing," Kessinger admitted. "We wouldn't be human if we weren't." The Mets went on winning, often in the most uncanny ways. On September 16, the Cardinals' Steve Carlton struck out 19 of them—but Swoboda socked a pair of two-run homers as the Mets won 4-3.

On Thursday, September 18, the Phillies pushed across three runs in the top of the eighth to beat the Cubs 5-3 at Wrigley Field. Meanwhile Seaver blanked the Expos 2-0 in Montreal. The Mets had opened up a five-game lead over the Cubs. Less than two weeks earlier, on the morning of September 5, their positions had been exactly reversed.

The Mets came to Wrigley Field on October 1 for two games that would conclude the season. The series that might have decided the race now meant nothing, for New York had clinched the division title a week before. Only 10,136 turned out to see the Mets win the first game 6-5 in 12 innings for their 100th victory of the season and their 38th (against just 10 losses) since August 13. The next day, 13,717 saw Banks's three-run homer propel the Cubs to a 5-3 win. The game was delayed when the Bleacher Bums set off a smoke bomb in the outfield and again when they marched into the more expensive seating areas in defiance of the outnumbered Andy Frain ushers. After the final out, a number of them traipsed about the field. Another group of young Cubs fans heckled the Mets from behind the New York dugout. "It's hard to admit you were not good enough," Swoboda said to them. "Isn't it? You were good, but not good enough."

The Mets went on to sweep Atlanta in the first National League Championship Series and, shockingly, to upset Baltimore four games to one in the World Series. When asked to explain the miracle that he and his players had wrought, Gil Hodges said simply, "Can't be done."

National League East Division standings—1969 (final)

	W.	L.	Pct.	G.B.
New York	100	62	.617	--
Chicago	92	70	.568	8
Pittsburgh	88	74	.543	12
St. Louis	87	75	.537	13
Philadelphia	63	99	.389	37
Montreal	52	110	.321	48

CHAPTER 25

Worst to First

"It's a job and it pays good, so I do it. But I don't like it. Who the hell likes to have pucks shot at them at a hundred miles an hour?"

-- *Tony Esposito, Blackhawks goalie, 1969-1984*

When the Blackhawks visited Montreal's Forum to play the Canadiens on October 25, 1969, they were winless in six games for the young season and seemed destined for a second straight last-place finish, while the Canadiens were heavy favorites to win their third consecutive Stanley Cup.

The Hawks had gone one game over .500 in 1968-69, but had nonetheless finished sixth and last in the NHL's powerful Eastern Division, missing the playoffs for the first time since 1958. They entered the next season with more questions than answers. First, Ken Wharram, the plucky winger who was one of the club's veteran leaders, suffered a heart attack that left him in critical condition for a time (he recovered, but his playing career was over). Then superstar Bobby Hull walked out of training camp, charging that the Hawks had reneged on certain promises made during his contract negotiations the year before. The goalie position was unsettled, with coach Billy Reay torn between Denis DeJordy, who had disappointed since replacing the great Glenn Hall two years earlier, and Tony Esposito, whose entire NHL experience consisted of 13 games with Montreal the season before.

With seven rookies, including Esposito, in the lineup, the Hawks were bombed 7-2 in the season opener at St. Louis. Then they lost four more games before managing a tie at New York. "It may take 30 or 35 games before we play the kind of hockey I believe we are capable of playing," Reay said, "but I am not discouraged."

The game in Montreal was the first portent of better things to come. Esposito, who had looked so bad in the opening-night debacle, was brilliant as the Hawks won 5-0. It was the Canadiens' first loss of the season and their first on home ice in 25 games dating back to the previous January. "I decided to go with Tony," said Reay, "in the hopes that he'd be fired up against the team that let him go, and it worked. I can't remember winning that decisively too often in Montreal."

The Hawks were a different team after Esposito's shutout of the Canadiens. They lost their next game, then reeled off a 10-game unbeaten streak of eight wins and two ties. Esposito played every minute of the streak and allowed a *total* of 10 goals. Two of the games were shutouts, one of them a 1-0 decision over Montreal at the Stadium.

Bobby Hull returned to the fold during the streak, his differences with the club's management put aside if not forgotten. General manager Tommy Ivan made it plain that Bobby would be expected to go along with the Hawks' new emphasis on defense. "Hockey is a team game," Ivan intoned. "We learned last season that individual records do not win championships." It was a blunt reference to Hull's record-breaking 58 goals in 1968-69.

Picking up where he had left off, Hull scored four goals in his first six games, giving the Hawks an emotional boost. Keith Magnuson, for one, was thrilled. "You can't appreciate Bobby until you've played with him," he said. "It's really nice, you know, to throw the puck up to Bobby on the left wing—and then watch it disappear."

Magnuson was himself a key factor in the Hawks' resurgence. The redheaded rookie proved a reliable stay-at-home defenseman who never shied away from a fight. He frequently took his lumps, but always came back for more. He would be the heart and soul of the Blackhawks for many years to come.

Another rookie, Cliff Koroll, was teamed with Stan Mikita and Dennis Hull on the Hawks' first forward line. "The kids will make a few mistakes," said Mikita, "but they're working hard, digging all the time. When we get used to each other, goals and points will start taking care of themselves." The diminutive center was right; he averaged two points per game for 20 games as the Hawks climbed into the playoff race.

Mikita was playing perhaps the best hockey of his career—quite a statement considering that he, like Hull, had twice won the Hart Trophy as the NHL's most valuable player. But the sensational Esposito was the real key. "If we're behind 1-0," said Reay, "he comes up with the big save and keeps the score from being 2-0, which is all the difference in the world."

In the first week of the 1970s, there was no question that the Hawks were beginning to come around, but they were still hovering at .500 and hard-pressed to stay out of the cellar. On January 7, Esposito blanked the Detroit Red Wings 7-0. The Hawks were now one point ahead of the sixth-place Toronto Maple Leafs and eight points behind fourth-place Detroit for the final playoff spot. They were 16-15-5, and their flirtations with the .500 mark would soon be over.

Esposito had back-to-back shutouts at Pittsburgh and Boston on January 14 and 17, respectively. The Hawks surged through the remainder of January and into February, going 10-2-1, but were unable to gain much ground on the Wings, who were also playing well. "Detroit and Toronto are the teams we've got to beat out," Reay declared, suggesting that New York, Montreal, and Boston were well out of reach. "We're going good now but you always worry there might be a letdown after a hot streak."

The letdown might have come after a 4-4 tie with the Philadelphia Flyers on February 7. In that game, defenseman Pat "Whitey" Stapleton dove headlong toward his own net to save a sure goal, then crashed into the goalpost. The gallant effort left the Hawks' captain with torn knee ligaments. He was lost for the season. The next night, defenseman Gilles Marotte tried to block a drive from 55 feet out and succeeded only in deflecting the puck past Esposito for the decisive goal in a 3-2 loss to Montreal.

With that, Tommy Ivan rolled the dice. He sent DeJordy, Marotte, and a minor-leaguer to the Los Angeles Kings for defenseman Bill White, goalie Gerry Desjardins, and center Bryan Campbell. White, a 31-year-old veteran, was the key man in the trade. "He's not spectacular," said Reay, "but he does a solid, workmanlike job. He doesn't make too many mistakes."

White's Blackhawk debut on February 21 at the Stadium was eventful. Midway through the second period, Bobby Hull scored the 500th goal of his career to join Gordie Howe and Maurice "Rocket" Richard as the only players to have reached that milestone. Seven minutes later, with White assisting, Bobby bagged his 501st. The Hawks beat the Rangers 4-2.

On February 26, the Hawks embarked on a six-game road trip that removed any lingering doubts as to whether they were for real. They beat Philadelphia, lost to Boston, then defeated New York, Los Angeles, Oakland, and Philadelphia again. They returned home in third place, only three points behind the second-place Rangers and six behind the Bruins. The Hawks were now legitimate contenders for more than just a playoff berth.

The last three weeks of the season offered the wildest stretch run in NHL annals. Five clubs had a chance to win the Prince of Wales Trophy as regular-season champions; one of them would miss the playoffs altogether.

The Hawks passed New York for second place on March 15. Three days later they beat Toronto to move within a single point of Boston. The first-place showdown at Boston Garden on March 19 went to the Bruins 3-1. "We haven't seen the last of Chicago," Boston goalie Eddie Johnston said darkly. As if to prove him a prophet, the Hawks again moved to within a point of the lead with a victory at Pittsburgh two nights later. At this juncture, Boston had 89 points, Chicago 88, Detroit 87, and Montreal and New York 85 apiece.

The five teams were as evenly matched as they could be, except that only one had Tony Esposito.

On March 22, Doug Mohns tallied in the third period to give the Hawks a 1-0 win over St. Louis. It was Esposito's 13th shutout of the season, equaling the league record. The Bruins also won to retain their slim one-point lead in the standings.

Four nights later in Detroit, the man who was now being called "Tony O" blanked the Red Wings 1-0 for an unprecedented 14th shutout. "I never thought I'd see the day that record would be broken," said Reay. "What Esposito has done is incredible." Appropriately, the game-winning goal was scored by Pit Martin, the feisty little center who had been jump-starting the Hawks' offense for weeks.

When Boston settled for a tie with Detroit on March 29, the Hawks achieved a share of first place by dispatching Toronto, in yet another shutout by Esposito, 4-0. Now the Hawks and Bruins each had 95 points, Detroit 91, Montreal 90, and New York 88. Each team had only three games left. Only New York could *not* finish first, but only the Hawks and Boston had clinched a playoff slot.

Montreal's victory over Boston on April 1 presented a golden opportunity for the Hawks—who squandered it, losing to Detroit to remain in a first-place tie.

The final weekend of the campaign featured home-and-home series between the Hawks and Montreal, Boston and Toronto, and Detroit and New York. The schedule favored the Bruins (who could be expected to handle the last-place Maple Leafs), while the Hawks had to contend with the defending champion Canadiens. On Saturday night, Boston beat Toronto. Not to be outdone, the Hawks gave perhaps their finest performance of the year, defeating Montreal 4-1 at the Forum in a game that included Dennis Hull's 100th career goal.

Then came Sunday, April 5, one of the most memorable days in the NHL's long history. The Hawks and Boston were battling down to the wire for first place, Detroit had clinched third place, and Montreal had the upper hand over New York for the fourth and last playoff berth. The Rangers not only had to win and hope the Canadiens lost, but they also had to finish the season with more goals scored than Montreal (a tall order, since they were five goals behind entering play).

New York held up its end of the bargain, blitzing Detroit 9-5 to finish the season 38-22-16 for 92 points. Boston defeated Toronto. So when the Hawks and Canadiens took the ice at the Stadium, each team knew what it had to do. If the Hawks won, they would tie the Bruins with 99 points but would be division champions because their 45 victories exceeded Boston's 40. If the Canadiens won or tied, they would be in the playoffs and New York would be out. If the Canadiens lost, their record would be identical to New York's but they could still make the playoffs by scoring five or more goals to top the Rangers' total of 246 for the season.

Before a standing-room-only crowd, the Canadiens struck first. Yvan Cournoyer's goal off a nice feed from Jean Beliveau gave Montreal a 1-0 lead at 9:12 of the first period. Fans began to wonder if perhaps the Hawks' Cinderella story wasn't meant to have a happy ending. Tension mounted as Montreal goalie Rogatien Vachon repelled one assault after another until 15:49 of the period, when Jim Pappin's slapshot from the blue line lit the lamp. Thus reassured, the Hawks took the lead just 95 seconds later when Doug Mohns set up a goal by Pit Martin. "I took my time, and I picked my spot," Martin said. "I didn't even see where the goalie was; all I saw was about eight inches of net."

The Hawks led 2-1 at the first intermission. Bobby Hull made it 3-1 at 1:24 of the second period, but Beliveau's tally put the Canadiens back in the game just two minutes later. For the rest of the second period and well into the third, the Hawks clung to a 3-2 edge.

Then it was Pit Martin time. After the previous season, Martin had called the Hawks the most selfish, underachieving team he'd ever seen, rubbing more than a few teammates the wrong way (it didn't help that future Hall-of-Famer Phil Esposito had been traded for him). Now Martin put his money where his mouth was. At 7:15 of the third period, he scored the goal that gave the Hawks a commanding 4-2 lead. Three and a half minutes later, he scored again to complete the hat trick.

The game was now out of reach, the champagne was on ice, and the Stadium rocked with chants of "We're Number 1!"

Montreal coach Claude Ruel realized that the Canadiens could not win the game, so he hatched a desperate plan to get the three more goals needed to surpass the Rangers for fourth place. For the last eight minutes of the game, goalie Vachon was replaced by an extra attacker each time Montreal got possession of the puck; this was the only way the Canadiens could get any pressure on Esposito.

Ruel's gamble backfired, to say the least. Almost every time Vachon skated to the bench, the Hawks stole the puck and gleefully swatted it into the empty net—first Eric Nesterenko, then Bobby Hull, Dennis Hull, Cliff Koroll, and Gerry Pinder. The fans were beside themselves, roaring more loudly after each goal. The final score was 10-2.

The somewhat bizarre ending disguised the fact that the game had been hard fought and well played for over 50 minutes. When the horn finally sounded, the Hawks had become the first team in NHL history to go from last place to first in one year—and they had earned it, winning twice against the fabled Canadiens to end the season. Beginning with Tony O's shutout in Montreal on October 25, they had gone 45-17-8. For the last 12 weeks of the season, they had gone 30-7-4.

Although their record of 38-22-16 would have easily won the Western Division (home of the six three-year-old expansion teams), the Canadiens were out of the playoffs for the first time since 1948. For the first time ever, the postseason would not include either Montreal or Toronto.

While his teammates showered each other with champagne and beer, Tony Esposito sat quietly in a corner of the Hawks' dressing room, exhausted. "He's the guy who made the difference," said Martin, indicating the man who seemed oblivious to the celebration going on around him. "He has made stops nobody could believe in game after game. He is the guy we've rallied around. I don't think there ever has been a goaltender with a season like the one he's had."

Esposito's season for the ages had carried the Hawks from last to first and had earned him the Vezina Trophy as outstanding goalie and the Calder as rookie of the year (he finished second to Boston's Bobby Orr in the MVP balloting). He had played 63 games, allowing just one goal in 15 of them and, of course, setting a record with 15 shutouts. As quick to refuse credit as he was to accept blame, Esposito was matter-of-fact about his feats. "All the guys worked so hard for me," he said. "They have all year. I kept thinking, 'Don't ease up; you don't want to let them down.'"

CHAPTER 26

Moments, 1970-1979

May 12, 1970
Milestone

Only Ernie Banks would have called the dreary Tuesday afternoon of May 12, 1970, "a beautiful day for baseball." It had rained throughout the morning, and there were puddles all over Wrigley Field when the Cubs took on the Atlanta Braves. Most fans assumed that the game had been called off, and only 5,264 diehards turned out.

They never regretted it. In the second inning, Banks stepped up to the plate against Pat Jarvis. On the count of 1-and-1, he swung and stroked a low line drive into the left-field bleachers for the 500th home run of his illustrious career. "I felt the ball had a real good chance," Banks said later. "Then when I saw [left fielder Rico] Carty turn and look into the seats, I knew it was in." The ball ricocheted out of the stands and back to Carty, who tossed it into the Cubs' bullpen for safekeeping.

Jack Brickhouse, of course, was calling the game on WGN television. He shouted, "On your feet everybody—this is it!"

Banks was the ninth player in major-league history to reach 500 homers. The fateful blow also marked his 1,600th run batted in; he was the 12th man to achieve that level. A generation later, either milestone would have held up the game for half an hour, but in Banks's day there was a minimum of fanfare. Richard Dozer described the scene in the *Tribune*: "[Banks] doffed his cap as he crossed the plate and shook hands with Rick Ferrari, Andy Frain usher chief who arrived conveniently at the plate with a new supply of baseballs for the umpire. Later, after he'd shaken the hand of every teammate in view, he went out to his first-base position, received another ovation, and got a congratulatory handshake from Carty on his way to the Atlanta dugout."

Atlanta's Hank Aaron also shook Banks's hand upon reaching first base later in the game. He had preceded Mr. Cub to the 500-homer and 1,600-RBI milestones, and he would eventually reach the unprecedented levels of 755 and 2,297, respectively, in the two categories.

The Cubs won the game 4-3 in 11 innings. It was strangely fitting that barely 5,000 spectators had witnessed the culmination of Banks's career—for the melancholy fact is that no other player ever performed as wonderfully for such listless teams and before so many empty seats. That he somehow managed to turn all this into a triumph was his greatest feat.

May 17 and 19, 1974
Cougar Town

The 1974 Avco Cup final series was the first, and presumably the last, championship of a major professional sports league to be played in northwest suburban Mt. Prospect.

The Chicago Cougars were charter members of the World Hockey Association, which was founded in 1972 as a rival to the National Hockey League, and the Avco Cup was the WHA's equivalent to the Stanley Cup.

Like other upstart leagues which have come along over the years, the WHA was initially regarded as something of a joke. But the NHL wasn't laughing after Blackhawks superstar Bobby Hull signed with the new league before its inaugural season. Hull's defection to the Winnipeg Jets gave the WHA instant credibility, and 67 other NHL players soon joined him.

Losing Hull proved calamitous for the Blackhawks. At 33, he had plenty of hockey left in him. He was coming off the fifth 50-goal season of his career and the 10th season in which he was one of the NHL's top three goal scorers. Hull's departure marked the beginning of a steady decline in the Hawks' popularity that persisted for decades.

The Cougars finished last in their division in the WHA's first season, but they made the playoffs the next year, led by three former

Hawks: center Ralph Backstrom, defenseman Pat "Whitey" Stapleton, and goalie Dave Dryden. The Cougars squeaked through two playoff series in seven games each and advanced to the Avco Cup finals against the Houston Aeros, who featured 46-year-old Gordie Howe—Mr. Hockey himself—and his sons Mark and Marty.

This was where the sublime met the ridiculous. The Cougars' usual home arena, the International Amphitheatre at 43rd and Halsted, had been available for the first playoff round, but not for the second round because it had booked a touring production of *Peter Pan*, starring former Olympic gymnast Cathy Rigby in the title role. As a result, the second playoff series had been moved to Randhurst Twin Ice Arena in Mt. Prospect, which was named for the vast shopping mall in whose parking lot it sat.

By the time the Cougars and Aeros were set to start the finals, *Peter Pan* had moved on—but the Amphitheatre's ice surface had been melted and, for whatever reason, could not be refrozen. The Cougars attempted to shift their home games to Chicago Stadium, but that plan fell through because the Hawks were still alive in the NHL playoffs and weren't willing to share. With tails between their legs, the Cougars returned to Randhurst for the Avco Cup finals.

The Amphitheatre was no great shakes, as anyone who attended an event there in those days could attest. But it could seat 7,000 spectators, whereas the Randhurst rink held less than 2,000. The venue had been designed to suit the needs of participants, not spectators, and it could not accommodate newspaper reporters, much less radio and television broadcasts, in any meaningful way.

It was probably just as well that Houston swept the series, sparing the Cougars the embarrassment of hosting more than the minimum of two games.

The shopping-mall ice rink made the Cougars a laughingstock, and they never recovered. During the 1974-75 season, the players themselves chipped in to buy the franchise from original owners Walter and Jordan Kaiser when the brothers failed to secure financing for a new arena in Rosemont. The Cougars folded at the end of the season.

The wished-for arena in Rosemont was eventually built, of course. It opened in 1980 as the Rosemont Horizon and was later renamed the Allstate Arena. It has been home to a highly successful franchise, the

Chicago Wolves of the American Hockey League, for many years. The Randhurst Twin Ice Arena, like the Amphitheatre, is no more.

The WHA outlasted its Chicago franchise by four years. When it disbanded in 1979, four of its teams joined the NHL: Edmonton Oilers, Hartford Whalers, Quebec Nordiques, and Winnipeg Jets. With them came a number of outstanding players, including Mike Gartner, Michel Goulet, Paul Holmgren, Rod Langway, Ken Linseman, Mike Liut, Mark Messier, Rick Vaive, and the Great One—Wayne Gretzky.

April 25, 1976
Lincoln, Washington, and Monday

As the United States prepared to mark its Bicentennial, most Americans were not in a particularly celebratory mood. Their confidence had been shaken by the Vietnam War, the Watergate scandal, the energy crisis, and other recent reversals. Then, a strange thing happened to cheer everyone up.

The Cubs were playing the Dodgers in Los Angeles. A man and his son climbed out of the stands and onto the field. "One of them had an American flag tucked under his arm," recalled Rick Monday, who was watching the pair from his vantage point as the Cubs' center fielder. The two went to a spot in left-center field, about halfway between Monday and left fielder Jose Cardenal, where the older man spread the flag out on the grass and began to sprinkle lighter fluid over it.

"The next thing I saw was the glint of the [lighter fluid] can," said Monday. "I figured it wasn't holy water. That's when I took off. They couldn't see me coming from behind but I could see one had lit a match. The wind blew it out, and just as they lit another and were about to touch it to the flag, I grabbed [the flag]."

Monday scooped up Old Glory just before it would have been set afire. He sprinted to the left-field bullpen and handed the flag over to Los Angeles pitcher Doug Rau. As the fans in the ballpark realized what had happened, they rose to give Monday a standing ovation. The Dodger Stadium message board flashed: RICK MONDAY, YOU MADE A GREAT PLAY.

205

The would-be flag burners were arrested and charged with trespassing. "If you're going to burn the flag," Monday later said, "don't do it around me. I've been to too many veterans' hospitals and seen too many broken bodies of guys who tried to protect it."

In the following weeks, ceremonies honoring Monday were held in every city the Cubs visited. Jose Cardenal, who'd witnessed the attempted flag burning up close, understood why Monday's actions had struck a chord. He had left his homeland of Cuba at the age of 17 in 1960, a year after it became a Communist dictatorship, never to return. Cardenal loved his adopted country and wasn't embarrassed to admit it. "Now we have three great patriots," he said. "Lincoln, Washington, and Monday."

April 8, 1977
"Coming on Like a Fire Truck"

Despite the acquisition of center Artis Gilmore, the 1976-77 Bulls got off to a horrendous start, losing a club-record 13 straight games early in the season. It seemed that their futility might even exceed that of the previous year, when they had struggled to an abysmal 24-58 record. Gilmore, a veteran of five outstanding campaigns in the recently defunct American Basketball Association, couldn't seem to get going in Chicago. His tremendous size and massive salary made him an easy target for increasingly frustrated Bull fans.

Gilmore and his teammates improved as the season went along, but the Bulls were still mired at 24-34 with just six weeks to go. From then on, with Gilmore leading the way, they played like men possessed. When the Bulls started winning, it appeared that they might salvage some sort of respectability out of an otherwise wasted season. Then it became reasonable to hope for a .500 finish. Finally, it looked as if they might even make the playoffs.

The stirring stretch drive galvanized Chicagoans, who began turning out in droves for home games, and captured the attention of the national media. "Chicago is coming on like a fire truck," said Don Criqui of CBS. The climb culminated on April 8. It was a Friday night, and the largest crowd ever to witness a Bulls game at the Stadium—21,652—was on hand. Fans were in the usual standing-room-only spots, behind the last row of seats, but they were also standing or sitting in every aisle of the first and second balconies.

The Bulls had won 18 of their last 22, and they needed just one more to clinch the coveted playoff spot. The Houston Rockets were their opponents, and it was a thrilling contest from the opening tipoff. The Bulls surged to an early lead, but an 18-4 rally by the Rockets sent the two teams into the halftime break tied 51-51. The two smallest players on the court, Calvin Murphy of Houston and Wilbur Holland of the Bulls, had done most of the damage, with 18 and 15 points respectively.

In the third quarter, with Gilmore tying up Moses Malone to the extent that it was possible, Bulls guard Norm Van Lier repeatedly sprung forwards Scott May and Mickey Johnson on fast breaks. As the huge crowd roared its approval, May scored 10 points and Johnson nine in the quarter. The running game carried the Bulls to a 98-82 lead with only 7:55 remaining, but the Rockets wouldn't go quietly. Determined play by Malone and Rudy Tomjanovich inside the paint brought them to within four points in the final minute.

Johnson's 18-footer in the closing seconds finally settled the issue, and the Bulls prevailed 113-109. It had been a smashing performance by the Bulls' starting five, each of whom played between 35 and 45 minutes. The key was Van Lier's astute distribution of the ball; he finished with 18 assists while ensuring a balanced attack that saw Johnson score a game-high 27 points, May 22, Gilmore 19, and Holland 16.

The Bulls closed out the regular season with another win, their 20th in 24 games. Coach Ed Badger said that his players had come to "accept the fact that if they played the same way every night, we could beat anybody." Suddenly the unthinkable—a world championship—was being discussed by the same fans who had showered the Bulls with catcalls only weeks before. So hot and so confident were the Bulls entering the playoffs that it was actually plausible. But they were turned back in the first round by a team with superior depth, the Portland Trail Blazers, in an epic best-of-three series. When the Blazers went on to win the title, to a man they said that the Bulls had been their toughest foe of the playoffs.

July 31, 1977
"I Hope We Don't Wake Up"

"Don't worry about doing a budget," Bill Veeck told general manager Roland Hemond upon reacquiring the White Sox in 1976. "We don't have any money." The two soon unveiled their "rent-a-player" strategy for 1977. Using players who were in their last year before free agency—such as sluggers Richie Zisk and Oscar Gamble—or who were bargain-priced because of previous injuries, Veeck and Hemond transformed their hapless team into one of the most exciting in franchise history. Led by easy-going manager Bob Lemon, the White Sox became known as the South Side Hit Men and emerged as surprising contenders in the American League West Division. Their boisterous fans introduced two rituals that quickly caught on: dugout curtain calls after home runs and the serenading of departing enemy pitchers with "Nah-nah-nah-nah, nah-nah-nah-nah, hey hey, goodbye!"

The high point of that memorable season came on Sunday, July 31. A lively crowd of 50,412 turned out for a sun-drenched doubleheader with the defending division-champion Kansas City Royals. In the first game, Kansas City's Marty Pattin led 1-0 and held the Sox hitless until Chet Lemon homered in the bottom of the sixth. A homer by Amos Otis the next inning gave the Royals a 2-1 lead, which they held until the bottom of the ninth. With one out, Alan Bannister reached on a two-base error. Jorge Orta's single to right scored Bannister and sent the game into extra innings.

White Sox starter Steve Stone retired the first two Royal hitters in the top of the 10th before issuing back-to-back walks to George Brett and Joe Lahoud. Stone headed for the showers, and successive singles by Cookie Rojas and Al Cowens scored Brett, then Lahoud. Further damage was narrowly averted when first baseman Jim Spencer speared a line drive off the bat of John Mayberry for the third out.

With the Sox now trailing 4-2, Spencer led off the bottom of the 10th with a single to left. Royal manager Whitey Herzog summoned righthander Doug Bird to face Chet Lemon, whose homer had tied the game earlier. This time, Lemon fell behind in the count 0-and-2, then socked a long home run into the center-field bleachers, again tying the score and sending the crowd into a frenzy. This occasioned another of the curtain calls that opponents found so annoying. "It's bush [league] what they do," Hal McRae declared. "It's a disgrace to baseball." After the commotion had died down, Eric Soderholm coaxed a walk, reached second on a sacrifice bunt by Brian Downing, and scored on a base hit by Ralph Garr.

The stirring 5-4 win was the ninth in the White Sox' past 10 games. It put them 25 games over .500, at 62-37, and 6½ games in front of the second-place Royals. "If we're all dreaming," said Stone, "I hope we don't wake up."

The second game was also quite eventful. The teams exchanged several knockdown pitches, and as umpire Art Frantz informed them that no further shenanigans would be tolerated on the field, a fight broke out in the stands near the press box. The one-legged, 63-year-old Veeck waded into the fray to act as peacemaker and came away with a bloody lip. "It's a hot day," he said cheerfully, "but all *I've* had is iced tea." Most of the fans, of course, had quenched their thirst with something stronger.

A good time was had by all, but the White Sox lost the second game 8-4. "We took three out of four [for the series]," said Zisk. "I'll take it." As July gave way to August, the White Sox and the equally unlikely Cubs were both in first place. Unfortunately, neither was able to go the distance. The Cubs dropped out of first place a week into August and faded fast thereafter to finish 20 games out. The Sox held on a while longer, occupying first place until August 19, but eventually finished 12 games behind the Royals. Still, the South Side Hit Men won 90 games and set a new franchise attendance record.

Veeck's second stint with the White Sox featured softball-style uniforms with untucked shirts and no stirrups, a shower in the center-field bleachers, and the infamous Disco Demolition Night in 1979 which forced the Sox to forfeit a game. It was fun while it lasted, but Veeck's shoestring operation was on borrowed time. Veeck sold the Sox in 1981 and never set foot in Comiskey Park again. He became a regular in the center-field bleachers at Wrigley Field, perched between the ivy he himself had planted and the scoreboard he had built while working for the Cubs in the thirties.

November 13, 1977
A Wing and a Prayer

With their miserable first-half performance at Soldier Field on November 13, the Bears seemed to confirm that the 1977 season, like the previous 13, would be a lost cause. They had come in expecting to improve upon their 3-5 record at the expense of the Kansas City Chiefs, who were 2-6. But the Chiefs piled up a 17-0 lead before halftime, and the Bears were serenaded with a chorus of boos as they trotted off for the intermission.

A substantial portion of the crowd of 49,543 didn't come back after halftime. Fortunately, the Bears did.

Brian Baschnagel's 42-yard punt return early in the third quarter set the Bears up at Kansas City's 31-yard line. Then Walter Payton showed the stuff of which legends are made. Taking a handoff from Bob Avellini, he started around the right end only to discover his path blocked by the Chiefs' lateral pursuit. He reversed his field and went back the other way, still parallel to and well behind the line of scrimmage. Spotting a hole, he cut back up the middle and bounced off five would-be tacklers like a pinball before he was finally dragged down after an 18-yard gain. "That's one of the most incredible runs I've ever seen," Kansas City linebacker Willie Lanier said after the game. "I thought he was down, and the next thing I knew he was still running." On the replay, which is still frequently shown on highlight reels, Payton does indeed disappear amidst several Chiefs at one point—only to emerge seconds later, still churning forward.

The magnificent effort turned an apparent dead end into a first down, and several plays later Payton vaulted into the end zone for the Bears' first touchdown. When Payton scored on another one-yard plunge with 7:39 left in the fourth quarter, the Bears were back in the game.

A pass-interference call on Gary Fencik prolonged Kansas City's next drive, which culminated in a Jan Stenerud field goal. With 3:21 remaining and the Bears behind 20-14, it was time for Payton to shine again. He made a sensational catch of a pass from Avellini for a 29-yard gain, but was shaken up in the process. He sat out one play, then made a dazzling touchdown run from 15 yards out. Bob Thomas's extra point gave the Bears a 21-20 lead with 2:02 left. Payton, who had rushed 33 times for 192 yards and three touchdowns, was carried off the field on the shoulders of teammates Ted Albrecht and Jim Osborne.

But quarterback Mike Livingston coolly drove the Chiefs into field-goal range with less than a minute left. With the ball on their own 14-yard line, the Bears sent an all-out blitz in a last-ditch effort to force a turnover. Recognizing it, Livingston quickly took the snap and pitched to Ed Podolak, who swept around right end for a touchdown. Stenerud's extra point gave Kansas City a 27-21 lead with 24 seconds remaining.

A squib kickoff gave the Bears possession at their own 43. On the first play, Avellini connected with Robin Earl for 20 yards to the Chiefs' 37.

Now there were 10 seconds left—time enough for one play, maybe two. The Chiefs were in a prevent defense, with their cornerbacks and safeties stationed well downfield. Avellini had James Scott wide right, Bo Rather in the right slot, and Greg Latta wide left. He went back to pass. Seeing that Latta had somehow gotten loose behind the Chiefs' secondary, Avellini heaved the ball down the left sideline. "It's a prayer, really," he said after the game. "Just throw it up and hope he's back there." Latta sprinted under Avellini's pass and made a fingertip grab in full stride for a touchdown. Thomas's extra point put the Bears ahead 28-27 with three seconds left. After the formality of the ensuing kick-off, the game was over.

The few fans who had stuck around for one of the most improbable and thrilling victories in Bears history cheered lustily as the players left the field. Linebacker Don Rives, a target of the boo-birds earlier in the day, said, "I wonder what would happen if we ever won two in a row."

He was soon to find out. The Bears defeated Minnesota the next week, with the astounding Payton rushing for a single-game record 275 yards. "You Chicago people are spoiled by Payton," said Vikings coach Bud Grant. "He's a phenomenon."

The Bears won four more in a row after that, ending the season with a six-game streak that propelled them into the playoffs for the first time since 1963.

December 16, 1979
A Little Help

The final Sunday of the 1979 NFL season dawned with a bolt from the blue. George Halas, Jr., son of the legendary Papa Bear and a respected football executive in his own right, died suddenly at his home. He was just 54.

Linebacker Doug Buffone was the first Bear to arrive at Soldier Field and thus the first to receive the news. For Buffone, it would have been an emotional day even without the shocking loss of the likable man called "Mugs." He was suiting up for his 186th regular-season game in a Bears' uniform (the most in franchise history to that time) and also his last. He had already announced that his stellar 14-year career would end with the Bears' season.

The Bears were scrambling for a playoff spot. If they beat St. Louis and Tampa Bay lost to Kansas City, the Bears would be in as champions of the NFC Central. If Tampa Bay won, the Bears would have to beat St. Louis and hope that Washington lost to Dallas. To complicate matters, the Bears would also have to make up a 33-point deficit to the Redskins in the categories of points scored and points allowed.

The Bears ran up a 21-0 lead in the first half of their game with the Cardinals. While they were in the locker room for the intermission, they learned that their division title hopes were gone because Tampa Bay had defeated Kansas City 3-0. Now the Bears' only hope was for their margin of victory and Washington's margin of defeat to total 34 points or more.

The Cardinals scored early in the third quarter to cut the lead to 21-6, but they missed the extra point. When Rickey Watts ran the ensuing kickoff back 83 yards for a touchdown, the floodgates were opened, and it was all Bears thereafter. The defense was stifling, quarterback Mike Phipps was sharp, and Walter Payton was Walter Payton. Buffone even caught a pass for 22 yards on a fake punt (the first and last pass reception of his career).

The Bears outrushed St. Louis 201 yards to 90 and outpassed them 295 to 23. With 157 yards, Payton narrowly wrested the NFC rushing title from Cardinals rookie Ottis Anderson, who was limited to 39.

The final score of 42-6 could have been even more one-sided, but it was enough. If Washington lost to Dallas by even a single point, the Bears would be in the playoffs. Buffone was in tears as he took off his uniform, realizing that even if the Bears made the playoffs, he would not play again before the Chicago fans. "I never wanted to be anything except a Chicago Bear," he said. "I never could have asked for anything better than the support of these fans. They made me play better football."

Buffone and his teammates huddled in the locker room listening to the Redskins-Cowboys game on the radio. Dallas led 21-17 after three quarters, but Washington rallied to claim a 27-21 advantage early in the fourth. When John Riggins' 66-yard touchdown run gave the Redskins a seemingly insurmountable 34-21 edge with only 8:06 remaining, the Bears began to head out, one and two at a time, to their cars. They had done, in Buffone's words, "everything a football team could be asked to do"—but apparently to no avail.

The Redskins had the ball again and were attempting to run out the clock when a fumble gave the Cowboys possession at their own 41-yard line with 3:49 left. The Bears still left in the Soldier Field parking lot gathered together to listen on someone's car radio. Three Roger Staubach passes later, Dallas had closed to within 34-28.

On the next drive, Larry Cole stopped Riggins on third down in Washington territory. After the Redskins punted, the Cowboys took over at their own 25 with 1:46 remaining. Staubach, no stranger to miracle finishes, hit Tony Hill for 20 yards and Preston Pearson for 22. Suddenly the Cowboys were at Washington's 33. Staubach's next pass fell incomplete, but then he connected with Pearson for 25 yards. Now the ball was on the Washington eight-yard line. The Bears crouched around the radio with their arms around each other. No one spoke, no one moved.

Staubach found Hill for the touchdown that made it 34-34. The Bears erupted, embracing and pounding each other on the back. Then more suspense as they waited for Rafael Septien to attempt the extra point.

The kick was good. The Bears were in the playoffs, and Doug Buffone's retirement would have to wait.

CHAPTER 27

A Long Time Coming

"I coached 1,078 games at DePaul and had the players and the good fortune to win 724 of them. Anybody who coaches that long ought to be stuffed and put in a museum."

-- *Ray Meyer, DePaul University men's basketball coach, 1942-1984*

When Chicago native Ray Meyer signed on as DePaul University's basketball coach in 1942, he agreed to a one-year contract for the modest sum of $2,500. He turned down a three-year deal, he later explained, "because I didn't know if I'd like the job or the profession." His first agenda item was to turn the gangly, six-foot-10 freshman George Mikan into a basketball player. The two had met before, when Meyer was an assistant coach at Notre Dame (where he had been a member of the 1936 national championship squad). When the awkward, bespectacled Mikan tried out for the Irish, Meyer was not encouraging. "He said I was so uncoordinated I tripped over the lines on the court," Mikan recalled. Head coach George Keogan suggested that Mikan try a smaller school where he might get to play some. Mikan heeded the advice and enrolled at DePaul, only to find when he got there that Meyer had been hired in the meantime. "I thought, 'Oh, no, here we go again,'" said Mikan.

But if Mikan's lack of polish was a problem, Meyer now made it *his* problem and project. "I knew the value of the big man in basketball," he wrote. "He gets more points by accident than a little guy [does] on purpose." Every day after the team's regular practice, Meyer put Mikan through a grueling regimen of skipping rope, shadow boxing, jumping over chairs, playing catch with medicine balls and tennis balls, and, almost incidentally, dribbling and shooting a basketball. In one drill, Mikan would stand under the basket and make a layup with his right hand, then rebound and make a layup with his left, rebound and layup with his right, etc., etc., etc. Known as the "Mikan Drill," this routine has been used for virtually all big men ever since; among its adherents are Kareem Abdul-Jabbar and Shaquille O'Neal.

"Mikan was raw material with a little talent," Meyer wrote. "His greatest asset was the desire to improve, which made him willing to listen and work. You can measure height and even talent, but not heart. Mikan showed me in the beginning he had the heart to be great."

Meyer's patient tutelage transformed the Clark Kent look-alike into a Superman. Mikan learned to execute hook shots deftly with either hand and to rebound and block shots like no one else. In his first season at DePaul, he led the Blue Demons to a 19-5 record and an appearance in the NCAA tournament's semifinal round (which hadn't yet been labeled the Final Four).

In 1943-44, Mikan and DePaul advanced to the championship game of the National Invitational Tournament, which was then equivalent to the NCAA in prestige, before losing to St. John's to conclude a 22-4 campaign. Mikan was chosen national player of the year. The next year, DePaul won 18 of 20 regular-season games and marched through the NIT with awe-inspiring ease, crushing West Virginia 76-54, Rhode Island 97-53, and Bowling Green 71-54. In the semifinal game, Mikan nearly outscored the other *team*, settling for a "tie" with 53. He was selected most valuable player of the NIT and repeated as national player of the year.

Following the title game at Madison Square Garden, the Demons remained in New York for a contest with NCAA champion Oklahoma A&M and its six-foot-11 center Bob Kurland, Mikan's only rival as the finest player in the country. Although the event was technically an exhibition to benefit the wartime Red Cross, it was hyped as a national championship game. DePaul had beaten the Aggies 48-46 several weeks earlier, and the rematch was expected to be a barn-burner. Unfortunately, it became somewhat anticlimactic when Mikan fouled out with six minutes left *in the first half* and three other starters soon followed. DePaul lost 52-44.

After three seasons at DePaul, Mikan had become so outstanding that the rules were amended to diminish his dominance. It had been his custom to station himself under the opposition's basket and simply swat incoming shots away or even catch them in midair and fling them ahead to teammates for easy fast breaks. Goaltending was outlawed prior to the 1945-46 season, but the change seemed not to bother Mikan, who continued to shine. He scored 555 points in 24 games (the previous year he had tallied 558 points, also in 24 games) and played superb defense. Rebounds were not counted in those days, but Mikan's excellence in that area is well documented in contemporary accounts.

DePaul rolled to a 19-5 mark in 1945-46, winning its final six games by an average of 20 points. Despite this, the Demons were snubbed by both the NCAA and NIT. Meyer suspected that his harsh comments about the officiating in the previous spring's Oklahoma A&M game had gotten him and the Demons blackballed from both tournaments, but he never knew for sure. With no postseason opportunities forthcoming, the Mikan era at DePaul ended with a lopsided 65-40 victory over Beloit College in the regular-season finale on March 9, 1946.

Meyer began to face life without the man who would later be voted the greatest player of the first half of the century. "While he was around," Meyer wrote, "I was a great coach." For his part, Mikan said of Meyer, "I'd be nothing without him." The Demons had won 81 of 98 games in the four years and finished third, second, and first in their three postseason tournaments. Now Mikan was bound for greater glory in the pro ranks, while Meyer was destined for decades of obscurity. The 32-year-old coach would see his age double before he and DePaul returned to national prominence.

Fast forward to March 9, 1978. The Blue Demons have concluded their regular season with 12 consecutive victories and a No. 3 national ranking, and they are awaiting the start of the NCAA tournament. Fame, that fickle companion, has returned to Meyer after all these years. In the meantime, seven Presidents have occupied the White House, and Meyer has gone to work at DePaul day after day with no fanfare and little reward beyond the enjoyment he derives from coaching. He and his wife Marge have raised their six children, all of whom call him "Coach."

Since Mikan's departure, the Demons had made six appearances in the NCAA tournament and five in the NIT. They had also endured a stretch from 1967 to 1973 in which they won 74 games and lost 75. The

1970-71 team, captained by Meyer's son Joey, inadvertently became the catalyst for DePaul's return to glory. After the Demons struggled to a record of 8-17, the university responded to the debacle by giving Meyer a recruiting budget and allowing him to hire an assistant coach for the first time. There followed a procession of top-flight players to DePaul: forward Bill Robinzine in 1972; center Dave Corzine, guard Ron Norwood, and forward Joe Ponsetto in 1974; guard Gary Garland and forward Curtis Watkins in 1975; and guard Clyde Bradshaw in 1977.

Like their forerunners of three decades earlier, the 1977-78 Blue Demons were led by an outstanding big man. At six-foot-11 and 250 pounds, Corzine was more or less the same size as Mikan, and comparisons between the two became inevitable. Meyer considered Mikan to have been quicker and generally more athletic than Corzine, while rating both as exceptionally intelligent and competitive. "There is not a better shooting center in the country," Meyer said of Corzine. "He's a better outside shooter than Mikan was. George could take the ball inside, though, and I'd sure like to have him back. I'd move Dave to forward and find a way to keep both of them happy."

Of DePaul's 12 straight wins to end the regular season, the biggest one by any measure was the seventh, on February 12 at Notre Dame. The Demons came into the game at 19-2 and ranked 11th in the nation; the Irish were 16-3 and ranked fourth. This was the game that made people take notice of the resurgent Blue Demons. It was a tough afternoon for Corzine, who was suffering from the flu and was double-teamed every time he touched the ball. He managed 23 points and played the entire game, but it was DePaul's guards who made the difference in the end.

"The din in Notre Dame's Athletic and Convocation center," Bill Jauss wrote in the *Tribune*, "defied description." Regulation play ended with the score tied 61-61. Notre Dame led 68-63 with 90 seconds remaining in overtime when DePaul's little guys took over. Garland scored off a rebound to make it 68-65. Then Bradshaw stole the ball and took it in for a layup to make it 68-67. As the clock ticked down into the final seconds, Randy Ramsey stole the ball and fired it to Garland in the corner for an open 15-footer—which missed. Bradshaw fouled Rich Branning as the latter grabbed the rebound for Notre Dame, sending him to the foul line for a one-and-one with 10 seconds left. "I was sure I'd blown it," said Garland.

But when Branning missed the first free throw, Corzine secured the rebound. "I knew we were out of timeouts," he said. "I looked up court for the first person I could see open. There he was." *He* was Garland, streaking up court. Garland fielded Corzine's baseball-style pass, dribbled to the top of the key, pulled up and let fly. The shot hit, as they say, nothing but net. Almost simultaneously the buzzer sounded. DePaul had won 69-68. "I knew it was going in," said Garland, who had gone from goat to hero in 10 seconds. "I definitely felt it."

"We don't know when we're beaten," Meyer said proudly.

Exactly a month after their victory at Notre Dame, the Blue Demons opened the NCAA tournament against Creighton. Thanks to red-hot shooting, Creighton led by 20 points late in the first half and by 14 at halftime, but the Demons kept their composure and doggedly battled back. DePaul eventually won 80-78 on two free throws by the virtually unknown William Dise, who'd come into the game when Watkins fouled out. Corzine notched 19 points and 11 rebounds, but it was the unsung Ramsey, normally a defensive specialist, who sparked DePaul's comeback. Focused to the point of obsession on Corzine, Creighton's defenders paid no attention to Ramsey, whose scoring average was four points per game. "I told Randy to *shoot!*" said Meyer. After scoring his usual two points in the first half, Ramsey tallied 12 points after the intermission. "The best half he ever played," Meyer said. "Without Ramsey, we wouldn't have won."

Corzine was absolutely unstoppable in the next game as DePaul subdued Louisville 90-89 in double overtime. He made 18 field goals, almost all of which were within several feet of the basket, including the game winner with six seconds remaining. He also went 10-for-10 from the free-throw line. His 46 points gave him 1,879 for his career—nine more than Mikan's previous school record.

DePaul was now 27-2 and one win away from the Final Four. To get there, the Blue Demons would have to get past none other than Notre Dame. The rematch with Meyer's alma mater was a compelling story—more compelling, it turned out, than the game itself. Corzine had dislocated a finger in practice the day before; the injury contributed to his relatively pedestrian output of 17 points and particularly hindered his rebounding. Notre Dame's 22-8 surge early in the second half transformed a one-point game into a rout. The final score was 84-64. "We just didn't come back," said Meyer. "The way they rebounded on us, they just took everything away. The well just ran dry."

Corzine's college career, as well as Ponsetto's and Ramsey's, ended with DePaul's departure from the 1978 NCAA tournament. Unlike in 1946, however, when Meyer had faced the dismal prospect of going forward without Mikan, this time DePaul had another superstar waiting in the wings. He was Mark Aguirre, a chunky, six-foot-six scoring machine from Chicago's Westinghouse High School and perhaps the most coveted recruit in the country. "Mark was a symbol of the revival of DePaul basketball," Meyer wrote, "for he was the sort of player we would have had no chance to get in our darkest days just a few years earlier."

Aguirre was joined in the starting lineup by holdovers Bradshaw, Garland, and Watkins, and center James Mitchem. His debut on November 25, 1978, at UCLA showed that he was intimidated neither by all the national championship banners hanging from the rafters of Pauley Pavilion nor by the Bruins themselves. On the first play of the game, Aguirre dunked resoundingly over UCLA's All-American center David Greenwood. He finished with 29 points in a 108-85 loss. "He's just going to keep getting better and better," said Meyer. "It's awfully tough to come onto UCLA's home court for your opener, but it didn't faze Aguirre. I don't think the [Los Angeles] Lakers would have fazed him."

After the defeat at UCLA, the Blue Demons won their next four games by an average margin of 22 points. They lost at Wichita State, then won eight in succession. They gathered steam as the season progressed. After two narrow losses in January, the Demons won eight more in a row before hosting Notre Dame on March 2. A boisterous overflow crowd at Alumni Hall saw DePaul upset the No. 2-ranked Irish 76-72. Playing his final home game, Watkins scored 21 points while holding Notre Dame's leading scorer, Kelly Tripucka, to eight. "You turn on the faucet and expect water to come out," Meyer said. "You put a uniform on Watkins and expect so many points and so many rebounds."

DePaul opened the 1979 NCAA tournament with wins over USC and Marquette, setting up a rematch with UCLA in Provo, Utah, on March 17. From the opening tip, the Demons showed that they were not the same team the Bruins had dispatched in November. Because Mitchem could not handle Greenwood by himself, DePaul abandoned its customary man-to-man defense in favor of a zone. "We have a very active zone," explained assistant coach Joey Meyer. "The guards go out to cover the passing lanes and make steals." Indeed, the quickness, athleticism, and general relentlessness of DePaul guards Bradshaw and Garland proved overwhelming as the Blue Demons built a 17-point lead by halftime.

After the intermission, Meyer and the Blue Demons were somewhat mystified when they emerged from the locker room to a thunderous standing ovation. They later learned that in returning to the floor themselves, the UCLA team had disrupted the performance of a dance troupe from Brigham Young University, which was hosting the game. The previously neutral crowd fervently cheered DePaul's every move from then on and might have helped the Demons withstand a frantic rally by UCLA in the closing minutes. The Bruins narrowed the gap to two points before Garland's layup with 10 seconds left decided the outcome. DePaul won 95-91, with the two seniors Garland and Watkins each tallying 24 points. "Now, when I walk down the street," Meyer said, "people will stop asking, 'Coach, where's DePaul?' Pretty soon, everybody will know."

DePaul was in the Final Four, and Meyer was becoming a favorite of even casual fans. His craggy, expressive face, gap-toothed grin, and ample midsection made him unmistakable either in person or on television. He was portrayed in the media as an affable, cuddly old grandpa, and his aw-shucks demeanor in interviews reinforced this impression. If he resented that he was just now being discovered by most of the audience, he never let on.

In their national semifinal game in Salt Lake City, the Blue Demons discovered why Larry Bird was the college player of the year and, not coincidentally, why Indiana State was undefeated. DePaul battled gamely throughout, and even took a one-point lead with 1:37 remaining, but Bird simply would not be beaten. The blond, six-foot-nine wizard hit 16 of 19 shots, grabbed 16 rebounds, and had nine assists as the

Sycamores prevailed 76-74. Between his 35 points and the assists, Bird was directly involved in 70 percent of his team's scoring. (Indiana State lost the championship game to Michigan State, in the first Chapter of the legendary rivalry that Bird and Earvin "Magic" Johnson continued in the NBA for a dozen more years.)

DePaul was at the peak of its success and notoriety for the next few years. The Blue Demons were arguably more popular than the Bulls in this pre-Jordan period. Meyer was now a beloved elder statesman, basking in the respect of opponents, fans, and the media; he was elected to the Basketball Hall of Fame in 1979, only the fourth active coach to be so honored. Aguirre proved to be the genuine article; his career output of 2,182 points and average of 24.5 per game dwarfed those of Corzine and Mikan, and he was the first player chosen in the 1981 NBA draft. Virtually every DePaul game was now televised, and a crowd of reporters followed the team even on the road. The Demons left the cozy 5,500-seat Alumni Hall at Belden and Sheffield, moving to the Rosemont Horizon, which held 18,000. The trickle of prize recruits coming to DePaul became a torrent. Whereas Meyer's previous teams had carried the aura of gritty underdogs with perhaps more heart than talent, the new Demons were a bunch of thoroughbreds.

For the 1979-80 season, Garland and Watkins were gone, but even so DePaul was loaded as never before. Aguirre, Bradshaw, and Mitchem were back, and Meyer had also landed guard Skip Dillard, forwards Teddy Grubbs and Bernard Randolph, and a real keeper, forward/center Terry Cummings. One that got away was the brilliant guard Isiah Thomas, who backed out of a verbal commitment to Meyer, enrolled at Indiana, and led the Hoosiers to the national championship in 1981.

The Blue Demons won their first 25 games before losing in double overtime at Notre Dame. They beat Illinois State to end the regular season with a record of 26-1 and a No. 1 ranking.

When DePaul lost 77-71 to UCLA in the first NCAA tournament game, it was the start of a wrenching and uncanny string of postseason failures. The next year, DePaul again lost only once during the regular season but bowed out in the first tournament game. And the *next* year, incredibly, it happened yet again.

The Demons lost only one regular-season game in each of the three years, compiling a record of 79-3. They were in 0-3 in the NCAA tournament over the same period. As the pattern repeated itself, it was heartbreaking not only for Meyer and his players but also for so many people in Chicagoland and across the country who were rooting for them. "I don't believe in jinxes," Meyer said. "We'll just have to try again."

Time was running out on Meyer's hopes for a national championship. He went through a transition in 1982-83, with the mainstays of recent years having departed. Most notably, Cummings had opted out of his senior season and joined the NBA, as Aguirre had a year earlier. The Blue Demons managed a 17-11 record in the regular season and did not qualify for the NCAA tournament. They settled for the NIT instead, winning four times before losing to Fresno State in the championship game.

It was understood that Joey Meyer would succeed his father when the latter retired, and this created a difficult situation for both men. Ray did not want to outlast his usefulness or to stand in his son's way, and Joey did not want to look as if he were pushing his father out the door. Some years earlier, Ray had told Joey that he would retire at the age of 70. Joey assumed that Ray would change his mind when the time came, but now Ray confirmed that he was sticking to the decision. He was not at all sure that he was ready, but he had given his word. For Ray Meyer, that was all there was to it.

Ray turned 70 on December 18, 1983. The 1983-84 season thus became his farewell tour, and he received gifts and other honors at almost every stop on the schedule. His team's performance was also a gift—the Blue Demons won their first 17 games. They lost to St. Joseph's (the same team that had upset them in the 1981 tournament), then beat Notre Dame and Loyola in Meyer's final meetings with those two old rivals. They split a home-and-home series against Dayton, another venerable Catholic-school rival, and ran the table thereafter, concluding the season with a triumph over Marquette and a sparkling record of 26-2.

DePaul opened the NCAA tournament against Illinois State on March 18 in Lincoln, Nebraska. The possibility that Meyer's illustrious career would end with yet another one-and-done was almost too excruciating to contemplate. It hung thickly in the air before the game but, fortunately, evaporated soon after the tip-off. The Blue Demons cruised to a 75-61 victory, DePaul's first NCAA tournament win since 1979. Although that particular monkey was off Meyer's back, the rest of the story did not adhere to the script. In the second tournament game, DePaul fell behind Wake Forest 2-0 and never trailed again until the overtime period. In the meantime, the Demons saw an eight-point edge disappear in the final two minutes of regulation. They missed free throws, threw passes out of bounds, and astonishingly, with a two-point lead and 26 seconds left, tried an alley-oop play that went awry. Wake Forest won 73-71. "I feel sad for the kids, not myself," Meyer said with typical graciousness. "It wasn't the way I planned to end my career."

It was sad that Meyer would not advance further in his final tournament and would never realize his dream of a national championship. It was also regrettable that the Blue Demons had allowed themselves to lose to a lesser opponent simply by their lack of poise and concentration in the clutch. In this respect, their exit from the tournament was identical to those in 1980, 1981, and 1982; only the specific details were different.

"This was a bitter defeat," said Joey Meyer, "but it doesn't take anything away from Coach's career." Ray Meyer's son and successor was prejudiced, of course, but he also was right. The accomplishments of four decades and the goodwill that Ray had earned in the process far outweighed the pain of the moment.

Joey took up the torch and carried it for 13 years as DePaul's head coach. When the Blue Demons trotted onto the court on November 17, 1997, it was the first time since March 4, 1942, that they had done so without Ray or Joey Meyer at the helm. In between, they'd taken the floor 1,467 times and had come away with a victory 955 times.

CHAPTER 28

How the West Was Won

"Their bubble has got to burst. They're not playing that well. They're winning ugly."

-- *Doug Rader, Texas Rangers manager, referring to the 1983 White Sox*

When he made an offhand comment about the White Sox, "They're winning ugly," Texas Rangers manager Doug Rader unwittingly created the South Siders' rallying cry for the 1983 season. The most successful Chicago baseball campaign in almost a quarter century began with the White Sox ugly, but not winning. They dropped the first three games of the season at Texas and in the process lost veteran reliever Jim Kern for the year with an elbow injury. In the home opener against Baltimore, starting pitcher Floyd Bannister was touched for seven runs in less than two innings, and the Sox lost 10-8. They finished April with a lackluster record of 8-10, and they were 12-12 on May 8 when *Sun-Times* columnist Ron Rapoport wrote them off. "It seems axiomatic," Rapoport intoned, "that if a month into the season a team does not have a shortstop, does not have a third baseman, does not have a center fielder, then no matter what its assets may be it forfeits its right to call itself a contender."

Shortstop Scott Fletcher, a rookie, was hitting .244 and struggling defensively. Third baseman Vance Law was hitting .204 with four runs batted in. Center fielder Rudy Law was hitting .217 with three runs batted in. These three were the main objects of Rapoport's disdain, but first baseman Mike Squires was mired at .186, with one RBI, and catcher Carlton Fisk at .169, with five RBIs. Among the pitchers, supposed aces Bannister and LaMarr Hoyt were 2-8 between them, with earned-run averages over 5.00.

After Rapoport's analysis appeared, the White Sox promptly lost eight of their next nine games to fall to 13-20. On May 26, with one quarter of the season completed, they were 16-24, seven games out of first place in the American League West. They had been shut out five times and had mustered only one run on seven occasions. By then, the buzzards were circling manager Tony LaRussa. The Sox' predominantly blue-collar fans had never warmed up to the fastidious LaRussa, and they showered him with boos every time he emerged from the dugout. "It's important to stay positive," said LaRussa, "but we've been struggling long enough."

LaRussa constantly tinkered with his lineup, trying to discover the right formula. "There has to be something I can do to help us get going," he said. "I've got to keep searching until I find it." Scott Fletcher and Vance Law began sharing time with journeyman Jerry Dybzinski and rookie Lorenzo Gray, respectively (neither of whom fared much better). Squires was relegated to late-inning defensive duty, while the lefty-righty platoon of Greg Walker and Tom Paciorek took over first base. Fisk was moved up to second in the batting order. Rudy Law, thankfully, had improved to .280 and stolen 16 bases. And no changes were contemplated in right field, where steady Harold Baines was stationed, or in left, where rookie Ron Kittle was among the league leaders in both home runs and RBIs.

As May gave way to June, the White Sox were still south of the .500 mark. A doubleheader sweep at Oakland on June 12 halted a four-game losing streak and probably saved LaRussa's job. On June 13, the Sox opened their longest homestand of the year with a 7-4 loss to California. The subsequent trade of solid second baseman Tony Bernazard to Seattle smacked of desperation and drew howls of protest, but newcomer Julio Cruz provided the lift that LaRussa had been looking for. The little Brooklyn native was an acrobatic fielder and daring baserunner whose enthusiasm sparked the ballclub.

On June 26, designated hitter Greg Luzinski launched a home run onto the left-field roof, and righthander Richard Dotson pitched creditably for six innings in 100-degree heat as the White Sox defeated Minnesota 9-7. "I was definitely relaxed," said Dotson, who had seen a hypnotist before the game. When asked if he too would consider undergoing hypnosis, LaRussa smiled and said, "I'd hate to give my many fans that much ammunition." The South Siders had won nine of 12 on the homestand to go over .500 for good. Their 36-34 record was mediocre to be sure, yet the Sox were within striking distance of the tepid pace set by the division-leading Rangers.

Comiskey Park hosted the All-Star Game on July 6, 50 years to the day since the inaugural midsummer classic at the same site. Ron Kittle was the home team's lone representative. The White Sox were 40-37 at the break, 3½ games behind Texas and 1½ behind California. They opened the second half with just four wins in nine tries at home against Milwaukee, Cleveland, and Toronto before Bannister handcuffed the Blue Jays on July 17. "He pitched like the Floyd Bannister I remember," said Fisk after the lefthander no-hit Toronto for six innings en route to a 3-2 decision. Bannister, a pricey free agent acquired the previous winter, had now won two in a row since closing the first half at 3-9. "That's in the past," he said of his early-season woes. "I want to look to the future."

The future to which Bannister and his teammates looked was bright. Although they'd managed just five wins and five losses on the homestand, the White Sox left town only half a game behind the skidding Rangers. 24 hours later, they were in first place. Fisk drove in four runs as Hoyt and Salome Barojas secured a 5-3 win at Cleveland. The Sox split two more games with the Indians, then lost three of four at Milwaukee to slip back into a first-place tie with Texas. On July 25 at Toronto, Dotson beat Dave Stieb and the Blue Jays 7-4; it was only the second defeat for Stieb in 10 career decisions against the White Sox. The following night, lefty Britt Burns was bombed for the third straight outing as the Sox lost the first game of a doubleheader. "Something's wrong," LaRussa said, "but you'll have to ask Burns for an explanation." In the second game, the bottom of the batting order, Fletcher and Cruz, combined for five hits and ignited two rallies as the Sox won 4-3 behind the pitching of Bannister and Dennis Lamp. Lamp, recently appointed chairman of LaRussa's bullpen by committee, had saved each of the Sox' last three victories. The road trip concluded with a 16-hit assault on Toronto pitching that produced an 11-3 victory for Hoyt. Fletcher rapped three hits, while Fisk, Baines, and Kittle all homered. "Awesome!" said Cruz. "I'm just happy to be with these guys."

Despite a lukewarm 11-10 mark since the All-Star break, the White Sox had gained six games in the standings. "We were second, half a game out, when we left home," LaRussa noted. "And we're coming home with a two-and-a-half game lead. It wasn't a bad trip." The Sox returned home to host the Yankees in a weekend series that stirred memories of their great rivalry two and three decades before. New York had won eight of its last nine, and was one of five East Division clubs that were 10 or more games over .500. Venerable Comiskey Park was packed to the rafters and at its maximum decibel level as fans demonstrated both their love for the first-place White Sox and their long-nurtured hatred of the Yankees. A total of 172,264 witnessed the four games, a new record for the old ballyard.

On Friday night, July 29, 40-year-old Jerry Koosman, the White Sox' very useful fifth starter, sailed to a 7-2 win aided by Fisk and Luzinski home runs. The next night, Dotson was in complete control as the Sox won 5-1. On Sunday, Burns was knocked out in the second inning; the Sox battled back from three different deficits before losing 12-6 in the 11th. This lively contest featured the ejection of New York's colorful manager Billy Martin early on. "[Umpire] Dale Ford doesn't know the rulebook," Martin said afterward, "and I'll bet you $100 he can't even read! All the rulebook is good for is to take along on a deer hunt."

In the series finale on Monday, August 1, Luzinski smashed a pair of two-run homers that provided all the offense Bannister needed for a tidy 4-1 victory. The first of these blows bounced on the roof, caromed off a light tower, and finally ended its journey back on the playing field. "The Bull" thus became the first player in Comiskey Park's long history to hit two rooftop home runs in the same season. Before him, only Jimmie Foxx and Ted Williams had ever hit two such shots in a career; 16 others had done it once.

The White Sox next took two of three from Detroit, then traveled to Baltimore. On August 5, former Cub Randy Martz made his first and only start of the season, replacing the slumping Burns. Martz pitched well enough, but the Orioles got to Lamp for three runs on five straight singles with two outs in the bottom of the ninth to win 5-4. The White Sox showed their resilience the next night. Back-to-back homers by

Baines and Luzinski and four hits by the surging Fisk carried Bannister to a 6-4 triumph. It was the Sox' first win after 10 consecutive defeats in Baltimore, and they enjoyed the experience so much that they repeated it the following afternoon. Luzinski and Paciorek knocked in two runs apiece, Cruz and Vance Law each made sparkling defensive plays, and Hoyt won 4-3. "They look like a rejuvenated team from the last time we played them [in May]," said Orioles manager Joe Altobelli. "They've covered a lot of ground to build up a good lead." The Sox' record of 58-50 would have placed them sixth in the crowded East race, five games behind Baltimore. In the West, however, it was good for a four-and-a-half game advantage over Kansas City.

Four days later, on August 11, the White Sox again faced the Orioles, this time at Comiskey Park. They had won two of three at Detroit in the meantime. Bannister dispatched Baltimore 9-3 in the series opener for his seventh consecutive win. The next night, Hoyt went the distance and subdued the Orioles 2-1 before a throng of 45,588. "He has courage, heart, guts," LaRussa said of the burly, bearded righthander who'd overcome a 2-6 start and now led both leagues with 15 victories. "There's no telling how many wins I can get," said Hoyt, "if I keep on pitching the way I have been."

Baltimore won the next two games to salvage a split of the series, and the Sox headed to New York. On August 15, Britt Burns got the starting assignment; he had spent two weeks in the bullpen after a string of poor performances. He made his return to the rotation a memorable one, tossing a complete-game, three-hit shutout at the Yankees and winning 1-0. After the game, Burns attributed his recent troubles to distraction and depression lingering from his father's death, which still haunted him after almost two years. "Tony LaRussa is the greatest manager in the major leagues," he said, "because he understood I had to deal with this problem. I have come to grips with it during the last few weeks, and I feel now like I have put it aside and can go on with my life."

The confident White Sox whipped New York 9-3 behind Bannister the next night, then completed the sweep with a 7-5 victory in 13 innings on August 17. In the latter, Rudy Law hit an inside-the-park home run, Barojas pitched three and a third scoreless innings, and the light-hitting Squires doubled home the winning run.

The two series against the Yankees bookended a stretch in which the White Sox won 14 of 20 against the reputedly superior East Division. Since the All-Star break, the Sox had played 41 consecutive games against Eastern foes, winning 25. They had built up a six-game lead over Kansas City, eight over Oakland and Texas, and nine over California. These would-be contenders in the West were as close as they were going to get. They'd had their chances earlier, while the White Sox were spinning their wheels. Now they were about to be steamrolled.

If Doug Rader and the Rangers entertained any thoughts of getting back into contention, they were squashed on Friday, August 19, when the White Sox swept a doubleheader in Texas. In the first game, Dotson pitched into the 10th inning, allowing just six singles and no walks, as the Sox prevailed 3-2. In the nightcap, Jerry Hairston started in left field in place of Kittle, who was slumping, and contributed two hits and two RBI's, while the unlikely Dybzinski rapped his first and only homer of the season. The Sox won 6-1, providing Koosman with the 200th victory of his career. They split the next two games to make it three out of four for the series. The Rangers, who had been in first place just a month before, were now 10 games behind the White Sox.

Then it was on to Kansas City, where the Sox all but eliminated the Royals by taking two of three. In the first game, Julio Cruz broke a 1-1 deadlock in the eighth with a two-run homer, his first round-tripper since joining the White Sox. Hoyt yielded just five singles and no walks in going the distance, and the Sox won 3-1. After losing the next night, the Sox closed out the series with a win that was perhaps the epitome of ugly. Baines was on first base and Rudy Law on third with one out in the top of the 10th when the slow-footed Kittle hit an apparent double-play ball to shortstop, but lumbered down the line just in time to beat the relay throw while Law crossed the plate with what proved to be the winning run. The Sox won 4-3, and the Royals were nine games out.

When the Sox returned to Comiskey Park on August 25 for a weekend series against Boston, they faced the pleasing fact that 21 of their next 26 games would be at home. Boston's 3-1 win Friday night was noteworthy in that it marked Bannister's first loss after nine consecutive victories. Saturday night, 43,556 saw Hoyt make Kittle's two-run homer stand up for a 2-1 win. On Sunday, Luzinski homered twice and Baines once as the Sox coasted to a 6-2 decision.

Texas came to town next, and Rader tried, somewhat clumsily, to clarify his earlier comments about the White Sox winning ugly. He was well aware that he had created a catchphrase, for it was staring back at him from T-shirts and handmade signs at Comiskey Park and around town. "Look, I didn't mean anything bad by that," Rader said. "I mean, nothing's really bad about winning no matter how it's done." The White Sox swept the two-game series, 2-1 and 5-0, then did the same to Kansas City in unequivocal fashion, 7-3 and 12-0. In the latter win over Kansas City, Hoyt twirled a complete-game four-hitter and, as usual, walked none. (For the year, he would average just over one walk per nine innings and rack up almost five times as many strikeouts as walks.)

It was September 1, the traditional date on which pennant races are supposed to enter the stretch drive. The "race" in the American League West was over. The Royals left town tied for second place, 11½ games behind the Sox.

Such was their situation at this heady time that the White Sox dropped two of three at Boston and still gained ground in the standings! They came home on Labor Day 12 games in front. After they swept three from Oakland and four from California, the margin was 16½, and the champagne was on ice.

A split of two games at Minnesota set up a four-game series at home against Seattle. On September 15, Hoyt blanked the Mariners 12-0 for his 10th consecutive win and 21st of the year. Luzinski, Kittle, and Vance Law each knocked in two runs, and Baines accounted for four with a grand slam. The next night, Baines broke a scoreless tie with a solo home run in the seventh inning, and the Sox added six runs in the eighth for good measure. Bannister struck out 12 in pitching a two-hitter, and no Mariner reached second base. The Sox won 7-0 to reduce their "magic number" to one. One more White Sox win *or* Kansas City loss would clinch the division title.

With his team's startling turnaround of the past 90 days about to reach its climax, LaRussa was in an introspective mood. "All I can hope for," he told Bob Verdi of the *Tribune*, "is that someday I'll earn the benefit of the doubt. That when I go out to change pitchers, maybe the people will say, 'Well, maybe he knows what he's doing.' Do you have to be 16 games up or win your division before you get that? I don't know."

On Saturday night, September 17, 45,646 passed through the turnstiles to push the White Sox' season total over two million (it was the first time that either the Sox or Cubs had achieved that figure). Koosman gave up an unearned run in the first, then settled down and pitched seven scoreless innings. The Sox scored single runs in the third and fourth, and when Baines cracked a home run in the bottom of the eighth to give them a 3-1 lead, the fans were beside themselves. But Seattle scored twice in the top of the ninth to put the party on hold.

In the bottom of the ninth, Hairston led off by lining out to pitcher Bill Caudill. Then Caudill walked the bases full—first Cruz, then Rudy Law, then Fisk. The ballpark, of course, was in an uproar. The unflappable Baines moseyed up to the plate; he was perhaps the only person involved who was unimpressed by the electricity in the park or the gravity of the moment. Lefty Ed VandeBerg replaced Caudill, and Baines lofted his first offering to medium-deep center field. It was deep enough to score Cruz standing up. The White Sox were division champions.

During the clubhouse celebration, LaRussa sought out a man whose confidence in him and support for him had never wavered. He enveloped general manager Roland Hemond in a bear hug. "I never lost faith in this team," said Hemond. "And I never lost faith in the manager."

Winning, ugly or otherwise, had become the White Sox' habit. They suffered no letdown after clinching the title. Although it wasn't strictly necessary, they beat Seattle again the next day for their 17th straight win at home. They went on to win 10 of the remaining 13 games to close the season at 99-63, an even 20 games ahead of the second-place Royals.

Here's how the West was won. The White Sox lost 32 of their first 59 games, then lost only 31 more for the rest of the season. Against their division foes, the Sox were 55-23 for the season and 31-6 in the second half. After the All-Star break, their top starting pitchers (Hoyt, Dotson, and Bannister) were a combined 42-5. After July 31, the Sox were 46-15. After August 26, they were 29-6 and never lost as many as two in a row. In their last 20 home games, they were 19-1.

All this, alas, did not prevent the Baltimore Orioles from defeating the White Sox in the American League Championship Series. The Sox had scored more runs than any other team in the majors during the season, but their bats fell silent against the Orioles. After Hoyt's 2-1 win at Baltimore in Game 1, the Sox scored only one more run in the series. In Game 4 at Comiskey Park, they had two on with nobody out in the seventh inning when Dybzinski failed to execute a sacrifice bunt, hitting into a forceout instead, and then committed a *faux pas* on the basepaths that led to the second out. Baltimore wriggled out of the inning with no damage done, and the game remained scoreless. Burns pitched heroically before yielding a home run to Tito Landrum with one out in the 10th. Agosto gave up two more runs, and that was that. The White Sox lost 3-0.

"I could see we were going to break out and start hitting again," LaRussa said sadly, "but we ran out of time. The series wasn't long enough for us to get it going." Nor was the series long enough for the White Sox to get LaMarr Hoyt onto the mound again. "No way did I want to see Hoyt tomorrow," said Baltimore's Ken Singleton. The Sox were convinced that Hoyt, who had not lost since July 23 and was soon to receive the Cy Young Award, would have won Game 5 for them—if only they had gotten there. The Orioles were content to leave the question open.

CHAPTER 29

"The Good Lord Wants the Cubs to Win"

"I don't give a damn about what happened in 1969. It has no interest or appeal to me at all."

-- Jim Frey, Cubs manager, 1984-1986

As the Cubs prepared for the 1984 season, there was little reason to suspect that it would be much different from the past 38 campaigns— each of which had ended with the Cubs finishing somewhere below first place (usually *far* below) and excluded from postseason play. The Cubs were entering the third season of Dallas Green's controversial administration as general manager, which had so far produced back-to-back records of 73-89 and 71-91.

Green's bluster and bombast had made him an easy target of critics who ridiculed his slogan "building a new tradition," pointing out that the Cubs' dreary performances in 1982 and 1983 indicated no departure from the same old story. "They all knew better than me what the Cubs needed," Green later remarked, "but nobody made an effort to find out what I was really like or how I work."

Those fans who *were* inclined to believe that Green's program was on the right track could not have been encouraged by the Cubs' 11-game losing streak in spring-training games; at one point the team's Cactus League record was an atrocious 3-18. When the regular season got going, though, so did the Cubs. At first, their unfailingly loyal and patient followers were relieved merely to find that the Cubs weren't as bad as in previous years. But they soon realized that "not bad" needn't be good enough in 1984.

March 27. The Cubs trade relief pitcher Bill Campbell and minor-league catcher Mike Diaz to the Philadelphia Phillies for left fielder Gary Matthews, center fielder Bob Dernier, and relief pitcher Porfirio Altamirano. "I can't see Bobby Dernier coming in and taking my job," says incumbent center fielder Mel Hall. "I don't think he qualifies, gentlemen." Nonetheless, the promising Hall is relegated to part-time duty. The deal also forces Leon Durham to first base, where he supplants the Cubs' best and most popular player of recent years, Bill Buckner.

Green, former Philadelphia manager, takes heat for his ever-growing collection of ex-Phillies, which now numbers 11 on the 25-man roster—including five of the eight everyday starters: left fielder Matthews, center fielder Dernier, right fielder Keith Moreland, shortstop Larry Bowa, and second baseman Ryne Sandberg. Skeptics nickname the Cubs "Phillies West," but Green is unconcerned. These players, in his estimation, are "gamers" who won't accept losing.

The trade turns out to be a monumental coup for Green. Dernier provides superb defense and joins with Sandberg at the top of the batting order to form a fleet-footed duo that jump starts the Cubs' offense. Matthews, a grizzled veteran known as "the Sarge," emerges as the Cubs' inspirational leader both on the field and in the clubhouse.

April 13. In the home opener at Wrigley Field, the Cubs host the only team in the National League that was worse than they were in 1983—the New York Mets. The Cubs' 11-2 victory, then, entertaining as it is, does not seem particularly meaningful. No one knows yet that the two clubs will be the top contenders for this year's East Division title.

April 24. At St. Louis, the Cardinals' ace reliever Bruce Sutter, unscored upon in 12 innings for the year, takes the mound in the top of the eighth with a 2-1 lead. Sandberg greets him with a double (the first hit of his young career against the former Cub), and later scores on a single by Durham. In the ninth, Richie Hebner blasts a line-drive homer to right, giving the Cubs a 3-2 lead, and Lee Smith nails down the save. The Cubs move into first place at 10-6. "First place!" says Durham. "We're in first place. That sounds awesome." Manager Jim

Frey is less impressed. "I think the only thing we've got to be excited about," he remarks, "is the game tomorrow afternoon."

May 24. The Cubs subdue the Atlanta Braves 10-7 and 7-5 at sun-kissed Wrigley Field for their first doubleheader sweep since 1980. In the first game, Dernier goes five-for-five, Hall and catcher Jody Davis hit home runs, and Durham belts a pair of three-run homers—"taters," in his lingo. In the nightcap, Davis clouts another homer to go with a three-run blast by third baseman Ron Cey. The Cubs have won six in a row and eight of their last nine. Their 16-4 start at home is the best since 1907, before the Friendly Confines existed. "For me," says Atlanta pitcher Pascual Perez, "I hate this team and this park." The Cubs are 26-15 overall and lead the division by two games over the Phillies.

May 25. Buckner is traded to the Boston Red Sox for righthanded pitcher Dennis Eckersley. The 34-year-old "Billy Buck" has spent more than seven years on the North Side and was National League batting champion in 1980. Although he has batted just 43 times in 41 games this year and made no secret of his displeasure, Buckner is still sorry to leave. "This is a very tough moment for me," he says.

Eckersley, 29, insists that his recent shoulder problems are behind him. "This year I'm throwing the ball better than the last year and a half," he says. His 24 starts for the Cubs between now and the end of the season will bear this out, and his ferocious competitiveness will enhance the burgeoning confidence of his teammates.

May 30. The Cubs have lost four straight when Steve Trout, the flaky lefthander called "Rainbow," holds Atlanta hitless for the first seven and two-thirds innings and Chicago wins 6-2. "With any luck at all, Rainbow's got a no-hitter," Frey says. "He was outstanding. With all our injuries to pitchers, we needed that."

The Cubs cling to a half-game lead over Philadelphia. Despite their success to this point, starting pitching remains a weakness. But Dallas Green has one more trick up his sleeve.

June 13. Green deals Mel Hall and three minor-leaguers (including future star Joe Carter) to the Cleveland Indians for starting pitcher Rick

Sutcliffe, reliever George Frazier, and backup catcher Ron Hassey. Regarding the 23-year-old Hall, Green asks the news media, "Who's going to talk about Lou Brock?" It is an unsubtle reference to the disastrous 1964 trade in which the Cubs gave up a future Hall of Famer for a broken-down pitcher supposedly in his prime.

Fortunately, Hall proves to be no Lou Brock. More importantly, Sutcliffe proves to be no Ernie Broglio. The towering righthander will be a tower of strength for the rest of the year. He will lose just *one* game between now and October, and will receive the National League's Cy Young award (becoming the first man to win the award after switching leagues so late in the season).

June 17. The Phillies beat the Cubs 9-7 to complete a four-game sweep at Wrigley Field that has reversed the teams' positions in the standings. The Cubs have gone from first place to third, two games behind Philadelphia. The surprising Mets remain in second place. The Cubs have slipped to only five games above .500 at 34-29.

June 23. On this sunny Saturday afternoon, Wrigley Field is packed to the rafters and a national television audience is tuned in. Sandberg is already three-for-four with four RBIs when he comes up to bat against the Cardinals' Sutter in the bottom of the ninth with the Cubs trailing by a run. Sandberg cracks a game-tying home run into the left-field bleachers.

The Cardinals waste no time in bringing the faithful back to reality; they score twice in their half of the 10th. Surely Sutter, a former Cub and future Hall of Famer, will not let another lead slip from his grasp. There are two outs and a man on when Sandberg's turn comes around again. Sutter can now redeem himself by closing out the game against the same man who extended it an inning before. Broadcaster Bob Costas announces that St. Louis's Willie McGee, who has hit for the cycle, is NBC's player of the game.

After all he has done, Sandberg finds himself in a position to make the last out. Incredibly, he blasts another home run over the left-field wall. Pandemonium reigns. It is the first (and last) time that anyone touches Sutter for two homers in the same game. Costas sheepishly mentions that he might need to rethink his choice for player of the game.

The Cubs finally win in the 11th inning on a base hit by reserve infielder Dave Owen. Sandberg, a budding star who heretofore has toiled in relative anonymity, ends up five-for-six with seven RBIs on the day. "The Sandberg game," as it comes to be known, catapults Ryno into his first All-Star Game and sends him on his way to the Most Valuable Player award.

July 5. "Sanderson's back, Cubs romp." The second word of this *Tribune* headline serves as both a verb and a noun: Scott Sanderson returns after being shelved by a sore back for five weeks, and he handcuffs the Giants 9-3. It is just the 10th start of the season for the fragile righthander, but he will be sturdy enough to make 13 more appearances down the stretch. Thanks to Sanderson's improving health, Trout's increasing reliability, and the acquisitions of Sutcliffe and Eckersley, opening-day starter Dick Ruthven now rates but fifth in the rotation, while erstwhile ace Rick Reuschel, a noble warrior, is reduced to mop-up chores. For the first time in many years, the Cubs possess genuine depth in the pitching department.

The season is exactly half over. The Cubs are 46-35; they lead the Mets by one game and the Phillies by two.

July 27. Dwight Gooden stifles the Cubs 2-1 in the opener of a critical four-game series at New York's Shea Stadium. Since being bombed in Chicago on April 13, the 19-year-old phenom has emerged as the most overpowering pitcher in the league. The Mets, 16-3 since midseason, have surged to a four-and-a-half game lead over the Cubs in the division race. Cubs fans wonder whether their heroes are embarking on another of the second-half swoons that have become so familiar since 1969. It seems an ominous sign that it is the Mets, of all teams, who threaten to quash the Cubs' hopes. As they did 15 years ago, the upstart New Yorkers have become instant contenders after finishing far back in recent years.

July 28-29. These Cubs are for real. Saturday night's game is tied 3-3 in the bottom of the seventh when Durham makes a sensational diving catch of a sinking liner and turns it into an inning-ending double play. The Cubs then score *eight* runs in the top of the eighth and roll to an 11-4 triumph.

On Sunday, the Cubs use just three pitchers and take barely four hours to win twice, 3-0 and 5-1. In the first game, Trout yields seven hits and no walks while going the distance for his first shutout of the year. Sanderson hurls seven and two-thirds solid innings in the nightcap before giving way to Smith, who retires the last four Mets hitters without incident. Davis calls two masterful games behind the plate and also knocks in four of the Cubs' eight runs.

The Cubs could have fallen all the way to seven and a half games out of first place in these two days. Instead, they leave New York only a game and a half behind. "I've been saying these games aren't that important," Frey says, "but it's getting a little late to be saying that now, isn't it?"

August 2. The Montreal Expos have men on first and third with one out in the ninth inning and the Cubs ahead 3-2 when Pete Rose smacks a line drive up the middle that appears certain to tie the score. But the ball hits Lee Smith in the shoulder and caroms right into the hands of shortstop Owen, who fires to Durham, catching the runner off first and completing an amazing double play to end the game. Broadcaster Harry Caray, not one to conceal his feelings in any case, is truly beside himself. "Cubs win, Cubs win!" he bellows. "Holy cow, the Cubs win! Oh, the Good Lord wants the Cubs to win!"

Rose, who has played over 3,300 games in his 23-year career, maintains that he has never seen such a play. Cubs fans call it the Immaculate Deflection. "When I saw that play happen," Durham says, "I just figured this has to be our year." The Cubs are back on top, a game and a half in front of the Mets.

August 6. The Mets trail the Cubs by only half a game when they invade Wrigley Field for a four-game series. The pennant race is heating up, and the atmosphere at the old ballpark is electric. The Cubs send a message in the series opener, bombarding Gooden for six runs in the first three innings en route to an easy 9-3 triumph. Davis drives in four runs with a prodigious 430-foot home run, a double, and a sacrifice fly.

"We weren't flat today," New York first baseman Keith Hernandez says. "They just whipped our butts."

August 7. Even the most wary of Cubs fans are forced to believe after a doubleheader sweep leaves the Mets scratching their heads and groping for answers. There is no denying anymore that the Cubs are, as Hernandez admits, "the team to beat."

In the first game, Moreland clubs a three-run homer in the fifth, erasing a 4-2 deficit and propelling the Cubs to an 8-6 win. "I would say that his hit was a very large one," says Frey, always a master of understatement. "Sutcliffe was struggling, and then Keith gives us all new life with one like that." Sutcliffe earns the victory, his seventh straight and ninth in 10 decisions since joining the Cubs. His ex-Cleveland teammate George Frazier picks up the save.

In the second game, reserve outfielders Henry Cotto and Thad Bosley combine for seven hits and three runs as the Cubs win again, 8-4. The fourth inning features a 20-minute brawl when Moreland charges New York pitcher Ed Lynch after being hit by a pitch. "I just went out there to get my point across," the former University of Texas linebacker says. "It's part of the game of baseball." Sanderson retaliates in the fifth, drilling Met third baseman Kelvin Chapman; Sanderson is ejected and thus doesn't get credit for the win, but he and his teammates are showing that they won't back down to anyone.

"Right now," says New York second baseman Wally Backman, "the Cubs have to feel like every time they go on the field, they can beat us." Chapman is more succinct. "We're getting the snot kicked out of us," he declares.

August 8. Moreland carries the day with three hits and four runs batted in; he now has 18 hits and 15 RBIs in his last 34 at-bats. He drives in a run in the first and two in the fifth, each time with two outs. In the seventh, he knocks in the run that proves decisive as the Cubs come from behind to win 7-6. The extracurricular activities continue: New York's Walt Terrell is ejected for hitting Dernier in the head with a pitch, Lee Smith is tossed for narrowly missing George Foster's chin, and several Mets attempt to climb into the stands after fans behind the dugout shower them with beer.

When it's all said and done, the Cubs have won their last seven games against New York and 12 of their last 14 overall. They have gained nine games on the Mets in 12 days. They are 68-45 for the season, and their lead has ballooned to four and a half games.

August 28. The Cubs are on cruise control. Moreland's three-run homer in the first inning of the first game ignites a doubleheader sweep of the Cincinnati Reds before another packed house at Wrigley Field. The stocky redhead is as hot as the weather—he also wallops a triple, two doubles, and a single, and collects six RBIs for the day. Eckersley and Ruthven pitch creditably as the Cubs win each game 5-2. Later, it is revealed that, in their excitement, Moreland, Davis, Bosley, Durham, and Sandberg have violated Matthews' rule prohibiting "high-fives" before the seventh inning. Matthews smilingly waives the requisite fines, but he admonishes the offenders not to let it happen again. "We just don't want to show anybody up," the old pro reminds his teammates.

September 14. "I'm running out of adjectives to describe Sutcliffe." So says Frey after Sutcliffe and Davis deliver the coup de grace to the Mets on a gloomy afternoon at Wrigley Field.

The Cubs already lead 3-0 in the sixth when New York manager Davey Johnson orders Cey intentionally walked to load the bases for Davis. While pitcher Brent Gaff executes the walk to Cey, the crowd of 32,403 takes up what has become a familiar chant in the Friendly Confines: "Jo-dee! Jo-dee! Jo-dee!" After Cey takes his base, the chanting increases, and Davis smashes Gaff's first offering into the bleachers in left-center field for a grand slam. The fans are delirious. Happy days are here again.

Sutcliffe scatters eight hits in going the distance, and the Cubs win 7-1. Chicago's advantage over the Mets is now a gaudy eight and a half games with only 14 games remaining on the schedule. "We're all trying to stay under control here," Frey says, "until someone comes in here and tells us we've won it."

September 24. During this Monday night game in Pittsburgh, a group of Cubs fans unfurls a banner that reads 39 YEARS OF SUFFERING ARE ENOUGH. By the end of the game, the suffering is over. Sutcliffe pitches a complete game, yielding but two hits, and strikes out Joe Orsulak to finish off the Pirates 4-1 and secure the Cubs' first championship since 1945. It is fitting that the "Red Baron" is on the mound when the magic moment comes, for the moment would not have come without him. Sutcliffe has now won 14 in a row and is 16-1 with the Cubs. He is only the second pitcher since 1904 to win 20 games while splitting a season between the two leagues (the other was Hank Borowy, who played an uncannily similar role for the 1945 Cubs).

"This is only perfect," Dernier says in the Cubs' champagne-soaked clubhouse. "It doesn't get any better than this."

Meanwhile, the curmudgeonly Frey vents the emotions he has kept in check all season. "We got the monkey off our backs!" he cries. "For seven months, we've been hearing about 1969 and the wind and the sun and the ivy and the moon. But it's over. It's over!" A newcomer to Chicago, Frey seems not to quite understand the intensity of Cubs fans or their morbid fascination with the heartbreak of 15 years ago. "Every time we lost two games in a row this year," he says, "30 guys would come into the clubhouse asking if we were about to fold. Well, we weren't and we didn't."

September 30. The Cubs score twice in the bottom of the ninth to defeat Sutter and the Cardinals 2-1 in the regular-season finale at Wrigley Field. The Cubs finish 96-65, six and a half games in front of New York. The Cubs won 46 games in the first half of the season and 50 in the second half; the Mets won 45 in each half.

After the game, Cubs fans release four decades' worth of frustration. They refuse to stop cheering long after the players have adjourned to the clubhouse. The ovation goes on and on, until finally the Cubs return to the field to bask in the adulation. "I was undressed in the clubhouse drinking a cup of beer," says Durham. "But I got dressed and went back out to see the fans. I had to get me some of that." The Cubs and their fans take the opportunity to thank each other for an unforgettable season.

Somewhere there exists a perfect ending to the story of the 1984 Cubs, but it was not the ending that fate selected.

The National League Championship Series between the Cubs and the San Diego Padres opened at Wrigley Field on October 2. The first game had Cubs fans pinching themselves—the Cubs swatted five home runs and obliterated the Padres 13-0 for the most lopsided shutout in postseason history. The next day, the Cubs eschewed the long ball in favor of aggressive base running, sparkling defense, and stingy pitching to record a crisp 4-2 decision. As the series shifted to San Diego, the Cubs needed just one more win to qualify for the World Series. That win never came.

CHAPTER 30

The Early Jordan

"Michael Jordan is the truth, the whole truth, and nothing but the truth."
-- *Caldwell Jones, Bulls center, 1984-1985*

The first NBA game that Michael Jordan saw in person, he played in. It was at Chicago Stadium on Friday, October 26, 1984. At one point in the second quarter, Jordan was soaring to the hoop for a dunk when the Washington Bullets' bruising center Jeff Ruland leveled him. Welcome to the NBA. Jordan landed on his neck and lay motionless while the crowd of 13,913 fell silent. Teammate Orlando Woolridge took off after Ruland, but Jordan himself later acknowledged that Ruland had only been trying to block the shot and had had no malevolent intent. Jordan got back to his feet, stayed in the game, and finished with 16 points, seven assists, six rebounds, and four blocked shots.

The star of the game was Quintin Dailey, who scored 25 points (including 12 in the fourth quarter) to lead the Bulls to a 109-93 win, but when it was over the media people were all clustered around Jordan. "I've got a sore neck and a big headache," he said. "I'm going to bed." Then he added, "This was a good start for my career." No one would know for several more years that it was the start of one of the greatest careers in the history of professional sports.

Jordan first came to the attention of basketball fans nationwide as a 19-year-old freshman at the University of North Carolina. In the final game of the 1982 NCAA tournament, the Tarheels—led by James Worthy and Sam Perkins—faced the Georgetown Hoyas and their intimi-

243

dating seven-foot center Patrick Ewing. The game more than lived up to its advance billing.

North Carolina trailed 32-31 at halftime and, after a second half in which neither team led by more than four points, 62-61 with less than a minute remaining. Tarheel coach Dean Smith called a timeout with 32 seconds left, and most in the Louisiana Superdome crowd of 61,612 (not to mention the television audience of tens of millions) believed that he would draw up a play for Worthy, an All-American who had three years of pressure games under his belt. Instead, Smith turned to Jordan and said, "Knock it down, Michael."

Jordan worked himself free to the left of the lane, took a pass, and, with 17 seconds left, attempted a jump shot from 16 feet. It was perfect. "I was all kinds of nervous," he said after the game, "but I didn't have time to think about doubts. I had a feeling it was going to go in."

The victory was sealed when Georgetown's Fred Brown, looking out of the corner of his eye, mistook Worthy for a teammate and threw him the ball with five seconds left. North Carolina's 63-62 win gave Smith his first national championship after several near misses.

By 1984, his third year at North Carolina, Jordan was the finest college basketball player in the nation. He declared himself eligible for the NBA draft. Bulls general manager Rod Thorn loved him, but whether the Bulls got him or not would depend on a coin flip. They had lost a coin flip with the Los Angeles Lakers for Magic Johnson five years before and had been in the doldrums ever since. This time Bulls held the third pick, while the Houston Rockets and Portland Trail Blazers were to flip for the top pick.

The key to the equation for the Bulls was that Portland was committed to the idea of drafting a big man. By consensus, center Hakeem Olajuwon of the University of Houston was the top center available. If the Blazers won the flip, they would take Olajuwon, and the Rockets would probably take Jordan. But if the Rockets won the flip, they would take Olajuwon and the Blazers would take the next-best big man, Sam Bowie of Kentucky.

How different the history of basketball would have been if Portland had won that coin flip! For one thing, the Bulls would have six fewer world championships to their credit. But Houston won the flip and drafted Olajuwon, and Portland chose the injury-plagued Bowie, leaving Jordan for the Bulls. "Nobody, including me, knew Jordan was going to turn out to be what he is," Thorn said later. "We didn't work him out before the draft, but we interviewed him. He was confident. He felt he was gonna be good. It was obvious that Michael believed in himself, but even he had no idea just how good he was going to be."

Before joining the Bulls, Jordan played for the United States in the 1984 Olympic Games in Los Angeles. Among his teammates were Sam Perkins and Patrick Ewing, who had played with and against him, respectively, in the NCAA championship game of 1982. Although coach Bobby Knight ran a highly structured offense that limited his opportunities to improvise, Jordan nonetheless made an impression with his gravity-defying athleticism. "Sometimes the players get into the habit of just watching Michael," said Steve Alford, "because he's usually going to do something you don't want to miss." With the Soviet Union and its satellites boycotting the Games, Jordan and the U.S. team easily won the gold medal.

The Olympics made Jordan a household name. When he appeared in the Bulls' training camp afterwards, head coach Kevin Loughery said to assistant Bill Blair, "Let's have a scrimmage and see if Michael's as good as we think he is."

"Michael took the ball off the rim at one end," Blair remembered, "and went to the other end. From the top of the key he soared in and dunked it, and Kevin says, 'We don't have to scrimmage anymore.'"

"We saw his skills," said Loughery, "but you've got to be around him every day to see the competitiveness of the guy. He was gonna try to take over every situation that was difficult. He was gonna put himself on the line. He enjoyed it."

Loughery had a habit in practice of splitting the Bulls into two squads and playing a game up to 10. Invariably, whichever team had Jordan would win. One time Jordan's team was ahead 8-0 when Loughery made him switch sides. "Michael was furious," trainer Mark Pfeil said. "He scored the first nine points himself, and his team won."

During his rookie year, Jordan's growing fame rubbed some people the wrong way. In the 1985 All-Star Game, Detroit's Isiah Thomas de-

245

cided to freeze Jordan out of the Eastern Conference's offense by simply refusing to pass the ball to him. In 22 minutes in the game, Jordan managed only nine shots. The Bulls and Pistons were scheduled to meet in the first game after the break, and by this time the All-Star snub had become a *cause celebre*. Jordan scored 49 points and pulled down 15 rebounds in leading the Bulls to an overtime victory. The moral of the story: it doesn't pay to make Michael mad.

Jordan was already known as the most exciting player in the world when he suffered a broken foot in the third game of his second year with the Bulls. He missed 64 games, then returned just in time to help the Bulls eke out the last playoff berth. The closing weeks of the regular season presented an interesting spectacle, as new general manager Jerry Krause imposed strict limits on how many minutes Jordan could play in each game. "I was scared to death," Krause explained. "I didn't want to go down in history as the guy who put Michael Jordan back in too soon." Meanwhile, Jordan kept begging coach Stan Albeck to let him play more. "I didn't want to watch my team go down the pits," he said. "I thought I was healthy enough to contribute something."

In the first round of the playoffs against the Boston Celtics, Jordan contributed something. He scored 49 points in Game 1, but the Bulls lost 123-104. In Game 2, he sank two free throws (his 53rd and 54th points of the game) to send the game into overtime. Then he scored seven more points in overtime, including a three-point play that gave the Bulls a 125-121 lead with 1:39 left. Two baskets by Boston forced a second overtime. Late in the second session, Jordan dunked over Robert Parish—giving him 63 points for the game, a new playoff record, and tying the game yet again. But despite his heroics, the Celtics finally prevailed 135-131.

Jordan had scored 104 points in two games against a team that was being touted as the best of all time. "I didn't think anyone was capable of doing what Michael has done to us the past two games," said Boston forward Larry Bird. "He is the most exciting, awesome player in the game today. I think it's just God disguised as Michael Jordan." But this one man, as great as he was, could not beat a great team by himself. This lesson would take a while for Jordan and the Bulls to absorb.

The Bulls entered the 1986-87 season with a starting lineup consisting of Jordan and Steve Colter at guard, Granville Waiters at center, and Earl Cureton and Charles Oakley at forward. It was "Michael and the Jordannaires." In the season opener at New York, Jordan scored the Bulls' last 18 points to carry them to a 108-103 come-from-behind win. His 50 points for the game were the most ever scored by a visiting player in Madison Square Garden. "I've never seen anything like Michael Jordan," said his new coach, Doug Collins. "Ever."

That year Jordan scored 40 or more points 28 times, 50 or more six times. He logged a record 1.4 million votes for the NBA All-Star Game and won the league's slam-dunk contest. In late February, he scored 58 points against New Jersey to best Chet Walker's single-game Bulls record by two. A few days later, he blitzed Detroit for 61 in an overtime win before over 30,000 fans at the Silverdome.

Jordan not only won his first scoring title in 1986-87, but he also became only the second man in NBA annals to score more than 3,000 points in a season (the first, Wilt Chamberlain, had done it twice). Michael's 37.1 average was the highest ever recorded by anyone other than Chamberlain.

After winning 30 games in 1985-86 and 40 in 1986-87, the Bulls—fortified by the addition of rookies Scottie Pippen and Horace Grant—turned the corner in 1987-88 and won 50 games. Jordan played at a rarefied level indeed: he led the league in scoring and steals, an unprecedented combination. The game's most potent offensive force was voted Defensive Player of the Year. Not surprisingly under the circumstances, he won his first Most Valuable Player award.

It was clear by now that Jordan was a unique phenomenon in the history of the NBA. He was the first and only man at the relatively small size of six-foot-six who could so thoroughly dominate a game at both ends of the court. Prior to this time, only giants—Chamberlain, Bill Russell, Kareem Abdul-Jabbar—had been thought capable of such a thing.

In the spring of 1988, Jordan and Charles Oakley were ringside at the Mike Tyson-Michael Spinks fight in Atlantic City when another spectator ran up and told them that Oakley had been traded to the New York Knicks for Bill Cartwright. "I was pretty upset about the deal," said Jordan, "and also to have to find out about it that way." It was the first time, but not the last, that Jordan openly criticized one of Jerry Krause's personnel moves.

"Michael really didn't know Bill Cartwright as a person," Krause recalled. "Michael made Bill prove himself. Michael did that with everybody. That was Michael's way. I told Bill, 'Michael's gonna drive you crazy.' Bill said, 'He ain't gonna do nothing to me.'"

"What made the trade so tough," assistant coach Johnny Bach said, "was that Michael looked at Oakley as a protector. Charles was ready to fly into any tangle. You hit Michael, you had to face Charles. But Bill toughened up the big guys we had, and, in his own quiet way, Bill became very much of a terminator. Things stopped at the basket." With Cartwright anchoring their defense, the Bulls became legitimate contenders.

In 1989, Jordan joined John Elway in infamy among Cleveland fans. In January 1987, Elway had guided his Denver Broncos 98 yards in the waning minutes of the AFC championship for a game-winning touchdown against the Browns. The effort went down in history as The Drive. Jordan's contribution to Cleveland lore was called The Shot.

The Cavaliers had improved steadily in Lenny Wilkens's three years at the helm, and in 1988-89 their young nucleus of Brad Daugherty, Ron Harper, Larry Nance, Mark Price, and John "Hot Rod" Williams carried them to a 57-25 record, second best in the NBA. They came into their first-round playoff series with the Bulls eager to avenge their elimination by Chicago the year before.

The Bulls, 47-35 for the regular season, were clearly on the rise but not yet regarded as a powerhouse. They scored an upset in Game 1 of the series at Cleveland, 95-88. The Cavaliers won Game 2 at home, and the Bulls won Game 3 at the Stadium. In Game 4, also at the Stadium, Cleveland stayed alive with a tough 108-105 win in overtime.

The teams returned to Cleveland for the fifth and deciding game. The Cavaliers had reason to be optimistic, for they had gone 37-4 at home during the regular season, winning 22 in a row at one point. It would be a tall order for the Bulls to win on Cleveland's home court for a second time in the same series.

Game 5 was an epic struggle in which the lead changed hands repeatedly throughout the fourth quarter, including six times in the last three minutes. Finally, with the Bulls trailing by a single point in the closing seconds, Brad Sellers inbounded the ball to Jordan in the frontcourt. Jordan was guarded by Craig Ehlo, a top defender and his shadow throughout the series. Jordan dribbled a step or two to his left, just inside the top of the key. The clock ticked down to three seconds, then two. Jordan went up for a jump shot. Preferring to take his chances on a shot from 17 feet out rather than to put Jordan on the free-throw line, Ehlo tried to contest the shot as closely as possible without fouling. He leaped high with his arm outstretched to disrupt the shot. Nance moved in to help him, too late.

Jordan appeared to hang in the air just long enough for Ehlo to fly into and then out of his way. Then he released his shot. It hit nothing but net. Time expired as the ball went through the hoop, and the Bulls had eked out a 101-100 victory. "I don't see how he stayed in the air that long," said Daugherty. "It's the most outstanding shot I've ever seen."

By the end of the eighties, there was no doubt that Jordan was the most electrifyingly entertaining player ever seen, but before people began to consider the possibility that he might also be the *best* ever seen, he would have to lead his team to the championship. It was often pointed out that Magic Johnson and Larry Bird elevated the play of their teammates, while Jordan seemed to be playing for himself. "I think there came a point where he understood his greatness was going to be defined by winning," said teammate John Paxson. "That's why I saw a change in his real commitment to winning championships and, to that end, dealing with teammates and getting guys he felt comfortable with, that were able to play with him. It was really the understanding that championships mean a lot, when it comes down to who's the greatest."

In 1989, Phil Jackson's first move as the Bulls' new head coach was to install an offensive scheme designed by Tex Winter called the triple-post, or triangle. It was a system that relied on ball movement and cutting rather than on set plays—and it was the key, Jackson believed, to turning Michael and the Jordannaires into a real team. "Usually coaches have to coax their star player to produce more," Jackson wrote; "in a way, I was asking Michael to produce less. How much less, I wasn't sure."

The triangle enabled Jordan to carry a somewhat reduced share of the load. His teammates became more involved, less inclined to stand around and watch him. "You ran cuts," said Jackson. "You did things off the ball. People were cutting and passing and moving the basketball. And it took the focus away from Michael, who had had the ball in his hands a lot, who had been a great scorer. That had made the defenses all turn and face him. Suddenly he was on the back side of the defenses, and Michael saw the value in having an offense like that."

"It took some time," Paxson said. "Michael was out there playing with these guys, and unless he had a great deal of respect for them as players, I think he figured, 'Why should I pass them the ball when I have the ability to do the job myself? I'd rather rely on myself to succeed or fail than some of these other guys.' The thing I like about Michael is that he finally came to understand that if we were going to win championships he had to make some sacrifices individually."

As Pippen and Grant matured and he came to trust in their abilities, Jordan grew to appreciate the triangle as a great system—except when it came down to crunch time. He still believed, for the most part, that the fourth quarter was his.

"Every now and then Michael would break loose and take over a game," Jackson wrote. "But that didn't bother me as long as it didn't become a habit. I knew he needed bursts of creativity to keep from getting bored, and that his solo performances would strike terror into the hearts of our enemies, not to mention help win some key games."

By 1990, the Bulls were knocking on the door. Jordan was better than ever (he had worked tirelessly to make his jump shot as devastating as his crowd-pleasing flights above the rim) and his supporting cast had become *very* good. Cartwright, admiringly nicknamed "Teach" by Jackson, was a calming influence in the locker room and on the court. He was an intimidator in the paint whose flying elbows were notorious throughout the league. Pippen and Grant—the "Dobermans," as Bach called them—had improved enormously on both offense and defense. Paxson and B.J. Armstrong harassed rival ballhandlers and were deadly when left alone on the offensive end. Their ability to hit the open shot prevented defenses from collapsing on Jordan with impunity.

The Bulls sailed through a 55-27 regular season, going 27-8 over the last two months. On March 28, against Cleveland (the team he invariably destroyed), Jordan scored 69 points for a career high. He captured his fourth consecutive scoring title and led the league in steals for the second time. The Bulls easily subdued Milwaukee and Philadelphia in the first two rounds of the playoffs and advanced to the Eastern Conference finals against Detroit. They split the first six games with the defending world champions, each team winning three times on its home floor.

The decisive Game 7 was at the Palace of Auburn Hills. It was, said Jackson, "my worst moment as a Bull." Paxson was out with a badly sprained ankle, Grant was a bundle of nerves, and Pippen was suffering from a migraine headache. Pippen went to trainer Mark Pfeil before the game and said he couldn't see. "Can you play?" asked Pfeil. As Pippen started to say no, Jordan interrupted: "Hell yes, he can play. Let him play blind." Pippen did play, but he was ineffective as Detroit jumped out to a big lead in the first half. The Pistons coasted to a 93-74 win and went on to claim their second straight championship.

It was a tough loss for Jordan and the Bulls, but the future was still bright. "I just knew we would win the next year," owner Jerry Reinsdorf said. "We had gotten close, and you could sense that we were going to beat them."

The loss to the "Bad Boys" in Auburn Hills marked the end of Jordan's early period and signaled a turning point for the Bulls as well. If the Bulls got another shot at the Pistons the next year, they vowed, the outcome would be different. "These guys are kicking our butt, taking our heart, taking our pride," Jordan said. "I made up my mind right then and there it was never going to happen again."

On the wings of the man known as Air Jordan, the Bulls were about to soar to heights which could hardly be imagined.

CHAPTER 31

Men Against Boys

"If it was a prizefight, they'd have to stop it."
-- *Dick Enberg, NBC broadcaster, speaking during Super Bowl XX*

In the first weeks of 1986, Chicago was transformed. The bronze lions guarding the Art Institute wore Bears helmets. The Picasso sculpture in Daley Plaza was decked out in a Bears jersey. Sir Georg Solti led the Chicago Symphony Orchestra in a rousing rendition of "Bear Down, Chicago Bears," while the black-tie audience clapped and stomped along. Chicagoans had caught Super Bowl fever.

The Bears' journey to Super Bowl XX in New Orleans had actually begun more than a year before, in the 1984 NFC championship game. The San Francisco 49ers ended Chicago's best season in two decades with a decisive 23-0 victory at Candlestick Park. As the teams were leaving the field, 49ers safety Ronnie Lott called out, "Next time, bring your offense."

The Bears entered the 1985 season with Lott's taunt ringing in their ears. "I don't know about you guys," coach Mike Ditka said on the first day of training camp, "but second best isn't good enough for me." The Bears believed they were ready to advance to another level, but there were some questions to be answered. Could their vaunted "46" defense, the finest unit in the league, withstand the loss of safety Todd Bell and defensive end Al Harris to salary holdouts? Could their quarterback, the tough and savvy Jim McMahon, stay healthy long enough to realize his potential? Could their featured running back, the great Walter Payton (already the NFL's all-time leading rusher), continue to perform with his usual brilliance for an 11th season? Could they go all the way with the youngest team in the NFL—whose 45 members included 24 with two years' experience or less, 10 of them rookies?

Week by week, the Bears turned every question mark into an exclamation point.

September 8. In the season opener at Soldier Field, McMahon completes a career-high 23 passes in 34 attempts and rushes for two touchdowns as the Bears roar back from a 28-17 halftime deficit to beat Tampa Bay 38-28. "I didn't recognize the Bear defense [in the first half]," says safety Gary Fencik, "and it had nothing to do with Todd or Al. Everybody was not playing well." What neither Fencik nor anyone else knows yet is that the Bears will allow so many points only once more in the next 18 games.

September 15. New England spends a total of 11 seconds in Bear territory, quarterback Tony Eason is sacked six times and intercepted three times, and the Patriots rush for just 27 yards. Middle linebacker Mike Singletary accounts for three of the sacks and one of the interceptions. "Singletary was great as usual," Ditka says. The Bears win 20-7, but McMahon and Payton are banged up and have little time to recuperate before a Thursday night contest at Minnesota.

September 19. McMahon doesn't start because a combination of ailments has kept him out of practice. Steve Fuller is at quarterback for the first two and a half quarters. "I was in Ditka's ear most of the time about putting me in," McMahon says later. "Steve wasn't playing all that bad; we just needed a spark." The Bears are trailing 17-9 with 7:22 left in the third quarter when McMahon enters the game. On his first play, at the Bears' 30-yard line, McMahon stumbles taking the snap, regains his footing, then sees that the Vikings' linebackers are blitzing. "What I also saw," he recalls, "was Willie Gault running free down the middle, so I just unloaded it to him, and it was a 70-yard touchdown."

After a Wilber Marshall interception, McMahon fires a 25-yard touchdown pass to Dennis McKinnon. He has now taken two snaps and thrown two touchdowns.

On the next possession, McMahon completes passes to Ken Margerum and Gault to move the Bears from their own 32 into Minnesota territory. Then he finds McKinnon streaking downfield for a 43-yard touchdown. There are 33 seconds remaining in the quarter, and the Bears now lead 30-17.

In less than seven minutes, McMahon has completed five of seven passes for 166 yards and three touchdowns, all on improvised plays that bear little resemblance to what Ditka has called. The Bears win 33-24. "The guy, I can't explain," says Ditka. "I don't know what he sees or how he sees what he sees."

September 29. Washington leads 10-0 early in the second quarter when Willie Gault takes a kickoff and returns it 99 yards for a touchdown. By halftime, the Bears are ahead 31-10. After Gault fires the first shot, Chicago's second-quarter blitzkrieg features three more touchdown drives consuming a *total* of nine plays. One of these culminates in a 13-yard touchdown pass from Payton to McMahon on that favorite sandlot play, the Statue of Liberty. Redskin quarterback Joe Theismann is pressed into service as an emergency punter and manages a boot of one yard. It's that kind of day: what is supposed to be a showdown between postseason contenders becomes a 45-10 rout for the Bears. "I don't know what happened out there," Ditka marvels. "We've tried to emphasize what a team can do—offense, defense, and kicking team—and today I think you saw the picture."

October 6. At Tampa Bay, Payton scores the 100th and 101st touchdowns of his career and Emery Moorehead catches eight passes for 114 yards (the biggest day ever for a Chicago tight end other than Ditka) as the Bears win 27-19. The winless Buccaneers again put up a good fight, but the Bears overcome a 12-point deficit for their fourth come-from-behind win in five games. McMahon recovers from a shaky start to find Moorehead in several key situations late in the game. Tackle Jimbo Covert says, "We kept plugging away, plugging away, plugging away."

October 13. Payback time for the 49ers. The Bears bring their offense, which is now the most potent in the league at 31.5 points per game. McMahon comes out winging (27 of Chicago's first 37 plays are passes), and the Bears open up a 16-0 lead early in the second quarter. By halftime the 49ers close to within 16-10, but the Bears soon quash any thoughts of a comeback. San Francisco manages but three first downs and 45 total yards in the second half. Defensive tackle Steve McMichael manhandles All-Pro guard Randy Cross and terrorizes quarterback Joe Montana, who's sacked seven times in all.

Payton rushes for 88 of his 132 yards in the second half as the Bears rely on the ground game to hold the lead. As the clock winds down on the 26-10 victory, Ditka inserts defensive tackle William "Refrigerator" Perry at fullback, and the 325-pound rookie carries twice for four yards. What begins as a way to tweak the 49ers for using guard Guy McIntyre in the backfield in the '84 title game ("I have a long memory," Ditka says) will spawn a national phenomenon almost overnight.

After the game, 49er coach Bill Walsh is asked to describe the Bear defense. "Use any adjective you want," he says. "I'll say it was intense and ferocious. They gave us a good, sound beating."

October 21. Monday Night Football comes to Soldier Field, and Perry becomes a household name. The Fridge lines up in the backfield at the Green Bay goal line three times: twice he steamrolls linebacker George Cumby to clear the way for Payton touchdowns, and once he scores himself from a yard out. After trailing 7-0, the Bears cruise to an easy 23-7 decision. Their fearsome pass rush knocks two Packer quarterbacks, Lynn Dickey and Randy Wright, out of the game with injuries.

October 27. The Bears intercept five passes (linebacker Otis Wilson runs one of them back for a touchdown) and Payton rushes for 118 yards on just 19 carries in a 27-9 win over Minnesota. At 8-0, the Bears are the only remaining undefeated team in the league.

November 3. The greatest rivalry in the NFL reaches a new low. In the first quarter, Green Bay cornerback Mark Lee runs Payton out of bounds and all the way over the bench; Lee is ejected. Several plays later, Matt Suhey is standing around the pile when safety Ken Stills levels him long after the whistle. "I don't mind that," Packer coach Forrest Gregg claims. "That's aggressive football."

"By the end," says Bears safety Dave Duerson, "there was something going on every play. Let's face it, it wasn't clean on either side." It is left to Walter Payton to raise the Bears up from the mire. His 27-yard touchdown run in the fourth quarter gives them a 16-10 win. Payton gains 192 yards on 28 carries, but is nearly overshadowed by the continuing saga of William Perry—who catches a touchdown pass from McMahon.

November 10. Payton rushes for 107 yards and Suhey 102 as the Bears roll over Detroit 24-3. With McMahon sidelined by a bad shoulder, backup quarterback Steve Fuller and the Bears play "keep away" from the Lions, starting the game with 21 consecutive running plays.

Chicago's offensive linemen (center Jay Hilgenberg, guards Mark Bortz and Tom Thayer, tackles Jimbo Covert and Keith Van Horne, and tight end Tim Wrightman) completely dominate the line of scrimmage; the Bears control the ball for over 41 minutes.

November 17. One for the books. The Bears annihilate Dallas 44-0 for the worst defeat in Cowboys' history. Even Ditka is amazed. "Our defense, what can you say?" he asks. Richard Dent, Dan Hampton, Wilber Marshall, and Otis Wilson are everywhere—the Bears come in waves that make it look as if they are playing with more than the requisite 11 men. Their frenzied pass rush accounts for six sacks, causes three interceptions (two are returned for touchdowns), and twice knocks Dallas quarterback Danny White out cold. "It was just a matter of playing the kind of defense we're capable of playing," says Singletary. "We're still getting better."

Perry provides some comic relief when he picks up ball carrier Payton at Dallas's two-yard line and throws him into the end zone; he is flagged for illegal use of hands. "I didn't know you weren't allowed to do that," he says. Even without Perry's help, Payton gains 132 yards to put him over 1,000 for the ninth time in his career, a record. Ditka awards a game ball to every man on the roster and promises a gold-plated one for Fuller, who gives another solid performance in place of McMahon.

November 24. The Bears demolish Atlanta 36-0. The Falcons manage to cross the 50-yard line just once; quarterbacks David Archer and Bob Holly complete only three passes while suffering five sacks, two interceptions, and a safety. The Bears' highlight on offense is a spectacular run by Payton, who tightropes 40 yards along the sideline for a touchdown. "We can play better offensively," says Ditka, "but I don't know how we can play any better on defense. It's hard to believe those guys." The Bears have allowed only three points in their last 13 quarters. They join the 1934 Bears and 1972 Miami Dolphins as the only teams to begin a season with 12 straight wins.

December 2. The Dolphins preserve the legacy of their 1972 forebears as the last team to have a perfect season, beating the Bears 38-24 in the Orange Bowl. Poor field position and turnovers are the Bears' undoing as Miami scores on its first five possessions to take a 31-10 halftime lead. When defensive coordinator Buddy Ryan stubbornly clings to the notion that his linebackers can cover Miami's fleet-footed receivers, Ditka challenges him to a fight. The Bears' fate is sealed when Hampton deflects a Dan Marino pass—and the ball flutters into the arms of Mark Clayton, who scampers 42 yards for the Dolphins' final touchdown.

Despite the loss, the Bears never doubt that they are headed to the Super Bowl. The very next morning, many of them are in a studio to record the "Super Bowl Shuffle," the audacious rap song that will be heard almost incessantly over the next two months. Featured "singers" are Payton, Willie Gault, Singletary, McMahon, Wilson, Fuller, Mike Richardson, Dent, Fencik, and Perry.

December 8. The Bears outlast Indianapolis 17-10 in the last home game of the regular season. McMahon is merely adequate in his first start in a month, and the Bears' defense gets no takeaways for the first time all year. But punter Maury Buford is superb, giving the Bears field position that sets up both of their touchdowns. The Bears hold the ball for almost 39 minutes, and Payton sets another record by gaining more than 100 yards for the ninth successive game. "Walter Payton is the greatest football player to ever play the game," says Ditka. "Other people who call themselves running backs can't carry his jersey."

December 14. In a nationally televised Saturday game at the Meadowlands, rookie Kevin Butler boots four field goals to lead the Bears to a 19-6 win over the Jets. His 27 field goals for the year and 12 straight successful attempts are both club records. The Bears' defense is magnificent; New York's five possessions in the third quarter produce "drives" of zero, six, two, four, and four yards. CBS analyst John Madden says, "I think the Bears will win the Super Bowl."

December 22. The Pontiac Silverdome crowd of 74,042 includes more Bears fans than Lion rooters, and when the Bears win 37-17 everyone but Ditka is happy. "We couldn't beat a playoff team today," he says. "We would have been eliminated." Later, after reviewing the game films, he changes his mind. The contest is memorable for Dennis Gentry's electrifying 94-yard kickoff return, for Marshall's devastating TKO of Detroit quarterback Joe Ferguson, and for Perry's slow-motion jaunt of 59 yards with a recovered fumble (he is brought down from behind after he all but stops at the Lions' 15-yard line).

257

Ditka always emphasized the contrast between his team and the defending world champions. He described the 49ers as a "finesse" team, which was not intended as a compliment. He was equally eager to distinguish his own style from that of San Francisco's "cerebral" coach Bill Walsh. "There are teams that are fair-haired and there are teams that aren't," Ditka said. "There are teams named Smith and teams named Grabowski. We're Grabowskis."

By going 15-1, the Bears equaled the 49ers' feat of the year before and ensured that if there were an NFC championship rematch between the two clubs, it would be at Soldier Field. They also earned a week off while other playoff qualifiers fought it out in wild-card games.

While the Bears were home relaxing, the New York Giants whipped San Francisco—so the Niners wouldn't be coming to Chicago after all. The Giants appeared at Soldier Field on January 5.

On this clear, cold, and blustery day, the wind off Lake Michigan became a 12th player for the Bears when New York's Sean Landeta went back to punt from his own goal line in the first quarter. A gust blew the ball away from Landeta at the instant his foot was coming through. The ball glanced off the side of his foot and wobbled to the five-yard line, where Shaun Gayle scooped it up and sauntered into the end zone. Landeta was credited with a punt of minus seven yards, and Gayle's touchdown made him the 22nd different Bear to score for the year (the ninth on defense).

The Giants were not in the game after Landeta's miscue. They went three-and-out on nine of their first 11 possessions. All-Pro running back Joe Morris rushed for 14 yards on his first carry but managed only 18 yards on 11 attempts thereafter. Quarterback Phil Simms was sacked six times. Richard Dent was all over the field, recording three and a half sacks and corralling Morris from behind several times. "The Giants came into the game with the No. 2 defense in the NFL," Don Pierson wrote in the *Tribune*, "and left knowing that Avis is a lot closer to Hertz than the Giants are to the Bears."

McMahon connected with McKinnon on two touchdown strikes in the third quarter to put the game out of reach. "When the game is on the line and you've got to perform," said Suhey, "[McMahon] is the kind of guy who turns it on. He has the mentality of a running back or an offensive lineman stuck in a quarterback body."

The final score was 21-0. Ryan had promised a shutout and his players had delivered. "We believe every thought Buddy shares with us," Duerson explained.

"We beat a good football team," said Ditka. He could scarcely conceal his glee when he added, "They manhandled the 49ers."

Next came the NFC championship game against the Los Angeles Rams on January 12. It was another cold and windy day in Chicago, and the Rams looked as if they longed for the temperate climes of southern California. Hampton said he could see defeat in their eyes even at the opening coin toss. When the Rams won the flip and elected to receive, the crowd of 63,522 cheered, figuring the Bear defenders would push them backward.

From the start, Los Angeles quarterback Dieter Brock (10-for-31 passing) and running back Eric Dickerson (17 carries for 46 yards) were wholly ineffective. Dickerson, supposed to be the man who would eventually break Payton's lifetime rushing mark, had gained a playoff-record 234 yards against Dallas the week before. The Bears held him to less than three yards per attempt and forced him to fumble twice. "If they would have run him more," said Ryan, who had predicted three fumbles by Dickerson, "he *would* have had three."

In the third quarter, Dickerson and Singletary—Southwest Conference rivals at S.M.U. and Baylor, respectively, renewed their acquaintance in the Rams' backfield. Dickerson had just taken a handoff when he blasted into Singletary filling the gap and stopped dead in his tracks; he moved not one inch forward after meeting up with the Bears' middle linebacker. "I *like* this kind of party!" Singletary shouted to the Rams. "I'm going to be here all day."

McMahon, meanwhile, was brilliant. Despite the weather, he hit on 16 of 25 passes for 164 yards. On the Bears' first series, he ran 16 yards for a touchdown on a play that was called as a pass. Later he passed for a touchdown on a play called as a run. "The coach sent in a play I didn't agree with," McMahon said, "so I called my own." His 22-yard strike to Gault put the Bears ahead 17-0, and the outcome was decided. The Bears would be NFC champions.

The fans began to chant: "Super Bowl, Super Bowl." Late in the fourth quarter, the hapless Brock dropped back to pass and was flung to the turf by Dent. The ball popped loose. Marshall picked it up at mid-field and headed into Rams territory with Wilson escorting him. Just then, it started to snow.

Marshall and Wilson romped 52 yards to the Los Angeles end zone all alone, while the crowd cheered both them and the snow. As the final minutes ticked away, the Bears briefly abandoned the business-as-usual demeanor that had characterized them all year. The embraced one another on the sideline, and Ditka congratulated each man individually. Duerson asserted that Ditka even became choked up. The final score was 24-0. "The way we were playing defense," said Ditka, "it didn't matter what we scored." The Bears became the first team ever to post back-to-back playoff shutouts.

In the two weeks between the Bears' dismantling of the Rams and their date with destiny in Super Bowl XX, Chicagoans were guardedly optimistic. Their teams had a history of near misses and other failures that made it impossible for many fans to fully savor the ride on which the Bears were taking them. Sure the Bears were great—they were having one of the most dominant seasons in the history of professional sports—but what if they *lost* the Super Bowl?

The Bears themselves were confident that they could not lose if they played anywhere close to their ability. Oddsmakers made them double-digit favorites, and the Bears swaggered into New Orleans as conquering heroes. Certainly no team ever entered the Super Bowl with a more colorful cast of characters. Their propensity for unpredictable quotes made the Bears an ongoing media event. One New Orleans sportscaster—not content with the *actual* outrageous statements of the Bears—falsely reported that McMahon had called the local women "a bunch of sluts." This was one rare instance in which the controversial McMahon was blameless. However, he *did* moon photographers at a workout to show them, he said, the part of his anatomy that was being treated with acupuncture.

The AFC champion New England Patriots were almost forgotten in the general hubbub surrounding the Bears. It wasn't that the Patriots weren't deserving (they had won 12 of their last 14 games); it was just that they weren't the Miami Dolphins—with whom the Bears wished to settle accounts. But the Dolphins hadn't made it to New Orleans, and the Patriots would have to do.

In a meeting of the Bears' defensive coaches and players the night before the Super Bowl, Ryan all but confirmed the rumors that he was leaving to become head coach of the Philadelphia Eagles. "Whatever happens tomorrow," he told the players, "I want you to know that you're my heroes." He then left the room, overcome with emotion. The group began watching some film of the Patriots. After just a few minutes, Hampton concluded that the session had gone on long enough; he kicked the projector off its stand. McMichael then hurled a chair through the chalkboard on which some plays had been diagrammed. "Let's get the hell out of here!" said Hampton. Without anyone saying another word, the players all got up and walked out of the room. The meeting was over, and the Bears were ready.

Once the game started, New England had a brief glimmer of hope. On the second play of the game, Payton fumbled at his own 19-yard line and the Patriots recovered. "Here we go again," thought all the Chicagoans who'd learned from bitter experience not to trust their teams too much. But New England quarterback Tony Eason misfired on three pass attempts, and the Patriots settled for a field goal.

Although they were behind 3-0 with the game barely a minute old, it was already perfectly plain by now that the Bears would win. The Patriots had no more idea how to move the ball against them than they'd had four months earlier. Convinced by the September 15 game that his team couldn't run on the Bears, New England coach Raymond Berry felt he had no choice but to come out throwing. Thus Eason felt the full force of the Bears' merciless pass rush on almost every play. "We knew that if we got them into a passing situation," Singletary said, "we'd have things wrapped up."

The Bears' next two possessions resulted in field goals by Butler. Then Dent stripped the ball from Patriot running back Craig James, and Singletary pounced on it at the New England 13. Two plays later, Suhey carried 11 yards for a touchdown.

At the end of the first quarter, the Bears led 13-3. New England had run 10 plays for minus 19 yards. "It was like trying to beat back the tide with a broom," said Patriot guard Ron Wooten. The second quarter saw more of the same. "I tried to scramble," Eason said, "but there was no place to go." The Patriots simply could not block the Bear defenders. Eason was 0-for-6 passing and had been sacked three times when he was removed from the game, for his own good, five minutes before halftime.

It was 23-3 at the intermission. By now even the most pessimistic Chicagoan must have known that nothing could stop the Bears. "It's the men against the boys out there," said NBC analyst Pete Axthelm.

Veteran Steve Grogan replaced the shell-shocked Eason and fared somewhat better, but the Bears continued to pour it on. McMahon hit Gault for 60 yards on their first play of the second half; he concluded the 96-yard drive eight plays later with a quarterback sneak from one yard out. A 28-yard interception return by Reggie Phillips and a one-yard plunge by Perry gave the Bears their last two touchdowns.

The score was 44-3 when Ditka called off the dogs and replaced his starters early in the fourth quarter. New England finally scored a touchdown on an eight-yard pass from Grogan to Irving Fryar after a 12-play drive against the Bears' second-team defense. Later, an obscure defensive end named Henry Waechter ended the day's scoring when he sacked Grogan in the end zone for a safety.

Ditka was roundly chastised for not trying harder to get Payton a touchdown at some point, particularly in light of the fact that Perry, the coach's favorite novelty act, got the chance to score from the one-yard line in the third quarter. Ditka admitted that he should have realized before it was too late that Payton hadn't scored in the game. But it was difficult to see how a token touchdown in a blowout game, even if it was the Super Bowl, would have added much luster to Payton's nonpareil career. What really mattered was that he and his teammates were world champions. No one had ever been more deserving of that honor.

When it was over, both Ditka and Ryan were carried off the field in triumph. The Bears had been splendid on both sides of the ball, and the final score of 46-10 made it the most lopsided Super Bowl up to that time. Practically any one of a dozen Bears could have taken MVP honors, which ended up going to Richard Dent. McMahon, for example, passed to six different receivers for 256 yards and ran for two touchdowns, while Gault caught four balls for 129 yards. Ryan's defenders disrupted everything that New England tried to do, limiting the Patriots to a mere 123 yards on offense—seven on the ground.

"It will be many years," Paul Zimmerman wrote in *Sports Illustrated*, "before we see anything approaching the vision of hell that Chicago inflicted on the poor New England Patriots in Super Bowl XX. It was near perfect, an exquisite mesh of talent and system, defensive football carried to its highest degree. It was a great roaring wave that swept through the playoffs, gathering force and momentum until it finally crashed home in New Orleans's Superdome in pro football's showcase game."

After exceeding even the wildest dreams of their fans all season, the Bears outdid themselves when it mattered most. In three postseason games, they scored 91 points and yielded only 10. Their opponents averaged fewer than 145 yards per game and converted *three* third downs out of 36.

The 1985 Bears showed football fans a level of excellence that had seldom been attained. They talked big, played bigger, and shuffled into a place in history.

CHAPTER 32

The Pistons Take a Powder

"I have nothing but contempt and disgust for the Pistons organization."
-- *Jerry Reinsdorf, Bulls owner, speaking in 1991*

The Bulls and the Detroit Pistons had a good deal of history between them when they met in the 1991 NBA playoffs—it was their third straight meeting in the Eastern Conference finals. The Pistons had defeated the Bulls in six games in 1989 and seven games in 1990, and had gone on to capture the world championship both times. For the Bulls to win a title of their own, they'd have to overcome Detroit's belligerent tactics; the Pistons had not only beaten them in recent years, but beaten them up as well. Bill Laimbeer and Dennis Rodman, in particular, used violence or the threat of violence to intimidate opponents. "When you were out there playing them," Scottie Pippen said, "that was always in the back of your mind, to kind of watch yourself."

The Pistons called themselves the Bad Boys, and indeed their style of play often suggested football or rugby rather than basketball. Laimbeer's specialty was the well-placed elbow to the back of the head; Rodman's was taking the legs out from under airborne opponents as they drove to the hoop. "At some level, you were gonna have to contest [the Pistons] physically if you were gonna stay in the game with them," Bulls coach Phil Jackson said. "If you didn't want to stay in the game with them, fine. They'd go ahead and beat you. But if you wanted to compete, you'd have to do something physically to play at their level."

Late in the season, the Bulls beat the Pistons in Detroit for the first time in almost two years. In that game, Chicago center Bill Cartwright was ejected after an altercation with Laimbeer. It was well worth it, for

Cartwright showed that the Bulls were no longer backing down. "Just winning a game in their building gave us confidence," John Paxson said, "because we'd had such a tough time beating them." The game was part of a streak in which the Bulls won 20 of 21; they finished with a record of 61-21 and wrested the division title from the Pistons.

The Bulls made quick work of the New York Knicks (three games to none) and Philadelphia 76ers (four games to one) in the first two playoff rounds to set the stage for the much-anticipated rematch with Detroit in the conference finals.

In Game 1 at the Stadium on May 19, the Bulls surged to a 20-8 lead in the first quarter and led 45-37 at halftime. Detroit rallied to take a one-point lead late in the third quarter, but the Bulls fought back to go in front 68-65 entering the fourth. Then reserves Cliff Levingston, Craig Hodges, and Will Perdue keyed a spurt that put the game away. The Bulls won 94-83. "Sometimes in the past, our bench has had trouble against this team," said Perdue. "But we accomplished our goal in playing well because the difference in this series will be whose bench plays better."

In fact, it was the Pistons' bench that made the game as close as it was; Mark Aguirre scored 25 points and Vinnie Johnson 21. Starting forwards Rodman, Laimbeer, and James Edwards combined for only 17. The Bulls enjoyed a 43-26 edge in rebounds. "We were slow afoot," Detroit coach Chuck Daly admitted, "and we struggled to get something going."

"They won today because we played like crap," said Rodman. "Now we'll see about Tuesday."

What Rodman and his teammates saw on Tuesday, May 21, was a pregame ceremony in which Michael Jordan received the NBA's Most Valuable Player award; they were forced to stand around uneasily while the Stadium crowd gave Jordan a lengthy standing ovation. When the game started, they saw a vintage performance by him—35 points on 10-for-20 from the floor and 13-for-14 from the line. Pippen added 21 points and grabbed 10 rebounds. The Pistons began to show their frustration; they committed 35 fouls, three of them flagrant.

The Bulls led by 16 after three quarters and coasted to a 105-97 victory. Again, Laimbeer and Edwards were all but invisible, scoring just three points between them. "Part of the problem," Laimbeer said in a classic understatement, "is their switching is hurting our scoring. We have holes on offense." Isiah Thomas managed 10 points. It fell to reserves Johnson and Aguirre to carry much of the load offensively. They succeeded in that regard, but their increased playing time left Detroit vulnerable on defense, where the six-foot-two Johnson was required to cover the six-foot-seven Pippen and the six-foot-six Aguirre had to guard the six-foot-10 Grant.

"To be honest," Pistons guard Joe Dumars said, "I guess we're in a tough spot. But what do you do? You just bounce back."

But Daly, for one, seemed to sense that Detroit's was a lost cause. "I'm not sure exactly what we can do now," he mused. "We didn't match their intensity on either end, but we've got to find it somewhere. They were a step faster, more aggressive, more intense. No question: they want it. They're very hungry."

"It was a big win," said Pippen. "We can smell it now."

As the series moved to Detroit, the Pistons sought to maintain their customary bravado. "This is where the series starts for us," said Thomas. "Unfortunately, we had to spot [the Bulls] 2-0 before we reached this point. But now we're ready to sink our teeth into it and make them start reacting to us."

When Game 3 began, though, it was the Pistons who again found themselves reacting. The Bulls took the action to them from the outset, stunning the crowd at the Palace of Auburn Hills by sailing away to a 24-8 lead in the first 10 minutes. "Getting out to that start was crucial," said Cartwright. "We play so well when we're out front and it took so much wind out of them." Only Johnson's hot hand kept the Pistons in the game in the first half. The Bulls led 51-43 at the intermission.

Detroit's starting forwards were so ineffectual that Daly virtually gave up on them; Rodman played only 21 minutes, Laimbeer 19, and Edwards nine. They combined for 12 points. Daly deployed a smaller lineup—Thomas, Dumars, Johnson, Aguirre, and John Salley—that proved somewhat better able to contend with the Bulls' quickness and athleticism. The Pistons played the Bulls to a draw in the third quarter and entered the fourth trailing 82-74.

They were behind by five with two minutes left when Aguirre stole the ball from Pippen and sent it ahead to Johnson, streaking down the left side of the court. Jordan was in hot pursuit. "I read Vinnie Johnson," he said after the game. "He knew I was right there. He kind of looked back, anticipating me fouling him.

"I wasn't going to foul him. I had four fouls. I was going to give him the layup. I basically had to maneuver defensively to confuse him. I anticipated correctly when he tried to throw back to Joe Dumars."

Johnson did pass across to Dumars, who tried to put up a running jumper with Jordan harassing him. Dumars's awkward shot rattled off the backboard and was rebounded by Jordan. He sent it ahead to Pippen, whose 15-foot jumper put the Bulls ahead by seven and all but wrapped up the game. Jackson described the play as the biggest of the playoffs so far—evidence, he said, of Jordan's "unquenchable spirit." Daly, on the other hand, believed that Jordan had fouled Dumars. "Jordan *evidently* made a great play," he remarked sarcastically. "As he always does."

Jordan scored 33 points, and the Bulls also got strong contributions from Pippen (26 points, 10 rebounds) and Horace Grant (17 points, eight rebounds). All three were tremendous on defense, as usual. Pippen and Grant, who had joined the Bulls as rookies in 1987 and had been inseparable ever since, were coming of age together. After some fits and starts earlier in their careers, they had developed rapidly—both physically and psychologically. "I think they exude confidence now," Jackson said. "They feel like they can take care of business on the floor."

The Bulls' 113-107 victory gave them a commanding 3-0 lead in the series and left the Pistons groping for answers. It wasn't simply that the Pistons were older, slower, and more tired than the Bulls—they had been all of these in 1989 and 1990 and had still won. What was different now was that they could no longer distract and intimidate the younger Bulls. "We've matured," said Pippen. "We've learned that when they're out there throwing the cheap shots and elbows, we try to play basketball."

At one point late in the fourth quarter, Rodman responded to a foul call by picking up the ball and heaving it into Jordan's chest. Jordan merely laughed at him, and the rest of the Bulls joined in. It had come to this: the Bulls were now laughing out loud at their former tormentors. "We're used to putting other people in this spot," Dumars observed. "We're not used to being in it ourselves. It's a terrible feeling."

"The Bulls stole our playbook," said Salley, "talking junk, talking garbage, their intensity on defense, making sure there's only one shot, keeping people out of the middle, making us beat them with the jump shot. That's what *we* usually do." Salley, like Dumars, at least had guts enough to comment after the game. Laimbeer, Rodman, Aguirre, and Johnson each dressed in the trainer's room and went out a side door to avoid the media.

"We definitely won't get swept." So said Isiah Thomas before Game 4 on May 27, Memorial Day. For a short time, it appeared that he might be right. Fired up by an ear-splitting crowd of 21,454 at the Palace, the Pistons came out with more intensity than they had shown in the early stages of the previous games. They led 22-20 late in the first quarter

Then came the turning point. As Paxson drove to the basket, Laimbeer shouldered him into the stands. Paxson got up, had a few choice words for Laimbeer (his fellow Notre Dame alumnus), and calmly converted the two free throws. "It got me going a little bit," Paxson said of Laimbeer's cheap shot. On the Bulls' next possession, Jordan made a fine gesture of support for and confidence in his teammate. He passed up a chance to dunk over Laimbeer and threw the ball out to Paxson, whose 18-footer was perfect. Paxson scored 10 straight points for the Bulls, and from then on the outcome was never seriously in doubt.

If they were destined to lose, though, the Pistons at least remained true to their identity as the Bad Boys. They heard no inner voices urging them to bow out with dignity. With the Bulls in front 42-34 in the second quarter, Rodman's body block sent Pippen skidding into the seats. Several players rushed off the Bulls bench expecting a fight to break out, but Grant calmed Pippen as the latter shook the cobwebs from his head.

"We knew what was coming," said Jordan. "You take the lumps, bruises, and cuts. You take every beating, elbow, and punch and be smart about it. You look left and right and still try to play your game." The Bulls kept their cool and gradually turned the game into a rout. They led 57-50 at halftime and 87-74 after three quarters. They were ahead by 20 two minutes into the fourth quarter, and that margin remained roughly unchanged thereafter. The Bulls won 115-94.

Jordan was superb, as expected, but Pippen was a revelation. His 23 points and 10 assists proved that he was not only an ideal sidekick for Jordan, but also a full-fledged star in his own right. For the series, he averaged 22 points, 7.8 rebounds, and 5.3 assists to emerge at least partially from Jordan's very long shadow.

As the clock ticked down toward Detroit's elimination, Laimbeer, Thomas, Rodman, and Aguirre managed to embarrass themselves more completely than even the Bulls' dominance had. By slinking off their bench and into the locker room before the game was over, the Pistons' veteran "leaders" apparently sought to deny the legitimacy of the Bulls' triumph—as if refusing to acknowledge the result would somehow erase it. They were widely and justly chastised for failing to congratulate the Bulls, but worse yet was how they so casually abandoned five teammates who happened to be on the court at the time. It was a fittingly shabby way for the Bad Boys to end their reign as champions.

To every question posed by the media after the game, Laimbeer had the same sneering reply: "They won." Rodman, too, claimed to be unimpressed by the team that had trailed for only 13 of the 192 minutes played in the series. "They still haven't proved anything," he said. "They've got to win about five or six championships before they're a great team." (Even by this unreasonably lofty standard, of course, the Bulls would qualify for greatness before the decade was out—with the unlikely Rodman sporting their colors for three championships.)

After their stunning sweep of the Pistons, the Bulls met the Los Angeles Lakers in the NBA Finals. People everywhere were talking about the intriguing matchup between Jordan, who was seeking his first title after seven years in the league, and the Lakers' Magic Johnson, who had already won five championships in his stellar 12-year career. There was no denying that the Lakers had the edge in experience; this was their ninth appearance in the Finals since 1980.

The series provided a reunion of sorts for Jordan and his old college teammates James Worthy and Sam Perkins of the Lakers. Worthy was nursing a sprained ankle that limited his impact, but Perkins was heard from—his late three-pointer gave Los Angeles a 93-91 victory in Game 1 at the Stadium.

It was only the second loss the Bulls had suffered in the playoffs, and it proved to be the last. During the next four games, they dismissed whatever doubts lingered about their talent, maturity, and heart.

In Game 2, desperately needing a win at home before heading off to Los Angeles, the Bulls overwhelmed the Lakers 107-86. Jordan shot 15-of-18 for 33 points, while Paxson was 8-for-8 in scoring 16 points. "Does Paxson ever miss?" Perkins asked.

Jordan's jumper with 3.4 seconds left sent Game 3 into overtime, whereupon the Bulls rolled away to win 104-96. The shot was just one of the countless clutch plays Jordan had made over the years, but the first that put the Bulls within striking range of a world championship.

Thanks to Chicago's relentless defense, the Lakers shot just 37 percent in Game 4. The Bulls prevented Magic from making the fancy passes that were his trademark, and their double-teaming in the post made life miserable for Worthy and Vlade Divac. The Bulls won 97-82; it was the Lakers' lowest offensive output since the introduction of the 24-second shot clock in 1954. "It's no surprise the way [the Bulls] have been defending," said Los Angeles coach Mike Dunleavy. "They are very athletic and very smart."

In Game 5, Jordan's penetration set up a wealth of opportunities for Pippen, who scored 32 points, and Paxson, who added 20—including five long-range bombs in the fourth quarter that sealed the game. The Bulls won 108-101 to wrap up their first world championship. Magic Johnson, as gracious in defeat as the Pistons had been boorish, went out of his way to find Jordan in the crush of players, fans, and media that swarmed the court after the game. "I saw tears in his eyes," he said. "I told him, 'You proved everyone wrong. You're a winner as well as a great individual basketball player.'"

Jordan cradled the championship trophy in his arms and wept for joy, certainly, but also for relief that he was no longer a superstar whose team had never won a title. He didn't know yet that this first ascent to the pinnacle was not the culmination of his career, but just the beginning of a new phase. Before long, the Bulls would rewrite the history of the NBA's greatest teams as thoroughly as Jordan had rewritten that of its greatest players.

CHAPTER 33

Moments, 1988-1993

December 31, 1988
The Fog Bowl

When Bears defensive coordinator Buddy Ryan resigned after the 1986 Super Bowl to become head coach of the Philadelphia Eagles, the uneasy truce that he and Mike Ditka had observed for four years was fractured forever. Since they no longer had to work together, each man was now free to say just what he thought of the other. Both men made full use of the privilege, and their long-simmering enmity bubbled over in a series of recriminations back and forth through the media.

The feud was good theater, and it sparked interest in the Eagles-Bears playoff game at Soldier Field on the last day of 1988. Unfortunately, the crowd of 65,534 and the national television audience saw only the first half. The second half was rendered all but invisible by fog.

Neal Anderson's four-yard touchdown blast put the Bears ahead 14-6 with 6:21 remaining in the second quarter. This took place under sunny skies. But when Kevin Butler added a field goal some four minutes later, the fog was rolling in from Lake Michigan and creeping over the stands. Within minutes, the whole field had been obscured.

For the rest of the game, the spectators could not see a thing. Nor could the TV cameras capture the action going on behind and within the soupy curtain of fog. "I felt like I was on another planet," a CBS producer remarked. For the players and officials on the field, visibility was better—but still less than 20 yards. "Have I ever played in anything like that before?" said Butler. "I haven't even driven in anything like that before."

Philadelphia's Luis Zendejas kicked two field goals (his third and fourth of the game) through the mist in the second half, and Butler booted another to make the final score Bears 20, Eagles 12. The game was quite unremarkable but for the fog. Quarterbacks Mike Tomczak of the Bears and Randall Cunningham of the Eagles tossed three interceptions apiece. The Eagles outplayed the Bears in most aspects, but they frittered away one opportunity after another—particularly in the first half, when Cunningham had two touchdown passes called back for penalties and another would-be touchdown strike dropped in the end zone.

Despite 430 total yards and 22 first downs, the Eagles never breached the Bears' goal line. "Credit the Bear defense," Ryan said. "Every time we got down there, we didn't make anything happen. We stopped ourselves. The effort was there, the heart was there, but it just didn't happen."

The Bears were delighted to have gotten away with the victory that few people saw. "One good thing will come out of this," said center Jay Hilgenberg. "We'll have a short film session tomorrow. I mean, what are the coaches gonna show us?"

Bob Verdi had the last word on the game that was known ever after as the Fog Bowl. "Somewhere over there on the lakefront," he wrote, "there's a guy who left his seat late in the first half to find a restroom and he's still out there, trying to find his wife."

September 9, 1989
"Better Than Yesterday"

One month to the day after entering first place in the National League East, the Cubs opened a three-game series with the St. Louis Cardinals to determine whether they would stay there. Like any weekend series between the Cubs and the Cardinals, it was sold out well in advance, long before anyone knew that these would be the most important games of the year for either club.

The Cardinals, who came into town only a game and a half behind the Cubs, rallied from a 7-1 deficit Friday afternoon to win 11-8 and reduce the margin to half a game. It was a horrendous defeat for the

Cubs, who gave up four runs in the seventh inning and another five in the eighth as victory slipped away. Their collars were a little tighter when they took the field Saturday knowing that a loss would drop them into second place.

It was a dark, drizzly afternoon, and Wrigley Field's one-year-old lights were on from the first pitch at 3:05. Both starting pitchers, Rick Sutcliffe for the Cubs and Jose DeLeon for St. Louis, performed admirably. The Cubs pushed across a run in the first, and the Cardinals scored two in the sixth. That was all the scoring for the first seven innings.

DeLeon maintained the precarious 2-1 lead into the bottom of the eighth. Dwight Smith led off with a single to right—a good start for the Cubs that almost turned disastrous when Smith took a wide turn around first base, then inexplicably stopped halfway to second. Cardinals right fielder Tom Brunansky hesitated to throw the ball back in, not sure whether Smith was headed to second or back to first. Finally, Smith bolted for second—and made it when Brunansky's throw was off the mark. "I waited too long," Brunansky admitted after the game. For his part, Smith justified the seemingly ridiculous risk he had taken. "If I screw up, I'm going to get a lot of questions for it," he said. "But if you're afraid to make a mistake, then you can't win."

So Smith, representing the tying run, was on second with nobody out. But Mark Grace fanned and Andre Dawson grounded out, and suddenly Smith was on third with two outs. Enter Luis Salazar, a journeyman third baseman who had been acquired 10 days earlier to bolster the Cubs' bench. Salazar's line-drive single to left tied the score at two apiece.

The game remained tied through the ninth inning and into the 10th. Grace led off the bottom of the 10th by popping out. Dawson coaxed a walk. And then Salazar stepped up to the plate again. With a count of 2-and-1, Cardinal lefty Ken Dayley threw a fastball well away from Salazar, who reached out and stroked it down the right-field line and up against the ivy. While Brunansky dug the ball out of the corner, Dawson ran for all he was worth. Dawson turned for home and kept on chugging as second baseman Jose Oquendo took the relay from Brunansky and fired it toward the plate—too late. Dawson's aching knees had carried home the winning run.

Shawon Dunston, the on-deck batter, leaped into Dawson's arms behind the plate while the rest of the Cubs piled on top of Salazar. The unlikely hero had batted but twice, delivering clutch hits that tied the game in the eighth and won it in the 10th.

"We were better than yesterday," said manager Don Zimmer. "There were a lot of little things that happened in this ballgame." It was a year in which a lot of little things added up to make the Cubs division champions. All season long, rookies and no-names like Smith, Jerome Walton, Joe Girardi, Mike Bielecki, Les Lancaster, Lloyd McClendon, Steve Wilson, and Salazar came through when it counted. The Cubs never looked back after the dramatic win on September 9. They won the division title going away, lengthening their margin to six games by the end of the season.

May 22, 1992
On a Roll

As the Bulls and Blackhawks advanced through their respective playoffs in 1992, Chicago fans entertained the novel idea of simultaneous world championships. The Bulls were heavy favorites to win their second consecutive NBA title, while the Blackhawks were longshots to win their first Stanley Cup in three decades.

The Hawks carried a seven-game winning streak into the conference finals, having won three in a row to close out their first playoff series against the St. Louis Blues and four straight to dispatch the Detroit Red Wings in the second round.

It was their fourth conference finals against Edmonton since 1983, and the first three tries had not gone well. But the team confronting the Hawks this time was not the unstoppable Oilers who had won five Stanley Cups in seven years. Wayne Gretzky, Mark Messier, Jari Kurri, and Paul Coffey were gone, and the Oilers had plodded through the season with a mark of 36-34-10.

The series began with a bang when Steve Larmer tallied for the Hawks only 47 seconds into Game 1 at the Stadium. But Chicago's all-star goalie Ed Belfour was shaky, allowing two soft goals later in the period. The score was 2-2 at the first intermission. "Eddie started slow," said center Jeremy Roenick, "but then he put it in overdrive."

So did the Hawks, who suddenly transformed the tie game into a rout. A three-goal barrage by Mike Peluso, Roenick, and Steve Smith started 2:51 into the period and concluded less than 90 seconds later. The Hawks now led 5-2, and Game 1 had been decided. For good measure, the Hawks lit the lamp three more times in the third period to make the final score 8-2.

Larmer, an unflappable 10-year-veteran and former Rookie of the Year, had scored the first and last goals of the game and assisted on two others in between. The four points put him over 100 in postseason games for his career, a level previously reached only by Stan Mikita, Bobby Hull, and Denis Savard in Blackhawks history. After the game, reporters asked if Larmer was excited about his performance and the Hawks' prospects. "Maybe," he replied. "I guess."

Edmonton coach Ted Green was more quotable. "We're certainly going to have to pick up our socks," he said, "or else it's going to be a very short series."

Green proved prophetic. In Game 2, Larmer's goal off a nifty pass from Michel Goulet tied the score 2-2 with 14 minutes left. Goulet tallied 10 minutes later, assisted by Larmer. Stephane Matteau's goal 45 seconds thereafter put the game away. Defenseman Chris Chelios assisted on all three Chicago goals in the third period.

Game 3 at Edmonton was deadlocked 3-3 after three periods. Two minutes and 45 seconds into overtime, Roenick received a pass from Chelios in the slot and cranked away. Edmonton goalie Bill Ranford never saw the shot. "I heard a chink when it hit the crossbar," he said. "I was waiting for a cheer [from the Edmonton crowd]. When I didn't hear a cheer, I knew it was over." It was indeed. Roenick's shot clanged off the bottom of the crossbar and spun into the net. The Hawks won 4-3.

The demoralized Oilers had little left for Game 4. The Blackhawks sailed away to a 5-0 lead in the first two periods and prevailed 5-1. Their postseason winning streak had reached 11, a new NHL record, and they were headed to the Stanley Cup Final for the first time since 1973.

By now the *Tribune* had taken to printing a "Championship Count-down" showing the "combined magic number of wins that would give the Bulls and Hawks championships." On Saturday, May 23, the number stood at seven for the Bulls (who were tied 1-1 in their conference finals) and at four for the Blackhawks. Alas, the Hawks' countdown went no further. They were swept by Mario Lemieux and the Pittsburgh Penguins in the finals, losing the four games by a total of five goals.

The Hawks qualified for the playoffs every year from 1970 through 1997, and made three appearances in the finals, but the ultimate prize continued to elude them, as it had since 1961.

June 14, 1992
Curtain Call

After winning their first world championship in 1991 and storming through the next season with a record of 67-15, the Bulls came into the 1992 playoffs with great expectations. But their road to a second title turned out to be bumpier than anticipated. The Bulls swept the Miami Heat in the first round. Then they were pushed to the limit in the second round, requiring seven games to dispose of the rugged New York Knicks. In the Eastern Conference finals, the Bulls had their hands full with the Cleveland Cavaliers (losing Game 2 by 26 points at home), before escaping in six games.

The Bulls faced the Portland Trail Blazers in the NBA Finals. Game 1 featured a superhuman exhibition by Michael Jordan, who hit six three-pointers and scored 35 points *in the first half* to propel the Bulls to an easy victory at the Stadium. The Blazers won Game 2 in overtime. In Portland, the Bulls won Game 3, lost Game 4, then won Game 5 behind a 46-point effort by Jordan.

When the series returned to Chicago, most observers considered it a foregone conclusion that the Bulls would wrap it up in Game 6. But someone forgot to tell the Blazers, who drew away to a 17-point lead late in third quarter. Entering the fourth quarter, the Bulls were still down 79-64, and coach Phil Jackson decided to try something different.

He sent Scottie Pippen out on the court with four reserves: B.J. Armstrong, Bobby Hansen, Stacey King, and Scott Williams.

"Phil told us, 'We need to get some momentum back,'" Hansen said later. "We had nothing to lose. All we could do was work hard and get it back so the horses could take over." The unorthodox move paid off immediately when Hansen knocked down a three-pointer to bring the Bulls to within 12 with 11:30 left. Then Hansen stole the ball, and King made one of two subsequent free throws. A layup by Pippen made it 79-70 with 10:50 remaining. After a running jumper by Portland's Cliff Robinson made it 81-70, the Bulls came charging back again.

With 10:21 left, King made two free throws.

With 9:45 left, Pippen hit a short bank shot off a nice feed from Armstrong.

With 9:31 left, Pippen forced Portland's Clyde Drexler to double dribble. Twenty seconds later, Armstrong popped a 14-foot jumper.

With 8:39 left, King's 14-footer off the glass made it 81-78.

By the time Hansen left the game with 8:36 remaining, making way for Jordan, the tide had turned. Now it was time for the Bulls' lead horse to take over. With the Bulls trailing 83-80, Jordan stole the ball and canned a running jumper. The Bulls had outscored the Blazers 18-4 in the first six minutes of the quarter. The Stadium crowd of 18,676 was in an uproar.

John Paxson came back in for Armstrong. There was 5:20 to go when Pippen's three-pointer tied the score at 85-85. 11 seconds later, Terry Porter's long jumper gave Portland the lead. Jordan answered with a jumper from 16 feet. With 4:24 remaining, Williams blocked a shot by Drexler, but Danny Ainge stole the Bulls' upcourt pass.

Jordan promptly stole the ball back, and his soaring layup put the Bulls ahead 89-87. It was their first lead since a 4-2 edge in the opening minutes. Drexler's layup tied it up again. Horace Grant returned, replacing King. "It was our job," said King of himself and his fellow bench players who had started the fourth quarter, "to hustle, to claw our way back."

The Bulls went ahead for keeps on Pippen's 16-footer with 2:21 left, and then Paxson's steal set up a jumper by Jordan that made it a four-point advantage. Jordan added a basket and two free throws in the final minute to preserve the Bulls' 97-93 victory. The Bulls' 33-14 blitzkrieg marked the greatest fourth-quarter comeback in the history of the NBA Finals. "I'm glad for Bobby Hansen," Jordan said of the obscure nine-year veteran who had sparked the run.

After the Bulls received their trophy and went through the obligatory champagne showers, it occurred to them that the fans had not left the Stadium. "Grab that trophy," Jackson yelled over the din in the locker room. "We're going back up to celebrate with our fans!" The players returned to the court, climbing atop the scorer's table to bask in the crowd's adulation. Later, Jackson reflected upon his team's achievement. "A back-to-back championship is the mark of a great team," he said. "We have passed the demarcation point."

June 20, 1993
Paxson for Three

The Bulls' hopes for a "threepeat" as world champions were in serious jeopardy in Game 6 of the 1993 NBA Finals. The Phoenix Suns were on their home court with a chance to win their third game of the last four. If they succeeded, they would have all the momentum—as well as the home-court advantage—in the decisive Game 7.

It had been a strange series, with the home team winning only one of the first five games. The Bulls had won the first two games in Phoenix, prompting visions of a sweep, since the next three games would be at Chicago Stadium. But in Game 3, the Suns battled to a 129-121 win in triple overtime. In Game 4, a 55-point effort by Michael Jordan carried the Bulls to a 108-98 win and the brink of the championship. Prior to Game 5, many merchants in the city boarded up their shop windows for fear that a Bulls' victory would provide an excuse for rioting and looting. When the Suns prevailed, their star forward Charles Barkley said, "We did the city a favor. You can take those boards down now."

Game 6 was a nailbiter from the opening tipoff. For the first three quarters both teams missed more than their share of opportunities—but Jordan, B.J. Armstrong, John Paxson, and Trent Tucker combined for *nine* three-pointers to make the difference for the Bulls, who led 87-79. The threepeat was just 12 minutes away. Incredibly, the Bulls then went six minutes without scoring, missing their first nine shots of the fourth quarter and turning the ball over twice for good measure. The Suns clawed their way back into the game.

Phoenix had a 98-94 lead and the ball with a minute left. Another basket would have iced it for the Suns, but Jordan grabbed a defensive rebound and went coast-to-coast to bring the Bulls to within two. There were 38 seconds left. On their next possession, the Suns used up almost the entire 24 seconds before Dan Majerle attempted a three-pointer. Majerle's long-range bombs had been a key weapon for Phoenix throughout the series, but this time he missed everything.

Now there were 14 seconds left. The Bulls called timeout and designed a play that would get the ball into Jordan's hands for the crucial shot. Jordan inbounded the ball to Armstrong, who sent it ahead to Scottie Pippen. Pippen sliced into the lane, looking to return the ball to Jordan. But Jordan was covered, and Phoenix center Mark West blocked Pippen's path to the hoop. Pippen spotted Horace Grant on the baseline and fired a perfect pass to set up an apparent game-tying layup.

Grant, who had scored but one point in the game, decided against trying the layup and threw the ball all the way out to Paxson, who was unguarded. Paxson caught it beyond the three-point line, just to the left of the circle, and went up for a shot. "I got a clean look at it," said Paxson. "There was no one around me, and it felt good when it left. I just caught the ball and shot it, as I have my whole life."

Paxson's shot swished through the net to put the Bulls ahead 99-98. America West Arena went deathly silent. "I knew it was in as soon as Pax shot it," Jordan said later. There were 3.9 seconds left. The Suns' last chance went for naught when Grant blocked Kevin Johnson's driving shot at the buzzer. The Bulls had accomplished their threepeat—something neither Larry Bird's Celtics nor Magic Johnson's Lakers had been able to do.

"It was like a dream come true," Paxson said after the game. "You know, it's just like when you're a kid. You go out to your driveway and start counting down 'Three, two, one....' I don't know how many shots like that I've taken in my lifetime, but this was the one that really counted."

September 27, 1993
"As Good as It Gets"

Bo Jackson's role as the glib celebrity pitchman in countless TV commercials tended to make people forget that he was not a cartoon character but a shy, modest man who was grateful for the gifts nature had given him. Jackson was an all-star in both the NFL and Major League Baseball—a unique achievement—until a 1991 football injury left him with an artificial hip.

His career seemed to be over, and when Jackson appeared at the White Sox' spring training camp in 1993, few observers gave him much of a chance to make the team. "I have a little hitch in my giddy-up," Jackson admitted, but he had put himself through a tortuous rehab program and claimed to be getting better every day. Jackson made the team, thus fulfilling a promise made at his mother's deathbed several months before.

Jackson's first at-bat of the year (and first in 18 months) came in the home opener at new Comiskey Park on April 9. He belted the second pitch he saw over the right-field wall for a home run. The crowd of 42,775 went wild, calling him out of the dugout after he had circled the bases. "The only thing I could think of at that time was my mother," Jackson said after the game. "I made myself a promise after she passed that when I got back in the game and got my first hit, I was going to give that ball to her." He had the ball bronzed, inscribed, and affixed to his mother's tombstone.

Although the Sox lost to the Yankees, it was a stirring start to what would prove a storybook season on the South Side. After a listless three months in which they flirted with the .500 mark, the Sox stormed through the second half to open up a comfortable lead over the Texas Rangers heading down the stretch. First baseman Frank Thomas, Jackson's football teammate at Auburn University, was having the greatest offensive season in White Sox history and would soon receive the first of back-to-back MVP awards.

By September 27, the White Sox were poised to clinch the American League West title. On this crisp Monday evening, the Sox' Wilson Alvarez and Seattle's Dave Fleming dueled through five and a half scoreless innings. In the bottom of the sixth, Ellis Burks led off with a single. Craig Grebeck followed with a bunt single, and the crowd of 42,116 began to stir. But Fleming settled down and retired the next two Sox hitters. Then Jackson stepped into the batter's box. Sensing the dramatic possibilities, the fans came to their feet cheering and waving a sea of white socks over their heads. Fleming approached Bo carefully, and the count went to 3-and-0. Given the green light, Jackson swung at the next offering and hit a sky-high drive to left field.

"I thought it was a pop-up," Jackson said. But the ball kept soaring up and out, up and out, until it finally landed beyond the wall for a three-run homer. "It was amazing," said the Sox' Lance Johnson. "I thought Bo missed it and popped it up, but the left fielder went back, back, back until he just ran out of real estate."

"That," Seattle manager Lou Piniella said, "is one strong man."

Bo's blow gave the Sox a lead they never relinquished as they won 4-2 to wrap up the division title. It was a miracle finish not only for Jackson, but also for Alvarez, who had returned from the minors in August to win his last seven starts.

After the game, the champagne-soaked Jackson went back out to the field to thank Sox fans for their support. Few had left, although the game had been over for half an hour. Jackson jogged around the field, waving a white sock of his own at the delirious fans. "This is as good as it gets," he said. "The most fun I've had as a professional athlete."

CHAPTER 34

Nowhere to Go But Up

"Hope we didn't hurt any of your boys."
   -- Hayden Fry, University of Iowa football coach, speaking to Northwestern
   coach Gary Barnett after Iowa's 56-14 victory over the Wildcats in 1992

In 1995, Northwestern University's football team had not had a winning season since 1971 (but had had four *winless* seasons since then), had not been to the Rose Bowl since 1949, and had not won the Big Ten championship since 1936. So which goals did coach Gary Barnett give his players on the first day of practice? 1) To have a winning season, 2) To go to the Rose Bowl, and 3) To win the Big Ten championship.

After their 7-4 campaign in 1971, the Wildcats had won a total of 38 games over the next 20 years. In the meantime they'd lost 179 games, for a winning percentage of .175. They'd lost 71 of 75 between 1975 and 1982, including 34 in a row. They'd gone five years without a win in the Big Ten. Attendance had gotten so bad that Northwestern sold a home game to Michigan in 1980 and to Ohio State in 1990.

A parade of coaches—Alex Agase, John Pont, Rick Venturi, Dennis Green, Francis Peay—had come and gone, but the dreadful legacy of losing had continued unabated. Northwestern's recruiting woes were almost always blamed on its rigorous admission standards; it was suggested that the university simply couldn't find enough top-flight football players who also excelled in the classroom. Northwestern students reflected this attitude with the chant they would direct at opponents in the waning minutes of the Wildcats' frequent defeats: "That's all right, that's okay; you're going to work for us one day."

Many observers, including some influential alumni, proposed that the time had come to drop out of the Big Ten (the University of Chicago had done just that when it de-emphasized athletics in the thirties).

Barnett would have none of it. "We'll take the purple to Pasadena," he said when he was hired—referring, of course, to the site of the Rose Bowl.

His positive attitude notwithstanding, Barnett's teams started out looking much like those of his predecessors. His first game, on September 5, 1992, was a resounding 42-7 loss to Notre Dame. The Wildcats finished the year 3-8. They slipped to 2-9 in 1993, failing to win a conference game. In 1994, Northwestern won three and tied one of its first seven games. "We're at a point," Barnett said, "that our coaches have wanted to see, that our players have wanted to be at, that our fans and our students have wanted us to get to. All this is an opportunity. Now it's time to step up." But, with visions of a bowl bid dancing in their heads, the Wildcats took a giant step backward. They were blown out in each of the last four games, and finished 3-7-1 (2-6 in the Big Ten).

There was nowhere to go but up. The 1995 Wildcats opened the season on September 2 at Notre Dame. The Irish had bombed the Wildcats in each of Barnett's first three years, by a combined score of 111-34. As Rick Telander wrote, the Irish were "supposed to be on their way to a national title, the Wildcats to grad school." Most of the 59,075 Irish faithful who came out to enjoy the perfect sun-kissed afternoon were only mildly perturbed when the first half ended with Northwestern leading 10-9; they were confident that the upstarts would shortly be put in their place. Those fans who'd wagered on the Irish were somewhat more concerned, for they'd had to lay 28 points to the Wildcats.

Early in the third quarter, 26-yard touchdown pass from Steve Schnur to D'Wayne Bates put Northwestern ahead 17-9. The scoring "drive" had covered 55 yards in 54 seconds, on just three plays. For the rest of the third quarter and most of the fourth, the Wildcats' defense held firm. "Notre Dame has a great system," explained Barnett. "They've used it for years. Part of a system is that it's predictable. We've known where they were going; we just haven't been able to stop them. We physically couldn't get there. This time, we had guys there who could make the play. And they did." Linebacker Pat Fitzgerald and safety Hudhaifa Ismaeli each made big plays to stifle Irish advances.

Northwestern was forced to punt from its own end zone midway through the fourth quarter, and Notre Dame soon turned the favorable field position into a touchdown that made it 17-15 with 6:16 left to play. On the try for a two-point conversion, though, Irish quarterback Ron Powlus got tangled up with his own center and fell to the turf. The Wildcats still clung to the lead.

On the next Irish possession, it was fourth and two when Randy Kinder took a handoff from Powlus at his own 44-yard line and ran smack into Northwestern defensive tackle Matt Rice. "Hindsight is always 20/20," Notre Dame coach Lou Holtz said later. "We had two timeouts left. We could have held them and gotten the ball back. We probably should have punted." The Wildcats took over with 4:02 remaining, and the Irish never got their hands on the ball again. Tailback Darnell Autry saw to that; he carried the ball repeatedly as the minutes dwindled down, and his 26-yard burst in the closing seconds ensured Northwestern's victory. He finished the day with 33 rushes for 160 yards.

To describe the outcome as stunning would be an understatement. The *Sun-Times* called it "the upset of the century." Holtz called it "very disappointing." It was the Wildcats' first triumph over Notre Dame since 1962 and their first season-opening win since 1975. Kicker Sam Valenzisi tore up a chunk of sod for a souvenir. For Fitzgerald and offensive guard Ryan Padgett, among others, the victory was particularly sweet. They had always wanted to play for Notre Dame, but the talent-laden Irish didn't want them. "The reason I came to Northwestern," said Fitzgerald, "was to beat Notre Dame."

The Wildcats had a layoff of 13 days between their historic win in South Bend and their home opener against Miami of Ohio. During this interval they appeared in the national rankings for the first time in a quarter century, eking out the 25th and final spot in the Associated Press poll.

Fans in Evanston were withholding judgment, and only 26,352 turned out for the Miami game on a golden, 75-degree day. The proceedings began on a somber note, as a moment of silence was offered for defensive back Marcel Price, who'd been killed in an accidental shooting over the summer. Seemingly inspired, the Wildcats exploded for three touchdowns in the first 20 minutes as two long passes from Schnur to Bates sandwiched a shorter strike to Autry.

By the end of the third quarter, Rodney Ray's 20-yard interception return had given Northwestern an apparently insurmountable 28-7 lead. Then the roof caved in. Miami scored three touchdowns in less than nine minutes, drawing to within one point with 2:22 remaining. A two-point conversion that would have put the Redskins ahead was no good. But in the final minute, an errant snap on an attempted punt gave Miami the ball on Northwestern's one-yard line. A chip-shot field goal as time expired gave Miami a 30-28 win.

"This is about as low as it gets," said Barnett.

The momentum generated by the Notre Dame upset was gone after the Miami game, but the Wildcats resolved to resurrect it somehow. The extent to which they succeeded surprised even themselves.

In back-to-back games at Dyche Stadium, the sensational sophomore Autry ran wild as the Wildcats blistered Air Force 30-6 on September 23 and Indiana 31-7 the next Saturday. With this, they popped back into the No. 25 spot in the AP poll. Then it was on to Michigan, where they hadn't won since 1959. The Wolverines were 5-0 and ranked seventh in the nation. The night before the game, Barnett denied that his players would be intimidated by the maize-and-blue mystique or by the 104,000 fans in Michigan Stadium. "We plan on winning this football game," he said.

The game was tied 6-6 at halftime. Michigan went in front 13-6 on a bootleg by quarterback Brian Griese from three yards out midway through the third quarter. After Northwestern fumbled the ensuing kickoff, Michigan tailback Tim Biakabutuka scampered 23 yards into the end zone. But a holding penalty negated the touchdown that would have given the Wolverines a comfortable margin. Two plays later, the Wildcats caught another break when a Michigan field-goal attempt went awry. Northwestern's next possession resulted in a 32-yard field goal by Valenzisi, and the Wildcats trailed only 13-9 at the close of the quarter.

The big break came on the second play of the fourth quarter. It had just started to rain when Griese dropped back to pass from his own 27. The intended receiver slipped in the wet grass, and Northwestern's Eric Collier intercepted the ball. The Wildcats' offense went for the jugular. On the first play, Schnur took the snap and pitched back to Bates, who—unbeknownst to the Wolverines—had been a quarterback in high school. Bates fired a perfect aerial to tight end Darren Drexler for a 26-yard gain to Michigan's five-yard line. A pair of plunges by Autry moved the Wildcats down to the two. From there, Schnur connected with fullback Matt Hartl for the touchdown that put Northwestern ahead. Valenzisi's extra point made it 16-13 with 12:42 to play.

Michigan's next drive abruptly ended when Fitzgerald sacked Griese at midfield, separating him not only from his senses but from the ball as well; Ismaeli recovered the fumble. A 46-yard completion from Schnur to Bates put the Wildcats within spitting distance of the Michigan goal line, but the Wolverine defense held. Valenzisi trotted out and booted his fourth field goal of the game with 8:42 left.

Northwestern led by six. Michigan could win with a touchdown and extra point. Biakabutuka, who ran for 205 yards on the day, almost singlehandedly moved the Wolverines into Wildcat territory as the clock ticked down. On a first down at the 34, Griese went for all the marbles, but cornerback Chris Martin (who, at five-foot-eight, was giving up eight inches to receiver Amani Toomer) broke up the play. Biakabutuka fumbled on second down, but Michigan recovered. On third down, Griese threw the ball away under pressure.

Now it was fourth down, and the Wolverines needed to gain at least 10 yards to keep their hopes alive. Northwestern blitzed, and Fitzgerald was all over Griese as he tried to throw. William Bennett picked off the pass, sealing Northwestern's victory.

With their fourth win of the season, the Wildcats established a new high-water mark for the Barnett era. But no one was satisfied. "Someone said to me the other day, 'You're playing with the big boys,'" Barnett remarked. "I said, 'No, we *are* the big boys, and now we're playing like the big boys.'"

Now ranked 14th in the nation, Northwestern journeyed to Minnesota on October 14. Autry rushed for 169 yards and three touchdowns, including one on a 73-yard jaunt that put the game away in the fourth quarter, as the Wildcats won 27-17.

On October 21, Wisconsin visited Dyche Stadium. So did 49,256 fans; it was Northwestern's first home sellout since 1983 (when a capacity crowd had shown up to cheer the Pasadena-bound Illinois team). Northwestern fans were coming around, but the bookmakers weren't—the 11th-ranked Wildcats, playing at home against the 24th-ranked Badgers, were two-point underdogs. Wisconsin had, after all, pasted Northwestern 53-14 and 46-14, respectively, in 1993 and 1994. As was becoming more and more evident, though, 1995 was different. The Wildcats forced seven turnovers and dominated throughout, winning 35-0. Their entire defensive unit shared Big Ten player-of-the-week honors. "People just sort of thought we were Cinderella," said Barnett, "and that sooner or later, the glass slipper was going to come off. That didn't look like Cinderella out there to me."

After their rout of Wisconsin, there was no denying that the Wildcats were for real. Their six victories had assured them of a winning season, and they'd moved up to No. 8 in the AP poll.

The confident Wildcats breezed into Champaign to battle Illinois amidst 25-mile-per-hour winds and light drizzle on October 28. The weather seemed not to affect the Illini, who executed a long drive with the wind in the first quarter and another into the wind in the second to grab a 14-0 lead. Thereafter, Northwestern scored 17 unanswered points. The indomitable Autry carried *41 times* for 151 yards, but it was his shortest run of the day, a one-yard touchdown dive with 6:14 remaining, that completed the comeback. Collier's interception in his own end zone with seven seconds left preserved the win. "I think we've pretty much locked ourselves into a bowl game now," said Autry. "We're definitely going to try to run the table."

"Running the table" would entail beating Penn State, Iowa, and Purdue to extend the winning streak to nine. The Wildcats themselves were sure that it could be done, and they were pulling many converts from the ranks of the erstwhile skeptics.

When 12th-ranked Penn State came to Evanston on November 4, Keith Jackson, "the voice of college football," was on hand to broadcast the game from coast-to-coast. "Often, television used to come here because of the opposition," Jackson said. "Today, we're here because of Northwestern." The Wildcats had climbed to sixth in the national rankings, yet they were installed as seven-point underdogs. Some people would need a little more convincing.

Penn State coach Joe Paterno wasn't one of them. "They're good!" he said. "People just don't seem to want to admit they're good." There was no way to escape the fact after Northwestern manhandled the Nittany Lions 21-10. Autry and Fitzgerald, standouts all year, were at their best. Autry rushed 36 times for 139 yards and three touchdowns behind a heroic effort from his offensive line, and Fitzgerald was involved in a season-high 17 tackles (11 of them unassisted). "Anytime you see a team play the way they're playing," said Paterno, "you've got to admire them. They just go out and win. They kind of plod along in there, and don't look spectacular doing it. But they're my kind of football team."

Barnett was ecstatic at his team's performance and at the way the community had responded. "That was a home-field advantage with a raucous home crowd [that was] into college football," he said. "I just can't think that there can be any better situation to experience than what we experienced Saturday. It was ours, it was purple, and it was loud."

For the first time since 1904, the Wildcats sported an 8-1 record. They were now ranked fifth in the nation. On November 11, they hosted Iowa, to whom they had lost 21 straight since 1973 (including an embarrassing 49-13 decision in 1994). When asked for his opinion of the Hawkeyes, Chris Martin said simply, "We don't really care for 'em." Iowa coach Hayden Fry took the bait. "I think Northwestern's players are just feeling their oats," he said. "Whatever is in their craw is in their craw. So be it."

The Hawkeyes had dropped three in a row since winning their first five, and they were desperate to salvage their season and a bowl bid with a victory in Evanston. Despite the temperature of only 26 degrees and a wind-chill factor of zero, another sellout crowd of 49,256 filled every corner of venerable Dyche Stadium for the final home game of the season. The purple-clad partisans were not disappointed. Northwestern stormed back from a 20-17 halftime deficit to win 31-20 on a three-yard run by Autry in the third quarter and a 31-yard fumble return by Ismaeli in the fourth. "I compliment a fine Northwestern team and effort today," said Fry. "They are just a heck of a football team."

The 9-1 record and eight-game winning streak were both unprecedented in Northwestern annals. The bad news was that Fitzgerald, inspirational leader of the Wildcats' swarming defense, had broken his left leg and would be out for the year. The Wildcats dedicated the season finale at Purdue to Fitzgerald, and Autry played like a man possessed. He gained 226 yards on 32 attempts as Northwestern overwhelmed the Boilermakers 23-8. Autry finished the season with 1,675 yards, 15 touchdowns, and a grand total of one turnover in 376 times handling the ball.

With an 8-0 slate in the Big Ten, the Wildcats could do no worse than tie for the conference championship. But they didn't know yet whether they'd be going to the Rose Bowl or to the less glamorous Florida Citrus Bowl. Worse, they could do nothing further to influence how it turned out. The Big Ten schedule was such that each team played every conference rival but two in any given year. As luck would have it, Ohio State and Northwestern missed one another in 1995, perhaps the only year in history that a matchup between them would have meant something. Second-ranked Ohio State was 7-0 in the Big Ten and 10-0 overall. The Buckeyes had one game remaining—their traditional season-ending contest with Michigan. If they won, they'd be headed to Pasadena; if they lost, all of Barnett's lofty preseason goals would have been fulfilled.

On November 25, the Wildcats' players and coaches gathered on the Northwestern campus to watch the ABC telecast of the Ohio State-Michigan game. The Wildcats' hopes rode on the padded shoulders of Michigan tailback Tim Biakabutuka, the man who had shredded their top-ranked defense for 205 yards on October 7. Could he come up with a similar effort against the unbeaten Buckeyes?

He could. Biakabutuka ran for 313 yards—the greatest performance by a running back in the history of the century-old rivalry. Meanwhile, Ohio State's Eddie George (who would receive that year's Heisman Trophy) was held to a relatively modest 104. Michigan won 31-23.

Rose Bowl president Bud Greist was at the game, ready to invite Ohio State in person if they'd won. Instead, he was connected via a video and audio hookup to Evanston so he could invite Northwestern electronically. Barnett milked the moment he had dreamed of for all it was worth. After a pregnant pause, he said, "I'll ask our guys if they want to go to Pasadena."

He didn't have to ask twice.

Northwestern's Cinderella story *almost* had a perfect ending. In the Rose Bowl, the Wildcats trailed USC 24-7 in the second quarter. They launched a stirring comeback, scoring on five straight possessions to take a 32-31 edge early in the fourth quarter. But they didn't quite get it done. A late Wildcat touchdown was called back for holding, and the Trojans eventually prevailed 41-32.

"Our kids fought hard enough," said Barnett. "There isn't anything I'd do over." He was justly proud of having kept his audacious promise to take the purple to Pasadena; it was no disgrace that the Wildcats had narrowly failed to bring home a victory. After 47 years, getting there had been considerably more than half the fun.

CHAPTER 35

72-10

"I love the way this Chicago Bulls team plays basketball."
-- *George Karl, Seattle SuperSonics head coach, 1992-1998*

With 17 games left in the 1994-95 regular season, the Bulls were struggling. "They had grown comfortable with the idea of being a .500 team," coach Phil Jackson wrote. "Then Michael Jordan walked in the door." On March 18, 1995, Jordan issued a statement consisting of two words: "I'm back." He thus confirmed that his career as a so-so minor-league baseball player was over and his career as the greatest basketball player of all time was about to resume.

Many people assumed that Jordan's return after almost two years away would automatically mean another championship for the Bulls. "But what happened instead," Jackson wrote, "was that the team lost the identity it had forged in Jordan's absence." Only three Bulls had played with Jordan before, and the others were understandably in awe of him. Their tendency to stand around and watch Michael worked out well enough when he torched the New York Knicks for 55 points in his fourth game back, but it didn't bode well for long-term success. The Orlando Magic ousted the Bulls from the playoffs in the second round. It marked the first time since 1990 that a Bulls team with Jordan had fallen short of the world championship.

The series against Orlando demonstrated two things. First, that Jordan's abbreviated season had not prepared him for the rigors of playoff basketball (he'd made several crucial gaffes and had appeared strangely uncertain throughout). Second, that the Bulls could not regain the title without a power forward to contend with the likes of Horace Grant, their former teammate who'd had a field day against them.

Jordan addressed the first point by putting himself through a murderous offseason workout regimen. He was almost 33, and he was determined to prove that he could still measure up to the incredible standard he had set before his retirement. "At my age, I have to work harder," he said. "I can't afford to cut corners. This time, I plan to go into the playoffs with a whole season of conditioning under my belt."

General manager Jerry Krause addressed the second point by trading Will Perdue to the San Antonio Spurs for Dennis Rodman. It was a bold move. Rodman's selfishness and lack of discipline had thoroughly alienated his coaches and teammates in San Antonio. He was a tattooed, body-piercing, cross-dressing free spirit who changed his hair color almost as often as most people change their socks. He was also indisputably the best rebounder in the league. That alone made him worth the risk in Krause's eyes.

Rodman was not effusively welcomed by his new teammates. Jordan and Pippen were skeptical, remembering Rodman's role with the Detroit Pistons' "Bad Boys," the Bulls' arch-enemies of the late eighties and early nineties. Toni Kukoc was even less enthusiastic, for Rodman's arrival meant his departure from the starting lineup. To ease Rodman's isolation, Krause signed journeyman forward Jack Haley, whom he had no intention of using on the court. Haley had befriended Rodman in San Antonio, and he became known as "Dennis's babysitter" with the Bulls.

Rodman was just beginning to adapt to the Bulls, and they to him, when a calf injury sidelined him three games into the season. Even without him, the Bulls won six of seven on a road trip through the West, while exhibiting the ferocious defense that would be their trademark all year. When Rodman returned after a month on the shelf, the Bulls stood at 13-2. In his first four games back, he showed why Krause had taken a chance on him. He pulled down 20, 21, 21, and 19 rebounds, respectively, as the Bulls defeated New York, San Antonio, Milwaukee, and Orlando.

The winning streak reached 13. "From the media's standpoint, it looks like we're toying with people," Jordan said. "But for us it's just a matter of making adjustments. We may take teams for granted a little bit early in games, but then we figure them out and apply our defense where necessary in the second half." Indeed, most games were decided shortly after intermission by a Bulls blitzkrieg that rendered the fourth quarter moot.

The combination of Jordan, Pippen, and Rodman—now nicknamed "Superman, Batman, and Rodman"—was proving unstoppable. Rodman flourished under Jackson's laid-back coaching style and won over Chicago fans by flinging his jersey into the crowd after each home game. His on-court antics occasionally got him ejected, fined, and/or suspended, and his off-court publicity stunts grew increasingly bizarre. But he showed up on time for practice, played hard in games, and generally got along with his teammates—none of which he'd done consistently in San Antonio.

While the Bulls' lesser lights didn't attract nearly as much attention, they too made key contributions. Guard Ron Harper became the perfect complement to the man he'd earlier been asked to replace; his stellar defensive work created myriad fast-break opportunities for Jordan. Center Luc Longley used his height and heft to disrupt opponents' drives down the lane. Kukoc and Bill Wennington provided scoring punch off the bench. Steve Kerr was a devastating long-range bomber. Randy Brown was a fleet-footed defender who could stick with the league's quickest point guards. Jud Buechler supplied Jackson's favorite ingredient, "good energy." The Bulls were hitting on all cylinders.

The Bulls lost at Indiana the day after Christmas. Three days later, they avenged the loss with a 120-93 rout of the Pacers in Chicago. Five weeks would go by before they tasted defeat again.

On January 3, the Bulls held the defending world champion Houston Rockets to one-of-15 shooting in the second quarter and cruised to an easy 100-86 win behind Jordan's 38 points. A week later, in a game with postseason implications, the Bulls humiliated the Seattle Super-Sonics 113-87 as Jordan grabbed 14 rebounds to go with his 35 points. On January 13, the Bulls visited the Philadelphia 76ers, whose rookie guard Jerry Stackhouse had recently announced, "Nobody can stop me in this league—not even Michael Jordan." Jordan scored 48 points and held Stackhouse to nine as the Bulls won 120-93. At New York on January 23, the Bulls bombed the Knicks 99-79. And so it went.

The month ended as it had begun, with a victory over the Rockets, this time in Houston (it was the Bulls' first win there in eight years). Pippen, who had emerged as a legitimate MVP candidate, topped the Bulls with 28 points, 12 rebounds, and five assists. "He's the leader of this team," Jordan said, exaggerating less than many people supposed.

January 1996 was the first perfect month in Bulls' history—14 games, 14 wins. By the time the winning streak reached 18 in early February, the Bulls had won 31 of their last 32. Their record stood at a stupendous 41-3. It was clear that they were taking aim at the single-season record of 69 wins in 82 games, set by the Los Angeles Lakers in 1971-72.

The Bulls had been in a similar situation in 1992. That year, Jackson deliberately pulled in the reins, allowing several late-season games to slip away while he rested his starters for the playoffs. The Bulls finished with "only" 67 wins but, more importantly, went on to take the world championship. Now Jackson again tried to downplay the regular-season record. "Playoff basketball totally changes everything," he said. "That's the mystery, as to whether we can play at this level all through the season and then come through with the championship drive."

The Bulls' unprecedented success and their panache both on and off the court made them the biggest phenomenon the NBA had ever seen. Every away game became an *event*, anticipated like a concert by the most famous of rock stars. In each city the Bulls visited, hundreds of fans turned out hoping just to catch a glimpse of them walking from their bus into the hotel.

A discordant note was sounded when Rodman was left out of the All-Star Game even though it was obvious that he was on his way to a fifth straight rebounding title. The game was played in San Antonio, and Rodman was bitterly disappointed that he could not return in triumph to the city from which he'd been banished. When the season resumed, the snub seemed to inspire him to play even harder and better than he already had for the Bulls.

In the second game after the break, at Detroit, Rodman had 19 rebounds, including an amazing total of 14 on the offensive side, as the

Bulls won 112-109. Three nights later at Indiana, he pulled down 23 rebounds while Jordan scored 44 points and Pippen added 40 as the Bulls subdued the Pacers. "They're the best," Indiana coach Larry Brown declared. "They wouldn't be 46-5 if they didn't try to make a statement every game."

The Bulls made a definitive statement a week later, blistering Orlando 111-91 at the United Center. Kukoc scored 24 points in 23 minutes, including 11 in a row to start the fourth quarter. He was showing signs of accepting, if not embracing, his role as sixth man. "I think he's shown that he can really contribute for us," Jackson said. "In big games, he plays big, and we're real comfortable with what he can do."

Kukoc came back with 23 points two nights later, while Jordan had 35 and Rodman secured a season-high 24 rebounds. The Bulls dismantled the Minnesota Timberwolves 120-99 for their 50th win of the season against six losses. It was February 27, and it marked the earliest date that any team had ever reached the 50-win milestone.

On March 18, Jordan celebrated the first anniversary of his return by scoring 38 points and hauling in 11 rebounds at Philadelphia. He played 47 of the 48 minutes, leading the Bulls to a hard-fought 98-94 victory. The club's record now stood at an almost unfathomable 58-7.

The Bulls were only three points shy of perfection for the rest of the regular season. They lost by a single point each at Toronto on March 24, to Charlotte on April 8, and to Indiana on April 20. The latter two were the Bulls' only defeats of the season at the United Center, costing them a chance to surpass or equal the Boston Celtics' home record of 41-1 in 1985-86.

The irresistible march into the record books culminated in Milwaukee on April 16. The 90-mile drive north to Milwaukee afforded many Bulls fans who couldn't hope to get tickets at the United Center (where the Bulls were drawing 109 percent of capacity) a rare opportunity to see their heroes in the flesh. Thus the sold-out Bradley Center was packed with Chicagoans for the historic game, which proved surprisingly difficult for the Bulls. "We came out totally lackluster," Jordan acknowledged. He and Pippen made only 16 of 46 shots, and the Bulls trailed for most of the contest. It fell to the diminutive and unsung Kerr to rescue the Bulls with a three-pointer, another long jumper, and two clutch free throws in the final minute. The Bulls won 86-80 for their 70th victory of the season.

On April 21, the Bulls dispatched the Washington Bullets for their 72nd win against 10 losses. The game was notable for being the last of the regular season and the first in which Jack Haley played. Haley, who had spent the prior 81 games on the bench in street clothes, cheering for his teammates, played seven minutes. He made two of six shots and one of two free throws for five points; he also grabbed two rebounds.

The Bulls' success as a team brought them a raft of individual honors. Jordan won his eighth scoring title and retained the highest career average of all time; he also won his fourth Most Valuable Player award. Pippen joined Jordan on the All-NBA first team and finished fifth in the MVP balloting. Rodman joined Jordan and Pippen on the All-Defensive first team and won his fifth rebounding title. Kukoc won the Sixth Man award. Kerr finished second in the league in three-point shooting but remained number one in career annals. Jackson was selected Coach of the Year and moved past Pat Riley for the highest winning percentage in NBA history. Krause was chosen Executive of the Year.

It had been a season for the ages, but the true test remained. "It don't mean a thing," Harper declared, "without the ring." The regular-season record would be all but meaningless if the Bulls failed to win the championship as well.

The Bulls' first playoff opponents were the Miami Heat, coached by Riley. "Never lose to that guy!" Jackson had told his players, for he and Riley shared a strong mutual dislike along with the distinction of being the most successful coaches in the league. The Heat tried to play the rough-and-tumble style that Riley had employed with the New York Knicks. But Miami didn't have the personnel to pull it off. Frustration got the better of center Alonzo Mourning, who repeatedly lost his composure and was even ejected from Game 1. The Bulls swept the series by the lopsided scores of 102-85, 106-75, and 112-91.

Next up were the very same Knicks whose tactics the Heat had lamely sought to adopt. Patrick Ewing, Charles Oakley, Anthony Mason, and John Starks were the genuine article, as tough and physical a bunch as could be found—but they could handle neither Jordan's offensive firepower nor the Bulls' defensive intensity. Jordan scored 44 points in Game 1 while he and his teammates forced 17 turnovers and did not allow a field goal in the last five minutes. The Bulls won 91-84. In Game 2, Ewing had 22 points after three quarters but was held to just one in the fourth as the Bulls won again, 91-80.

Jordan was truly heroic in Game 3 at New York. He scored eight points in the final 71 seconds as the Bulls rallied to push the game into overtime. He played 51 minutes in all and totaled 46 points, but the Knicks won 102-99. Game 4 found the Bulls at their most vulnerable. Kukoc was out with a sore back, Pippen wrenched *his* back and missed considerable playing time, and the exhausted Jordan made only seven of 23 shots. But Rodman was superb, grabbing 19 rebounds and dishing out a pair of crucial assists in the final two minutes—both of which were coolly finished by Wennington, who explained, "Dennis got me the ball, I was open, and I hit the shots." The Bulls escaped with a 94-91 triumph that sealed the Knicks' fate. In Game 5 in Chicago two nights later, the Bulls were in command throughout as they won 94-81. The Bulls advanced to the series they had waited for all year, a playoff rematch with Orlando.

What a difference a year made. In 1995, Horace Grant was carried out of the United Center on the shoulders of his teammates as they celebrated their victory over the Bulls. In 1996, Grant scored zero points and had one rebound in 28 minutes *for the series*. He was completely outplayed by Rodman (who scored 13 points and had 21 rebounds) in Game 1, then watched the remaining games from the bench, nursing an injured elbow.

The Magic were wholly inept in Game 1. Like Grant, Dennis Scott did not score, while Nick Anderson managed two free throws—so three Orlando starters *combined* for two points. The Bulls, on the other hand, got double-digit scoring from six players en route to an overwhelming 121-83 victory.

In Game 2, Orlando's mammoth center Shaquille O'Neal was dominant (he finished with 36 points), and the Bulls found themselves trailing by 18 midway through the third quarter. Then they tightened the screws on defense and outscored the Magic 20-4 to close the quarter behind by only two. "We lost our poise," Orlando guard Anferne "Penny" Hardaway admitted. The Bulls' pressure defense continued to stifle the Magic down the stretch, and the Bulls prevailed 93-88.

Games 3 and 4 were played in Orlando, where the Magic had lost only twice all season. In Game 3, the Magic were limited to 67 points—the second lowest output in any playoff game since the advent of the 24-second shot clock some 40 years earlier. The Bulls sailed to a 19-point win. "We just overpowered them," said Pippen, who scored 27 points. The Magic improved in Game 4, but not enough. Jordan's 45 points sparked the Bulls to a 106-101 win that completed the series sweep. This time, Orlando players offered no disparaging comments about Jordan's age or effectiveness.

"It's not our goal," Rodman said of the world championship, "it's our destiny."

It certainly seemed so in light of the Bulls' astounding 72-10 regular season and 11-1 romp through the first three playoff rounds. Most experts had already anointed the Bulls as the greatest team of all time. There was, though, one more team to beat: the Seattle SuperSonics, who had outlasted the Utah Jazz four games to three in the Western Conference finals. No slouches themselves with 64 wins in the regular season, the SuperSonics nonetheless were 10-1 underdogs against the Bulls.

In Game 1 at the United Center, the Sonics held tough for three quarters, after which they trailed only 69-67. But then it was Toni Kukoc time. The lanky Croatian notched 10 points in the first five minutes of the fourth quarter, igniting a surge in which the Bulls drew away to win 107-90. Kukoc's 18 points were part of an exceptionally balanced attack by the Bulls: Longley finished with 14, Harper 15, Pippen 21, and Jordan 28. Rodman had 13 rebounds and watched, bemused, as Seattle's Frank Brickowski was ejected for trying to goad him into a wrestling match.

"A lot of people don't give me enough credit for being an adult," Rodman said. He gave a grown-up performance in Game 2, pulling down 20 rebounds, including 11 on offense, to keep the Bulls in the game despite their 39 percent shooting. "He was probably their MVP tonight," said Seattle coach George Karl. Rodman and Kukoc keyed a 15-4 spurt in the late third and early fourth quarters that put the Bulls ahead 81-68. Although Kukoc's tip-in with six minutes left proved to be Chicago's last field goal, the Bulls held on to win 92-88.

Ron Harper's ailing knees were so stiff and sore after Game 2 that he could not continue effectively. The Bulls would be without him for all but a few minutes of the next three games. It made little difference in Game 3, as the Bulls put on an almost frightening display. They led 34-12 after a quarter and 62-38 at halftime, then coasted to a 108-86 decision before a stunned, silent crowd at Seattle's Key Arena. Again the overwrought Brickowski was ejected, this time for a flagrant foul. Jordan scored 36 points and Longley, who'd struggled badly in Game 2, added 19. When asked what had accounted for Longley's improvement, Jackson had a candid and succinct reply. "Verbal bashing by everybody on the club," he said.

The champagne was on ice. One more win would give the Bulls not only their coveted world championship, but also, at 15-1, the finest playoff run in NBA history—a bookend to their phenomenal regular season. But, to their credit, the Sonics did not roll over and play dead. They had never led in Game 3, but in Game 4 they took control early in the first quarter and rolled to a 108-86 win. Game 5 was a seesaw battle until Seattle's 11-0 run with eight minutes broke it open; the Sonics won 89-78.

The back-to-back defeats in Seattle marked only the second time in 99 regular-season and playoff games that the Bulls had lost twice in a row. They were a jolt of reality, proving that even the Bulls couldn't beat as good a team as the Sonics merely by showing up. They also showed how much the Bulls needed the vastly underrated Harper, the catalyst of their pressure defense.

Game 6 was on June 16 at the United Center. Jordan promised his family a win for the man whose absence was a presence in their lives—Michael's father, James, who'd been murdered shortly after the Bulls' last title run in 1993. It was, after all, Father's Day.

The 24,544 fans on hand were ready to rock, and they did their best to make sure the Bulls were too. They impersonated Blackhawk fans by cheering throughout the national anthem. Then they roared even louder when the Bulls' starters were introduced. Among the five who trotted into this cauldron of sound was the courageous Harper; determined to play as hard as he could for as long as he could, he wound up logging 38 minutes.

With the raucous crowd revving them up, the Bulls were the aggressors from the outset. But each time they threatened to turn the game into a rout, Seattle climbed back into it. The Bulls led 45-38 at halftime. In the third quarter, a 19-9 surge gave Chicago a 15-point edge, but the Sonics responded with a 9-0 run of their own. A long three-pointer by Kerr made it 67-58 as the quarter ended.

In the fourth quarter, the Sonics double- and triple-teamed Jordan, daring the other Bulls to shoot. Kukoc obliged and hit two three-pointers, the second of which extended the lead to an apparently insurmountable 75-61. When Shawn Kemp, Seattle's heart and soul, left the court after fouling out a few minutes later, any hope for a comeback went with him. Kemp had just sat down when Pippen launched a long three-pointer that put the game away. What the last three minutes lacked in suspense they made up for in decibels, as the huge throng saluted the Bulls with a lusty and prolonged ovation.

The final score was 87-75. Jordan scored a modest (for him) 22 points to close the playoffs with a 30.7 average, almost identical to his 30.4 for the regular season. He was, of course, voted Most Valuable Player of the series. Rodman had 19 rebounds, matching the NBA Finals record with 11 offensive boards for the second time in the series. He had repaid Krause many times over for taking a chance on him. Pippen had, as usual, wreaked havoc at both ends of the floor.

"I think we can consider ourselves the greatest team of all time," Pippen said, grinning and puffing on a king-sized Cohiba. It would be difficult to dispute that assertion or any of the accolades heaped upon the 1995-96 Bulls. They won 87 of 100 games, a feat unlikely to ever be repeated, and embodied the cliché of being greater than the sum of their parts. "They play as a team," said the longtime coach and commentator Jack Ramsay, "and there appears to be no selfishness. There's no evidence of ego. They all know their roles, and they all can fill their roles."

Jackson received far less credit than he deserved for fostering this ethic of old-fashioned teamwork in an era of colossal player salaries and even larger egos. Though justly proud of what he and the Bulls had done, he left it to others to assess his team's place in history. "Let's just say that we are honored to take our place among the select few," he wrote. "Unless, however, somebody invents a time machine. Then I think maybe I could convince Michael and these guys to lace up their sneakers to settle the issue once and for all."

Even for Jordan, whose career had been marked by one unforgettable achievement after another, the 1995-96 campaign was a particular high point. Far from being diminished, his individual brilliance was only enhanced by the fact that it now shone within a team system functioning at a level very near to perfection. He could have been speaking for the teammates and fans to whom he'd given so much over the years when he said simply, "I've been very blessed."

CHAPTER 36

From Citation to Cigar

"Secretariat is the most capable horse I ever saw, and geriatrics defeat any thought of seeing his like again."

-- Charles Hatton, Daily Racing Form *writer, 1928-1975*

When the great Cigar visited Arlington Park in Arlington Heights on July 13, 1996, seeking to equal the all-time record with his 16th consecutive victory, the occasion was bittersweet. On one hand, it enabled Chicagoland racing fans to witness history in the making, and it showcased the magnificent Arlington facility (rebuilt from the ground up after the grandstand was destroyed by fire in 1985) to a national television audience. On the other, it demonstrated that the track now needed to stage a truly extraordinary event in order to attract the kind of crowd that used to show up almost every Saturday and Sunday.

There was a time when the best thoroughbreds came through the Chicago area every year. Throughout the forties, fifties, and sixties, many of the top trainers and jockeys spent the entire summer here, and even those who were based elsewhere made frequent appearances at Arlington, Hawthorne Park in Cicero, and Washington Park in Homewood to race for purses ranking among the richest offered anywhere.

Since its halcyon era (when, not coincidentally, the racetracks were the only places outside of Las Vegas where people could legally gamble), racing has endured a steady decline. But many Chicagoans still recall the glory days and the immortals who made their mark here. A few stood out even among the other champions of their time. These were the best of the best.

Citation

Owned by Chicagoan Warren Wright and named after the baking-powder company he had founded, Calumet Farm was the most illustrious stable in racing history. A long line of champions carried its devil-red and blue silks to glory in the forties: Whirlaway, Armed, Twilight Tear, Coaltown, Bewitch, and Citation. The last of these was exceptional even by Calumet's rarefied standards. While it was not particularly uncommon at the time for the best horses to compete in one top race after another with hardly a pause to catch their breath between starts, it was quite uncommon for any horse to win 19 races in a single year, as Citation did. "He could outsprint the fastest," Edward L. Bowen wrote, "outstay the stoutest, and do it all with a mechanical rhythm invested of perfection."

Citation first came to Chicago in the summer of 1947, his two-year-old season. On July 24, he captured the Sealeggy Purse at Arlington Park, covering the five furlongs in 58 seconds flat for a new track record. He won his first stakes race, the Elementary, six days later at Washington Park. On August 16, he and two stablemates entered the Washington Park Futurity. They were trained by the famous father-and-son team of Ben and Jimmy Jones, who won the Kentucky Derby eight times between them.

"We ran three horses in the Futurity that year," Jimmy Jones later recalled, "and we figured we'd take the first three places with Citation, Bewitch, and Free America. So we told the riders before the race that we would split the fees three ways. That way nobody would do anything foolish in the drive. Bewitch, with Doug Dodson up, got the lead and finished a length in front of Citation, with Free America third. Steve Brooks, on Citation, said he could have gone by [Bewitch] at any time." It was the only defeat of the year for Citation, who went eight-for-nine and was voted champion two-year-old colt. Bewitch was champion two-year-old filly.

In 1948, Citation enjoyed the greatest three-year-old campaign of all time. He won 19 of 20 starts and earned $709,470 (the previous record was $424,195). He not only swept the Triple Crown races with astonishing ease, but he also won the Jersey Derby between the Preakness and the Belmont! "Citation is by far the greatest horse I've ever ridden," said jockey Eddie Arcaro, and even curmudgeonly old-timers began to mention him in the same breath as the legendary Man O' War, who had died at the age of 30 the year before.

Fresh from his Triple Crown triumph, Citation returned to Arlington Park for the Stars & Stripes Handicap against older horses on July 5. That no three-year-old had won, and only one had run in the money, in the 20-year history of the event was of no concern to Citation. Before a huge crowd of 46,490, he romped to a two-length victory and tied the track record for a mile and an eighth at 1:49.2. He got a well-deserved six-week vacation, then devastated his rivals in an allowance sprint at Washington Park on August 21. A week later, the entry of Citation and Free America was sent off at odds of 1-10 in the American Derby, also at Washington Park. The race went true to form, as Citation scored by a length over Free America in a brisk 2:01.6 for the mile and a quarter. It was his ninth consecutive win. By the end of the year, the streak had reached 15, and Citation's career mark stood at 27 wins and two seconds in 29 starts.

An ankle injury sidelined Citation for all of 1949, but, because his owners were intent on making him the first equine millionaire, he came back to race 16 more times in 1950 and 1951. He lost on several occasions, in the words of racing writer Joe Hirsch, to "horses who couldn't warm him up when he was right." Nonetheless, he went out in style, winning his last three races to bring his lifetime earnings to $1,085,760.

Citation made his final public appearance on July 29, 1951. While thousands cheered, he galloped down the home stretch at Arlington Park, then was led to that place he knew so well—the winner's circle.

Native Dancer

Racing was a popular feature on television in the fifties, and Native Dancer's distinctive gray coloring made him instantly recognizable even on the comparatively primitive black-and-white sets of the day. It hardly mattered that the "Gray Ghost" was so easy to pick out of a crowd, though, for he was seldom in one. His usual practice was to bide his time in the early stages of a race, then fly past his rivals with a burst of almost frightening power. "Words can't explain it," said jockey Eric Guerin. "You have to be on his back to feel it."

Native Dancer won all nine of his starts in 1952. The next spring, he came into the Kentucky Derby as an overwhelming favorite. As was his wont, he started casually and relaxed near the back of the pack while Guerin looked ahead for the most advantageous route. Seeing what appeared to be a likely opening between horses, Guerin was about to go through when a 46-1 shot named Money Broker abruptly swerved into his path. Thrown offstride by the collision, Native Dancer dropped further back and raced well wide into the far turn before fully recovering his bearings. He rallied courageously down the stretch but barely ran out of real estate, losing to Dark Star by a head.

The details of the 1953 Derby wouldn't matter much but for the fact that it was the only defeat that Native Dancer ever experienced.

He won the Withers Stakes, the Preakness, the Belmont, and the Dwyer Stakes before appearing at Arlington Park on July 18 for the Arlington Classic. Its purse of $154,300 made the Classic the richest event for three-year-olds in the history of racing up to that time. The track was heavy, and the crowd of 39,460 was relatively cautious in its support of Native Dancer, making him a 2-3 favorite. Van Crosby led around the turn, with the Dancer stalking him. "I was out there in front going into the stretch," said Bobby Baird, Van Crosby's rider, "and on the heavy track I couldn't hear what was behind me. We just kept going. Then I heard a horse coming to me and by the time I could look around, he was past me. I never saw anything like it!"

The horse that went past, of course, was Native Dancer, who rolled away to a nine-length victory. "When we were halfway around the bend, I asked him to turn it on," said Guerin. "I knew the race was over. I never had to touch him with the whip. All I did was yell at him."

In his next start, the Travers Stakes at Saratoga, Native Dancer prevailed by five and a half lengths at odds of 1-20. Then it was back to Chicago for the American Derby at Washington Park on August 22. Guerin was serving a suspension for a riding infraction, so Eddie Arcaro got the mount. The crowd of 37,108 bet Native Dancer down to 1-5 and applauded warmly when he came onto the track. He responded by giving his fans a few anxious moments. Native Dancer was 11 lengths off the pace after half a mile and not showing much interest in the proceedings. He was still six lengths back turning for home. That's when Arcaro roused him with a couple taps of the whip. In just a few strides, the Dancer was in front, and he was still pulling away when he swept across the finish line two lengths clear of his nearest rival. His time of 1:48.4 was just a fifth of a second slower than the track record. "Sheer power!" Arcaro exclaimed after the race. "He's everything they said he was."

Native Dancer was champion two-year-old in 1952, champion three-year-old in 1953, and champion older horse and Horse of the Year in 1954. His career record of 21 wins and one second in 22 races is the best of all time among horses that started more than 15 times, slightly surpassing Man O' War's mark of 20 wins and one second in 21 races.

Round Table

Racing on grass has been the norm in Europe for centuries, but it wasn't a prominent aspect of American racing until after World War II. Round Table was the first great American "lawnmower"; he won 14 of 16 races on the grass, including a perfect 10-for-10 at Chicago tracks.

Among the top-flight horses of the 20th century, none had a stronger Chicago connection than Round Table, who made a total of 23 starts among Arlington, Washington, and Hawthorne, and won 15 of them—including almost all of the major races those tracks had to offer on grass or dirt: the American Derby, the Arlington Handicap (twice), the Laurance Armour Handicap, Hawthorne Gold Cup (twice), the Stars & Stripes, and the Washington Park Handicap.

Round Table won 14 races in 1958, his four-year-old season. He concluded the campaign with a triumph in the Hawthorne Gold Cup on October 11, in which he broke the track record for a mile and a quarter. He received Eclipse awards as champion grass horse, champion older horse, and Horse of the Year.

In 1959, Round Table won "only" nine races, but his best performances were as good as any of his career. He made his first Chicago-area start of the year on June 13, in the Citation Handicap at Washington Park. Although he'd been on the shelf almost four months with an injury and had been assigned to carry 130 pounds, Round Table did not disappoint. Going a mile on the dirt under Steve Brooks, he prevailed by a neck over Etonian, who carried only 104 pounds. On July 4, Round Table won the Stars & Stripes at a mile and an eighth on the turf, also at Washington Park. Ridden by Bill Shoemaker, he pulled away in the stretch and "scored cleverly," in the words of *Daily Racing Form*, by three and a half lengths.

Round Table made the last Chicago appearances of his career in the Arlington Handicap on grass and the Washington Park Handicap on dirt, both contested at Arlington Park.

The Arlington Handicap was run on August 22. Round Table was made to carry 132 pounds, while his eight opponents ranged from 104 to 112. Sent off at odds of 4-5, Round Table was restrained by Shoemaker for the first five furlongs while remaining close to the pace. Shoemaker let out the reins on the far turn, and Round Table soon charged into the lead. He extended the advantage to two and a half lengths in mid-stretch, then withstood a furious rally by Manassas in the final sixteenth of a mile. "He was all out," said Shoemaker. "No question about that." Round Table held off Manassas by a head, and the time of 1:53.4 lopped four-fifths of a second off the American record for a mile and three-sixteenths on the grass.

Maurice Shevlin of the *Tribune* reported that the result "had the crowd of 22,517 standing in the aisles for an ovation seldom given any thoroughbred in Chicago."

The Washington Park Handicap was run on Labor Day, September 7. Again Round Table was assigned 132 pounds, conceding at least 18 to each of his five rivals. Unconcerned, the crowd of 33,184 bet him down to 7-10. Breaking from the No. 2 post position, Round Table and Shoemaker were in no hurry in the early going. They were next to last, some six or seven lengths back, as first Terrang, then Better Bee, and finally Belleau Chief held the lead for about a quarter mile each.

Round Table was still fourth, but gaining, as the field approached the far turn. "I just let the horse out a little bit," Shoemaker said. On the turn, Round Table made an electrifying move that shot him into the lead. In the home stretch, he drew clear by three lengths, then five. At the wire, he was six and a half lengths in front. The time of 1:47.2 improved the track record for a mile and an eighth on dirt by one and one-fifth seconds, or approximately six lengths. Therefore the runner-up, Dunce, narrowly missed the previous track record even while finishing far behind Round Table. "Nobody was going to beat that horse today," declared Dunce's rider, Johnny Rotz.

When he retired at the end of the 1959 season, Round Table's lifetime bankroll of almost $1.75 million was unprecedented, and his total of 43 victories was the highest since Exterminator logged 50 from 1917 to 1924. Not even the most durable champions of subsequent decades (Kelso, Forego, and John Henry) have reached 40.

Dr. Fager

Many racing people believe that at top speed (going all-out for half a mile or so), Dr. Fager was the fastest thoroughbred ever to race in North America. His record makes that difficult to dispute. William Nack wrote after one race that he "blew around [the track] like a malevolent wind."

Dr. Fager visited the Chicago area three times. First, in June 1967, he captured the Arlington Classic for three-year-olds by 10 lengths over a sloppy course, at odds of 2-5. Then, in October of the same year, he scored a two-and-a-half length victory in the Hawthorne Gold Cup for three-year-olds and up, at odds of 3-10.

Late in the summer of his four-year-old season, on August 24, 1968, Dr. Fager returned to Arlington for the Washington Park Handicap. By this time he was known throughout the racing world for his tremendous speed, and he was assigned to carry 134 pounds to make things more competitive. No horse in the history of the race had ever been given a burden of that magnitude. Even so, the fans made him a 3-10 favorite.

A week of intense heat and no rain had rendered the track bone-dry. Dr. Fager broke from post position No. 9 under the great Panamanian jockey Braulio Baeza. Baeza bided his time in the middle of the pack for the first quarter mile, then sent the Doctor flying. After half a mile, they had moved up to contend for the lead—but the pace, 44 seconds flat, seemed to be far too fast. Wouldn't the Doctor run out of gas along the turn or in the stretch?

The answer was no. One rival after another took a run at him, but Dr. Fager pulled away to a three-length lead after six furlongs in the astounding time of 1:07.6. (To put this in perspective, consider that the Breeders' Cup Sprint, which pits the fastest sprinters in the world against one another for six furlongs, was run that fast only twice in its first 25 years.) With a quarter mile to go, Dr. Fager continued to draw off. Through the stretch he extended his advantage to 10 lengths. When he hit the wire, the timer showed 1:32.2—two-fifths of a second faster than the world record set by Buckpasser on the same track, also under Baeza, two years before.

"I don't care about setting world records or financial records," said owner/trainer Johnny Nerud. "My concern is winning and winning alone. I'm prejudiced but I have to say that this is as good a horse as ever raced on American tracks." At the close of the 1968 season, Dr. Fager received Eclipse awards as champion sprinter, champion grass horse, champion older horse, and Horse of the Year. It was, and remains, an unprecedented sweep.

Dr. Fager retired with 18 wins in 22 starts, with one second and one third. (In the only race in which he was officially out of the money, he finished first by six and a half lengths but was disqualified for rough riding by his jockey and placed fourth.) At the time, he was one of a mere handful of horses to have earned more than $1 million. His world record for the mile was still holding up nicely as of the end of the century.

Secretariat

In the 1973 Triple Crown races, a colt named Sham admirably demonstrated both talent and heart. He ran the mile and a quarter of the Kentucky Derby faster than it had ever been run in the 99-year history of the race. Likewise, he covered the mile and three-sixteenths of the Preakness in record time. But he finished second in both races, beaten by two and a half lengths each time. In the Belmont Stakes, he battled gamely with the horse that had defeated him in the other two races. Finally, the strain of trying to keep up with the immortal Secretariat proved to be too much for Sham, who faded out of contention on the backstretch and eventually finished last. He never raced again.

Having disposed of Sham, Secretariat continued to accelerate—though no other horse was in a position to challenge him. He was running now only against the limits of his own greatness. Jockey Ron Turcotte, who had been in the habit of restraining Secretariat at times to conserve his strength, let him go. "Secretariat is moving like a tremendous machine!" cried track announcer Chic Anderson.

In the home stretch, Turcotte heard the cheering of the crowd, but he could hear no other horses. He turned around to look over his left shoulder and was astonished to discover that there were none in sight. Secretariat crossed the finish line 31 lengths ahead of his nearest pursuer. When the timer showed 2:24 flat, trainer Lucien Laurin thought it had malfunctioned. But the time was correct: Secretariat had beaten the world record for the mile and a half by two full seconds—or about 10 lengths! The people who were fortunate enough to be at Belmont Park that day saw not only what they'd come hoping to see, the coronation of the first Triple Crown champion in a quarter century, but also the greatest race ever run.

The Triple Crown series is a grueling ordeal, and most horses are given time off afterwards for rest and relaxation. But Secretariat wasn't like most horses. Just three weeks after his brilliant victory in the Belmont, he was on the track at Arlington Park. Realizing that the Secretariat had won with something in reserve despite the incredible time, Laurin advised owner Penny Chenery Tweedy to run Secretariat in the hastily arranged Arlington Invitational Stakes on June 30. Mrs. Tweedy agreed. She saw it as her duty to give something back to the sport, and she felt that fans in the Midwest deserved a chance to see her famous big red colt in the flesh.

Only three other horses showed up at Arlington to challenge him, but 41,223 humans were on hand—and they were not disappointed.

Secretariat was sent off at odds of 1-20. Though he was left behind at the gate, he wasted little time in overpowering his three adversaries. He assumed command shortly after entering the clubhouse turn, even with Turcotte keeping a tight hold on him. Once Secretariat got to the front, the race was over. He galloped to the finish line nine lengths ahead of My Gallant, a veteran of the Kentucky Derby and Belmont who was already familiar with the view of Secretariat from behind. The time was 1:47 for the mile and an eighth, only one-fifth of a second slower than the track record by Damascus.

"I could have broken the track record if I wanted," said Turcotte. "The horse was not quite on his feet when the gate was sprung. Rather than rush him, I let him settle himself. I kept him 10 to 12 feet off the rail all the way."

Track record or not, Secretariat gave Chicago-area racing fans a shining moment and almost single-handedly salvaged a profitable season for Arlington. "It was a wonderful thrill, the reception we got here," Laurin said. "I'm glad we brought him."

Spectacular Bid

Spectacular Bid was sold as a yearling for a mere $37,000. Before long, however, trainer Grover "Bud" Delp called him "the best horse to ever look through a bridle," and the legendary jockey Bill Shoemaker concurred.

Spectacular Bid won seven of nine starts in 1978, including the last five in succession, and was voted champion two-year-old. He won his first seven starts in 1979, including the Kentucky Derby and the Preakness, by a combined 44 lengths. He carried a 12-race winning streak into the Belmont Stakes, and racing fans considered it a foregone conclusion that he would win easily to complete the Triple Crown. But it didn't happen. First, according to Delp, Spectacular Bid stepped on a safety pin the morning of the race. Then, for reasons known only to jockey Ronnie Franklin, he was sent winging from the gate to chase an 85-1 shot that had no chance. Used up too early, Bid staggered home third. He was given 10 weeks off after the Belmont, and from then on he was ridden by Shoemaker—who was elected to the National Racing Hall of Fame the year before Franklin was born. Bid suffered the last defeat of his career in October, finishing a game second to Affirmed, the previous year's Triple Crown winner, in the Jockey Club Gold Cup. He finished the year with 10 wins, a second, and a third in 12 outings.

In 1980, his four-year-old season, Spectacular Bid went undefeated, equaling Tom Fool's achievement of 1953 and presaging Cigar's of 1995. He was bet down to far less than even money in every race; the *highest* price he went off at was 3-10. In his third start of the year, in February, he won the Strub Stakes at Santa Anita and established a world record for the mile and a quarter (1:57.8) that still stands. He dominated three more top-caliber stakes in California that spring and summer, then came to Arlington Park for the Washington Park Stakes on July 19.

The crowd of 29,611 bet over $650,000 on the big race and $3.5 million for the day, both Illinois records at the time. One man bet $120,000 on Spectacular Bid to place. Although the odds on Bid were 1-20, the law required that each winning ticket be paid $2.10 for every $2 wagered. Therefore, the track ended up paying out some $98,000 more than was wagered on the race.

Spectacular Bid broke slowly from the gate, as was his custom, but soon moved up outside the others to draw within striking range of the pacesetting Hold Your Tricks on the backstretch. The powerful gray colt assumed the lead on the far turn and began to pull away. Now the question was not whether he would win, but whether he'd break Damascus's track record for the mile and an eighth. "I went to dinner with Shoemaker on Friday," Delp said after the race, "and the only thing I said about the race is that Bid has never been better. I told him if he felt he could get a track record and hold the horse within himself, then it was entirely up to him."

Shoemaker decided to go for it. Never resorting to the whip, he simply clucked in Spectacular Bid's ear down the stretch to keep him driving. "He was tired at the end," Shoemaker said. "It was hot and he hadn't raced for a while." Even so, they flashed under the wire 10 lengths to the good of Hold Your Tricks, stopping the timer in 1:46.2. Damascus's track record had fallen by three-fifths of a second, or about three lengths.

"The Meyerhoffs [the horse's owners] could have retired him after last year," said Delp, "but, thank God, we have people who still look at racing as a sport and not just a business." The owners were amply rewarded for being good sports: Spectacular Bid's share of the purse that day put him over $2.5 million in career earnings, a new record.

Two months after visiting Arlington, Spectacular Bid ended his career in a most memorable fashion. That he was literally in a class by himself was nicely demonstrated when no other horse was entered to face him in the Woodward Stakes at Belmont Park. Bid ran the mile and a quarter all alone but for the company of Shoemaker, earning his ninth victory in nine tries for the year and the 26th in 30 attempts for his career. It was the only uncontested race, or "walkover," at a major track in the last half of the century.

John Henry

John Henry was on the small side and nothing much to look at, as befitted the son of an obscure sire with the somewhat comical name Ole Bob Bowers. He was sold as a yearling for only $1,100, and then—to add injury to insult—was gelded in a futile attempt to curb his nasty temper. He spent his early career running at cheap tracks in Louisiana, with little success.

His record stood at three wins in 17 tries when he was bought by Sam and Dorothy Rubin in May 1978. Shipped to New York, John Henry became a winner from the instant he walked off the van. He won his first start in the Rubins' colors on May 21 at Aqueduct, paying odds of 12-1. On June 1 at Belmont Park, he raced on grass for the first time and won as he pleased—by 14 lengths. This was the turning point for John Henry. Running on grass and at longer distances, he was an entirely different horse.

On September 16, 1978, John Henry paid his first visit to Arlington Park and notched his first major stakes victory, capturing the Round Table Handicap by 12 lengths.

John Henry was on his way. He had a good campaign as a four-year-old in 1979, finishing first or second in nine of his 11 starts. The next year John Henry had eight wins, three seconds, and a third in 12 starts; he received the first of his four Eclipse Awards as best male grass horse of the year.

In 1981, the six-year-old John Henry won five of his first six starts in top-quality stakes competition. Then he came to Arlington for the inaugural running of the Arlington Million, the first race in the world to offer a million-dollar purse. The Chicago area had been hard hit by rain for several days prior to the race on August 30, and Arlington's turf course was very soft and spongy. John Henry had tried soft turf only once before, and had been well beaten on that occasion. To make matters worse, he drew the outermost post position in the field, No. 12.

Sent off at odds of 11-10, John Henry was the heavy favorite of the crowd. But in the early stages of the mile-and-a-quarter race, it was obvious that he did not like the boggy footing. He was far out of contention for the first half mile. "It was terrible," said jockey Bill Shoemaker. "He wasn't handling it at all down the backstretch, and I didn't think we'd be close. I was trying to urge him a little, without making him sour, but he was struggling." Key to Content led all the way down the backstretch and into the far turn, with 40-1 longshot The Bart in hot pursuit. John Henry was eighth as they entered the far turn.

Turning for home, Key to Content yielded command to The Bart. John Henry had moved up to fifth, but he was still six lengths from the front with only a quarter mile left to go. "He began to pick it up on the turn and moved through the upper stretch pretty good," Shoemaker recalled, "although he was still a beaten horse at the eighth pole. I was trying to hold him together at that point, for he was working very hard and beginning to tire."

John Henry, furiously charging on the outside, was giving Shoemaker everything he had—but it didn't seem to be enough. Inside the final furlong, The Bart was still holding him off by a full length. John Henry kept coming. He edged ever closer to The Bart until, finally, with the cheers of the crowd rising to a crescendo, the two flashed across the finish line together. It was impossible to tell which horse had won. NBC originally identified The Bart as the winner, but the photo-finish pictures confirmed that John Henry had prevailed by a nose.

"He overcame everything," trainer Ron McAnally said. "He had the worst post position and this soft turf wasn't his type of racetrack. But I never saw him run a better race."

The little gelding's thrilling triumph in the first Arlington Million catapulted him to Horse of the Year honors in 1981. He finished the year with eight victories in 10 outings and earned almost $1.8 million. In 1982, physical problems prevented John Henry from defending his title in the Million; he won twice in only six starts that year. He was on the sidelines again for much of 1983, his eight-year-old season. The third Arlington Million, on August 28, was only his second start of the year—but John Henry was game, losing by merely a neck to Tolomeo.

John Henry had perhaps his finest year in 1984, at the ripe old age of nine. He won six of his last seven races, finishing second in the other. He earned a staggering $2,336,650, and was again voted Horse of the Year. Along the way he won his second Arlington Million. A crowd of 39,053 turned out on the perfect afternoon of August 26 to cheer him on. Again the bettors' favorite at 11-10, John Henry bided his time in third position under Chris McCarron while remaining always within striking range. At the head of the stretch McCarron angled him right to make his customary outside run to the wire, and he easily ran down the pacesetting Royal Heroine to score by a length and three quarters. The victory put John Henry over the $5 million mark in career earnings—at a time when no other horse in history had collected even $3 million.

Cigar

Cigar's early career gave little indication that he was destined for greatness. He never raced at age two, and he won just two of his first 13 starts—11 of these on the grass, which his breeding suggested he should prefer. With nothing to lose, trainer Bill Mott moved Cigar back to the dirt late in his four-year-old season—and the rest, as they say, is history. Cigar won his last two starts of 1994, then went 10-for-10 in 1995. That year, he became the oldest horse to have a perfect season and earned a record $4,819,800.

Rather than retire Cigar after his sensational 1995 campaign, owner Allen Paulson decided to keep him in training for another year so as to give the racing game a much-needed shot in the arm. Cigar won his first three races in 1996 to extend his winning streak to 15, one short of the mark established by Citation between 1948 and 1950. When a minor injury prevented Cigar from making his next scheduled start, in the Hollywood Gold Cup on June 30, Arlington chairman Dick Duchossois stepped into the breach. Working with Paulson's cooperation, he scheduled the Arlington Citation Challenge for July 13, rounding up a field of nine challengers to face Cigar at a mile and an eighth for a purse of $1,050,000.

Cigar was given a police escort from O'Hare Airport to Arlington. Mott participated in a question-and-answer session with fans on the morning of the race, and jockey Jerry Bailey signed autographs for more than an hour in the afternoon. Eighty-nine-year-old Jimmy Jones, Citation's trainer, was on hand as well. The weather was perfect, further adding to the carnival atmosphere.

Cigar had drawn the outermost post position, No. 10. He had also been assigned to carry 130 pounds, thus conceding between eight and 14 pounds to each of his rivals. The crowd of 34,223 gave him a standing ovation when he appeared in the paddock to be saddled, when he stepped onto the racetrack, and when he entered the starting gate. "He really seems to enjoy it," Mott said of the hubbub surrounding his horse, "and I'm not so sure he doesn't know this great crowd is for him."

Cigar broke leisurely and was five wide around the first turn, about six lengths behind the front-running Honour and Glory. With Bailey content to remain wide and stay out of traffic trouble, Cigar gradually advanced along the backstretch. On the far turn, Dramatic Gold threatened the leader while Cigar moved into striking range, only a length from the front. "And now Jerry Bailey sets Cigar alight!" track announcer Michael Wrona exclaimed as Honour and Glory, Dramatic Gold, and Cigar passed the quarter pole virtually three abreast.

Honour and Glory soon called it a day, but Dramatic Gold stubbornly refused to give in. By the eighth pole, though, Cigar had finally managed to get in front by half a length, and from then on he continued driving to draw off by three lengths at the wire. Bailey held his cap aloft to acknowledge the tumult of cheers as he guided Cigar back to the winner's circle for the 16th consecutive time. "I can't put into words how proud I am of Cigar," he said.

It was a thrilling day for Chicago racing fans (and one that took on added significance when Cigar ran second in his next start, thus failing to break the record he had tied at Arlington). When Paulson said that it had been an honor to bring Cigar to Chicago, racing writer Sharon Smith gently took issue with him: "It was a gracious thought," she wrote, "but inaccurate. It was the tracks and the sport itself who were honored by Mr. Paulson's horse in 1996, not the other way around."

CHAPTER 37

Moments, 1997-2001

July 6, 1997
Tigermania

When Tiger Woods arrived at Cog Hill in Lemont for the 1997 Western Open, he was the biggest phenomenon not only in golf, but in all of sports. The 21-year-old prodigy was 10 weeks removed from his astonishing triumph in the Masters—in which he'd become the youngest champion and recorded the lowest score (270 for the 72 holes) in tournament history, while enjoying the widest margin of victory (12 strokes) in any major tournament since 1870.

Woods's presence swelled attendance at the Western to 199,955, breaking the old tournament record by 30,000. There were 156 players in the field, but the spectators seemed intent on watching only one. "I feel for the guys who play in front of me and behind me," said Woods. "Their concentration sometimes is interrupted. As I always tell people, you've got to understand that not only myself but other players are out here on tour, and we're actually trying to make a living here."

On Thursday, July 3, Woods shot a five-under-par 67 to trail his playing partner Mark O'Meara by a stroke after one round. On Friday, Woods's 72 and O'Meara's 73 were the worst scores among the leaders; they ended the second round tied with four others for seventh place—four strokes behind Justin Leonard, who had carded a 64 to go nine under par for the tournament.

O'Meara continued to slide on Saturday, shooting a 75 to drop out of contention. But Woods climbed back up the leader board. His 25-foot birdie putt on the 18th gave him 68 for the day and 207 for the tournament. It also triggered a deafening roar from the gallery. "Yeah, the people were going crazy," Woods said. "It was kind of wild, especially since it's late afternoon, and it's kind of warm and they've been sipping."

Woods was now tied with Leonard and Loren Roberts for the lead at nine under par. A crowd of 49,462 turned out for the final round on Sunday, erasing the single-day attendance record that had been established Saturday.

Sunday's spectators saw just what they had come hoping to see—eventually. There was a touch of doubt early on: Woods shot even par for the first five holes, while Roberts carded two birdies to take the lead. On the sixth, a challenging 213-yard par three, Woods placed a four-iron within 12 feet of the cup and knocked it down for birdie. Roberts began to implode; he lost three strokes to Woods on the next four holes and gave up the lead for good.

Woods bogeyed the par-four 10th hole to fall back into a tie with Leonard and Frank Nobilo. Thereafter he put on a clinic. On the par-three 12th, he sank a birdie putt from 25 feet out. On the 14th, another par three, his tee shot landed a mere foot from the cup, and he made birdie. Woods added another birdie on the par-five 15th for good measure. As he strode up the 18th fairway with victory securely in his grasp, hundreds of spectators broke through the ropes on either side and fell in behind him, their Pied Piper, and marched to the green en masse. "I really didn't see them," Woods claimed, "because I'm facing forward. I definitely heard them, but when I got up to the green, I was just looking at my putt."

After Woods putted out, he hurled his ball into the gallery. His 34 on the front nine and 34 on the back gave him 68 and a four-day total of 275 (13 under par). Leonard managed a 72 to finish tied for third. Nobilo shot 70 to end up second, three strokes behind Woods.

Woods's win was his sixth in less than 11 months since his graduation from the amateur ranks. He ended 1997 as the first golfer ever to earn more than $2 million in a single year. There was no telling how many more victories or dollars lay before him. "If I play my normal game," he said, in a monumental understatement, "I should be able to win out here on tour."

June 14, 1998
"You Know You're There"

Michael Jordan was so great that we came to take his incredible feats for granted. Finally, he could surprise us only by being ordinary.

For most of Game 6 of the 1998 NBA Finals, Jordan was surprising. He made just 13 of his first 33 shots as the Bulls engaged in a nip-and-tuck battle with the Utah Jazz. A win would give the Bulls their sixth world championship; a loss would introduce the uncertainties of a Game 7, also on Utah's home court.

With Scottie Pippen all but incapacitated by a sore back, Ron Harper hampered by stomach flu, and Luc Longley wholly ineffective, it fell to Jordan to carry the load for the Bulls. Despite his struggles, the Jazz couldn't put the Bulls away. They led 25-22 after a quarter, 49-45 at the half, and 66-61 after three quarters.

Utah led 86-83 after John Stockton popped a three-pointer with 42 seconds left in the game.

This was when Michael Jordan stopped surprising us. Now he demonstrated why he was still, at the relatively advanced age of 35, the best player in the world. Receiving an inbounds pass from Pippen in the Bulls' frontcourt, Jordan stutter-stepped to throw defender Bryon Russell off balance, then drove around Russell and soared to the hoop for a layup to make it 86-85.

There were 37 seconds left when Stockton brought the ball up and tossed it to Karl Malone in the low post. Guarded by Dennis Rodman, Malone began to back in toward the basket. As Malone maneuvered into position to shoot, Jordan pounced from the blind side. "[Jeff] Hornacek was trying to set a pick," said Jordan, "but it fell through. Karl never saw me coming, and I was able to knock the ball away." Jordan not only slapped the ball loose but also recovered it when it bounced off Malone's shin.

Now 20 seconds remained. Jordan took the ball upcourt and drove to the top of the key with Russell trying gamely to guard him. He made a quick hesitation move that fooled Russell, who slipped and fell. Russell's misstep left Jordan wide open. "That's when the moment becomes the moment for me," Jordan said. "Once you get to the moment, you know you're there." His jump shot from 17 feet out was perfect. The Bulls led 87-86 with five seconds left.

Stockton's desperate three-point attempt was slightly deflected by Harper and rimmed out as the buzzer sounded. The Bulls were world champions again.

It was not surprising that Jordan had been the hero or that he was selected MVP of the Finals for the sixth time. It was fitting that this turned out to be his last appearance in a Bulls uniform, for how better to bow out? "I think everybody knows how he should be remembered," said Utah coach Jerry Sloan. "As the greatest player that has ever played."

September 12-13, 1998
Slammin' Sammy

Late in the 1998 season, Sammy Sosa was chasing the ghosts of Babe Ruth and Roger Maris and the real, live Mark McGwire for the title of greatest single-season home-run hitter of all time. The Cubs were chasing the National League's final playoff berth. They hosted the Milwaukee Brewers on September 11, 12, and 13, knowing they'd have to win at least two of the three games to keep pace with the New York Mets.

On Friday, Sosa socked his 59th home run of the year, but the Cubs lost 13-11.

Now in dire need of a win, the Cubs managed to fall behind 10-2 on Saturday. They were still trailing 12-5 in the seventh inning when Sosa blasted a three-run homer that turned the game around. It was his 60th home run of the season, equaling the standard set by Ruth in 1927.

Solo homers by Glenallen Hill and Tyler Houston made it 12-10 going into the bottom of the ninth. Sosa was the first batter, and the fans rose to their feet anticipating another long ball. Instead, Sosa rapped a single that ignited the game-winning rally. Hill followed with a single up the middle, and Gary Gaetti sacrificed the runners to second and third. Mickey Morandini coaxed a walk. A seeing-eye bouncer by Houston scored Sosa and Hill.

Then, with Houston on first, Morandini on third, and the score tied, pinch-hitter Orlando Merced belted Bob Wickman's second pitch into the right-field bleachers. A sacrifice fly would have sufficed, but the home run was a lot more fun. The 39,170 fans cheered for 15 minutes after Merced touched home plate.

On Sunday, Sosa launched a two-run shot that flew 480 feet and landed across Waveland Avenue. It was his 61st homer of the season, equaling Maris's mark in 1961. The blow put the Cubs ahead 8-3 in the fifth inning. But thanks to some atrocious Cub pitching, Milwaukee scored the next seven runs to lead 10-8 going into the bottom of the ninth.

Was it too much to expect another last-minute miracle? It appeared so when Mark Grace led off the inning by striking out. Then Sosa strode to the plate. He worked the count to two-and-one, then swung and launched a tremendous drive over the left-center-field wall and onto Waveland Avenue. It was his 62nd homer of the season, tying the new record set by McGwire five days earlier against the Cubs. A lengthy delay followed as Sosa acknowledged the ovation from the crowd. When the game resumed, the Cubs promptly tied it up on a double by Henry Rodriguez and a single by Gaetti. They won it on Grace's homer leading off the 10th. Grace and Sosa were carried off the field on their teammates' shoulders.

Three nights later in San Diego, Sosa hit a grand slam that drew him even with McGwire again at 63 homers apiece. It came in the eighth inning, breaking a 2-2 deadlock and catapulting the Cubs to another much-needed win. Although McGwire finally won the home-run race, Sosa didn't lose. He succeeded in carrying the Cubs into the playoffs, and he was named the National League's Most Valuable Player.

October 28 and November 4, 2001
Fantastic Finishes

The 2001 Bears lost their season opener to the Baltimore Ravens, defending Super Bowl champions, and then reeled off four straight wins. The winning streak was in danger on October 28 when the Bears spotted the San Francisco 49ers two touchdowns in the first quarter and lost quarterback Jim Miller with a hip injury in the second. Halfway through the third quarter, 49ers safety Zack Bronson intercepted a pass from Miller's backup, Shane Matthews, and returned it 97 yards for a touchdown. The Bears trailed 28-9.

Rookie running back Anthony Thomas rambled 19 yards for a Bears touchdown late in the quarter, and Paul Edinger's extra point made it 28-16. San Francisco's first possession of the fourth quarter resulted in a field goal, and, more importantly, took seven and a half minutes off the clock. The 49ers now led 31-16. Matthews engineered a drive that culminated in a 13-yard touchdown strike to wide receiver David Terrell. Edinger's kick made it 31-23 with 4:08 left to play. Now the Bears were within striking distance, and their defense rose to the occasion, forcing a three-and-out on the 49ers' next possession.

After San Francisco punted, the Bears started from their own 33-yard line with 2:46 remaining. Again, Matthews coolly drove his team downfield. Another touchdown pass to Terrell made the score 31-29 with 26 seconds left. Matthews had completed 25 of 31 attempts for 166 yards and three touchdowns, while Thomas had rushed 27 times for 127 yards—but it would be all for naught unless the Bears made the two-point conversion.

They did, on a straight-ahead plunge by Thomas, and the game was tied 31-31.

The overtime period lasted only 16 seconds. The 49ers won the coin flip and received the kickoff. On the first play from scrimmage, quarterback Jeff Garcia dropped back, saw Terrell Owens slanting across the middle, and let fly. The pass bounced off Owens and popped right into the arms of Bears safety Mike Brown. "I couldn't believe it," Garcia said. Neither could Brown believe his good fortune. He tucked the ball away and scurried 33 yards for a touchdown. The Bears won 37-31. "We are a pretty opportunistic team," said linebacker Brian Urlacher.

The next Sunday, the Bears took on the Cleveland Browns, also at Soldier Field. Again they dug themselves a hole, trailing 21-7 after three quarters. They were still behind 21-7 when they took possession of the ball at their own 20-yard line with 1:52 remaining in the game. Matthews completed six consecutive passes as the Bears advanced and the clock ticked down. On the eighth play of the drive, Matthews connected with Marty Booker for a touchdown from nine yards out. Edinger's extra point made it 21-14, but there were only 28 seconds left.

The Bears, naturally, lined up for an onside kick. It worked to perfection. Edinger's kick tumbled into a crowd of players from both teams, and the Bears' Bobbie Howard came away with the ball after a spirited scrum at midfield. "There's no telling how many times it changed hands," said Bears head coach Dick Jauron.

Starting from the Cleveland 47-yard line, Matthews completed two short passes to running back James Allen. Now the Bears had 34 yards to go and time enough for one more play. Matthews took the snap, stepped up in the pocket, and flung a Hail Mary pass into the end zone. Of course, a number of players were waiting for the ball to come down. When it did, it ricocheted off a helmet or shoulder and fluttered onto the outstretched fingertips of Allen, who was in a full-out dive. He secured it just inches above the ground for one of the most sensational catches that anyone would ever see. The clock read 0:00. "Can you believe a running back ran all the way down the field to catch that pass?" Browns safety Devin Bush asked incredulously. Edinger's extra point tied the score, and the game went into overtime.

This time, the extra period lasted almost three minutes—but it ended with déjà vu all over again. After the Bears won the coin toss and failed to move the ball, the Browns took over at their own 28-yard line. On first down, Bears linebacker Rosevelt Colvin sacked Cleveland quarterback Tim Couch. On second down, Couch again went back to pass. Bears defensive end Bryan Robinson tipped the ball, which spun in the air and (wouldn't you know it?) was caught by Mike Brown, who returned it for his second overtime touchdown in as many weeks. That particular feat had never been done before and is unlikely to be repeated. "When the ball was up in the air," said Brown, "I was like, 'I can't believe it. Here we go again.'" The Bears won 27-21.

The Bears had pulled off two of the most miraculous wins in their history in back-to-back games. They won the rest of their regular-season contests except the two against the arch-rival Green Bay Packers, finishing at 13-3 and capturing the NFC Central title. Their playoff loss to the Philadelphia Eagles on January 6, 2002, was the last game ever played at the original Soldier Field.

CHAPTER 38

Five Outs Away

"One of the things we're trying to get through to our fans is 'Feel free to believe in us.' Don't worry about getting hurt."
-- Mike Remlinger, Cubs pitcher, 2003-2005

"Why not us?" Dusty Baker asked hopefully when he was introduced as the new manager of the Cubs in November 2002. The question became a slogan for Baker, but the answer was somewhat complicated, as experienced Cubs fans knew all too well. The Cubs were coming off a disastrous 67-95 campaign and had not been to the World Series in 57 years. Baker had been to the World Series just three weeks earlier as manager of the San Francisco Giants.

"I came here to win," Baker continued after trying on the Cubs' familiar blue cap and pinstriped jersey. Then he backed off a bit, saying that, after all, he was no miracle worker. "My name is Dusty," he said, "not Messiah." Many of his constituents preferred to believe otherwise, and T-shirts proclaiming IN DUSTY WE TRUSTY were strong sellers as the 2003 season got under way.

The Cubs routed the New York Mets 15-2 in the season opener on March 31. They moved into first place on April 15 with an 11-1 drubbing of Cincinnati, then beat the Reds 10-4 the next day and 16-4 the next. They remained in first place or within a single game of the lead from April 13 through July 3.

It was an eventful time for Sammy Sosa. On April 4 at Cincinnati, the slugging right fielder notched the 500th home run of his career. On April 20 at Pittsburgh, he clubbed a two-run homer in his first at-bat, then was hit by Salomon Torres' pitches the next two times up. The second of these shattered Sosa's batting helmet and left him with facial lacerations. Sosa was not seriously hurt, but he appeared uncomfortable at bat for quite a while thereafter. He began taking his stance farther away from the plate than ever before, and he often backed up still more as pitches were in flight.

On June 3, in a game against the Tampa Bay Devil Rays at Wrigley Field, Sosa squibbed a ground ball to the second baseman and broke his bat in the process. Tampa Bay's catcher retrieved the business end of the bat and was about to hand it to the Cubs' bat boy when he noticed something strange about it. What was strange was that the inside of the bat had been hollowed out and filled with cork. Umpire Tim McClelland ejected Sosa for using the illegal bat. "I didn't want to do it," said McClelland, who, of course, was well aware of Sosa's superstar status. "But obviously the evidence was right there. You've got to go by the rules."

Sosa explained that he kept the corked bat on hand for batting practice only, in order "to put on a show for the fans." He was suspended for seven games nonetheless.

The Sammy Sosa of 2003 was not the smiling, apparently carefree sprite who had captivated fans in 1998. His fame had become a double-edged sword. On one hand, Sosa blithely exercised the perks of his celebrity. He was surrounded by a retinue of hangers-on who were given free reign of the Cubs' clubhouse, his notorious boom box ensured that his taste in music trumped that of any and all teammates, and his personal assistant Julian Martinez not only traveled with the team but even appeared in uniform (No. 80) in the dugout and on the field.

On the other hand, the media spotlight that Sosa craved was now increasingly harsh in its glare. The record-smashing feats of Sosa, Mark McGwire, Barry Bonds, and others were coming under suspicion as the widespread use of steroids during the period became undeniable. If many of the unprecedented performances of recent years seemed too good to be true, fans concluded, they probably were. Sosa tried to laugh off questions about his own transformation from the 160-pound greyhound who joined the White Sox in 1989 to the lumbering 235-pound block of solid muscle he'd become. He credited the change to a daily regimen of Flintstones vitamins.

Sosa's suspension was still pending when the New York Yankees invaded Wrigley Field just three days after the corked-bat episode, so he was in the lineup against the 26-time world champions, who were playing the Cubs for the first time since the 1938 World Series.

The park was absolutely packed for all three games, and the atmosphere was fully charged. The first game, on Friday, June 6, was played in a light mist under cloudy skies. The Yankees led 5-0 after two and a half innings, but Cubs starter Carlos Zambrano and four relievers held them in check after that. A two-run homer by second baseman Ramon Martinez in the third and a solo shot by center fielder Corey Patterson in the eighth got the Cubs back in the game. In the bottom of the ninth, the Cubs had the tying runs on second and third and the winning run at the plate when Hee Seop Choi struck out swinging.

Saturday's game matched Cubs righthander Kerry Wood against Roger Clemens, a six-time Cy Young award winner who was still potent as ever at the age of 40. Wood had exploded onto the scene five years earlier, striking out 20 Houston Astros on May 6, 1998, in just his fifth major-league outing. Only two Astros reached base, one on a scratch single off the glove of third baseman Kevin Orie and the other when he was hit by a pitch. Eight pitches were hit into fair territory, just two beyond the infield. With 20 strikeouts in a single game, Wood had joined a very exclusive club whose only other member was Clemens. He'd won 13 games for the season, fanned 233 batters in 167 innings, and been named Rookie of the Year. He had battled injuries and inconsistency since then, but he was coming into his own by 2003, and he made the all-star team for the first time.

Wood admitted he was thrilled to be facing Clemens, a fellow Texan and (along with Nolan Ryan) his idol. Adding some spice to the mix was the fact that Clemens was seeking his 300th victory.

Both pitchers were sharp. A solo homer by Hideki Matsui in the fifth was the Yankees' lone hit off Wood for the first seven innings. Clemens retired 15 straight Cubs in one stretch and carried a two-hit shutout into the bottom of the seventh. With two on and one out, New York manager Joe Torre removed Clemens and handed the ball to reliever Juan Acevedo. Clemens did not appear to be happy, and he was less so when Cubs first baseman Eric Karros drove Acevedo's first offering into the left-field bleachers to give the Cubs a 3-1 lead.

The drama wasn't over yet. With two on and two out in the Yankees' eighth, Wood issued a walk to Derek Jeter. Baker called for lefty Mike Remlinger to face the next hitter, Jason Giambi. Wood departed to a standing ovation; he had allowed just three hits and three walks while striking out 11. Giambi, a former American League MVP, had already clouted 14 homers on the season, including one the day before. After a swinging strike and a called strike, he waited out three deliveries that were off the mark. Then, with the crowd roaring, the baserunners going, and no margin for error, the crafty Remlinger threw a changeup, right over the heart of the plate. Giambi swung through it for strike three.

The Cubs won 5-2. "The most electric game I've ever been a part of," said Karros.

The Cubs won again Sunday night, defeating the Yankees 8-7. Entertaining as it was, the series against the New Yorkers was hardly crucial, for there were still 101 games left in the season. But the Cubs were gaining credibility and confidence. "You don't know," Baker said, "if this is a defining moment or a turning point until down the road."

Baker's caution seemed well-founded when the Cubs lost 25 of their next 42 games, including a stretch of four out of five that dropped them under .500 for the first—and last—time. They were 51-52 after losing to Houston on July 26, five and a half games behind the Astros and two behind St. Louis.

The promising Patterson had been lost for the season with a knee injury, but general manager Jim Hendry had an answer for that. In a lopsided trade with Pittsburgh, the Cubs acquired veteran Kenny Lofton to fill Patterson's spot in center field and budding star Aramis Ramirez to fill a void at third base that had existed, with a few short breaks, since the departure of Ron Santo 30 years earlier. Later, the obliging Pirates sent over first baseman Randall Simon as well. All three ex-Pirates proved indispensable, especially Lofton. The Cubs' first prototypical leadoff hitter in recent memory hit .328 and scored 39 runs in 56 games.

The turning point for the Cubs was a five-game series against the Cardinals at Wrigley Field beginning on September 1. On that date, righthander Mark Prior scattered five hits over eight innings and also swatted an RBI single as the Cubs won 7-0. It was Prior's sixth victory without a loss since a short stint on the disabled list; he had now allowed just three runs in his last 47 innings.

The Cubs and Cardinals split a doubleheader the next day. The Cubs won the first game 4-2 on a home run by Sosa in the 15th inning. In the nightcap, they trailed 2-0 and had the bases loaded in the bottom of the seventh when Moises Alou stroked an apparent extra-base hit down the left-field line. But umpire Justin Klemm called it foul. The Cubs said that chalk had flown up from the foul line. Alou and reliever Antonio Alfonseca were ejected for arguing, the call stood, and the Cardinals won 2-0. The game was also notable for some bad blood generated when Wood twice buzzed St. Louis pitcher Matt Morris high and tight while the latter attempted to bunt.

The next day, the Cubs overcame a 6-0 deficit with three runs in the sixth, three in the seventh, and two in the eighth. Alou went five-for-five with four RBIs, including the go-ahead run in the eighth. The Cubs won 8-7. "As far as bad losses go," St. Louis manager Tony LaRussa said, "this is tied for first [place] with any that I can remember." It was more of the same in the series finale. The Cardinals led 2-0, and the Cubs went ahead 3-2. The Cardinals led 5-3, and the Cubs went ahead 6-5. The Cardinals tied it up at 6-6, and the Cubs came back *again* to win 7-6.

The series turned the season around for both teams. The Cardinals fell from first place to third and were not a serious factor in the race thereafter. The Cubs embarked on a march to the division title. They went 19-8 during September, clinching the crown with a doubleheader sweep of the Pirates on the next-to-last day of the season. On the last day of the season, the Cubs retired Santo's No. 10, rested their regulars, and looked ahead to the postseason.

In the first round of the playoffs, the Cubs outlasted the Atlanta Braves three games to two for their first win of any postseason series since 1908. In the decisive Game 5 at Atlanta, the crowd of 54,357 was heavily weighted with Cubs fans, who saw Wood yield only one run and five hits in eight innings as the Cubs won 5-1. For the series, Wood and Prior were a combined 3-0 with a 1.48 earned run average. "We just couldn't beat their big guys," said Braves manager Bobby Cox.

So far, so good. The Cubs advanced to the National League Championship Series against the Florida Marlins. In Game 1 at Wrigley Field, Sosa's two-out, two-run homer in the bottom of the ninth sent the crowd into delirium and the game into extra innings. The Cubs eventually lost 9-8, but they rebounded to take the next three games. They routed the Marlins 12-3 in Game 2 behind another strong effort by Prior. In Game 3, Doug Glanville's pinch-hit triple scored Lofton with the deciding run in the 11th inning. Game 4 was not as suspenseful: Ramirez cracked a grand slam in the first inning, and the Cubs coasted to an 8-3 victory. Ramirez knocked in another run with a single in the third and yet another with a solo homer in the seventh.

Now the Cubs were just one win away from their first World Series since 1945. "The forecast for hell," Dan McGrath wrote in the *Tribune*, "calls for rapidly falling temperatures and a frost warning."

As in 1984, the Cubs would have three chances to win the one game needed.

Florida's Josh Beckett summarily removed one of those chances. Only three Cubs reached base, and none got past first base, as the flame-throwing Beckett blanked them 4-0 in Game 5. "We would've rather wrapped it up," said Baker, "but we've got a chance now to win it at home and let Chicago go crazy."

Heading back to Chicago for the final two games, the Cubs were optimistic—and why not? They had their pair of aces, Prior and Wood, lined up to start Game 6 and Game 7 respectively. The Cubs were a perfect 5-0 in the duo's postseason starts so far. Daniel G. Habib of *Sports Illustrated* had even suggested that the presence of Prior and Wood ensured that the Cubs *couldn't* lose the series: "In a seven-game NLCS," Habib wrote, "they would pitch at least twice each. You do the math."

When Prior took the mound for Game 6, on Tuesday, October 14, the math was looking pretty good. Including the postseason, he had won 12 of his last 13 decisions with a 1.55 ERA. There were 39,577 fans inside Wrigley Field and thousands more milling around outside, poised for a celebration. The Cubs scored single runs in the first, sixth, and seventh innings. Meanwhile, the Marlins managed three hits and two walks, but no runs, against Prior.

Mike Mordecai led off the eighth inning for Florida. When he flied out to Alou in left field, it appeared that Prior was on cruise control. Eight consecutive Marlins had been retired. All the fans were on their feet by now, and many were holding up five fingers, signifying the number of outs between the Cubs and the World Series.

The next hitter, Juan Pierre, slapped a double to left. Then Luis Castillo came to bat. After working the count to 3-and-2, Castillo lofted a pop fly down the left-field line. Alou ran over into foul territory, behind the Cubs' bullpen, and leaped against the brick wall to attempt a backhanded catch. Just as the ball came within reach of Alou's outstretched glove, it was tipped by a fan and bounced away.

It's impossible to know what would have happened if the fan had not touched the ball. Alou *might* have caught it. If he had, the Marlins would've been down to their last four outs, still trailing by three runs. Prior and/or closer Joe Borowski *might* have made short work of them thereafter. We can only guess what might have happened, but we know what did happen. Alou angrily slammed his glove down and berated the fan. Prior stalked around the infield, asking in vain for the umpires to call fan interference. Baker sat impassively in the dugout, chewing on his ubiquitous toothpick.

Castillo eventually coaxed a walk, after nine pitches. Ivan Rodriguez singled, scoring Pierre with the Marlins' first run.

If Cubs shortstop Alex Gonzalez had fielded a routine bouncer off the bat of Miguel Cabrera, the inning would have ended with the Cubs still ahead 3-1, and the incident in the left-field corner would have been forgotten. Alas, Gonzalez muffed the likely double-play ball to load the bases. Then Derrek Lee hit the very next pitch for a double. The game was tied, Prior was done, and worse was yet to come.

Kyle Farnsworth relieved Prior and issued an intentional walk. A sacrifice fly gave the Marlins a 4-3 lead. Another intentional walk loaded the bases. Mike Mordecai came to bat for the second time in the inning. A utility infielder who had hit only .213 with eight runs batted in for the season, Mordecai delivered the coup de grace, lacing a double to center that scored all three baserunners. Mike Remlinger replaced Farnsworth. A single by Pierre scored Mordecai, and then—finally—Castillo popped up to end the inning.

The damage totaled eight runs. As the nightmare inning concluded, the fan who had deflected the ball away from Alou was escorted out of the ballpark for his own safety. When his name was subsequently revealed in the media, he went into hiding. His life was changed forever.

Ugueth Urbina needed only 16 pitches to dispatch the Cubs over the final two innings and seal the Marlins' 8-3 win.

The Cubs had suffered a bitter loss, but couldn't they still bounce back and win Game 7? Baker, for one, seemed to think so. "Anyone that thinks this is over," he said, "they're not a Cub fan."

The Cubs turned to Wood, who had performed brilliantly in the do-or-die Game 5 against Atlanta. Again, the old ballpark was packed to the rafters, and the nearby streets were teeming with people who couldn't get in, but wanted to be as close to the action as possible and also wanted to be on hand for the celebration that was now more hoped-for than expected.

Florida's Miguel Cabrera clouted a three-run homer in the first inning, sucking all the air out of the park and encouraging the defeatists (or were they realists?) in the crowd to say, "I told you so." The Cubs weren't done just yet, however. They tied it up in the second on a single by Karros, a double by Gonzalez, and a two-run homer by Wood himself. When they took a 5-3 lead on Alou's two-run homer onto Waveland Avenue the next inning, it looked as if everything might turn out all right.

But the Marlins touched Wood for three runs in the fifth and another in the sixth. They scored two more in the seventh off Farnsworth. Meanwhile, Florida manager Jack McKeon had called upon Josh Beckett to hold the lead. Having had just two days' rest since his complete-game outing in Game 5, Beckett pitched the fifth through eighth innings, allowing but one run on one hit (a pinch-hit home run by Troy O'Leary) and effectively extinguishing the Cubs' hopes.

The final score was 9-6, and the Marlins were National League champions.

Wood blamed himself for the loss. "I choked," he said. "I let my teammates down, I let the organization down, and I let the city of Chicago down." Others blamed the unfortunate fan who had grabbed for the fateful foul ball the night before. The fan was a convenient scapegoat, but in truth there was plenty of blame to go around for the Cubs' defeat. The Marlins deserved the largest share, because they were simply better than the Cubs when it counted. "They don't give up and they don't give in," said Wood.

It had been the nearest miss in a long time, but the fact remained that another year had come and gone without a world championship or even a National League pennant for the Cubs. Baker sought to distance himself from the franchise's gnawing history of failure, pointing out that he'd only been around for one season. But he had already learned all he needed to know about Cubs fans. "I've seen people who enjoy their baseball [before]," he remarked, "but here it's life and death." He had also learned more than he cared to know about the mythology of omens, jinxes, and curses that surrounded the franchise. "Seems like there's nothing you can do about it but win," he said, "and then when you win, they've got to come up with something else [to talk about] for the next 95 years."

CHAPTER 39

The White Sox Bring It Home

"We're not the Cubs, so we're doing the best we can."
-- A.J. Pierzynski, White Sox catcher, 2005-2012

On August 1, 2005, the White Sox led the American League Central Division by 15 games over the Cleveland Indians. On September 7, the lead had diminished, but was still comfortable at nine and a half games. Over the next two weeks, the margin evaporated almost completely. On September 22, the Sox lost to Minnesota in extra innings while Cleveland won. The lead was now a game and a half. Were the White Sox about to join the 1951 Dodgers, 1964 Phillies, 1978 Red Sox, and 1969 Cubs among the most famous losers of pennant races that had seemed to be in the bag?

It was surprising to see the White Sox in such dire straits. From the start of the season, all indications had been that this was their year.

The Sox beat Cleveland 1-0 on Opening Day, April 4, at U.S. Cellular Field (the new name for the new Comiskey Park) behind a masterful performance by lefthander Mark Buehrle. The Indians sent only 28 batters to the plate as Buehrle and Shingo Takatsu dispatched them in just an hour and 51 minutes.

Buehrle, always a model of efficiency, allowed a single in the fifth (the runner was promptly erased in a double play) and another in the seventh. He walked one and struck out five. "That's what we expect from him," Sox manager Ozzie Guillen said matter-of-factly. First baseman Paul Konerko was more effusive. "The guy is unbelievable," he said of Buehrle. "If it is a seven-run game, he gives up runs when he knows he can do it. If it's a 1-0 game like it was, he just bears down. You can't put your finger on it. He's good."

In the second game of the season, Konerko and Jermaine Dye clubbed back-to-back homers as the White Sox rallied for four runs in the bottom of the ninth inning to win a 4-3 thriller. The Sox won eight of their first 12 games, after which they were tied for first place. Then they won eight in a row and began to pull away from their rivals.

The White Sox set a blistering pace early in the season, going 17-7 in April, 18-10 in May, and 18-7 in June. At the end of June, they sported a gaudy record of 53-24 and had opened up a 10½-game advantage over the Minnesota Twins and 11 over the Indians. They had not been hot for a couple weeks or a month; they had been hot since Buehrle's first pitch of the year.

The White Sox picked up where they left off after the All-Star break. Righthander Jose Contreras blanked the Indians 1-0 on July 14, and the Sox went on to sweep the four-game series at Cleveland. They completed another four-game sweep in Baltimore on August 1. At this point, the White Sox stood at 69-35. They were 15 games in front of Cleveland and 15½ ahead of Minnesota.

Eight defeats in nine games between August 12 and August 23 narrowed the White Sox' lead to seven games. But it was back up to nine and a half after a 1-0 victory over Kansas City, the Sox' seventh in a row, on September 7. Then things started to get hairy. The Sox dropped three straight to the Los Angeles Angels at home, then went 3-3 on a road trip to Kansas City and Minnesota. They returned home on September 19 to face the rampaging Indians, who had won 12 of their last 13.

Cleveland made it 13 of 14 in the series opener, plating two in the eighth and one in the ninth to turn a 5-4 deficit into a 7-5 win. The lead was down to two and a half games. The next night, the White Sox trailed three different times, blew a one-run lead in the ninth inning, and finally won on a solo home run by third baseman Joe Crede leading off the bottom of the 10th. Crede was mobbed at home plate by his teammates, whose reaction was equal parts joy and relief. "We want to get to the playoffs," said Crede, "but we've got nothing clinched yet." As if to confirm that point, the Indians routed the White Sox 8-0 in the series finale.

Phil Rogers of the *Tribune* wrote that if the White Sox failed to win the division, they wouldn't be guilty of the absolute worst late-season collapse in history; it would only be the second worst after the 1964 Philadelphia Phillies. On September 22 against Minnesota, the Sox stranded the potential winning run in the eighth, ninth, and 10th innings; they lost 4-1 in the 11th. They had now dropped 10 of their past 14 games. "I don't want to talk about my team," Guillen told reporters, "because I might say something you guys or my team don't want to hear."

The lead was down to a game and a half. The next night, Dye walloped a three-run homer in the first inning, and Contreras made it stand up. He went the distance, scattering six hits and striking out nine as the Sox won 3-1. But Cleveland also won.

Dye hit another three-run homer the next night, part of a six-run third inning, and the White Sox coasted to an 8-1 victory. But they still they gained no ground because Cleveland won yet again. The Indians had gone 16-2 since Labor Day. "I don't expect Cleveland to lose another game," said Guillen. But the Indians did lose on September 25 at Kansas City, while the Sox won their third straight over Minnesota, 4-1, thanks to a typically fine effort by Buehrle.

They weren't out of the woods yet, but the White Sox now led by two and a half games. There were seven games remaining on the schedule: four in Detroit and the last three in Cleveland. "If you go into the last week of the season holding your destiny in your own hands," said Konerko, "what more can you ask for?"

Despite dropping the first two games at Detroit, each by a single run, the White Sox lost only half a game in the standings, as the Indians were idle the first night and lost themselves the second night. The Sox beat the Tigers 8-2 the next night, while the Indians lost their third straight. The White Sox now led the division by three games. They took the field in Detroit the next afternoon, September 29, with a chance to make the season-ending series in Cleveland irrelevant. If they beat the Tigers, the Sox would clinch the division title. Even if they were swept in Cleveland and both teams finished at 96-66, the White Sox would be division champions because of their advantage over the Indians in head-to-head competition. Under that scenario, the Indians would also quali-fy for the postseason, as the American League's wild-card team.

The White Sox struck in the first inning. Designated hitter Carl Ev-erett laced a two-out triple off the center-field fence to score Dye, who had doubled, and Konerko, who'd walked. The Sox added a run in the second on a double by catcher A.J. Pierzynski, a sacrifice bunt by short-stop Juan Uribe, and a sacrifice fly by left fielder Scott Podsednik. Konerko homered in the sixth for the Sox' fourth run. Meanwhile, Chi-cago starting pitcher Freddy Garcia was sharp. He yielded only one run on seven hits in the first seven innings, while walking no one.

Garcia departed after Detroit's Placido Polanco singled leading off the eighth. Cliff Politte retired the first man he faced, then surrendered a run-scoring double to former White Sox star Magglio Ordonez. Neal Cotts and Bobby Jenks each recorded an out as the Sox escaped the in-ning still in front 4-2. Jenks, a burly, hard-throwing righthander, had recently succeeded Dustin Hermanson as Guillen's closer, just as Her-manson had replaced Shingo Takatsu earlier.

The Tigers mounted a threat against Jenks in the ninth. A single and an error put the tying runners on base and brought the winning run to the plate. Jenks was equal to the task—he needed only six pitches to strike out the next two hitters, Dmitri Young (swinging) and Curtis Granderson (looking). Then Polanco smacked a line drive right into Konerko's glove at first base, and the ballgame was over.

The resilient White Sox were division champions. "We stuck to-gether and talked about team chemistry when we were winning early on in the year," center fielder Aaron Rowand said, "and everybody said, 'Yeah, well, it's easy when you're winning.' But when you're losing and everybody in the papers is doubting you and all that, everybody still stuck together. And that showed the character of this team."

The White Sox went to Cleveland for the series that had loomed so threateningly less than a week earlier (and still meant something to the Indians, who had a slim chance to make the playoffs). The Sox, feeling their oats now, swept the three games. They entered the postseason having won eight of their last 10 games and having thoroughly turned their fortunes around.

Many players had contributed significantly to the Sox' 99 wins. The offense featured a little bit of speed—from Podsednik, Rowand, and second baseman Tadahito Iguchi—and a lot of power. Podsednik, who stole 59 bases, was the only regular not to hit 13 or more home runs (he had none). As a team, the White Sox blasted an even 200 homers, led by Konerko's 40.

Impressive as the offensive fireworks were, the real key to the Sox' success was pitching. None of the primary starting pitchers—Buehrle, Garcia, Contreras, and Jon Garland—missed a turn all season, logged fewer than 200 innings, won fewer than 14 games, or had an earned-run average over 3.90. As a group, they compiled a record of 63-33. The bullpen corps was equally effective. Righthanders Politte and Luis Vizcaino and lefties Cotts and Damaso Marte gave Guillen a number of viable options to set up the Sox' closers, who combined to lead the league in saves.

"We know we've got the pitching to do something here [in the postseason]," Konerko declared. Events would soon prove him right.

The White Sox opened the postseason against the Boston Red Sox at U.S. Cellular Field on October 4. The Red Sox had won their first World Series since 1918 the year before, leaving Cleveland (1948) as the only franchise within a few decades of the White Sox (1917) and Cubs (1908) in the category of longest world-championship droughts. Neither Chicago team had even *been* to the World Series since 1959, much less won it, while each of the other franchises in existence at that time had appeared in the fall classic at least twice since then.

The Sox' injured slugger Frank Thomas threw out the first ball before the game. Thomas was greeted warmly by the 40,717 fans—who, like him, didn't know that he had already played his last game for the Sox. After 16 years, two Most Valuable Player awards, and 448 home runs (more than twice as many as any other player in White Sox history), Thomas was cut loose during the following offseason.

The fans had hardly sat down after the national anthem when the White Sox brought them back to their feet with a five-run rally in the bottom of the first inning. Boston starter Matt Clement, a mainstay of the 2003 Cubs team that almost won the pennant, hit two batters with pitches and yielded two singles before Pierzynski clubbed a three-run homer. Konerko added a solo shot in the third, and shortstop Juan Uribe's two-run homer in the fourth sent Clement to the showers. Podsednik hit his first home run of the entire year with two on in the sixth, and Pierzynski cracked his second of the game in the eighth. Contreras allowed eight hits and no walks in seven and two-thirds innings before Cotts and Politte finished up. The White Sox won 14-2 for their first postseason victory at home since the similarly one-sided 11-0 verdict over the Dodgers in Game 1 of the 1959 World Series.

The next night, the White Sox fell behind 4-0 in the early innings, then plated five in the fifth, with one run scoring on a double by Rowand, another on a single by Crede, and three on a homer by Iguchi. Buehrle was not at his best, but he was good enough—with Jenks's help—to make the five-spot hold up as the Sox prevailed 5-4.

Game 3 at Boston was tied 2-2 when Konerko homered with Dye aboard in the sixth. After Manny Ramirez led off the Red Sox' half with a homer, Garcia was replaced by Marte, who promptly allowed a single and two walks to load the bases with nobody out. With this, Guillen called for Orlando Hernandez, who'd been the Sox' fifth starter during the regular season. Hernandez induced two infield pop-ups and struck out the next batter to wriggle out of the jam. He pitched two more innings, yielding just one harmless single, before passing the baton to Jenks, who earned another save.

"Every day it's somebody different on this team," said Guillen. "I'm so proud of the players because they just go out there to bust their tails. They do a tremendous job and they never panic. That's why we are where we are."

Where the White Sox were now was the American League Championship Series vs. the Los Angeles Angels.

In Game 1 on October 11 in Chicago, Contreras was touched for three runs in the first three innings. The Sox chipped away with single runs in the third and fourth, but they did not score again, leaving the tying and go-ahead runs on base in the eighth and the tying run on in the ninth. "We just didn't execute very well tonight," said Pierzynski, who himself missed a sign and was thrown out stealing in the seventh. For Contreras, who deserved better, it was the first defeat after nine consecutive victories.

Game 2 was crucial, because the White Sox could hardly hope to win the series if they lost the first two games at home. The game and the series (and, arguably, the Sox' entire postseason) hinged on a bizarre play that, not surprisingly, featured Pierzynski in the central role. Pierzynski was often called an instigator, agitator, and worse, and he relished it. "When you play against him, you hate him," said Guillen. "When he's on your side, you hate him less." The game was tied 1-1 when Pierzynski came to bat with two outs and nobody on in the bottom of the ninth. With the count at 3-and-2, Angels reliever Kelvim Escobar delivered a low fastball. Pierzynski swung and missed to send the game into extra innings.

Or did he? With nothing to lose, the resourceful Pierzynski broke for first base. It would be hard to say who was more confused at this point—home-plate umpire Doug Eddings, who appeared to signal the third out, or catcher Josh Paul, who nonchalantly rolled the ball back to the mound and started jogging off the field. Pierzynski reached first base and was called safe on a dropped third strike. "You're taught that if the third strike is in the dirt you run," Pierzynski said, "and Josh didn't tag me. I think he thought he caught it. I just ran, and luckily it worked out." Replays were inconclusive as to whether Paul had caught the ball on the fly or trapped it against the ground. For his part, Eddings claimed he had only signaled the third strike, not an out. In any event, the White Sox had the winning run on base.

Pablo Ozuna pinch ran for Pierzynski and immediately stole second. Then Crede banged a line drive off the left-field wall, and that was that. The Sox won 2-1, with Buehrle going the distance.

Buehrle's complete-game victory set a precedent that Garland, Garcia, and Contreras dutifully observed for the remainder of the series. In Game 3 at Anaheim, Garland got all the support he needed in the first inning, when Dye doubled home Podsednik and Konerko followed with a homer. The lanky righthander allowed two runs on just four hits as the White Sox won 5-2. In Game 4, the Sox again scored three in the first, this time on a three-run homer by Konerko, and cruised to an 8-2 decision behind Garcia. In Game 5, the Sox trailed 3-2 before scoring one in the seventh, one in the eighth, and two in the ninth. They won 6-3, with Contreras yielding five hits and walking two. "Four complete games in a row," said Konerko, who was named MVP of the series. "You have to be kidding me."

The White Sox were headed to the World Series. "No matter what happens," said chairman Jerry Reinsdorf, "when you win the American League pennant, you've had one wonderful year. But then you get greedy, and you want to get four more [wins]. It's only been since 1917, so I think it's time, and hopefully these guys can get the job done."

The South Siders' opponents in their first World Series since 1959 were the Houston Astros, who had come into being in 1962 and were appearing in their first Series ever.

Game 1 was played in Chicago on October 22. Roger Clemens started for Houston and was not effective, leaving with a sore hamstring after two innings and three White Sox runs. Crede made the difference for the Sox with both bat and glove; his fourth-inning home run snapped a 3-3 tie, and he made diving stops at third base in the sixth (with a runner on third and one out) and the seventh (with two on and two out). The Sox added a run in the eighth on Podsednik's triple with Pierzynski aboard. Jenks struck out three of the four batters he faced to preserve the 5-3 win for Contreras.

Game 2 was one of the most entertaining games ever played in Chicago—or anywhere else, for that matter. The cold, wet weather did not dampen the enthusiasm of the 41,432 who turned out. Buehrle pitched seven innings for the White Sox, allowing four runs on seven hits. His counterpart, Andy Pettitte, left after six innings with a 4-2 lead. Dan Wheeler started the seventh for Houston and retired Crede on a foul pop-up. Then Uribe stroked a double to center. Podsednik struck out. Iguchi coaxed a walk. Dye was up next; he worked the count to 3-and-2 before the next offering hit his bat—but was ruled to have hit his arm. Now the bases were loaded, and the crowd was in an uproar.

Chad Qualls replaced Wheeler on the mound. Konerko stepped up to the plate. He swung at Qualls's first pitch and drilled it over the wall for a grand slam. It was one of the most electrifying moments in Chicago's long baseball history. Konerko circled the bases and then took a curtain call to acknowledge the tremendous ovation from the rain-soaked crowd. After the game, Konerko maintained that he'd been focused on getting a hit to tie the score and that the idea of hitting a home run hadn't occurred to him. "That's usually when you get them," he said, "when you're not trying to."

Politte retired the Astros in order in the eighth, and Jenks came on in the ninth with the Sox still ahead 6-4. With two outs and runners on second and third, pinch hitter Jose Vizcaino lined a single to left, and the game was tied. Cotts replaced Jenks and got the third out with no further damage.

Houston manager Phil Garner handed the ball to all-star closer Brad Lidge for the bottom of the ninth. Lidge retired Uribe for the first out, but then the unlikely Podsednik belted a home run to right-center field, and the White Sox were 7-6 winners. After hitting no homers during the regular season, Podsednik had now hit his second of the postseason. Few home runs, even by the most illustrious sluggers, have been more impactful. It was only the 14th game-ending (or "walk-off") homer in World Series history, and it gave the Sox a commanding 2-0 lead in the Series. "Clearly, everything they're doing now is right," Garner said. "They can't do anything wrong."

Game 3, the first World Series game ever played in Texas, was a classic. It looked bleak for the White Sox early, as the Astros built up a 4-0 lead for their ace righthander Roy Oswalt in the first four innings. Crede started the top of the fifth with a home run and ended the inning standing on first base after being hit by a pitch. In the meantime, RBI singles by Iguchi and Dye and a two-run double by Pierzynski had given the Sox a 5-4 edge.

Garland settled down and retired nine of the last 10 batters he faced. He left after seven innings with the Sox still ahead 5-4. In the bottom of the eighth, with two on and two out, Houston's Jason Lane doubled off Hermanson to tie the score. Then, with the go-ahead run on third and a potential insurance run (Lane) on second, Hermanson caught Brad Ausmus looking to end the inning.

Both teams were scoreless in the ninth inning. And the 10th. And the 11th, 12th, and 13th. A parade of pitchers, pinch hitters, and pinch runners cluttered the scorecard for both sides, and still the game remained tied. Dye led off the White Sox' 14th with a single, a hopeful sign, but Konerko bounced into a double play on the very next pitch. Geoff Blum, a backup infielder who'd been acquired late in the season, came up to bat. After taking two balls from pitcher Ezequiel Astacio,

Blum connected with a low fastball and sent it over the right-field fence. "I didn't know if I got it high enough," he said. "Somebody was watching out for me." The home run was the first and last at-bat of the Series for Blum, a former Astro. The Sox added another run on two singles and two walks, and they took a 7-5 edge into the bottom of the 14th.

Marte, the Sox' eighth pitcher of the night, was on the hill for his second inning of work. With two outs and a man on first, an error by shortstop Uribe put the tying runs on and brought the winning run to the plate. Guillen called for Buehrle, who had concluded his seven-inning stint in Game 2 just 51 hours earlier. Buehrle got Adam Everett on a pop-up to Uribe, who had no mishap this time. The Sox won to take a 3-0 lead in the Series.

The Astros had managed just one hit after the fourth inning and had stranded 15 base runners in all. They'd left the potential winning run in scoring position in the ninth, 10th, and 11th. Houston manager Garner did not offer any platitudes. "This is embarrassing," he said, "the way it's played out." Garner saw what was obvious to anyone by now: that the White Sox would soon be world champions.

In Game 4 on October 26, Garcia and Astros righthander Brandon Backe each tossed seven shutout innings. Lidge came on in the eighth for Houston. Willie Harris, pinch hitting for Garcia, led off the inning with a single. Podsednik sacrificed him to second. Harris advanced to third on a groundout and scored on a clutch two-out single by Dye. "I just stayed with my game plan," said Dye. "I didn't try to do too much, just tried to hit it hard somewhere and found a hole up the middle."

The lone run was enough. Politte and Cotts held the lead through the eighth, and Jenks closed the Astros out in the ninth. The game, the series, the season, and White Sox' 88-year wait ended on a ground ball to Uribe, who tossed to Konerko for the out. Konerko held onto the ball for a couple days, then presented it to Reinsdorf at the Sox' victory celebration in Chicago. The latter was overcome with emotion at the gracious and surprising gesture.

"It was only fitting it ended up 1-0," Pierzynski said of the final game. "That's the way we started the year [on Opening Day], that's the way we started the second half, and that's the way it should have ended."

It really should have ended, in a perfect world, on the South Side of Chicago. It was mildly disappointing that all four clinching games—for the division title, the first playoff series, the American League Championship Series, and the World Series—had been on the road. Thus the White Sox and their fans hadn't had the chance to celebrate these victories together. Nonetheless, it had been a spectacular and satisfying run: 11-1 in the postseason and 19-3 overall since the nerve-wracking September slump. The White Sox had spent every day of the season in first place, they had beaten back all comers, and they had earned the mantle of world champions in every way.

"People are looking for big theories," general manager Kenny Williams said. "We've just got 25 hard-working, grind-it-out guys. We asked them one thing—each and every one of them to leave it all out on the field. They did that more than any team I've ever seen."

As White Sox fans basked in the glory of the achievement they had always imagined but never quite expected, they paused to recall other faithful fans who hadn't lived long enough to see it. Although many of these parents, grandparents, siblings, spouses, and friends had been deceased for decades, they weren't really gone—at least in the minds of their survivors. The Sox had won for them, too.

CHAPTER 40

Here Come the Hawks

"Anything can happen if you dream big."

-- Rocky Wirtz, Blackhawks owner, 2007 –

When Blackhawks owner Bill Wirtz died at age 77 on September 26, 2007, the venerable franchise was in a bad way.

The Hawks had missed the playoffs in eight of the past nine seasons. Attendance had fallen to less than 13,000 a game—down 40 percent from the United Center's inaugural season of 1994-95.

Pat Foley, voice of the Hawks for 25 years, had been cut loose and had signed on with the minor-league Chicago Wolves (who, some argued, were now more popular than the Hawks).

Inexplicably, Bob Pulford was still running the Hawks' hockey operations. During his 30-year tenure as general manager and then executive vice president, the Hawks had made it to the Stanley Cup Final only once—and failed to win a game. In one period that was abysmal even by his standards, Pulford had traded three future Hall of Famers (Jeremy Roenick, Ed Belfour, and Chris Chelios) in just two and a half years, getting next to nothing in return.

A fan poll by *ESPN: The Magazine* in 2004 ranked the Hawks as the very worst among all 122 franchises in the NHL, NBA, NFL, and MLB.

At the Blackhawks' 2007-08 home opener, the crowd was asked to stand and observe a moment of silence in Bill Wirtz's memory. (Wirtz had been dead less than two weeks.) The fans stood as requested and then, rather than remain silent, they booed at the top of their lungs.

Wirtz's son and successor Rocky knew that he had his work cut out for him. Rocky had loved and respected his father, but he recognized that the franchise had all but petrified over the years. There was no denying that drastic changes were required.

Rocky immediately rolled up his sleeves and got to work. His first agenda item was to reverse his father's longest-held and most controversial policy, the refusal to televise home games in the Chicago area. Selected home games were televised during the 2007-08 season, and *all* games, home or away, were televised starting with the following season.

John McDonough was lured from his role as president of the Cubs, bringing his organizational skills and marketing prowess to the Blackhawks. McDonough wasted no time building bridges to a fan base that had been alienated and insulted for decades.

Pat Foley was welcomed back with open arms. Likewise, Blackhawk legends Bobby Hull, Stan Mikita, and Tony Esposito returned to the fold and were put on the payroll as goodwill ambassadors.

The above changes might have been regarded as merely cosmetic if the new regime had not proved its seriousness with substantive, even drastic, moves in the hockey operations.

Pulford was quietly moved to an innocuous position with the Wirtz Corporation from which he could do no further damage.

Scotty Bowman, winner of more regular-season games, more playoff games, and more Stanley Cups (nine) than any other coach in NHL history, signed on as a senior advisor. So did former Colorado Avalanche and St. Louis Blues coach Joel Quenneville. Bowman's son Stan soon replaced general manager Dale Tallon, and Quenneville supplanted head coach Denis Savard.

Within a year of his father's passing, Rocky Wirtz had transformed the Blackhawks' organization from a laughingstock into a model of professionalism and efficiency. And within two more years, he was hoisting the Stanley Cup in his hands.

The newly relevant Blackhawks had their coming-out party on New Year's Day of 2009. On that date, the Hawks took on their old rivals (and defending Stanley Cup champions) the Detroit Red Wings before 40,818 frozen fans at Wrigley Field, in the NHL's second annual Winter Classic. The largest television audience for any NHL game since

1975 was introduced to Chicago's core of exciting young players, including center Jonathan Toews and right wing Patrick Kane (both age 20), left wing Kris Versteeg (22), and defensemen Brent Seabrook (23) and Duncan Keith (25).

The Hawks lost to Detroit in the Winter Classic, but by the end of the season they had compiled an estimable record of 46-24-12, good for their first 100-point season since 1993 and their first playoff berth since 2002. They advanced beyond the first round for the first time in 13 years and eventually made it to the conference finals, where they were eliminated by the Red Wings.

Having gotten a taste of success, the young Blackhawks entered the 2009-10 season hopeful that they could go all the way.

Toews, the third player chosen in the 2006 NHL draft, had shown himself to be an exceptionally intelligent and gritty two-way player whose leadership qualities were so obvious that he already wore the captain's "C" on his sweater despite his tender years.

Kane, the first player chosen in the 2007 draft, possessed electrifying skating, stickhandling, and shooting skills that marked him as a superstar in the making. Accordingly, he wasn't bashful about wearing number 88, drawing inevitable comparisons to all-timers such as Wayne Gretzky (99) and Mario Lemieux (66).

Keith, a big and rugged defenseman, was as reliable as anyone behind his own blue line while also presenting a formidable threat in the offensive zone, especially on the power play. His efforts earned him the Norris Trophy as the league's top defenseman in 2010.

Toews, Kane, and Keith were joined by several others who lifted the Blackhawks into the top tier of teams in the league. In addition to the aforementioned Seabrook and Versteeg, mainstays included left wing Patrick Sharp, defensemen Brian Campbell and Dustin Byfuglien, and right wing Marian Hossa, a future Hall of Famer from Slovakia who had signed with the Hawks as a free agent after leaving Detroit.

In the goaltending department, there was no latter-day Chuck Gardiner, Glenn Hall, or Tony Esposito on the roster to carry the team on his back. Journeyman Cristobal Huet held down the job until he was replaced by Antti Niemi late in the season.

The Hawks started the season with two games against the Florida Panthers in Helsinki, Finland. They returned to North America and lost at Detroit to make their record an even 1-1-1, which proved to be the low-water mark of the entire season.

After that the Hawks embarked on a relentless march to their first division title since 1993. By the end of October, they were 8-4-1. On the 24th of that month, the Hawks overcame a 5-0 deficit to defeat the Philadelphia Flyers 6-5 in overtime for the greatest comeback in NHL history. By the end of November, the Hawks were 16-6-3. By the end of December, they were 27-10-3. January, 37-14-4. February, 41-15-5. You get the picture.

February included a two-week break for the Winter Olympics, in which Canada, with Toews, Keith, and Seabrook, earned the gold medal and the United States, featuring Kane, took the silver. "You don't want this to slip away," said Toews, "because it's an unbelievable feeling and something that maybe comes once in a lilfetime."

The Hawks lost the regular-season finale 3-2 in overtime to their old nemesis Detroit, thereby missing a chance to clinch the top playoff seed in the Western Conference. Nonetheless, they finished at 52-22-8, easily breaking the franchise records for wins and points (112) in a season.

Even the most casual hockey fan knows that regular-season results don't necessarily translate to postseason success, and the Washington Capitals proved that point by getting bounced in the first round of the playoffs after breezing through the regular season with 121 points.

The Hawks got off on the wrong foot themselves by losing their first playoff game against the Nashville Predators at home by the lopsided score of 4-1.

The series was tied two games apiece when the Predators visited the United Center for Game 5 on April 24. The Hawks found themselves trailing 4-3 in the third period and facing the prospect of returning to Nashville for a potential elimination game when the situation went from bad to worse. Hossa was sent off for boarding with only a minute and three seconds left.

As the clock ticked down, Nashville's Martin Erat got possession of the puck behind his own net and attempted to clear it along the boards, hoping to spring one of his teammates for a shot at Chicago's empty net.

Sharp intercepted the puck, pushed it over to Seabrook in the corner, who slid it to Toews in the slot. Toews flipped a wrist shot that Nashville goalie Pekka Rinne stopped with his pads but allowed to bounce toward Kane, who was camped just to the left of the goal mouth.

Before you knew it, Kane shoveled the biscuit into the basket, and the game was tied with 13.6 seconds remaining. It was the first game-tying, shorthanded goal inside the final minute of a playoff game in the long history of the NHL, and it saved the Hawks' season.

The Hawks won 5-4 when Hossa tallied four minutes into overtime. "I don't even remember the game, to be honest," Kane said. "I just remember us winning. From death to the door opening is a really good feeling."

The Hawks advanced to the second round by defeating the Predators 5-3 in Game 6 at Nashville.

The opener of the conference semifinal series against the Vancouver Canucks was eerily similar to the opener against Nashville; the Hawks were routed 5-1 at home. "We can't be pleased in any respect with what took place tonight," Quenneville said. Huet played the third period in relief of Niemi in what proved to be his only appearance of the playoffs and his last appearance in the NHL.

In Game 2, also at home, the Hawks fell behind 2-0 within the first five minutes. They still trailed 2-1 early in the third period. The crowd was growing progressively more anxious when a shorthanded goal by Sharp, assisted by Seabrook, turned the whole series around. The fired-up Hawks swarmed Vancouver goalie Roberto Luongo relentlessly until Versteeg lit the lamp with only a minute and a half remaining. Kane's empty-net tally made the final score 4-2.

The Hawks dominated the next two games, both on the Vancouver ice that had recently hosted the Olympics. Agitating by Hawks role players such as Byfuglien, Dave Bolland, and Adam Burish drove the Canucks to distraction time and again in Game 3. Of Vancouver's nine penalties, five were for roughing or misconduct. Byfuglien not only goaded the Canucks into several of these penalties, but he also earned a hat trick with his first three goals of the playoffs.

Game 4 saw more of the same. A series of ill-advised Vancouver penalties led to three consecutive power-play goals by the Hawks in the second period, turning a 2-2 tie into a blowout. The final score was 7-4.

"We lost our composure again," said Luongo. "We talked about it. We were all on the same page before the game started. I don't know."

At the United Center for Game 5, the Blackhawks were greeted by a raucous sellout crowd that fully expected to see the series wrapped up with a ribbon and a bow. Alas, the Hawks showed little in losing 4-1.

But not to worry. Back in Vancouver, the Hawks scored three unanswered goals in the second period to put Game 6 and the series away. In the third period, Byfuglien scored the last goal and assisted on the next-to-last; he was the difference maker for Chicago throughout the series. The final score was 5-1, bringing the total count to 17-7 in the three games the Hawks won at Vancouver.

It might have been said in hindsight that the Blackhawks were happy just to make it to the Western Conference finals in 2009, since they had not even made the playoffs at all for the previous five seasons. In 2010, though, just getting there wouldn't be good enough. Both the Hawks themselves and their ever-growing corps of diehard fans, returning fans, and new fans expected more—and they got it, in the form of a four-game sweep of the San Jose Sharks.

Perhaps it was just as well that the series opened in San Jose, in light of the Hawks' dismal performance in home openers in the previous two series. Accordingly, the Hawks won 2-1 behind a sensational performance by Niemi, who stopped 44 shots by the Sharks. In Game 2, the Hawks jumped out to a 3-0 lead before the contest was halfway through and sailed away to a 4-2 victory.

Now the Hawks had won seven straight road games in the playoffs, tying the NHL record, while performing somewhat poorly at home. Quenneville therefore contrived to make Game 3 at the United Center *seem* like a road game by having his players stay in a Chicago hotel rather than at their homes.

Quenneville's ploy worked—although, of course, we'll never know what would've happened in its absence. Game 3 was tied 2-2 at the end of regulation, with the unsung Niemi again playing superbly and turning away 44 of 46 San Jose shots. Byfuglien, a beefy (six-foot-five and 265 pounds) defenseman and part-time forward, notched the game winner from Bolland and Campbell a little more than 12 minutes into overtime.

In Game 4, the Sharks jumped out to a two-goal lead, but the Hawks tied it up by the end of the second period. The game-tying goal, with 1:22 left in the second, came off the stick of Bolland, assisted by Ben Eager and Keith, who had just returned to the ice after losing *seven* teeth when he caught a puck square in the mouth. "They [his team-mates] didn't say much when I came off," said Keith, "because they didn't want to scare me about the way it looked. No stitches. They just stuck a bunch of needles in there and froze it all up."

That probably tells us all we need to know about the toughness and fortitude of the man who became known thereafter as "Duncan Teeth."

The score was tied 2-2 when the unlikely Byfuglien stepped up yet again, lighting the lamp with assists from Kane and Toews with 5:55 left in the third period. For good measure, Versteeg added an empty-netter in the final minute to make the final score 4-2.

Byfuglien, who'd scored 17 goals in 82 regular-season games, ended up with 11 in the 22 playoff games. He played the role that had made Al Secord a fan favorite many years earlier—camping out in front of the net, daring rival defenseman to try and move him, and offering to drop the gloves if they so much as gave him a dirty look.

The series sweep was now complete, and the Hawks were headed to the Stanley Cup Final for the first time since 1992. A comical scene unfolded when the Clarence Campbell Bowl, emblematic of the Western Conference championship, was wheeled onto the ice and presented to Toews. The Hawks' captain refused to even go near the trophy, let alone touch it.

"Jonny and I talked about it," said Sharp, "and thought it was best to just leave that one there. We're proud of being Western Conference champions, but we've got our eyes on the bigger trophy."

The battle for the bigger trophy—the greatest trophy in all of sports—began on May 29 at the United Center.

Game 1 was a wild affair, described by Quenneville as "the shootout at the O.K. Corral." The Hawks and Philadelphia Flyers combined for six goals (three for each team) in the first 21 minutes and 10 goals (five each) after two periods.

Only one goal was scored in the third period—by the Hawks' Tomas Kopecky after a nifty pass from Versteeg. The relatively unknown Kopecky had sat out the previous five games and was in the lineup only because of an injury to Andrew Ladd. After Kopecky's tally with 11:35 remaining, Niemi and the Hawks held on for a 6-5 victory. "We were lucky to steal that one," said Toews. It was the franchise's first win in the Stanley Cup Final series since 1973.

Game 2 was a highly physical contest that remained scoreless until Hossa buried a rebound of a shot by Troy Brouwer with three minutes left in the second period. "It's been a long time," said Hossa, who despite contributing two assists in Game 1 and playing his typically effective two-way hockey throughout the playoffs, had failed to score a goal for the past eight games. "It bugged me, definitely," he said. "I tried to create offense, but when I shot the puck it didn't want to go in. I tried not to get frustrated, but I did."

Only 28 seconds after Hossa's tally, Eager lit the lamp with a wicked wrist shot from the top of the faceoff circle. It was the first and only goal of the playoffs for Eager, who played just four minutes in the game and averaged six minutes a game for the postseason.

Three minutes into the third period, Sharp was sent to the penalty box for tripping, and Philadelphia cashed in. Simon Gagne scored with one second remaining on the power play to cut Chicago's lead in half. For the last fifteen minutes, though, Niemi was equal to everything the Flyers threw at him. After he dropped to his knees to stop a point-blank attempt by Ville Leino with about two minutes left, the United Center crowd of 22,275 chanted his name until the final horn sounded. "What an unbelievable feeling," Niemi said.

So far, so good. The Blackhawks took a potentially commanding 2-0 series lead to Philadelphia, but they soon discovered that the series was far from over.

The Hawks were strangely undisciplined in Game 3. A slashing penalty by Hossa in the first period and a similar infraction by Byfuglien in the second each led to power-play goals by the Flyers. The game was tied 2-2 after two periods and 3-3 after regulation. The overtime period was almost six minutes old when the Hawks got caught in a bad line change that left them with only three skaters (Keith, Seabrook, and Bolland) on the ice when Claude Giroux hit the back of the net to give the Flyers a 4-3 victory. "It shouldn't happen," said Keith. "We need to be a little smarter."

As ragged as the Blackhawks' performance had been in Game 3, their next effort was well worse. In Game 4, the normally heady defenseman Niklas Hjalmarsson committed two bad turnovers in the first period, both of which resulted in goals for the Flyers. The Hawks took seven penalties, and none of them was what Quenneville might have called "good" (meaning necessary). The penalties included one for interference, one for cross-checking, two for high-sticking, and three for slashing. The Hawks were fortunate to lose only 5-3 and not by a wider margin.

When the series returned to the United Center for Game 5, the Chicago fans showed they were ready by roaring even more rousingly than usual during Jim Cornelison's singing of the national anthem and by springing to their feet and cheering virtually every time the Hawks got possession of the puck. Quenneville was ready, too. He reshuffled his forward lines in an effort to wear down the Flyers' star defenseman Chris Pronger. Quenneville broke up his most productive line—Toews, Kane, and Byfuglien—on the theory that Pronger (who averaged 30 minutes a game for the playoffs) couldn't stay on the ice long enough to keep tabs on all three players. Toews skated with Hossa and Kopecky, Kane with Ladd and Sharp, and Byfuglien with Versteeg and Bolland.

Seabrook opened the scoring with a power-play goal at 12:17 of the first period, assisted by Versteeg and Brouwer. When goals by Bolland and Versteeg followed at roughly three-minute intervals, the Hawks led 3-0 and the rout was on. The Hawks won 7-4, and Byfuglien made Quenneville's lineup changes look like a work of genius by racking up two goals and two assists. "He got rid of us," Kane said, with tongue in cheek, "and started performing." Pronger, with the taunts of the faithful ringing in his ears, had perhaps the worst night of his great career, earning a minus-five in the box score.

For the Hawks, it was an exceptional performance from beginning to end. "We found energy," Hossa said, with his typical understatement, "from shuffling the lines."

June 9, 2010. The home team has won each of the first five games of the Stanley Cup Final when the Blackhawks and Flyers take the ice for Game 6 in Philadelphia. Kane assists on the Hawks' first goal, by Byfuglien, and their third, by Ladd, as Chicago takes a 3-2 lead into the third period.

But the Flyers' Scott Hartnell scores his second goal of the game with 3:59 remaining in the third period, and neither team scores again in regulation. The Hawks have the better of it all night, peppering Philadelphia goalie Michael Leighton with 41 shots in all, while Niemi faces only 24, but the Flyers hold on to force overtime.

Four minutes into the extra period, Kane receives the puck from Brian Campbell near the left circle. He advances on Leighton and fires from an apparently impossible angle, almost parallel to the goal line. Somehow, the puck travels between Leighton's pads and deep into the far side of the net.

The Hawks are Stanley Cup champions, but for an awkward stretch of time no one other than Kane knows it—because only Kane is certain that the puck is in the net (actually it has become lodged underneath the backing of the net).

Kane single-handedly begins the celebration, skating the length of the ice, yelling "It's in! It's in! The game's over!" as he passes the Hawks' bench. He then jumps into the arms of Niemi, while the Flyers and their fans look on in stupefied silence. Almost a full minute elapses before the officials finally confirm that Kane has indeed scored and that the Hawks' 49-year Stanley Cup drought is over.

"I can't believe it," Kane says. "We just won the the Stanley Cup!"

CHAPTER 41

"A Fun Time to Be a Blackhawk"

"I think everyone that has success wants to sustain that over a period of time. It's a challenge to do it."
-- *Stan Bowman, Blackhawks general manager, 2009 --*

The Blackhawks team that won the Stanley Cup in 2010 might have done so over and over if not for the NHL's salary cap, which came into being after the labor dispute that forced the cancellation of the entire 2004-05 season. Its effect became obvious when seven different teams won the Cup in the first seven years of the salary-cap era. Gone were the days when a handful of teams could monopolize the Cup like the Montreal Canadiens, New York Islanders, and Edmonton Oilers did by winning 14 of the 15 championships between 1976 and 1990.

Thanks to the salary cap, Hawks general manager Stan Bowman had to wave goodbye to many players he'd have preferred to keep after the 2010 championship. The Hawks were good but not great for the next two years, losing in the first round of the playoffs both times. "We had to change the whole makeup of our team, basically half the team, after winning," said head coach Joel Quenneville. "It was kind of a new team for a couple years there."

When you were named after the Stanley Cup, as Bowman was, perhaps you have a more than ordinary desire to win it. By the 2012-13 season, the Hawks were back. The core group—center Jonathan Toews, wingers Patrick Kane, Marian Hossa, and Patrick Sharp, defensemen Duncan Keith, Brent Seabrook, and Niklas Hjalmarsson, and goalie Corey Crawford—hadn't gone anywhere. And Bowman had managed, after some hard work, to surround them with a mix of promising young-sters (winger Brandon Saad, defenseman Nick Leddy, and center Andrew Shaw), and productive veterans (defensemen Johnny Oduya and Michal Rozsival, winger Viktor Stalberg, and backup goalie Ray Emery) that made the Hawks believe they could go a long way. "We like our team," said Quenneville. "We think we've got all the right ingredients."

With the Blackhawks chomping at the bit, another NHL labor dispute delayed the start of the season from October 2012 until January 2013 and reduced the schedule from 82 games per team to 48.

The Hawks opened the season by routing the Kings 5-2 in Los Angeles, with Hossa scoring two goals in his first game back from the concussion that knocked him out of the 2012 playoffs. They reeled off five more wins before suffering a shootout loss at Minnesota. After another shootout loss at Vancouver on February 1, they won four more in a row. With a quarter of the abbreviated season behind them, the Hawks were 10-0-2. Even more impressive was the fact that they'd compiled such a record while having played 10 of the 12 games on the road.

The second quarter of the shortened season went even better. After falling to Anaheim in a shootout, the Hawks really started cooking. They won the next 11 games, defeating Colorado 3-2 at home on March 6 to arrive at the halfway point of the season with a stupendous record of 21-0-3. Their 45 points to date represented 94 percent of the points they could have possibly accumulated. By opening the season with 24 straight games in which they earned at least one point, they obliterated the previous record of 16.

All good things must come to an end, as the Hawks' streak did with a thud in a 6-2 loss at Colorado on March 8. "We should be very proud of what we accomplished," Quenneville said. "It's a great feather in our cap, but let's move forward here and try to get better as we go along."

A 6-5 defeat at Edmonton two nights later gave the Hawks their first losing streak of the season. (They ended up losing two in a row only one other time, and never lost three straight until the playoffs—but we're getting ahead of ourselves.) They continued at a lukewarm pace for the better part of a month, compiling an unimpressive record of 6-5-1 for the third quarter of the season.

Then the Hawks got it back together. They won seven straight from April 6 to April 19. The second win of the streak clinched a postseason berth. "We obviously want to stay in the spot we're at [first overall]," said Toews, "but first and foremost, our number-one goal coming in every season is we want to make the playoffs." The streak began and ended with victories over Nashville and also included wins over future playoff opponents Minnesota and Detroit. By the time it ended, the Hawks had wrapped up first place in the Western Conference. A victory at Edmonton on April 24 clinched the Presidents' Trophy, emblematic of first place overall, and with it home-ice advantage throughout the playoffs.

The Hawks ended the regular season with a record of 36-7-5, good for 77 points (more than 80 percent of the possible total of 96). They finished 11 points ahead of Anaheim in the Western Conference and five points ahead of Pittsburgh for the Presidents' Trophy. Kane led the club with 55 points, while he and Toews tied for the lead with 23 goals apiece. Crawford and Emery shared the Jennings Trophy, awarded to the team allowing the fewest goals.

It had been a truly great regular season, the first in the Blackhawks' long and distinguished history in which they'd earned more than 70 percent of the possible points, let alone 80 percent. But as Quenneville and his players understood, it would ultimately count for very little unless the Hawks won the Stanley Cup.

The first round of the playoffs went pretty much according to plan. The Blackhawks dispatched the Minnesota Wild four games to one, routing them 5-1 in the last game while the United Center crowd chanted "Corey! Corey!" in honor of Crawford. "I think the past two years we felt we could've gone further," said Crawford, who'd won the first playoff series of his career. "This is definitely a good start for us."

The Hawks opened the next round, the Western Conference semifinals, by scoring three unanswered goals in the third period to subdue the Detroit Red Wings 4-1. "It doesn't matter who scores," said Sharp, who had a goal and two assists. "Our team is going to produce goals, and whoever is doing it doesn't matter to us."

But then, after winning five of the first six postseason games, outscoring their opponents 21-8 and killing off all 20 enemy power plays in the process, the Hawks suddenly went ice cold (no pun intended). They scored only two goals, allowing nine, as they dropped the next three games to Detroit. "We played our tails off and did a lot of good things," Toews said after the third straight loss. "We just couldn't find the back of the net." The three-game losing streak was the first of the whole year for the Hawks, who now were confronted with the possibility, even likelihood, of being eliminated.

Showing what they were made of, the Hawks came back with a vengeance in Game 5 before a raucous crowd at the United Center. Bryan Bickell opened the scoring 14 minutes into the first period, from Kane and Michal Handzus. After Detroit tallied halfway through the second, Shaw notched the go-ahead goal, on the power play, at 13:08 when he redirected Keith's shot from the blue line. Less than three minutes later, Toews scored on another power play, assisted by Hossa and Keith. It was his first goal of the playoffs, and it galvanized the whole team. "They [the Red Wings] have been all over him," Shaw said, "but it just shows he's a great captain. He sticks with it and was rewarded tonight."

Shaw lit the lamp again almost seven minutes into the third. The Hawks won 4-1, outshooting the Red Wings 45-26. "They were better than us today," Detroit captain Henrik Zetterberg said. "That's a fact."

"We have to go back to Detroit and win a game," said Quenneville. Wouldn't you know it, the Hawks did just that. Trailing 2-1 after two periods, they tied it up in the first minute of the third and scored twice more in the next nine minutes to put the game away. "It was just pure confidence," said Toews, "and our heads were in the right spot. We knew what we had to do, and we weren't panicking."

The series returned to the United Center. If going to a Game 7 is the limit, then going to overtime in a Game 7 is beyond the limit—and that is what the Blackhawks and Red Wings did. After a scoreless first period, Sharp scored for the Hawks barely a minute into the second, and Zetterberg tallied for the Wings less than half a minute into the third.

It appeared that Hjalmarsson had scored the game winner with 1:47 remaining in regulation, but the goal was waved off because of coincidental penalties well behind the play. "That was a tough call," said Kane. "It was a tough break for us, but we wanted to regroup and get back at it in overtime."

The real game winner came just three and a half minutes into the extra period. Dave Bolland leveled a monster hit on Gustav Nyquist along the boards, and the puck squirted free to Seabrook, who buried a wrist shot from just inside the blue line for his first goal of the playoffs. "I don't even know if I saw it go in, to be honest," Seabrook said after the game. "I just heard the horn going and saw the boys jumping out. You don't get to do that too many times, and it'll be something I'll remember for the rest of my life."

"I think we might have needed a little adversity to get us going here in the playoffs the last three games," Kane said in the victorious dressing room. "It's a fun time to be a Blackhawk. We have a great opportunity to do something special."

The Western Conference finals vs. the defending Stanley Cup champion Los Angeles Kings offered a reunion of sorts with Darryl Sutter, current head coach of the Kings, former head coach of the Blackhawks (1992-1995), and one of the gamest, most popular Hawks players of the 1980s.

Riding the momentum from the stirring comeback against Detroit, the Hawks won the first two games against Los Angeles, both at the United Center, to make it five in a row. In Game 1, second-period tallies by Sharp and Hossa erased a 1-0 deficit and proved decisive as the Hawks prevailed 2-1. In Game 2, the Hawks scored four times in the first 30 minutes and held on to win 4-2.

"We're feeling good about where we are in the series," said Toews, "but that's not a team that's going to give up easy." Sure enough, the Kings won Game 3 in Los Angeles by the score of 3-1.

The Hawks reclaimed the upper hand in Game 4. After the teams traded goals in the first period, the Kings went ahead 2-1 early in the second. Late in that period, Quenneville decided to juggle his lines. Kane and Hossa traded places, with Kane joining Toews and Bickell on the first line while Hossa teamed with Sharp and Handzus on the second. The change paid off handsomely when both reworked lines scored within three minutes to turn the game around. Kane notched the game-tying goal, assisted by Bickell and Hjalmarsson, with less than two minutes left in the second. Then Hossa dented the twine, from Handzus and Oduya, barely a minute into the third. Hossa's goal proved to be decisive as the Hawks won 3-2, breaking the Kings' 15-game winning streak at home.

Game 5, back in Chicago, was an entertaining back-and-forth affair in which Kane played the leading role. He scored in the first period to give the Hawks a 2-0 lead. After the Kings fought back to tie the game, he scored again to put the Hawks ahead with less than four minutes left in the third. Finally, after the Kings tied it up again with nine seconds remaining in regulation, he completed his hat trick on a nifty two-on-one rush with Toews. Receiving Toews's pass just inside the right circle, Kane took his time, got Quick to commit too soon, and then fired the puck into a wide open net—ending the game and the series at 11:40 of the second overtime.

When asked in the postgame press conference for his analysis of the game winner, the laconic Sutter gave an answer that would do as well as any. "In the end," he said, "probably their two best offensive guys [Kane and Toews] made a great play to score a goal."

After taking four and a half periods to win the last game of the conference finals, the Blackhawks played five and a half periods in the first game of the Stanley Cup Final against the Boston Bruins.

The Hawks trailed 3-1 in Game 1 when Bolland scored off Shaw's perfect pass through traffic with exactly eight minutes left in the third period. Oduya tied it up just over four minutes later when his shot hit a Bruin defenseman's skate and trickled past goalie Tuukka Rask. Neither team scored again until 12:08 of the third overtime, when a shot by Rozsival was tipped first by Bolland and then by Shaw on its way to the back of the net. The Hawks won 4-3. Crawford was sensational, making 51 saves, 29 of them in overtime—including a point-blank attempt by Shawn Thornton in the first extra period. "You just have to stick with it," Crawford said. "You have to keep going until you win."

The two teams also required overtime to resolve Game 2. The Hawks peppered 19 shots at Rask in the first period, but only one (a drive by Sharp) got past him. The Hawks didn't score again. The Bruins scored with five minutes left in the second period and again at 13:48 of overtime. "If somebody would watch the first period," said Boston's Jaromir Jagr, "I would've said, 'Oh, give [the Hawks] the Cup right now.' If somebody watched the overtime, they'd say, 'It's gonna be a long series.'"

The series shifted to Boston for Game 3, and the Blackhawks' offense again turned up missing. Hossa sat out with an undisclosed upper-body injury, which didn't help, but Quenneville attributed the 2-0 defeat to the Bruins' overwhelming dominance in the faceoff circles (71 percent) and the Hawks' continued futility on the power play (0-for-4). "The last two series, there have been times when we had trouble scoring goals," said Toews. "Sometimes it happens. We've just got to be better."

The Hawks were indeed better offensively in Game 4, but not good enough to win by a comfortable margin, or even in regulation. They spent the majority of the game in the Bruins' zone, eventually getting 47 shots on goal to Boston's 33. They also gained, and then gave up, leads of 1-0, 3-1, 4-2, and 5-4 before the game went into overtime knotted up at 5-5.

A loss would put the Hawks in a three-games-to-one hole—and maybe this time they wouldn't be able to dig out of it, as they had done against Detroit. Fortunately, they never had to find out. The man whose goal rescued them at 9:51 of overtime was the same man whose overtime goal had ended the Detroit series. Seabrook whistled a slapshot from the right point, through Toews's screen, and into the net. Rask never saw it. Toews didn't get credit for an assist because he didn't touch the puck, but he managed to occupy two defenders—including the massive (six-foot-nine, 250 pounds) former Norris Trophy winner Zdeno Chara—in front of the net.

"We feel good about going home," Sharp said. "Best of three with two home games, but I don't think it matters where we play. Boston has been tough to play against in their building and they've been tough in Chicago."

Quenneville needed very few words to aptly describe the Bruins: "They keep coming."

Back on home ice for Game 5, Kane came through, as he so often did when the glare of the spotlight shone brightest. He first lit the lamp at 17:27 of the first period when he corralled the rebound of a shot by Oduya and tucked it into the net behind Rask. He tallied again at 5:15 of the second, this time on a rebound of a wraparound attempt by Bolland. "He's very good at kind of finding those quiet areas," Boston coach Claude Julien said, "and sliding into the right spot."

"I think everyone wants to be that guy in big-time games," Kane said, "and I've been lucky enough in a couple to step up." Toews assisted on both of Kane's goals, but he sat out the entire third period after having his bell rung twice (by Johnny Boychuk and Chara). The Hawks maintained the 2-0 lead until Chara scored early in the third. From then on, the Bruins furiously attacked, but Crawford and the Hawks held them off until Bolland's empty-net goal with 14 seconds left confirmed the outcome.

The Blackhawks were now one win away from another Stanley Cup. "We know the situation," said Keith, "but we're not going to get ahead of ourselves. There's a lot of work to be done yet."

It had been a thrilling series so far, and Quenneville, for one, was impressed. "You look at every minute from Game 1 to where we're at today," he said. "It's been an amazing series, and relentless hockey. I commend the guys on both teams for leaving it out on the ice."

On their home ice for Game 6, the Bruins came out flying, running the Hawks ragged, abusing them physically, and outshooting them 12-6 in the first period. Chris Kelly scored for Boston, assisted by Tyler Seguin and Daniel Paille, at 7:19 (these fourth-liners combined for four goals and seven assists in the series). Only heroic work by Crawford enabled the Hawks to escape the period trailing just 1-0.

The second period started much the same way. The Bruins were already having the better of it when Shaw was sent off for roughing at 2:24. Thus began Boston's third power play of the game, against none for the Hawks.

Great players are recognized as such because they perform great feats on a regular basis. And so it was that Toews gained possession of a loose puck in the neutral zone, streaked down the right side, and fired a wrist shot that landed in the far corner of the net, just below the crossbar. The unassisted goal was not credited as short-handed because it occurred at 4:24, just as Shaw was stepping out of the penalty box.

Seabrook was called for tripping less than a minute after Toews's goal, but the Hawks killed that penalty as effectively as they had killed the previous three. Finally, the Bruins' Seguin was sent off for hooking with six minutes left in the period to give the Hawks their first power play, which paid no dividends. The score remained 1-1 at the second intermission.

Boston went ahead when Milan Lucic was left unattended in front of the net and swatted one past Crawford with just under eight minutes remaining in the third period. Then, the Bruins clung to the tenuous lead for almost seven minutes, while the Hawks kept on grinding and hoped to make something good happen.

It happened. Toews spotted Bickell moving unmolested toward the net and flipped a pass right onto his stick. "Tazer got it in front," said Bickell, "and I just buried it." Bickell's ninth goal of the playoffs tied the game with 1:16 left in regulation. Toews and Keith got the assists.

What happened next ensured that the phrase "17 seconds" will conjur up fond memories for every Hawks fan for many years to come. Almost simultaneously with the customary public-address announcement "One minute to play in the period," Oduya sent the puck toward the net and Bolland, camping in front, redirected it. Bolland's goal, from Oduya and Michael Frolik, came only 17 seconds after Bickell's, putting the Hawks ahead 3-2. "It was the best goal I ever scored," Bolland said. "It's better than sex, almost."

The rest is history. Fifty-nine seconds later, the Blackhawks were Stanley Cup champions. Kane received the Conn Smythe Trophy as most valuable player of the playoffs. "My head is spinning," he said. "I don't even know what's happened the past 20 minutes, to be honest with you. You can't write the script any better."

Only eight of the Hawks who took a turn hoisting the Stanley Cup in 2013 had done so in 2010. Remarkably, Bowman had turned over the other two-thirds of the team.

"We want to be positioned to win every year," said owner Rocky Wirtz. "We know we can't win it every year, but if we get in position, that's our job. We want to be very, very good every year." With Wirtz himself, Bowman, Quenneville, Toews, Kane, Keith, and other key contributors in place for the foreseeable future, there was no reason to doubt that such would prove to be the case.

CHAPTER 42

Moments, 2007-2015

February 4, 2007
Almost Super

Super Bowl XLI was the first Super Bowl played in a driving rain, the first to feature even one African-American head coach (let alone two), and the first in which the opening kickoff was returned for a touchdown.

The Bears had rolled through a league-best 13-3 regular season. They scored 427 points (including an incredible 65 by the defense and special teams), while allowing only 255. Eight Bears were selected for the Pro Bowl: center Olin Kreutz, guard Ruben Brown, defensive end Tommie Harris, linebackers Brian Urlacher and Lance Briggs, special teamer Brendan Ayanbadejo, kicker Robbie Gould, and return man Devin Hester.

Quarterback Rex Grossman had excelled while leading the Bears to wins in their first seven games, but struggled as the season wore on. After Grossman committed 19 turnovers in the second half of the season, sportswriters asked head coach Lovie Smith whether he might make a change for the playoffs. Smith's answer has lived on as a sound bite ever since. "Rex is our quarterback," he said in his syrupy Texas drawl.

Smith's trust in Grossman was rewarded when the Bears squeaked past the Seattle Seahawks in overtime and then routed the New Orleans Saints to punch their ticket to the franchise's first Super Bowl since the legendary 1985 season.

When Smith met his counterpart and old friend, Indianapolis Colts head coach Tony Dungy, on the field at Miami's Dolphin Stadium before the game, they shook hands as the first African-American head coaches in Super Bowl history. "I just told Lovie how proud I was of the moment," said Dungy.

Then the Colts' Adam Vinatieri kicked off to Hester, and the sensational rookie who'd set an NFL record with six return touchdowns on the year did not disappoint. He raced 92 yards to the opposite end zone. After Gould added the extra point, the Bears led 7-0.

Fourteen seconds had been played. Fifty-nine minutes and 46 seconds remained, but Hester (who eventually proved to be the greatest returner of all time) was done for all intents and purposes. From then on, the Colts squibbed every kickoff and punted the ball near him only once.

The Colts' first possession ended with safety Chris Harris intercepting a Peyton Manning pass at the Bears' 29-yard line. Alas, the Bears failed to move the ball and were forced to punt. A 53-yard strike from Manning to Reggie Wayne got the Colts onto the scoreboard, but a botched extra point left the Bears ahead 7-6.

The Bears fumbled the ensuing pooch kick (while Hester waited in vain at his own goal line), and Indianapolis recovered. The Colts returned the favor on the very next play when running back Joseph Addai coughed up the football to Bears defensive end Mark Anderson. On the next play, Bears running back Thomas Jones scampered 52 yards down to the Colts' five-yard line. Then Grossman found Muhsin Muhammad in the end zone, extending the Bears' lead to 14-6.

The Bears did not score again until Gould booted a 44-yard field goal with 1:14 left in the third quarter. In the meantime, Prince delivered a stupendous halftime show and the Colts delivered a touchdown and three field goals against the Bears' bend-but-don't-break defense.

At the outset of the fourth quarter, the Colts were ahead 22-17, not an insurmountable lead by any means. But then came the play of the game. Grossman's pass intended for Muhammad was picked off by Kelvin Haynes and taken 56 yards for a touchdown. The Bears had now been outscored 23-3 since the first quarter. The ensuing kickoff was soon followed by the coup de grace, another interception of Grossman.

The final score was 29-17. "A frustrating loss," Grossman said. "There were definitely opportunities for us to take that game, and we didn't do it." For his part, Manning was later overheard saying that the Colts "should've scored 70 [points]." They had controlled the ball for 38 minutes, earning 24 first downs to the Bears' 11 and amassing 430 yards of offense to the Bears' 265. The Bears had lost to a superior team and to perhaps the greatest quarterback of all time.

September 30, 2008
The Blackout Game

On September 23, 2008, the first-place White Sox brought a two-and-a-half-game lead into Minnesota for a three-game series with the second-place Twins.

If the Sox won all three games, they would clinch the American League Central Division title outright. If they won two, they would clinch a tie for the crown. And even if they won just one, it wouldn't be a disaster; they would still leave town a game and a half in front.

Alas, the Twins showed why White Sox manager Ozzie Guillen called them "piranhas." They swept the series, overcoming a five-run deficit in the third game. The Sox skulked out of town in second place. They would conclude the season with three games at home against Cleveland (plus a makeup game with Detroit if it were necessary). The Twins would host three games against Kansas City.

Both contenders lost their next two games and staggered into the final day of the regular season, Sunday, September 28, with the Twins ahead by half a game. If the Sox lost, they would be eliminated no matter what Minnesota did.

Old reliable Mark Buehrle had something to say about that. While everyone kept one eye on the scoreboard to track the progress of the Minnesota-Kansas City game, Buehrle scattered nine hits over seven innings and pitched the Sox to a 5-1 victory. When the Sox headed into their clubhouse at 3:35 p.m., Minnesota led Kansas City 2-0 in the top of the seventh. But the Twins scored two in the seventh and two more in the eighth to defeat the Royals and end their regular season at 88-74.

The White Sox were 87-74, so the Tigers were obliged to postpone their tee times and visit Chicago to make up a game that had been rained out two weeks earlier.

The Sox trailed 2-1 when Dewayne Wise drew a lead-off walk in the bottom of the sixth. Wise stole second, advanced to third on a wild pitch, and scored on yet another wild pitch. The game was tied until rookie second baseman Alexei Ramirez blasted a grand slam later in the same inning. The Sox won 8-2. Gavin Floyd earned the victory with help from four relievers.

So the White Sox and Twins were tied for the division championship. Game number 163 to unbreak the tie took place in Chicago, the Sox having won a coin flip.

Marketing director Brooks Boyer came up with a clever idea to energize Sox fans and enhance their team's home-field advantage. It was "the Blackout Game." Fans were asked to show up dressed in black, and virtually all of the 40,354 obliged. They turned U.S. Cellular Field into a sea of black and hollered their lungs out from the first pitch to the last.

The Sox sent southpaw John Danks to the mound against Minnesota righthander Nick Blackburn. Danks had been bombed in his previous start vs. Cleveland, but he was sharp on this occasion. So was Blackburn.

Neither team seriously threatened until Michael Cuddyer doubled to lead off the Twins' half of the fifth inning. Delmon Young's deep fly ball to Sox center fielder Ken Griffey, Jr., moved Cuddyer to third.

Then Brendan Harris lifted a rather shallow fly to Griffey, a late-season acquisition by the Sox who, at age 38, was nearing the end of his great career. The 10-time Gold Glover made the catch and fired a perfect strike to catcher A.J. Pierzynski, who made the tag despite being steamrolled by Cuddyer. "I don't know how A.J. held onto the ball," Danks said admiringly.

The scoreless tie remained in place until Jim Thome led off the bottom of the seventh for the Sox. Like Griffey, Thome was a future Hall of Famer whose best years had been spent elsewhere. At six-foot-four and 250 pounds, he was also the very definition of what the late, great Harry Caray used to call a "hairy-chested slugger."

With the count at two and two, Thome did what he did best. Blackburn delivered a changeup. Thome swung from the heels, connected, and drove the ball over the center-field fence, over the shrubbery behind the fence, and onto the concourse behind the stands—some 460 feet from home plate.

Danks carried the precarious 1-0 lead into the eighth. With one out, he yielded a single to Harris, then induced Nick Punto to bounce into a

6-4-3 double play. Danks, overjoyed, pumped his fist and started to skip to the dugout before he realized what he was doing and resumed a normal gait.

The Sox did no damage in their half of the eighth, and Bobby Jenks relieved Danks to start the ninth. With the black-clad spectators roaring, Jenks needed only eight pitches to retire the Twins in order and record the save.

The South Siders had pulled out three consecutive elimination games against three different opponents, a first in baseball history. They were division champions—and so were the Cubs. Now that was news, because the two clubs hadn't both finished first in the same year since 1906. But hopes for another crosstown World Series evaporated when the Sox won only one game in the postseason (one more than the Cubs).

January 23, 2011
Rivalry

For the first 90 years of their existence, the Bears met their ancient rivals from up north, the Green Bay Packers, only once in posteason play—in 1941, when the two teams tied for the Western Division title and needed a special playoff game to decide which would go to the NFL championship game. The Bears won on that occasion by the lopsided score of 33-14 and went on to capture the world championship the following week by drubbing the New York Giants.

The Bears and Packers met for the second time in postseason play following the 2010 season, again with a trip to the NFL championship game (now known as the Super Bowl) at stake.

The Bears had gone 4-3 to start the season, won seven of eight after their bye week, then lost the final game at Green Bay to finish 11-5, a notch ahead of the Packers for the NFC North division title.

Bears fans came to the NFC championship game at Soldier Field on January 23 with high hopes. They started the "Let's go, Bears!" chant while tailgating in the parking lot, continued it while waiting in line to enter the stadium, and kept at it after reaching their seats. The game presented an interesting matchup between two of the NFL's most promising young quarterbacks—Jay Cutler of the Bears and Aaron Rodgers of the Packers.

Only Rodgers was left standing at the end. Cutler completed six of 14 passes for 80 yards and one touchdown, plus two interceptions, before he was injured early in the third quarter with the Bears trailing 14-0. Backup Todd Collins misfired on four attempts before he too was injured. Third-stringer Caleb Hanie led the Bears on an eight-play, 67-yard touchdown drive early in the fourth quarter. The score was now 14-7, and the Bears' defense was performing heroically. Green Bay's first drive of the second half ended with an interception by Brian Urlacher, and the next four Packer possessions ended with punts. The game was there for the taking. But with barely five minutes left and the Bears at third and five on their own 15-yard line, Hanie's pass intended for Matt Forte in the left flat was picked off by the massive defensive tackle B.J. Raji, who dragged his 335 pounds into the end zone for a touchdown.

After the Bears lost 21-14, Cutler—always a lightning rod for critics—was forced to explain why he hadn't soldiered on with a torn medial collateral ligament in his left knee! Some players in the league, observing from the comfort of their living rooms, questioned his toughness and commitment via social media. Rodgers called these sallies "disrespectful." Broadcaster and former quarterback Troy Aikman called them "stupid."

Meanwhile, the Packers went on to win the Super Bowl.

April 28, 2012
Turning Point

The Bulls took the court for their first playoff game of 2012 with high hopes—and why not? They had rampaged through the regular season with a record of 50-16, they were seeded No. 1 in the Eastern Conference (thus earning home-court advantage through the conference finals), and they had the NBA's reigning Most Valuable Player, point guard Derrick Rose, on their side to take over close games when it came down to crunch time.

The story of Rose's career so far seemed almost too good to be true. A local kid from the blighted Englewood neighborhood on the South Side, he had added to his glittering resume every year.

In 2007, he was Illinois' Mr. Basketball and a McDonald's High School All-American for Chicago's Simeon Career Academy, which won its second consecutive state championship. In 2008, his first and only year of college ball, he was a third-team All-American for the University of Memphis, which finished second in the NCAA tournament. Also in 2008, he was the first player selected in the NBA draft—by his hometown team, the Bulls. In 2010, he was an NBA All-Star reserve and Rookie of the Year. In 2011, he was an All-Star starter and NBA Most Valuable Player (the youngest in league history at age 22).

If the above statements reflected Rose's resume, the following quotes could have served as references. Indiana Pacers head coach Frank Vogel: "That kid is out of this world." Bulls head coach Tom Thibodeau: "He has handled everything with such grace and class." Bulls chairman Jerry Reinsdorf: "If you don't see something special in Derrick Rose, then you're blind."

No one could have known it at the time, but the pinnacle of Rose's career with the Bulls had already come and gone. Rose appeared in only 39 games in 2011-12, due to a variety of relatively minor injuries. Despite his frequent absences from the lineup, the Bulls tied for the best record in the league and entered the playoffs as favorites to reach the NBA Finals.

In the first game of the first round of the playoffs, the Bulls led the Philadelphia 76ers 99-87 with 1:22 left on the clock when Rose leapt off his left foot, appeared to land awkwardly, and then collapsed to the floor in obvious pain, as the United Center crowd fell silent. Tests soon confirmed that Rose had suffered a torn anterior cruciate ligament in his left knee. The Bulls held on to win the game, but they lost four of the next five to make an embarrassingly early exit from the postseason.

Rose did not play again for 18 months. He played 10 of the first 11 games in the 2013-14 season, then injured the other knee and was lost for the season. He managed to play 51 regular-season games in 2014-15, but it was obvious that he was a mere shadow of his former self. Though he was still only 26 years old, his explosive, acrobatic flights to the basket were now few and far between. He resorted more and more to shooting long-range jumpers, hardly a strength of his.

Thibodeau was let go after a five-year run in which the Bulls won almost 65 percent of their regular-season games but invariably disappointed in the playoffs. In 2015-16, the Bulls limped to a 42-40 record under rookie coach Fred Hoiberg. Rose was healthy enough to play in 66 games, but his performance continued to decline. When the Bulls missed the playoffs for the first time in his pro career, it was high time to admit that their window of opportunity to win a championship with Rose as their centerpiece had long since closed. He was traded to the New York Knicks. Both he and the Bulls then looked forward to a future offering far more questions than answers.

May 27 and 30, 2015
Pivotal

In every sport that features playoff series (rather than single games, like football), it seems that the fifth game of a series that's tied two games apiece must be called "pivotal" by all broadcasters and writers. When the Blackhawks and Anaheim Ducks played such a pivotal game in the NHL Western Conference finals of 2015, the Hawks erased deficits of 3-0 and 4-2 before finally succumbing in overtime.

The Hawks were now on the brink of elimination, but they weren't panicking. "We feel that we're a tough team to get rid of," said captain Jonathan Toews.

Toews disdained the idea of offering any pep talks before Game 6 at the United Center. "Anything over the top just adds to any sort of anxiety," he said. "We know to expect every guy in here to be ready and to bring their best game." Sure enough, he was proven right. After the game remained scoreless for almost 30 minutes, the Hawks tallied three times in less than four minutes midway through the second period.

The great defenseman Duncan Keith assisted on all three goals, but he wasn't done yet. Late in the third period, with the Hawks now ahead only 3-2, Keith alertly corralled a loose puck that was headed for the net (while goalie Corey Crawford was caught out of position in a scrum

370

in front of the net). Andrew Shaw's goal at 16:28 gave the Hawks some breathing room, and his empty-netter at 19:11 made the final score 5-2.

Keith ended up with a plus-three rating on the scoresheet while logging a game-high 28 and a half minutes of ice time. "There are games when you see how great he can be," Toews said, "how pivotal, how much he means to our team, especially in these big games."

The two teams headed back to Anaheim for Game 7, with a trip to the Stanley Cup Final in the balance. Playing in a seventh game, Toews said, "is the ultimate challenge to see what you've got as a player." Then he went out and put his money where his mouth was, showing why he already ranked among the greatest players in franchise history despite his relative youth (he had recently turned 27). The Ducks came out flying from the opening faceoff, while their fans roared their approval—but Toews promptly stopped the Ducks' momentum and silenced the crowd when he scored at 2:23 of the first period, shoveling a rebound of Niklas Hjalmarsson's shot past Anaheim goalie Frederik Andersen. He tallied again at 11:55, on the power play, flicking a wrist shot into the net off a nice pass from Brad Richards, while Shaw tied up a defenseman and also managed to screen Andersen in the process.

After Brandon Saad lit the lamp barely a minute into the second period, a Blackhawks win looked very likely. When Marian Hossa scored at 13:45, the outcome was all but certain. The final score was 5-3. Patrick Kane notched three assists, Richards and Keith two each. Crawford turned aside 30 shots. The somewhat one-sided Game 7 didn't tarnish the quality of the series as a whole. "When you review the games," said Blackhawks coach Joel Quenneville, "watch them, it's an amazing series. It has been great."

Although his team came up on the losing end, Anaheim coach Bruce Boudreau agreed. "I asked the question to somebody," he said, "I asked, 'Has this been a good series?' They laughed at me. They said, 'Are you kidding? It has been as good as it gets.'"

The Anaheim series served as the Blackhawks' springboard to the Stanley Cup championship. They vanquished the Tampa Bay Lightning four games to two in the Stanley Cup Final. Oddly, the Hawks scored exactly two goals, no more and no less, in five of the six games—but it was enough. They won Games 1, 4, and 5 by identical scores of 2-1 and won Game 6 by the margin of 2-0.

The Blackhawks had won their third Stanley Cup in six years, equaling the number of championships accumulated in the first 82 years of the franchise. They had also won the Cup-deciding game at home for the first time since 1938. "We love this city," said Hossa. "We love the crowd; they're spoiling us every year with sellouts. We're just so happy to be able to give this back to the city and the people who love the Blackhawks."

The people who loved the Blackhawks had grown exponentially in both numbers and devotion since Rocky Wirtz and John McDonough took over the franchise in 2007. Meanwhile, the perennial excellence of the players wearing the club's classic sweater spoke for itself. Lest anyone wonder whether the immensely successful organization was in danger of becoming complacent, McDonough had an answer. "We're not done," he said. "We're not done."

CHAPTER 43

At Last

"Everybody wants to talk about how we haven't done it since 1908, but who cares?"

-- Jake Arrieta, Cubs pitcher, 2013 –

"Sure as God made green apples," the legendary broadcaster Harry Caray said as he signed off for the 1991 season, "the Chicago Cubs are gonna be in the World Series. And maybe sooner than we think."

We'll never know exactly what Caray meant by "sooner than we think," but it's safe to assume he didn't mean another quarter of a century. By the time his prediction came true in 2016, Harry had long since passed away, as had Ron Santo, Ernie Banks, and an untold number of ever loyal, ever hopeful Cubs fans. In the meantime, the Cubs had suffered through the excruciating near miss of 2003, three different postseason appearances in which they failed to win a single game, and quite a few nondescript seasons in which they finished well off the pace.

The Cubs' meandering journey to their first World Series since 1945 took a decided turn in the right direction on October 21, 2011. That was the day that chairman Tom Ricketts hired Theo Epstein, the most capable executive in baseball. Epstein was the youngest general manager in major-league history when he took over the Boston Red Sox in 2002, at the tender age of 28, and the Red Sox won the World Series two years later—ending a drought that stretched back to 1918 (when they had beaten the Cubs four games to two, with their young lefthander Babe Ruth notching a pair of victories).

In the category of droughts, of course, the Red Sox had nothing on the Cubs, who (as goes without saying) had not won it all since 1908. Epstein's plan required the faithful to be patient a while longer. "If it meant taking a step back at the major-league level for a few years," he later said, "trading some established players for some younger, lesser-known prospects, then that's what we would do."

The first thing Epstein did as president of baseball operations was persuade his former Red Sox colleague Jed Hoyer, general manager of the San Diego Padres, to assume the same position with the Cubs. And just about the first thing the reunited Epstein-Hoyer team did was trade for 22-year-old first baseman (and cancer survivor) Anthony Rizzo, who'd been drafted by Epstein in Boston and traded for by Hoyer in San Diego. "I saw his strength and character, which are incredible," Epstein later said. "I loved his swing, loved his makeup, and, for a bigger guy, loved his sneaky kind of athleticism. And he was always a team leader."

The Cubs lost 101 games in 2012, which was pretty bad but hardly surprising. They lost "only" 96 in 2013 and 89 in 2014, by which time the franchise's future looked promising indeed.

Their poor performances on the field had enabled the Cubs to move to the head of the line in the annual draft of amateur players, and they had made the most of it. They landed infielder Javier Baez (selected by former general manager Jim Hendry) with the ninth overall pick in 2011, outfielder Albert Almora with the sixth pick in 2012, third baseman Kris Bryant with the second pick in 2013, and catcher Kyle Schwarber with the fourth pick in 2014.

Meanwhile, the Cubs made some trades for which the term "shrewd" is hardly sufficient. Starting pitcher Kyle Hendricks (a minor-leaguer at the time) was acquired from Texas in 2012, starter Jake Arrieta and reliever Pedro Strop were acquired from Baltimore in 2013, and shortstop Addison Russell (also a minor-leaguer at the time) was acquired from Oakland in 2014.

Finally, in the 2014-15 off-season, Epstein and Hoyer shifted into a new phase of their rebuilding program. After several years of trading veterans for untested youngsters, they decided it was time to bring in some experienced players to fortify a club that seemed ready to turn the corner. They traded for center fielder Dexter Fowler and catcher Miguel Montero. Then they landed the biggest free agent available, lefty starter Jon Lester (and also signed his preferred catcher, David Ross, for good measure).

A key puzzle piece fell into place when Joe Maddon, universally regarded as one of the best managers in the game, elected to cut ties with his current employers, the Tampa Bay Rays. Epstein and Hoyer flew down to Florida to have a talk with Maddon. By the time the group's 12-pack of Pabst Blue Ribbon was exhausted, Maddon had agreed to take over as skipper of the Cubs. "It was a game changer," Epstein said of hiring his new manager.

Maddon and the Cubs spent the early part of the 2015 season getting used to each other. Most of the players had never had a manager who, for example, hired a magician to entertain them in the clubhouse, installed a petting zoo in the outfield several hours before a game, or mandated that they all wear one-piece pajamas ("onesies") when heading out on a road trip. "He understands that this is a really long season, you know," Rizzo said. "So he keeps it really loose and really easy for us to just come in and be ourselves and play."

After 99 games, the Cubs were 52-47. What would happen next? Would they a) fade away as the pennant race heated up? b) continue to muddle along near the break-even mark? or c) prove to be genuine contenders?

The correct answer is "c." The rebuilt Cubs were for real. They won 15 of their next 16 games, including a four-game sweep of the San Francisco Giants (one of their main rivals for a postseason berth) at Wrigley Field. They won more games after August 1 than any other team in either league. They ended up at 97-65, an amazing achievement for a club which featured *four* rookies (Bryant, Russell, Schwarber, and outfielder Jorge Soler) in the starting lineup and whose oldest regular (Montero) was just 31.

The Cubs' record was the third best in all of baseball—but also third in their own division, behind St. Louis and Pittsburgh. Therefore, they needed to win the National League wild-card game vs. the Pirates in order to go any further. Fortunately, the right man for the job was on hand; Arrieta was in the midst of one of the greatest stretches for any pitcher in history. Over his last 20 starts, he had gone 16-1 with an 0.86 earned run average and three shutouts, including a no-hitter at Los Angeles on August 30. He was soon to receive the Cy Young Award.

Arrieta remained true to form in the wild-card game. He went the distance in blanking the Pirates on five hits and no walks, while striking out 11. Fowler scored three runs, Schwarber knocked in three, both homered, and the Cubs won 4-0. After the game, Maddon was asked if he'd had a maximum pitch count in mind for his ace. "Yes, I did," he replied. "Infinity."

Next, the Cubs dispatched the arch-rival Cardinals in the National League Division Series. After dropping the first game 4-0, the Cubs bludgeoned St. Louis pitchers for 20 runs in the next three games, all victories. They also pounded 10 home runs, including a truly monumental shot by Schwarber that landed atop the new video board behind the right-field bleachers at Wrigley.

The Cubs advanced to their first National League Championship Series since 2003 with high hopes and growing respect from all quarters. Alas, they ran into the proverbial buzzsaw in the form of the New York Mets' outstanding starting rotation. The Cubs were swept out of the postseason in four games.

It was a disappointing end to a thrilling season, but in truth the Cubs had been playing with house money. The rebuild was about a year ahead of schedule, and it was hard to imagine how it could have gone any better to this point.

Epstein and Hoyer stepped hard on the accelerator during the 2015-16 off-season. They landed three of the most attractive free agents on the market: second baseman/outfielder Ben Zobrist, outfielder Jason Heyward, and righthanded starter John Lackey (the latter two from the Cardinals).

As splashy (and pricey) as the signings of Zobrist, Heyward, and Lackey were, the return of Dexter Fowler was even more impactful. Fowler had rejected an earlier qualifying offer from the Cubs and elected to try free agency. On February 25, with news reports indicating that he'd already agreed to a three-year deal with the Baltimore Orioles, Fowler instead signed for one year with the Cubs. When he strolled unannounced onto the practice field at Sloan Park in Mesa, Arizona, still in his street clothes and accompanied by Epstein, he got a hero's welcome from his teammates. "These are my boys," Fowler said. "And I feel like we have some unfinished business."

Fowler resumed his customary place at the top of the Cubs' batting order, and Maddon required few words to impress upon him how important he was to the team's offense: "You go, we go."

Maddon's knack for pithy sayings produced several that made it onto T-shirts during the 2016 season: "Try not to suck," "Never let the pressure exceed the pleasure," "Do simple better," and "Embrace the target." The last one meant, essentially, We know we're the team to beat, and the other teams know it, so why pretend otherwise?

As the season got underway, the Cubs proved more than equal to the sky-high expectations placed upon them. They won eight of the first nine games. On April 21, Arrieta tossed a no-hitter as the Cubs bombed Cincinnati 16-0; it was Arrieta's second no-no in his last 10 starts. On May 8, Mother's Day, Baez belted a walk-off homer to complete a four-game sweep of the Washington Nationals. The Cubs had won 24 of the first 30 games.

On June 19, Father's Day, the Cubs pounded the Pirates in a nationally televised Sunday night game at home. Five Cubs homered, including rookie catcher Willson Contreras, who knocked the first pitch he ever saw in the majors over the center-field wall. The Cubs were now 47-20 and led their division by 12½ games.

Fowler's value was underscored when he went on the disabled list with a hamstring pull on June 20 and the Cubs lost 15 of the next 21 games. The few wins in that period did provide some highlights, though. On June 27, Bryant went five-for-five with three homers and two doubles in an 11-8 win at Cincinnati; it was the first time that any player had that particular combination of hits in a major-league game. The next night, Maddon had some fun by using pitchers Travis Wood, Spencer Patton, and Strop in left field, and the former two also on the mound, after running out of position players in extra innings. Wood even made a fine catch of a drive up against the wall. The Cubs eventually prevailed 7-2 in 15 innings.

Having endured a very rough three weeks, the Cubs nonetheless arrived at the All-Star break with a seven-game cushion over St. Louis for the division lead. They supplied the National League's entire starting infield for the midsummer classic in San Diego: first baseman Rizzo, second baseman Zobrist, shortstop Russell, and third baseman Bryant (who cracked a first-inning homer off Chris Sale of the White Sox).

Lester, Arrieta, and Fowler were also All-Stars, although the latter two did not play in the game. The American Leaguers won 4-2, meaning that (thanks to a nonsensical rule dreamed up by former commissioner Bud Selig) neither the Cubs nor any National League team could have home-field advantage for the World Series, even if they had a better record than the American League champions.

The Cubs returned from the break looking more like themselves, winning 11 of 17 for the rest of July. On July 31 against Seattle, they rallied from an early 6-0 deficit to force the game into extra innings. After Heyward led off the bottom of the 12th with a double and advanced to third on a flyout, Maddon looked down his bench and called upon Lester to pinch hit for Hector Rondon. It was an unlikely choice, in that Lester's lifetime batting average stood at .051. With the count at two-and-two, Lester laid down a perfect bunt between the mound and the first-base line, and Heyward's headlong dive carried the winning run across the plate.

The Cubs won the next 10 games as well, making it 11 straight with a 13-2 rout of the Cardinals on August 12. After dropping the next two to St. Louis, the Cubs took nine of 11. On August 26, they won in extra innings at Los Angeles, with flame-throwing closer Aroldis Chapman earning the save. For Chapman, the hardest thrower in baseball history to date (at up to 105 miles per hour), it was already the 10th save since his acquisition from the Yankees a month before.

Having won 29 of 39 since the All-Star break, the Cubs were now 82-45 for the season. They led the Cardinals by 14 games and the fading Pirates by 16½. There would be no wild-card game for them to get through in 2016.

The countdown to the division title was almost over when Hendricks held the Cardinals hitless for the first eight innings of a 4-1 win on September 12. The unflappable 26-year-old who'd started the season as the Cubs' fifth starter ended it with the best ERA (2.13) in the majors and a third-place finish, one notch behind Lester, in balloting for the Cy Young Award.

On September 14, Rizzo blasted two homers in a 7-0 win over St. Louis that reduced the Cubs' magic number to one. The Cubs lost to Milwaukee at home the next day, but clinched the division title overnight when the Cardinals lost at San Francisco. On September 16, the

Cubs showed up at Wrigley Field planning to celebrate win or lose, then pulled off a come-from-behind victory that made the postgame champagne party more satisfying. They scored twice in the the ninth and once in the tenth, on a leadoff homer by Montero, to beat the Brewers 5-4.

In practical terms, it would've made no difference if the Cubs had lost the regular-season finale at Cincinnati on October 2—but even so, they did not. Instead, they showed the resilience that had defined them all year and would serve them so well in the coming postseason. They trailed 4-3 with two outs and nobody on in the top of the ninth. Albert Almora walked, then Munenori Kawasaki lined a single to center. Matt Szczur worked the count to three-and-two, then smashed a double into the right-field corner to score the tying and go-ahead runs. Montero followed with a two-run homer. Just like that, the Cubs led 7-4. When Carl Edwards retired the Reds one-two-three in the bottom of the ninth, the regular season was over.

It had been the best regular season for the Cubs in a long, long while. They won their division by 17½ games. Their 103 wins were the most for the franchise since 1910; their .640 winning percentage the best since 1935. The Cubs had done as much as they could have done so far. They needed 11 more wins to do all that could be done.

In the division series, the Cubs were tasked with breaking the San Francisco Giants' curious habit of winning the world championship in even-numbered years (2010, 2012, and 2014).

Game 1 featured a scoreless duel between Lester and the Giants' Johnny Cueto until Baez came up with one out in the bottom of the eighth and hit a tremendous drive that seemed destined for Waveland Avenue. Baez stood at the plate admiringly watching the ball sail into the night, having forgotten that the wind was blowing a gale back toward the infield. Fortunately, the ball's truncated journey ended in the basket in front of the left-field bleachers, saving Baez some embarrassment and giving the Cubs the game's only run. "Thank God for that basket," said Ross.

In Game 2, the Cubs touched up former teammate Jeff Samardzija for four runs in the first two innings, including a pair on a broken-bat single by Hendricks. Hendricks had to leave in the fourth inning after taking a line drive off his right forearm, but five relievers—Wood, Edwards, Mike Montgomery, Rondon, and Chapman—combined to blank the Giants for the rest of the way. Wood also chipped in with a home run. After the Cubs won 5-2, Lester suggested that he was dreading the flight to San Francisco. "It's gonna be four and a half hours of listening to the recap of Woody hitting a home run," he said. "I already told him he's not allowed to talk."

The Giants staved off elimination by winning the hard-fought Game 3 in 13 innings; it was their tenth consecutive win in a potential elimination game. "We are hard to kill," pitcher Madison Bumgarner remarked. Matt Moore confirmed the point in the next game, limiting the Cubs to two runs on only two hits over eight innings. But in the ninth, *five* Giants relievers paraded to the mound vainly attempting to hold a three-run lead. The Cubs scored four times to go ahead 6-5, and Chapman struck out the side in the bottom of the ninth to wrap up the game and the series.

Next up was another old rival, the Los Angeles Dodgers, in the National League Championship Series. Game 1, at Wrigley Field, began swimmingly when Fowler singled and Bryant doubled him home in the bottom of the first. In the second, Heyward led off with a triple. Baez doubled to score Heyward, advanced to third on a wild pitch, then stole home.

The Cubs' 3-0 lead evaporated when the Dodgers tallied once in the fifth and twice in the eighth. In the bottom of the eighth, the Cubs had two on and two out when the Dodgers intentionally walked Chris Coghlan to get to Chapman's spot in the batting order. Maddon sent Montero up to bat for Chapman. Los Angeles reliever Joe Blanton quickly got two strikes across, then came back with a slider that got too much of the plate. Montero was ready. He belted a grand slam just inside the right-field line. "Wrigley is shaking!" radio announcer Ron Coomer yelled. "If this place could get any louder, I'd like to see it."

The Cubs held on to win 8-4, breaking a seven-game losing streak in NLCS play that dated back to 2003. A game-winning grand slam in the postseason would be a great thrill for anyone, of course, but it was especially meaningful to Montero, who'd gone from first to third (behind Contreras and Ross) on the Cubs' depth chart at catcher and had even expected to be released before the end of the season. "Obviously, as a kid, you dream about these situations," he said. "It's what you live for."

The Cubs' victory in Game 1 proved to be not only exhilarating but also crucial when they failed to score a single run in the next two games. Their stretch of scoreless innings had reached 21 when Zobrist led off the top of the fourth in Game 4 with a perfectly placed bunt single up the third base line. Baez and Contreras followed with singles, the latter scoring Zobrist, and then Baez scored on a groundout by Heyward. Russell knocked one over the center-field fence, and the Cubs were in business. When Rizzo homered the next inning, the rout was on. The Cubs won 10-2, with Russell and Rizzo—their two coldest hitters of the postseason so far—combining for six hits, four runs scored, and five RBIs. It was the most important win of the year to date. "Everybody had us buried yesterday," said Ross. "Today we're on top of the world."

Lester was typically sharp in Game 5, allowing but one run on five hits over seven innings. Russell confirmed that his slump was behind him by clouting two homers. The Cubs busted the game open with five runs in the eighth and won 8-4.

As in 2003, the NLCS returned to Chicago with the Cubs needing to win one of the last two games to advance to the World Series. It was a vaguely interesting coincidence, but the 2016 Cubs didn't need a billy goat, a deflected foul ball, or any other excuses. They offered the faithful an efficient, relatively stress-free victory to capture the pennant with one game to spare.

Hendricks retired the Dodgers in order in the first. Fowler led off the bottom of the frame with a double and scored on a single by Bryant. After Rizzo reached on a two-base error, a sacrifice fly scored Bryant. The Cubs added single runs in the second, fourth, and fifth. That was all she wrote for the Dodgers' ace lefty Clayton Kershaw, who had befuddled the Cubs in Game 2. Meanwhile the Dodgers could do nothing against Hendricks. When it was all said and done, he and Chapman had faced the bare minimum number of batters (27), three of whom reached base, none of whom scored, and all of whom were erased on double plays—including one from Russell to Baez to Rizzo that ended the game.

The final out brought forth an outpouring of emotion in the stands, in the streets surrounding the ballpark, and in living rooms and barrooms everywhere that Cubs fans were gathered. The big prize was still out there, but in winning the National League pennant the Cubs had done something that the vast majority of their fans had never seen before. "We played our best game of the year," said Hoyer. "I think the players played their best because they know what this means to these people."

"It all started with a bunt," Maddon said, recalling the hit by Zobrist in Game 4 that had turned the whole series around.

The Cubs were opposed in the World Series by the Cleveland Indians, who were replete with storylines themselves. They had not won it all since 1948, the longest current drought except for that of the Cubs. They had won the American League pennant despite missing their best player, left fielder Michael Brantley, for the final five months of the season and starting pitchers Carlos Carrasco and Danny Salazar for the last two months. Finally, manager Terry Francona was not only a former Cub (1986), but had also managed the Red Sox under Epstein for eight years and two world championships.

The Cubs provided an interesting wrinkle when they revealed that Schwarber, sidelined since tearing knee ligaments in the third game of the season, was being added to their active roster for the Series. Schwarber's hard work in rehab had accelerated the timeline for his recovery, and a few promising at-bats in the Arizona Fall League convinced the Cubs' management that he was ready. He'd been cleared medically to hit and run the bases, but not to play the field; therefore he would be designated hitter for away games and be available only as a pinch-hitter for home games. Schwarber's return gave the Cubs an emotional lift and profoundly affected the outcome of the series.

Schwarber's ringing double off the right-field wall was the lone highlight for the Cubs in Game 1, a 6-0 defeat at the hands of Indians ace Corey Kluber. Some said the Cubs were just rusty, since it was their first World Series game in 71 years.

The Cubs didn't show any lingering signs of rust in Game 2. They scored in the first inning on a single by Bryant and a double by Rizzo. Schwarber later contributed a pair of run-scoring singles. (After the game, Francona jokingly texted Epstein: "You guys should really be a little more cautious with Schwarber.") Zobrist also had two hits, including a triple that sparked a three-run rally in the fifth. Meanwhile, Arrieta held the Indians hitless until the sixth. He, Montgomery, and Chapman eventually allowed just one run on four hits. The Cubs won 5-1.

The series shifted to Chicago for the next three games, and the hype surrounding them was something to behold. Even standing-room-only tickets brought four figures apiece on the resale market. The games were on a Friday, Saturday, and Sunday, enhancing the party atmosphere for which Wrigleyville has long been famous. "The fact that people are flying in just to be in a bar," Maddon remarked, "not even at the ballpark—that's pretty impressive."

The Cubs took the field for Game 3 full of piss and vinegar, as the saying goes, but the biggest cheer they got all night was the moment they first stepped over the foul lines. There was little to cheer about thereafter, as the Indians won 1-0.

Game 4 produced a similar result. Fowler scored in the first when he doubled and Rizzo singled him home, and he scored again in the eighth on his own home run. But in between, Cleveland tallied seven times. Northbrook native Jason Kipnis delivered the coup de grace with a three-run homer in the seventh.

Backs against the wall, do or die, now or never—use any cliché you like. The fact was that the Cubs came into Game 5 needing a win to avoid an embarrassing oh-fer and an Indians celebration on their home field and, not incidentally, to keep their flickering hopes for the world championship alive.

The Cubs trailed 1-0 after three innings. They had now produced only two runs and 13 hits in 21 innings at Wrigley Field. Time was running short. Like Zobrist in Game 4 of the NLCS, Bryant came to the plate knowing he had to get something going. The 24-year-old had been a revelation since coming up from the minors early in the 2015 season. Everyone knew about his prodigious power all along, but his defensive skills, baserunning, and precocious maturity had come as surprises to most. By the end of 2016, he had been College Player of the Year, Minor League Player of the Year, National League Rookie of the Year, and National League Most Valuable Player in successive years.

Hall of Famer John Smoltz, broadcasting on Fox TV, said, "The Cubs really need to score this inning." Bryant obliged by driving Trevor Bauer's third pitch over the wall in left-center. Then, it was as if a switch had been turned on. Rizzo followed with a line shot off the ivy in right field for a double. Zobrist singled. Russell singled, scoring Rizzo. After Heyward struck out, Baez bunted for a single to load the bases. Ross strode to the plate. With the count at two-and-two, he lifted a fly ball to left that was deep enough to score Zobrist. The Cubs didn't score again, but the three runs held up. Lester departed after yielding two runs in six innings, Edwards got the first out of the seventh, and Chapman got the last eight outs for the longest save of his career.

After singing "Go Cubs Go" and watching the "W" flag flying atop the scoreboard for the last time in 2016, the crowd of 41,711 didn't want to leave. The Cubs seemed to feel the same way, for many of them came out of the clubhouse and back onto the field to savor the moment. Especially for the 39-year-old Ross, who was due to retire at the end of the series, the occasion was bittersweet.

In Game 6, back in Cleveland, the Cubs did themselves and their fans a favor by removing any suspense as to the outcome early in the proceedings. Bryant homered with two outs and nobody on in the first inning. Rizzo and Zobrist followed with singles, and Russell knocked both of them in with a double. In the third, Russell cracked a grand slam to put the game away. All told, the middle of the Cubs' order—Bryant, Rizzo, Zobrist, and Russell—went 11-for-19 with eight runs scored and nine driven in.

The Cubs won 9-3. Maddon took a lot of flak for using Chapman in a blowout game, rather than trying to keep him rested for Game 7, but the bottom line was that the Cubs had survived to fight another day. "It's just correct and apt that we would go seven games," Maddon said.

Then came the moment of truth. Game 7 of the World Series is a special occurrence in any case, but the 2016 Cubs and Indians produced one of the most dramatic of all time.

Hendricks was on the mound for Cubs, while Kluber made his third start of the Series for Cleveland. Fowler, following the "You go, we go" script, led off the game with a home run. The Cubs led 1-0 until the bottom of the third, when Coco Crisp led off with a double, was bunted to third, and scored on a single by Carlos Santana. With that, Lester got up in the bullpen; he had volunteered to work if needed, and Maddon seemed antsy to take him up on it. Next came an error by Baez, his second of the game, but Hendricks retired the next two batters to get out of the inning with no further damage.

Finally getting to Kluber after he'd vanquished them in Games 1 and 4, the Cubs scored twice in the fourth to get some breathing room and twice more in the fifth. They now led 5-1. Cubs fans everywhere pinched themselves and thought, *It's really going to happen.*

Hendricks required only 10 pitches to set the Indians down in the fourth. He was getting sharper as the game went on, but meanwhile Lester continued toiling in the bullpen. In the fifth, Hendricks got two quick outs on an infield grounder and a strikeout. Then, with a count of three-and-two, he froze Santana with a slider that appeared to hit the outside corner for strike three—but umpire Sam Holbrook wasn't convinced. While Santana was trotting down to first, Maddon popped out of the dugout. Seeing this, Hendricks screamed something into the inside of his glove that probably wasn't very nice.

Lester was lathered up and ready to go, and Maddon knew that if he didn't use him now, he wouldn't be able to use him at all. Therefore Hendricks went to the showers just as he seemed to be taking complete command of the game. Kipnis was the first batter to face Lester. When he topped a little spinner between the mound and the third-base line, Lester didn't move. He watched as Ross (who'd just entered the game himself) pounced on the ball and then sailed it well over Rizzo's grasp. Now there were runners on second and third with the dangerous Francisco Lindor at bat. Lester struck out Lindor to end the inning, but not before uncorking a wild pitch that bounced away from Ross far enough to score both runners.

When Ross went deep in the sixth, atoning for his misadventures behind the plate in the previous half inning, he became the oldest man ever to homer in a World Series game. That it was the last game of his career made the achievement all the more significant.

The Cubs led 6-3. Lester settled in and got through the sixth, seventh, and two-thirds of the eighth with no trouble. But after he yielded a two-out single in the eighth, Lester departed and the ubiquitous Chapman took the ball. Just as Lester had replaced Hendricks with two outs, a runner on first, and no apparent danger on the horizon, so did Chapman take over for Lester.

Brandon Guyer greeted Chapman with a double off the wall in right-center, scoring Jose Ramirez from first. It was evident from the get-go that Chapman didn't have his normally sizzling fastball. Accordingly, he tried to sneak a slider past Rajai Davis down and in, but Davis golfed it into the left-field seats to the tie the game.

Chapman gave up a single to Crisp just as the tumult over Davis's homer was subsiding, but then he fanned Yan Gomes to escape the inning. The Cubs failed to score in the ninth despite having a man on third with one out. Then, to his great credit, Chapman managed to retire the Indians one-two-three in the bottom of the ninth, even though he was obviously spent both physically and emotionally.

The umpires called a brief rain delay before the Cubs came to bat in the tenth inning. "That rain delay," said Rizzo, "was the most important thing to happen to the Chicago Cubs in the past 100 years. I don't think there's any way we win the game without it."

During the delay, Heyward called the players together to make sure they weren't discouraged by the events of the past couple innings. The game was still theirs for the taking. "We're the best team in baseball," Heyward told his teammates, "and now we're going to show it."

When play resumed, Bryan Shaw was on the mound for Cleveland. Schwarber smashed a single (his third hit of the night) through the Indians' shift into right field. Almora pinch ran for him. Bryant hit a long drive to right-center that looked as if it might leave the yard. Standard procedure for Almora in this case would've been to station himself a step or two from second base, so he could score if the ball dropped. Instead, he went all the way back to first, tagged up, and took second when the ball was caught on the warning track.

Rizzo was up next, and he drew an intentional walk. Zobrist lined a double over the first-base bag and into the right-field corner, scoring Almora and sending Rizzo to third. After Russell was intentionally walked, Montero (the Cubs' third catcher of the game) grounded a single through the left side to score Rizzo. Now the Cubs led 8-6 with the bases loaded and only one out, but Bauer entered the game and retired Heyward and Baez to keep the Indians relatively close.

Edwards, a six-foot-three, 170-pound stringbean, took the mound for the bottom of the tenth, the most momentous half inning for the Cubs in 108 years. The rookie righthander struck out Mike Napoli and induced a groundout from Ramirez. The Cubs were one out away from that which their fans had dreamed of for so many decades. Then Guyer coaxed a walk and, with the Cubs paying no attention to him, took second on the first pitch to Davis. The intrepid Davis rapped the next pitch over second base to score Guyer.

Maddon called on Montgomery to face the next hitter, Michael Martinez. Martinez took Montgomery's first offering for a called strike. He swung at the next pitch and chopped it to the left of the mound. Bryant charged in, made a nifty pickup, and fired the ball to Rizzo in time. And that was that.

The Cubs had done it. Over the next few days, their fans celebrated in various ways, both public and private. A million or more flocked to the city's parade and rally on November 4. Hundreds, maybe thousands, scrawled poignant messages in chalk on the outside walls of Wrigley Field. And every last one of them paused to consider what it all meant to him or her.

Anthony Rizzo's statement will do nicely to conclude this narrative. "We're world champions," he said after taking a champagne shower from actor Bill Murray. "The Chicago Cubs are world champions. Let that sink in."

Bibliography

Ahrens, Art, and Eddie Gold. *The Cubs*. New York: Macmillan, 1986.

Angell, Roger. *Season Ticket*. Boston: Houghton Mifflin, 1988.

Barnett, Gary, with Vahe Gregorian. *High Hopes: Taking the Purple to Pasadena*. New York: Warner Books, 1996.

Baseball-reference.com. <http://www.baseball-reference.com>

Bowen, Edward L. *The Jockey Club's History of Thoroughbred Racing in America*. Boston: Bulfinch Press, 1994

Brown, Warren. *The Chicago Cubs*. New York: G.P. Putnam's Sons, 1946.

Brown, Warren. *The Chicago White Sox*. New York: G.P. Putnam's Sons, 1952.

Bunce, Steve, with Bob Mee. *Boxing Greats*. Philadelphia: Courage Books, 1998.

Chicago Tribune. Various editions from 1906 through 2016.

Chen, Albert, ed. *Cubs Win! A Sports Illustrated 2016 Commemorative Issue*. New York: Time, Inc., 2016

Cronin, Tim. *Purple Roses: Northwestern's Glorious March to Pasadena*. Champaign, Illinois: Sagamore Publishing Inc., 1996.

Ditka, Mike, with Don Pierson. *Ditka: An Autobiography*. Chicago: Bonus Books, 1986.

Durocher, Leo, with Ed Linn. *Nice Guys Finish Last*. New York: Simon & Schuster, 1975.

Funk, Joe, ed. *Hawks Dynasty: The Chicago Blackhawks' Run to the 2015 Stanley Cup*. Chicago: Triumph Books, 2015.

Funk, Joe, ed. *Unstoppable! The Chicago Blackhawks' Dominant 2013 Championship Season*. Chicago: Triumph Books, 2013.

Goldberg, Seth. "Cardinal Chronicle." <http://www.angelfire.com/fl/TheCard>

Goldstein, Richard. *Spartan Seasons*. New York: Macmillan, 1980.

Golenbock, Peter. *Wrigleyville: A Magical History Tour of the Chicago Cubs*. New York: St. Martin's Press, 1996.

Halas, George, with Gwen Morgan and Arthur Veysey. *Halas by Halas*. New York: McGraw-Hill, 1979.

Halberstam, David. *October 1964*. New York: Ballantine, 1995.

Hayner, Don, and Tom McNamee. *The Stadium*. Chicago: Performance Media,1993.

Helyar, John. *Lords of the Realm*. New York: Ballantine Books, 1994.

Hirsch, Joe. *The First Century*. New York: Daily Racing Form Press, 1996.

Hockey-reference.com. <http://www.hockey-reference.com>

Holtzman, Jerome, and George Vass. *The Chicago Cubs Encyclopedia*. Philadelphia: Temple University Press, 1997.

Honig, Donald. *The Chicago Cubs: An Illustrated History*. New York: Prentice Hall Press, 1991.

Jackson, Phil, and Hugh Delehanty. *Sacred Hoops*. New York: Hyperion, 1995.

Kellams, Mike, ed. *Hawkeytown: Chicago Blackhawks' Run for the 2010 Stanley Cup*. Chicago: Triumph Books, 2010.

Lazenby, Roland. *And Now, Your Chicago Bulls! A Thirty-Year Celebration*. Dallas: Taylor Publishing Company, 1995.

Lazenby, Roland. *Bull Run!* Lenexa, Kansas: Addax Publishing Group, 1996.

Leiker, Ken, ed. *Cubs Win! Cubs Win! A Sporting News Special Commemorative Issue*. Charlotte, NC: Sporting News Yearbooks, 2016.

McAvoy, John. *Through the Pages of Daily Racing Form*. New York: Daily Racing Form Press, 1995.

Meyer, Ray, with Ray Sons. *Coach*. Chicago: Contemporary Books, 1987.

Milbert, Neil. *Arlington Park (1927-1986)*. Arlington Heights, IL: Arlington Park Racetrack, Ltd., 1986.

Milbert, Neil. "Praise for a Forgotten Foe." In *Chicago Tribune*, December 15, 2007.

Nack, William. "Next Year Is Here." In *Sports Illustrated*, October 1, 1984.

Okrent, Daniel, and Steve Wulf. *Baseball Anecdotes*. New York: Harper Collins, 1989.

Pro-football-reference.com. <http://www.pro-football-reference.com>

Ribowsky, Mark. *A Complete History of the Negro Leagues, 1884 to 1955*. New York: Birch Lane Press, 1995.

Ritter, Lawrence S. *The Glory of Their Times*. New York: William Morrow, 1984.

Seymour, Harold. *Baseball: The Golden Age*. New York: Oxford University Press, 1971.

Stout, Glenn. *The Cubs*. Boston: Houghton Mifflin, 2007.

Thomas, John C. "Loyola Basketball History." *Ramblermania.com*. <http://www.ramblermania.com>

Townsend, Doris, ed. *This Great Game*. Englewood Cliffs, NJ: Prentice Hall, 1971.

Vass, George. *The Chicago Black Hawks Story*. Chicago: Follett, 1970.

Verdi, Bob. *Chicago Blackhawks: Seventy-Five Years*. San Diego: Tehabi Books, 2000.

Veeck, Bill, with Ed Linn. *Veeck—As In Wreck*. New York: G.P. Putnam's Sons, 1962.

Ward, Geoffrey C., and Ken Burns. *Baseball: An Illustrated History*. New York: Alfred A. Knopf, 1994.

Whittingham, Richard. *The Bears: A 75-Year Celebration*. Dallas: Taylor Publishing Co., 1994.

Whittingham, Richard. *The Chicago Bears: An Illustrated History*. Chicago: Rand McNally, 1979.

Whittingham, Richard. *The White Sox: A Pictorial History*. Chicago: Contemporary Books, 1983.

Zimmerman, Paul. "Bearing Up Mighty Fine." In *Sports Illustrated*, October 21, 1985.

Zimmerman, Paul. "Black and Blue Day in Big D." In *Sports Illustrated*, November 25, 1985.

Zimmerman, Paul. "Domination Under the Dome." In *Sports Illustrated*, February 3, 1986.